HUSSERL, HEIDEGGER, AND THE SPACE OF MEANING

Northwestern University
Studies in Phenomenology
and
Existential Philosophy

HUSSERL, HEIDEGGER, AND THE SPACE OF MEANING

Paths toward Transcendental Phenomenology

Steven Galt Crowell

Northwestern University Press
Evanston, Illinois

Northwestern University Press
Evanston, Illinois 60208-4210

Printed in the United States of America

10 9 8 7 6 5 4 3 2 1

ISBN 0-8101-1804-1 (cloth)
ISBN 0-8101-1805-X (paper)

Library of Congress Cataloging-in-Publication Data

Crowell, Steven Galt.
Husserl, Heidegger, and the space of meaning : paths toward transcendental phenomenology / Steven Galt Crowell.
p. cm. — (Northwestern University studies in phenomenology & existential philosophy)
Includes bibliographical references and index.
ISBN 0–8101-1804–1 (alk. paper) — ISBN 0–8101-1805-X (pbk. : alk. paper)
1. Husserl, Edmund, 1859–1938. 2. Heidegger, Martin, 1889–1976. I. Title. II. Series.
B3279.H94 C76 2001
142'.78—dc21 00-046032

The paper used in this publication meets the minimum requirements of the American National Standard for Information Sciences—Permanence of Paper for Printed Library Materials, ANSI Z39.48-1984.

To my mother,
and to the memory of my father

Contents

Acknowledgments

I would like to thank the following publishers for kind permission to reprint here the works for which they continue to hold the copyright.

Chapter 1 first appeared as "Neo-Kantianism" in *A Companion to Continental Philosophy,* ed. Simon Critchley and William Schroeder (Oxford: Basil Blackwell, 1998). Chapter 2 was first published in *Kant-Studien* 87 (1996), but it had been written for another project in 1985 and had been in circulation since then. Chapter 3 was published in *Husserl and the Phenomenological Tradition,* ed. Robert Sokolowski (Washington, D.C.: Catholic University of America Press, 1988). Chapter 4 first appeared in *The Journal of the British Society for Phenomenology* 23, no. 3 (1992). Chapter 5 was published as "Making Logic Philosophical Again (1912–1916)," in *Reading Heidegger from the Start: Essays in His Earliest Thought,* ed. Theodore Kisiel and John van Buren (Albany: State University of New York Press, 1994). Chapter 6 appeared in *Man and World* 28, no. 4 (1995). Chapter 7 appeared in *Phenomenology Japanese and American,* ed. Burt C. Hopkins (Dordrecht: Kluwer, 1998). Chapter 8 was published in *History of Philosophy Quarterly* 14, no. 2 (1997). Chapter 9 was originally published in *Philosophy and Phenomenological Research* 50, no. 3 (1990). Chapter 10 was published in *Husserl in Contemporary Context,* ed. Burt C. Hopkins (Dordrecht: Kluwer, 1997). Chapter 11 first appeared as the entry "Phenomenology and the Question of Being: Heidegger" in *The Edinburgh Encyclopedia of Continental Philosophy,* ed. Simon Glendinning (Edinburgh: Edinburgh University Press, 1999). Chapter 12 appeared in *Philosophy and Phenomenological Research* 60, no. 2 (2000).

Having incurred many debts, intellectual and otherwise, during the fifteen years sedimented in the chapters of this book, it would be hard to do justice here to the specific ways in which I have benefited from the help, criticism, and support of so many people. I would have to start by thanking Karsten Harries and Robert Sokolowski, both of whom have been mentors of the first rank, and I would have to acknowledge in memoriam an even deeper debt of gratitude to Maurice Natanson, who introduced me to phenomenology and so, in a sense, to philosophy. More concretely, my work has been materially supported by the generous travel stipends and enlightened leave policy of the School of Humanities at Rice University, and I would express my gratitude to Allen Matusow, former dean of the school, and to Judith Brown, the current dean, for fostering, in this and other ways, an environment in which scholarship can flourish. In the same vein, I should thank the members of the Philosophy Department at Rice for their collegiality; it is hard to overestimate the importance of mutual respect in these contentious times. The members of the Continental Theory Workshop, an interdisciplinary faculty group sponsored by the Center for the Study of Cultures at Rice, also deserve thanks for the constant intellectual stimulation that has kept me focused on fundamental issues. In particular Jack Zammito, Harvey Yunis, Lane Kauffmann, and Tullio Maranhão have forced me to be very specific about what phenomenology can contribute to interdisciplinary discussion.

But how would it be possible to acknowledge all those who have done so much to foster my thinking about Husserl and Heidegger? Many of these chapters were aired in their raw, naked form at meetings of the Husserl Circle and of the Society for Phenomenology and Existential Philosophy, and a list of those to whom I owe thanks would have at least to include those who attended these sessions. But even so it would be wrong not to express special thanks to Burt Hopkins, who has provided an outlet for several of my essays and has always been a trenchant interlocutor in matters concerning the Husserl-Heidegger relation. Similarly, much of what I have done over the past several years would not have attained whatever acuteness it possesses had it not been for Theodore Kisiel, whose generosity with his time and great knowledge of Heidegger have been a constant provocation to my thinking. A different sort of provocation, and one for which I am no less grateful, has been provided by Hubert Dreyfus and the many who, having learned from him, do not, in our discussions together, make my Husserlian reading of Heidegger any easier, only better—among whom special thanks go to Charles Guignon, William Blattner, and John Haugeland. All the more grateful am I, then, for the many conversations about matters Husserlian that I have been fortunate to have had with John Drummond, whose work is a model of the genre. Perhaps the most up-to-the-minute note of gratitude would go to an anonymous reader for Northwestern University Press, whose several excellent suggestions regarding the argument, to which I could respond here mostly only by way of promissory notes, point toward just the sort of discussion of these issues I hope will be the ultimate product of this book.

This book is dedicated to my parents, since it is thanks to them that I not only came to appreciate the life of the mind but had the resources to live it. My fondest hope is that my work will not fail to reflect their virtues. At the same time, I am a man who, like every other, lives from day to day, and those days are shared, gloriously, with my wife, Laura Lark. To her, then, the last best word of thanks.

Abbreviations

References to the writings of Husserl and Heidegger have, where possible, been included in the text according to the following abbreviations of Heidegger's *Gesamtausgabe* (GA) and the *Hussserliana* (Hua) series. The German pagination is given directly after the colon, and where an English translation is readily available, I have listed that page after a slash. However, I have sometimes altered the published translation. Where such translations are not available, I have made my own. References to works not found in these series are given in the notes and the list of works cited.

Heidegger's Works

GA 1	*Frühe Schriften,* edited by Friedrich-Wilhelm von Herrmann (Frankfurt: Vittorio Klostermann, 1976).
GA 2	*Sein und Zeit,* edited by Friedrich-Wilhelm von Herrmann (Frankfurt: Vittorio Klostermann, 1976); translated by John Macquarrie and Edward Robinson under the title *Being and Time* (New York: Harper and Row, 1962).
GA 3	*Kant und das Problem der Metaphysik,* edited by Friedrich-Wilhelm von Herrmann (Frankfurt: Vittorio Klostermann, 1976); translated by Richard Taft under the title *Kant and the Problem of Metaphysics* (Bloomington: Indiana University Press, 1997).
GA 9	*Wegmarken,* edited by Friedrich-Wilhelm von Herrmann (Frankfurt: Vittorio Klostermann, 1976); includes "Letter on Humanism," translated by Frank Capuzzi, and "What Is Metaphysics?" translated by David Farrell Krell, in *Basic Writings,* ed. David Farrell Krell (New York: HarperCollins, 1993).
GA 17	*Einführung in die phänomenologische Forschung,* edited by Friedrich-Wilhelm von Herrmann (Frankfurt: Vittorio Klostermann, 1994).

GA 19	*Platon: Sophistes,* edited by Ingeborg Schüßler (Frankfurt: Vittorio Klostermann, 1992).
GA 20	*Prolegomena zur Geschichte des Zeitbegriffs,* ed. Petra Jaeger (Frankfurt: Vittorio Klostermann, 1979); translated by Theodore Kisiel under the title *History of the Concept of Time: Prolegomena* (Bloomington: Indiana University Press, 1985).
GA 21	*Logik: Die Frage nach der Wahrheit,* edited by Walter Biemel (Frankfurt: Vittorio Klostermann, 1976).
GA 24	*Die Grundprobleme der Phänomenologie,* edited by Friedrich-Wilhelm von Herrmann (Frankfurt: Vittorio Klostermann, 1975); translated by Albert Hofstadter under the title *The Basic Problems of Phenomenology* (Bloomington: Indiana University Press, 1982).
GA 25	*Phänomenologische Interpretationen von Kants Kritik der Reinen Vernunft,* edited by Ingtraud Görland (Frankfurt: Vittorio Klostermann, 1977).
GA 26	*Metaphysische Anfangsgründe der Logik im Ausgang von Leibniz,* edited by Klaus Held (Frankfurt: Vittorio Klostermann, 1978); translated by Michael Heim under the title *The Metaphysical Foundations of Logic* (Bloomington: Indiana University Press, 1984).
GA 29/30	*Die Grundbegriffe der Metaphysik: Welt, Endlichkeit, Einsamkeit,* edited by Friedrich-Wilhelm von Herrmann (Frankfurt: Vittorio Klostermann, 1983).
GA 40	*Einführung in die Metaphysik,* edited by Petra Jaeger (Frankfurt: Vittorio Klostermann, 1983); translated by Ralph Manheim under the title *An Introduction to Metaphysics* (New Haven, Conn.: Yale University Press, 1959).
GA 56/57	*Zur Bestimmung der Philosophie,* edited by Bernd Heimbüchel (Frankfurt: Vittorio Klostermann, 1987).
GA 58	*Grundprobleme der Phänomenologie (1919/20),* edited by Hans-Helmuth Gander (Frankfurt: Vittorio Klostermann, 1993).
GA 59	*Phänomenologie der Anschauung und des Ausdrucks: Theorie der philosophischen Begriffsbildung,* edited by Claudius Strube (Frankfurt: Vittorio Klostermann, 1993).
GA 61	*Phänomenologische Interpretationen zu Aristoteles: Einführung in die Phänomenologische Forschung,* edited by Walter Bröcker and Käte Bröcker-Oltmanns (Frankfurt: Vittorio Klostermann, 1985).

GA 63 *Ontologie (Hermeneutik der Faktizität),* edited by Käte Bröcker-Oltmanns (Frankfurt: Vittorio Klostermann, 1988).

GA 65 *Beiträge zur Philosophie (Vom Ereignis),* edited by Friedrich-Wilhelm von Herrmann (Frankfurt: Vittorio Klostermann, 1989).

Husserl's Works

Hua I *Cartesianische Meditationen und Pariser Vorträge,* edited by S. Strasser (The Hague: Martinus Nijhoff, 1963); translated by Dorion Cairns under the title *Cartesian Meditations* (The Hague: Martinus Nijhoff, 1969).

Hua II *Die Idee der Phänomenologie: Fünf Vorlesungen,* edited by Walter Biemel (The Hague: Martinus Nijhoff, 1958); translated by William P. Alston and George Nakhnikian under the title *The Idea of Phenomenology* (The Hague: Martinus Nijhoff, 1964).

Hua III *Ideen zu einer reinen Phänomenologie und phänomenologischen Philosophie: Erstes Buch,* edited by Walter Biemel (The Hague: Martinus Nijhoff, 1950); translated by F. Kersten under the title *Ideas Pertaining to a Pure Phenomenology and to a Phenomenological Philosophy: First Book* (The Hague: Martinus Nijhoff, 1983).

Hua IV *Ideen zu einer reinen Phänomenologie und phänomenologishen Philosophie: Zweites Buch,* edited by Marly Biemel (The Hague: Martinus Nijhoff, 1952); translated by R. Rojcewicz and A. Schuwer under the title *Ideas Pertaining to a Pure Phenomenology and to a Phenomenological Philosophy: Second Book* (Dordrecht: Kluwer Academic Publishers, 1989).

Hua V *Ideen zu einer reinen Phänomenologie und phänomenologischen Philosophie: Drittes Buch,* edited by Marly Biemel (The Hague: Martinus Nijhoff, 1952); translated by Ted E. Klein and William E. Pohl under the title *Ideas Pertaining to a Pure Phenomenology and to a Phenomenological Philosophy: Third Book* (The Hague: Martinus Nijhoff, 1980).

Hua VI *Die Krisis der Europäischen Wissenschaften und die transzendentale Phänomenologie: Eine Einleitung in die phänomenologische Philosophie,* edited by Walter Biemel

	(The Hague: Martinus Nijhoff, 1954); translated by David Carr under the title *The Crisis of European Sciences and Transcendental Phenomenology: An Introduction to Phenomenological Philosophy* (Evanston, Ill.: Northwestern University Press, 1970).
Hua VII	*Erste Philosophie (1923/24): Erster Teil: Kritische Ideengeschichte,* edited by Rudolf Boehm (The Hague: Martinus Nijhoff, 1956).
Hua IX	*Phänomenologische Psychologie: Vorlesungen Sommersemester 1925,* edited by Walter Biemel (The Hague: Martinus Nijhoff, 1962).
Hua XVII	*Formale und transzendentale Logik,* edited by Paul Janssen (The Hague: Martinus Nijhoff, 1974); translated by Dorion Cairns under the title *Formal and Transcendental Logic* (The Hague: Martinus Nijhoff, 1969).
Hua XIX/1	*Logische Untersuchungen,* edited by Ursula Panzer (The Hague: Martinus Nijhoff, 1984), vol. 2, pt. 1; translated by J. N. Findlay under the title *Logical Investigations,* 2 vols. (London: Routledge and Kegan Paul, 1970).
Hua XIX/2	*Logische Untersuchungen,* edited by Ursula Panzer (The Hague: Martinus Nijhoff, 1984), vol. 2, pt. 2; translated by J. N. Findlay under the title *Logical Investigations,* 2 vols. (London: Routledge and Kegan Paul, 1970).
Hua XXIV	*Einleitung in die Logik und Erkenntnistheorie,* edited by Ulrich Melle (The Hague: Martinus Nijhoff, 1984).
Hua XXV	*Aufsätze und Vorträge (1911–1921),* edited by Thomas Nenon and Hans Rainer Sepp (The Hague: Martinus Nijhoff, 1987); includes "Philosophy as Rigorous Science," in *Phenomenology and the Crisis of Philosophy,* translated by Quentin Lauer (New York: Harper and Row, 1965).

HUSSERL, HEIDEGGER, AND THE SPACE OF MEANING

Introduction

Reconsidering Transcendental Phenomenology

The theme of this book is the space of meaning and the path opened up to its philosophical elucidation by Husserl and Heidegger. The space of meaning is familiar to philosophers under many names, reflecting diverse views of what is most important about it. Recently, Wilfred Sellars's name for it—the "space of reasons"—has come into vogue, signaling an interest in distinguishing between explanations that also provide justifications (reasons) and those that do not (causes). Earlier it was common to talk in Wittgensteinian terms of "logical space" in which individual phenomena (or sentences) had their "place." Earlier still, neo-Kantian philosophers spoke of the *Geltungsbereich,* or "realm of validity," to distinguish the specific theme of philosophy from that of the empirical sciences of nature or the historical sciences. In the tradition that informs the approach taken in the present volume, the space of meaning has also been identified in various ways. Early Husserl (followed by the earliest Heidegger) called it the field of "phenomenological immanence." Later, he would rechristen it "transcendental consciousness," while Heidegger preferred simply to speak of "world." A philosophical *topos* capable of being approached under so many designations will not be surveyable in a single pass. Indeed, as the messianic faith in something called the "linguistic turn" shows every sign of having receded in late-twentieth-century philosophy, it becomes possible to recognize that what has distinguished philosophy in the twentieth century is not that it has concerned itself with language, but that, whether through the prism of language or not, it has concerned itself with *meaning.* The present volume aims to contribute something to this ongoing inquiry. Specifically, it argues that transcendental phenomenology is indispensable to the philosophical elucidation of the space of meaning.

No doubt this argument flouts the spirit of the times—whether measured in "analytic" or "continental" terms—and this along two axes.

First, in spite of important work by Mohanty, Sokolowski, and others, transcendental phenomenology is still too often simply dismissed as a relic, as "Cartesian," "foundationalist," "idealist"—all terms of deepest opprobrium in contemporary philosophy. But Husserl's thought has not been well understood, because it has not been read, by most of those who criticize it. And among those who are well positioned to understand it, that philosophy has long been held hostage to animosities stemming from the collapse of the personal relationship between Husserl and Heidegger. For too long the philosophical significance of *phenomenology* has been hostage to the clannish behavior of *phenomenologists* such that the only possible conjunction between Husserl and Heidegger appears to be an either/or. Which brings me to the second axis: Among students of Husserl and Heidegger, it will likely seem perverse to identify as "transcendental phenomenology" Heidegger's contribution to an elucidation of the space of meaning. Heidegger takes center stage in this book, but it is a Heidegger whose philosophical relevance depends largely on our being able to recollect the Husserlian infrastructure of his work and to carry out new constitutional analyses within the framework Heidegger provides. Thus, I claim that his decisive contribution remains within the horizon of transcendental phenomenology and does not lie in some sort of hermeneutic, pragmatic, or postmodern "break" with that horizon. Such a claim obviously requires much defense, some of which can be found in the chapters that follow. These take up the challenge of suggesting not only how a successful philosophical grasp of the space of meaning demands transcendental phenomenology, but also how the Husserl-Heidegger relation can be understood so as to make the distinctive contributions of each accessible within that ongoing phenomenological project.[1]

In carrying out this task, an interpretation of the early Heidegger—the one who is still on the way to *Being and Time*—proves crucial. Parts 1 and 2 of this book reflect this in different ways. Part 1 concerns the tradition of transcendental logic as developed in neo-Kantianism (especially by the most original member of the Baden school, Emil Lask) and as appropriated by Heidegger during his student years at Freiburg. Focus on Lask and the issue of transcendental logic achieves two things. First, it becomes clear how third-generation neo-Kantians like Lask, whose work was deeply informed by motifs from German idealism, were alive to aspects of the philosophy of meaning that have surfaced in more recent approaches to the "space of reasons." Lask, for instance, offers an account of the relation between meaning and truth, and the rudiments of a nonmentalistic (nonrepresentational) concept of mind, that strongly anticipate the post-Quinean efforts of those whom I would call the neo-neo-Kantians.[2] Then as now, however, we find lacunae, blind spots that come into view only by adopting a more phenomenological approach. A look at the differences between Lask, Heidegger, and Husserl on the topic of meaning, then, provides insight into those places where appeal to phenomenology might even now be necessary if the "unboundedness of the conceptual" is to be made perspicuous. Second, we thereby gain a platform for a new reading of the Husserl-Heidegger relation itself, one oriented toward their interest in a common philosophical problem.

The beginning of such a reading is attempted in part 2. Again focusing on the early Heidegger—his lecture courses from the 1920s and especially those given in Freiburg between 1919 and 1923—these chapters explore Heidegger's relation to the problematic of transcendental phenomenology and seek a more nuanced understanding of his criticism of Husserl. They emphasize in the early Heidegger's work a proximity to Husserlian thinking which is otherwise easy to ignore[3] and provide the basis for a general reading of *Being and Time* that treats its continuity with the transcendental tradition as philosophically decisive. Heidegger's achievement would thus consist in his systematic effort to respect the difference between straightforward (positive) and reflective (critical) inquiries—the difference between entities and the meaning of entities—while simultaneously doing justice to the demand that philosophy demonstrate the grounds of its own possibility as an inquiry into meaning. It is as a philosophy of meaning that Heidegger's thought is essentially phenomenological; it is as a philosophy of philosophy that it is essentially transcendental.

To say that Husserl and Heidegger share an orientation toward a common philosophical problem—the phenomenon of meaning—is not, however, to say that their *conceptions* of meaning are the same. While I hold that Heidegger's philosophy cannot abandon essential tenets of Husserlian phenomenology, I also see a philosophically decisive development "from" Husserl "to" Heidegger precisely in the working out of a richer conception of meaning. That development can be characterized, roughly, as an increasing appreciation for the existential ground of meaning. Husserl's breakthrough to transcendental phenomenology, to a genuinely universal theory of meaning, came with the recognition that the notion of signification (*Bedeutung*), which "originally . . . concerned only the linguistic sphere," can "find application of a certain kind to . . . all acts, be they now combined with expressive acts or not." Meaning (*Sinn*) now designates the signification that pertains to "all intentive mental processes" (Hua III:256/294). But meaning in *that* sense is a far richer phenomenon than even Husserl recognized, and an account of it (beyond what has thus become only an *analogy* with linguistic signification) points toward the embedding of acts, or "intentive mental processes," in something phenomenologically more primordial. Thus, for Heidegger, like Husserl, "meaning is that wherein the intelligibility of something maintains itself"; however, it is not originally the correlate of an act but the "upon which of the project in terms of which something becomes intelligible *as* something" (GA 2:201/193). Act analysis will have to be founded in project analysis, yet I shall argue that this does not render act analysis otiose; nor does existential supplant transcendental phenomenology.

Though the chapters in parts 1 and 2 were written at different times and for different occasions, each arose as an argument within the project horizon just described. And though the structure pretty closely follows the chronology of Heidegger's thinking, the chapters retain a certain autonomy within the whole. Readers who prefer to browse by topic, then, should not find the going difficult. At the same time, because of a fairly tight thematic unity, I have found it neither necessary nor desirable to revise extensively—though obviously much more could be said on the issues. Specifically, I have not tried to draw connections between the approach to the space of meaning found in neo-Kantians such as Lask and the approach that is pursued in recent neo-neo-Kantianism. To those familiar with these contemporary philosophers the connections will be apparent, but to have drawn them into the discussion would have distracted from the flow of an argument whose primary concern is with a chapter in the history of phenomenological philosophy. A debate between the old neo-Kantians and these new ones would require a fresh start. In addition, the terms in which Lask poses the problem have, on their own, much to recommend them, and perhaps essays that take those terms seriously might spark a deeper reception of Lask than has been evident so far in the Anglophone world. Nevertheless, it will be useful to say a word or two about John McDowell's position further along in this introduction, for it shows quite clearly where transcendental phenomenology finds its natural place in the reflection on meaning pursued in a nonphenomenological idiom.

A second area where I have resisted the temptation to revise concerns the interpretation of the "young" Heidegger's position. Much work has been done on these matters in recent years as more scholars have taken up the challenge of the early lecture courses. My own interpretation has developed over the past decade and a half in light of the problematic that interests me—certainly not the only possible angle on Heidegger's *Denkweg*—and though I have occasionally reviewed my differences with other researchers (notably Theodore Kisiel), I have generally avoided forays into polemics. However, since his forceful, comprehensive, and learned interpretation of the "young Heidegger" contrasts in so many important ways with my own far less ambitious reading, it was tempting to graft a critical dialogue with John van Buren onto the following chapters. Ultimately, that too would have proved a distraction; yet it will serve the purpose of introducing what is at stake in this volume to take a moment here to outline the hermeneutic basis for my differences with van Buren.

Readers of Heidegger quickly sense the presence of two voices in his work. There is, first, the Heidegger who seeks the proper name of being; the Heidegger who, in spite of his best insights into the ontological difference, often seems to imagine being as some sort of primal cosmic "event," a hidden source or power. Seeking the "meaning of being," this Heidegger appears to want philosophy to "eff the ineffable." There is, second, the Heidegger who is concerned with the reflexive issue of the possibility of philosophy itself, the Heidegger who constantly chastises other thinkers for not being rigorous enough, for succumbing to metaphysical prejudice and losing sight of the things themselves. This Heidegger seems precisely to shun the excesses of what the first Heidegger appears to embrace. Though these voices are indelibly entwined in Heidegger's text, there is a real temptation to separate them out and to weight them relative to each other. Both van Buren and I give in to this temptation, but our estimation of which voice is worth attending to is quite different. Van Buren gives the palm to the first, "mystical" and "antiphilosophical," voice, while I follow the second "transcendental" and "critical" one. This stems less from specific differences over Heidegger interpretation than from serious differences concerning what is the best lesson to be drawn from the history of philosophy.

The real hero of van Buren's story is not Heidegger, but Derrida, and his view seems to be that if philosophy is anything more than a personalistic appropriation of an ultimately mystical "sending," it consists in deconstructing putative claims to philosophical knowledge. In contrast, the real hero of my Heidegger story is neither Heidegger nor Derrida, but Husserl; or rather, a transcendental phenomenology that, inaugurated by Husserl and carried on in Heidegger's best moments, cannot be deconstructed because it is presupposed in every deconstruction—not as a set of first-order claims but as that which underwrites the meaning of the practice itself. Phenomenology in this sense has by no means lost its relevance for addressing questions of meaning in a philosophically compelling way. Having chosen different heroes, van Buren and I proffer very different interpretations of Heidegger's early writings and their relation to *Being and Time.* I argue that *Being and Time* brings to fruition Heidegger's early project of combining the "transcendental" philosophies of Aristotle and Kant by means of Husserlian phenomenology. Relentlessly explored in the early Freiburg lectures under the heading of philosophy as "primal science," the basic question of this project is how philosophy itself, as an inquiry into meaning as opposed to entities, is possible. Van Buren, on the contrary, sees *Being and Time* as an "aberration" in Heidegger's thinking, a "plodding scientific treatise" that, by "entangling itself in the subjectivistic metaphysical language of Kant's and Husserl's transcendental thinking," squandered the philosophical capital accumulated in the early Freiburg lectures, namely, their plans for an "end of philosophy and a new beginning." Carried out through "an-archic personalist formulations of the being question," what is best about the early lectures (and what is absent from *Being and Time*) is thus a "negative, deconstructive, skeptical thinking . . . close to Derrida."[4]

Hence, van Buren sees the early Freiburg work as a "dangerous supplement" that undermines the story of Heidegger's itinerary authorized by Heidegger himself. Having characterized the earliest work—notably Heidegger's two dissertations (1914, 1915)—as a metaphysical "neo-neo-Scholasticism" that remains only a "more sophisticated and enlightened form of idealism," van Buren constructs an "anti-metaphysical" (which, for him, means an anti-transcendental, anti-*philosophical*) Heidegger from the lectures beginning in 1919 where, it is said, Heidegger "deconstructs his own earlier metaphysics."[5] This is the Derridean heart of Heidegger's "real" project. Misled by the "dead hand" of Heidegger himself, the *mens auctoris,* the Heidegger industry has been on the wrong track all along: Heidegger's first question was not really "what is being" but rather "the more radical question of what gives or produces being as an effect," his real topic the "anarchic temporalizing of being out of an original concealment and impropriety."[6] From this perspective, then, Heidegger's so-called turn after *Being and Time* is a re-turn to his earlier an-archic, anti-metaphysical ways.

At the heart of van Buren's wide-ranging reading is attention to what John Caputo first called the "mystical element" in Heidegger's thought and to the influence on it of religious sources—medieval Scholasticism, first of all, then the "authentic religious experience" of early Christianity which set in after Heidegger abandoned Catholicism and its "eternal worldview." The point is to show that "the existentialist or transcendental reading of Heidegger's youthful texts is bewitched by their surface and fails to see the depth of their *Vorhaben,* which often can be sounded out only by a sensitivity to the historical context in which Heidegger was working at the time (for example, his continued interest in mysticism into the early twenties)." A veneer of transcendental language, then, serves only to conceal Heidegger's real interest in a "step-back and turn from being to the lethic anarchic *Sache* of the differentiated temporal giving of being in and through concrete life." But is the transcendental motif really so absent even from this formulation of Heidegger's "genuine" *Vorhaben?* Is this solely the descendant of Heidegger's earlier "philosophical mysticism," now in the form of an "anti-philosophy" reflecting Heidegger's "passionately anti-Greek Christian heritage"?[7] Or might the last five words of the citation testify to a continuing concern not *simply* to acknowledge the "lethic anarchic" character of the giving, but to reflect critically on that "in and through" which it *is* giving? For van Buren, Heidegger's interest in this critical question, evident in the Freiburg lectures' pursuit of a primal science and a theory of categories, is merely misleading and superficial, a dead end that will celebrate its apotheosis in *Being and Time* before Heidegger returns to his senses and turns away from philosophy for good.

Such a thesis deserves the closest scrutiny, especially when worked out in the detail van Buren devotes to it. Some of these details can be questioned. For instance, van Buren's story employs the term "metaphysics" in the global sense it came to have in Heidegger's later writings, thus eliding the careful distinctions Heidegger was anxious to draw between metaphysics, logic, transcendental philosophy, worldview, and phenomenology in his early work. To restore these distinctions (as I shall do in the chapters below) is to place some of van Buren's arguments for the supposed genuine *Vorhaben* of Heidegger's thought in a very different light. However, it is not really necessary to enter into details to dispute the thesis that the existential and transcendental aspects of Heidegger's thought are superficial window dressing. Van Buren's judgment here is simply one way of weighting the two Heideggerian voices I noted at the outset. One might well agree that the mystical element is present in the Freiburg lectures while continuing to argue that the critical interest is in fact an integral aspect of Heidegger's thinking.[8] For just this coincidence of criticism and mysticism seems to be at stake in what van Buren himself recognizes as Heidegger's desire to establish a "new conception of philosophy." If one takes seriously the fact that Heidegger never sees his project simply as mystical antiphilosophy, one can admit that the desire to put an "end" to philosophy (specifically, to the epistemological philosophy of neo-Kantianism and the metaphysical philosophy of neo-Scholasticism) is central to Heidegger's 1919 project and still insist that the desire to reflect critically upon the *possibility* of philosophy (as phenomenological "primal science") is no less central. To do so, however, is to shift emphasis from the *an-archic* potential of the mystical "primal something" to the *alethic* potential of reflection on the space of meaning. It is to inquire not only into that which makes that space possible (constitution questions) but into that which makes our philosophical grasp of it *as* the space of meaning possible (transcendental questions). From this point of view, the mystical element in Heidegger's thought begins to look rather uninteresting. It is there, certainly, but what makes it of interest to philosophers is the way Heidegger forces it to become accountable to *thinking*. This commitment to thinking remains the irreducible trace of the supposedly superficial transcendental moment in Heidegger's project, and he never abandons it.

This, however, raises another controversial point. On van Buren's reading, the mysticism in Heidegger's *Vorhaben* is correlated to a new "personalistic" conception of philosophy, one whose goal is life transformation rather than knowledge. Van Buren cites Kisiel's claim that "Heidegger urged his students to adopt a more 'phronetic approach' to their chosen science [philosophy], contrary to the traditional equation of scientific comportment with *theorein*."[9] While there is certainly some truth to this idea—and we shall examine it further in later chapters—here one should note that such a transformation of philosophy is not straightforward. There is, for example, a clear tension between this notion of philosophical "phronesis" and Heidegger's pursuit of philosophy as primal science. While the latter does have a crucial existential dimension, its aim more resembles that of Aristotle's *Nichomachean Ethics* itself than it does what Aristotle calls *phronesis*. The *Ethics,* like Heidegger's primal science, *reflects* upon the terrain of the ethos; it is not just another example of practical wisdom. So what is the nature of such reflection, in Heidegger or in Aristotle? We get no answer if we simply adopt a personalist idea of philosophy as self-transformation.

Van Buren comments on this tension in the course of his description of young Heidegger as a "philosophical Luther" completing the task of deconstructing the hegemony of Aristotelian metaphysics. He writes that "one of Heidegger's great contributions in the early twenties was his providing an ontological language and an opening within academic philosophy for such marginal traditions in which the end of philosophy and new post-metaphysical beginnings had already occurred." And again, "he attempted to create an opening within academic discourse for precisely those concerns that traditionally had been considered beyond its reach."[10] This is in fact an important aspect of what Heidegger—and the phenomenological tradition generally—promised, and continues to promise, to do. But one should mark well that the project is one of clearing a space *within* academic discourse—a term that does not finally stand for some particular school or movement but for the project of a *publicly accountable* practice of philosophy—*not* the outright dismissal of it in favor of a personalistic mysticism that simply calls itself "philosophy." In these terms, the primary question concerns what measures success or failure in such a project. Even the deconstructive process of clearing space for marginal traditions must appeal to more, in its critical practice, than to the purity of heart of its practitioners.

Here lies the deepest division between the mystical and the transcendental readings of Heidegger's early work. If one emphasizes the "concerns that had traditionally been considered beyond the reach" of philosophy (chiefly, whatever appears to elude the "universal": the *jeweilig*, the "cross of facticity," etc.), questions about how such things can actually be brought to bear in a philosophical discussion will seem secondary, artifacts of that contingent historical and cultural situation it is supposedly the task to overcome. One then highlights all those places in Heidegger's early writings where he seems to "join forces with his early opponents"—proponents of "historicism, psychologism, and scepticism"—against traditional "platonistic" and idealistic, metaphysical, "transcendental" universalistic conceptions of philosophy. The Husserl-Heidegger relation will appear to support this: Husserl's transcendental-phenomenological pursuit of essences can only seem to Heidegger a "fantastic path to the ahistorical"—a sheer impossibility—"doomed not just in practice but rather in principle, since it ignored the a priori of temporality, historical difference, finitude, exile, way, non-arrival." If Heidegger explicitly invokes Husserl's "principle of all principles"—the demand that philosophical thinking proof itself against direct intuition of the things themselves (*Evidenz*)—this will be understood not as a call to philosophical responsibility in the public "academic" context of discourse and thinking but as a personalistic reflection of the mystical "devotion" or submission (*Hingabe*) to what gives itself in pretheoretical life.[11] However, if instead of emphasizing the "concerns traditionally excluded from philosophy," one emphasizes the attempt to clear a space *for* them *in* the discourse of the academy, then the very same passages will read differently, and one will be forced to ask some critical questions.

For instance, is it not odd to speak of an "a priori" of temporality, finitude, exile, and so on? Is it enough simply to claim that there is such a thing? How is it discovered—not how do I discover myself as a historical being, but how is my *essential* historicity established? Indeed, if we agree to set aside the contentious and misleading characterization of Husserl's position and assume, as van Buren claims, that Heidegger wanted to show that "Husserl's promised *ideal* of a universal, transtemporal eidetic kingdom of transcendental subjectivity was in principle unfulfillable through the praxis of *actual* phenomenological investigations,"[12] what claim upon us do these latter "investigations" make? Will they not have the character of "essential insights" or "a priori truths"? What is the ground of their validity? In the following chapters I explore the hypothesis that Heidegger took such questions quite seriously as part of his project of making room in the academy—that is, within the ethical protocols of rational grounding and public debate—for experiences left out of traditional philosophy. This is precisely what makes his work during this period so exciting. Much of the excitement dissipates, however, if those protocols are simply abandoned. For example, if Heidegger's appropriation of Husserl's principle of all principles is not understood as the basis for reformulating the theory of evidence so as to incorporate the existential dimension, but is seen instead simply as a restatement of the idea that I am always already "in the truth" in pretheoretical life, it may serve to edify, but it remains philosophically lifeless. No space for critical discussion of any particular experience, marginal or otherwise, is cleared by it. On my reading Heidegger was never content with such reductions but always respected the truth that philosophy necessarily includes both a private (existential) and a public (transcendental) dimension. What is philosophically interesting in the early Heidegger, then, are the resources he provides for thinking these two together. The existential loses all significance for philosophers (though not, of course, for persons) if it is separated from the transcendental.[13]

Thus, I agree fully when van Buren claims that Heidegger's pre-1919 "phenomenological suspension of the flux of spatiotemporal reality was also a suppression of his own philosophical impulses,"[14] if by "phenomenological suspension" is meant only that certain issues were inadequately thematized in Heidegger's earliest work. The argument of the following chapters will show that that work is aporetic and cannot reach the genuine constitutional problems in the theory of meaning. However, if the "flux of spatiotemporal reality" is given a mystical interpretation ("mysticism" being van Buren's name for Heidegger's "own philosophical impulses"), and if this is invoked as a reason to trivialize Heidegger's continuing interest, after 1919, in questions of constitution, validity, and the possibility of philosophy (phenomenology), then I would argue that Heidegger's best work comes precisely when he works *against* his "own philosophical impulses" by trying to frame his insights in the language of transcendental philosophy, the academy, and the public protocols of "scientific" discourse. The phenomenology of evidence, even as radicalized by Heidegger, respects these protocols—is, indeed, nothing but their trenchant exploration—whereas the "mystical impulse" leads beyond all that toward something that, if it does not lack all claim upon others, certainly lacks the claim that a work like *Being and Time* possesses for anyone interested in the possibility of philosophy.

With that I articulate the hermeneutic principle of my own highly selective reading. Heidegger's interest in the transcendental problematic (in the conditions of possibility of meaning, together with the conditions of possibility of our philosophical *grasp of* those conditions) may be an "aberration" when seen in light of his "own impulses," but if that is so, then Heidegger's most significant work emerges in struggling *against* the wholesale embrace of those impulses, in disciplining them by an "ontological" or philosophical idiom. For me, then, the biographical Heidegger more or less drops out. If it is admitted—as it must be—that the transcendental project is part of Heidegger's thinking from the 1912 essays to the publication of *Being and Time* in 1927, then it doesn't matter whether the transcendental *Ansätze* in the Freiburg lectures are seen as essential to Heidegger's project or as constraints on the "true" Heidegger. One who is not convinced that deconstruction represents the last word on the question of meaning can explore Heidegger's early writings for the phenomenologically attestable insights they contain, as material with which to build. This is what I have tried to do in the present volume.

Suppose there is, then, headway to be made in metaphysics, epistemology, or philosophy of mind by a renewed focus on the space of meaning. Is it really likely that this will come through transcendental phenomenology, innocent of the linguistic turn—through an approach that takes neo-Kantianism seriously and insists on a symbiosis between Husserlian eidetics and Heideggerian hermeneutics? Such doubts being easy to anticipate, it has been a constant temptation to pepper the margins of my chapters with references to current work where the approach, though couched in terms very different from those of Husserl and Heidegger, could be materially advanced by incorporating a transcendental-phenomenological perspective. Yet such picking at the edges would finally satisfy nobody—neither those who need convincing of the relevance of transcendental phenomenology, nor those who, needing no convincing, want to see the payoff spelled out in detail. Still, this introduction might be the place to indicate, with one example, how debates between Husserl, Heidegger, and neo-Kantians like Emil Lask have unexpectedly taken on renewed currency.

Under the heading of "transcendental logic," the neo-Kantian philosophers of the late nineteenth and early twentieth centuries pursued several investigations that we would now identify with epistemology, philosophy of mind, philosophy of language, and metaphysics. Emerging as a reconfiguration of transcendental logic, phenomenology promised a comprehensive new approach to all these fields, starting from the thesis that meaning (*Sinn*) is prior in the order of inquiry to all "positive" (scientific *and* metaphysical) thematics. The question of the meaning of meaning set the terms of the debate between phenomenologists and neo-Kantians. Emil Lask, for instance, understood the space of meaning (which he called the *Geltungssphäre*) in quasi-Aristotelian fashion not as a propositional space but as a space of meaningful *objects,* the "original" measure or tribunal for propositions. In this way he hoped to avert Kantian "skepticism." Since "the object is itself nothing other than meaning," the supposed "gap between meaning and object turns out to be a distance between meaning and meaning."[15] Though critical of Lask, Heidegger praised him precisely for his "attempt to bring Aristotle and Kant as close to one another as possible" (GA 1:33). This very attempt has recently emerged as a desideratum in the work of John McDowell, who calls for a "reconciliation" that can "recapture the Aristotelian idea that a normal mature human being is a rational animal, but without losing the Kantian idea that rationality operates freely in its own sphere."[16] Does McDowell's approach to the space of meaning exhibit lacunae similar to those Husserl and Heidegger discerned in Lask's transcendental logic? If so, a strong case might be made for reconsidering the contribution of transcendental phenomenology.[17]

McDowell wants to recover a philosophically defensible empiricism by overcoming the impasse—precipitated by Sellars's critique of the Myth of the Given and extended to its apparently logical conclusion in Davidson's coherentism—of a "reflection about experience that disqualifies it from intelligibly constituting a tribunal." How can our thinking be "answerable to the world" at all if we reject as myth the notion that the world impinges on our thinking by way of "givens" that are not produced by the spontaneity of thought? If all warrant takes place within the "space of reasons," that is, in terms of the conceptual relations of "implication or probabilification" that make up the idea of justification, then no appeal to something given outside that space can provide rational *grounds* for what we say, but only "exculpations"—not normative justifications but naturalistic explanations in terms of "brute impacts from the exterior."[18] Conversely, if the given is conceived as belonging *within* the space of reasons (identified with our spontaneity, our capacity for thinking and judging), we seem to lose the necessary "friction" between thought and the world without which the idea of empiricism is idle and collapses into a kind of idealism.

Yet this is very nearly what McDowell proposes, and in so doing he comes into proximity with Lask. McDowell argues that the conceptual sphere, or the space of reasons, is "unbounded": It is wrong to imagine that what impinges on our thinking and acts as its warrant is entirely nonconceptual; indeed, "experiences themselves are already equipped with conceptual content." "*That things are thus and so* is the conceptual content of an experience, but if the subject of the experience is not misled, that very same thing, *that things are thus and so,* is also a perceptible fact, an aspect of the perceptible world." Thus *that things are thus and so* is something (passively) "seen" *and* it is "the sort of thing one can also, for instance, judge."As Lask put it, "the gap between meaning and object turns out to be a distance between meaning and meaning."[19] Framing his position in the Kantian terms of "receptivity" and "spontaneity," McDowell's response to the apparent justificatory irrelevance of givenness is to claim that receptivity includes conceptuality without, however, ceasing to be receptive. It therefore remains serviceable as a check on our thinking.

McDowell associates this revision of Kant with Hegel's philosophy, but it more closely resembles the Fichte-tinged neo-Kantianism of Lask. Lask too argued that logical content "reaches right into the object itself,"[20] but like McDowell and unlike Hegel, Lask wished to preserve a genuine distinction between spontaneity and receptivity. Thus, Lask criticizes Hegel's *Panlogism* (the claim that content just *is* the concept) and defends a more modest "hegemony of the *logos*" that allows him to address the friction problem and to avoid idealism through a theory of the "material determination" of logical form *within* the space of meaning. Against Hegel, this implies that perception and thought have independent, irreducible roles to play in the theory of meaning, a position McDowell also appears to adopt in his account of how perceptual color discriminations can be said to be conceptually informed.[21] For both, then, epistemological dilemmas are to be overcome through the recognition that meaning spans the traditional divide between perception and conception. Yet to work out the difficulties facing such a view requires a phenomenological perspective that remains largely absent in both Lask and McDowell. In its absence the twin dangers of dogmatism and "idealism" (a danger only if incorrectly understood) reappear in the theory of meaning itself.

Consider how Lask strives to avoid the charge of idealism (Kantian psychologism or phenomenalism) by conceiving the conceptually informed object ultimately as a radically "transcendent" entity, untouched by all subjectivity and so, strictly speaking, beyond the bounds of experience. He means by this only that the conceptual content of the entity is not a function of subjective forming or "spontaneity," but because his nonphenomenological concept of experience leaves no room for any other way of conceiving the presence of the meaningful object to consciousness, his theory as a whole falls victim to dogmatism—the positing of something transcendent without an account of the conditions that make its supposed presence intelligible. McDowell, by contrast, believes that he can defuse idealism by distinguishing, in the concept of experience itself, between experienc*ing* and the experi*enced.* If "thought" is understood as the "act" of thinking, and this is distinguished from the "content" of the act, then what constrains thought from "outside" need only be external to the act of thinking, it "does not need to be from outside *thinkable contents.*" Thus, while McDowell highlights the normative role of what transcends thinking (what Lask calls the "universe of the think*able*"), he also goes further to say that the "thinkable contents that are ultimate in the order of justification are contents of *experiences.*"[22] Seeing-as is seeing what is.

As a bit of phenomenology this point is, I take it, unobjectionable. But McDowell, like Lask, appears to believe that any further move in the direction of constitutional analyses of seeing-as would land him in idealism. Thus, instead of exploring the implications of the phenomenological fact that perception, "seeing-as," is not a simple act but one that takes place through law-governed constitutional syntheses of modes of givenness, McDowell uses his insight into the givenness of meaning as warrant for a new *naturalism,* or better, a renewed Aristotelianism in which the modern "anxiety" about reason being cut off from the world is no longer felt. On this view we are to see the supposed gap between the conceptual (meaningful) and the real not as a feature of nature but as an artifact of the attitude of modern natural science, solely a function of its form of explanation in terms of rigorous, nonmeaningful "laws."[23] Against the "bald naturalism" that seeks to reduce the space of meaning to this realm of law (and so, in its own way, "get rid of the anxiety"), McDowell suggests that we need not equate nature with the subject matter of this "naturalistic" science, and if we do not, we are free to view nature as a space in which meaningful rationality (spontaneity, thinking) is integrated.

But on what basis is this new sense of nature established? It cannot be on the basis of contemporary natural science—for *its* sense of nature ("law") is just what gives rise to the anxiety. But nor does it seem to result from metaphysical inquiry; or at any rate if it is the sort of metaphysical Aristotelianism it sometimes appears to be, it will certainly be subject to the same critical reservations Kant (and indeed Hegel) leveled at the original. It is one thing to say that it is simply our "nature," as rational animals, to dwell within the space of meaning—what McDowell calls "second nature," a function of *Bildung* as culture, language, and inculcation in what it means to give reasons. It is quite another thing to distinguish this position from dogmatism on the one hand and skepticism (McDowell's "idealism") on the other. Viewed through the prism of transcendental phenomenology, McDowell's vague references to *Bildung* indicate just where a genuine *phenomenological* idealism (transcendental constitution theory) must insist on its contribution. One cannot simply posit a correlation between experience and nature, between seeing-as and seeing what-is; one must show what this sense of nature *amounts* to through an account of the evidence *in* which it is given *as* nature. Here

Husserl and Heidegger have provided some of the crucial tools in their reflections on the constitution of the space of meaning.

McDowell, though, is uninterested in constitutional issues and elides their importance by substituting for them a series of metaphors about how "our environment is *taken up into* the ambit" of spontaneity, or how our "conceptual capacities are *drawn into operation*" by impressions of outer sense.[24] Intent on avoiding what he believes to be the idealism and skepticism of Kantian transcendental philosophy, he implies that once one has dismissed the relevance of the naturalistic "machinery of thinking," nothing stands in the way of a kind of Aristotelian realism.[25] Assuming that if a constitutive account is not a naturalistic "explaining away" of the space of meaning there is not much else it *could* be, McDowell suggests that there is no "constructive account of what responsiveness to meaning is" beyond simple reference to "the fact that normal human maturation includes the acquisition of a second nature, which involves responsiveness to meaning." Hence "the response we should aim at being entitled to, if someone raises a question like 'What constitutes the structure of the space of reasons?' is something like a shrug of the shoulders." Like Rorty, he believes that such questions only arise against an "assumed background that is supposed to make them urgent," a background that *his* notion of second nature aims precisely to dislodge.[26] The phenomenologist must insist, however, that *her* interest in the constitution of meaning is not anxiously motivated by a background gap between reason and nature, but precisely by a *reflective* interest in getting clear about how the space of meaning, the successor to that bad picture of the world, is structured in its details. This is a task for constitutive transcendental philosophy, not for those sciences of the "world" that investigate things appearing *within* the space of meaning. Without it, McDowell's Aristotelian conception of nature comes off as little more than a deus ex machina compared with the well-wrought conception of meaningless "nature" established by natural science.

The sort of new naturalism McDowell has in view—the basis for an empiricism that would no longer be hostage to modern concepts of the mind as a *forum internum* or space of representations—has been a staple of the phenomenological tradition, especially in the figures of Husserl, Heidegger, and Merleau-Ponty, since Husserl introduced the notion of the lifeworld in the 1920s. This does not mean, however, that the phenomenological tradition as a whole has been any more successful than McDowell in establishing a convincing account of nature. The issue concerns precisely the question of how one can "step out" of modernity without simply pretending that it is possible to go back to Aristotle—how, in other words, we are to "bring Aristotle and Kant as close to one another as possible" without imagining that our desire to escape modern predicaments makes it acceptable to forget all that is just in the modern critique of ancient metaphysics. I shall have a good deal more to say about all this in the following chapters, since their aim is to suggest how transcendental phenomenology, as "first philosophy," provides an alternative to the ancient metaphysical paradigm and the modern epistemological one. On such a view, the new sort of empirical realism McDowell proposes—based on the hegemony of the space of meaning—must be grounded in an equally new transcendental idealism. Neither a doctrine of otherworldly cognitive capacities nor a quasi-psychological theory of the synthesis of representations, this idealism corresponds to what McDowell himself claims would be difficult "but perhaps not impossible" to do, namely, to "rehabilitate" the "idea of a transcendental constitution of consciousness."[27]

At bottom this has nothing to do with the desire to revive a superannuated form of philosophy but is forced upon us once we recognize that McDowell's empirical realism is formulated with the help of a term—"meaning"—that is not itself an empirical concept, that does not name one feature of things among others. It thus requires clarification by way of an inquiry showing that, and how, it is the "condition of possibility" of knowledge of objects. That sort of inquiry is a transcendental one, and it is "idealism" to the extent that it cannot say how *things* are bound up with the space of meaning without also saying how *thoughts* are as well—not the logical content of thought but their first-person aspect, the experiencing of the experienced. From this perspective, McDowell's own theory of meaning remains dogmatic. It may be that by starting with the transcendental concept of meaning we gain the resources for a pluralistic empiricism in which the concept of the object, the "given," is *functionally* defined in terms of conceptual content (what it is given "as") and not rigidly defined in terms of some predetermined material (sense data or what have you) lying outside the space of reasons. Thus, "conceptual schemes or perspectives need not be on one side of the exploded dualism of scheme and world." However, it is not enough to speak of the subjective correlate of this functional object concept as being our "unproblematic openness to the world."[28] Unproblematic it may be with regard to old positivist threats of skepticism, but it is certainly not monolithic, nor is it possible to construct any metaphysical or epistemological position from this "new naturalism" without taking into account *how* objects of experience come to be able to serve *within* the space of meaning as constraints on what we say about them.

It is just here that transcendental phenomenology becomes relevant, for what distinguishes it from positions like McDowell's (and Lask's) is that it offers a functional concept of *intuition* to go along with the functional object concept. Intuition is defined not in terms of the "receptivity" of the "senses" but rather functionally, in terms of the structure of givenness itself. Intuition is that through which the (meaningful) object or state of affairs is given "in person" or "as" itself. Only on this basis will an empiricism that recognizes not only quarks and trees, but numbers, battles, and passions, be in a position to resist not only skepticism, but reductionism as well. It is through intentional (phenomenological) analyses of how objects like chess pieces or insults come to be given as what they are—analyses that go far beyond the claim that we are simply "open to" such things—that the concept of meaning can be *shown* to have priority over other (metaphysical or epistemological) philosophical starting points.[29]

With that, however, we already touch on one of the main substantive issues to be dealt with in this book. To conclude the introduction we need note only that the transcendental phenomenological criticism of McDowell's position—that it lacks the necessary theory of perception or intuitive givenness to remove the appearance of dogmatism in its appeal to the space of meaning—takes place against a shared commitment to a kind of empiricism in philosophy. It is precisely in defense of a philosophical empiricism that transcendental phenomenology conflicts most directly with neo-Kantianism, whose attitude toward appeal to the given, to *Evidenz,* was entirely critical. If the point of philosophy is not simply to gain knowledge, but to account for the very *possibility* of knowledge, these philosophers argued that no appeal to *Evidenz* can be any more than question begging. What is required is some principle, some basis for an argument, to show that, and how, the connection between knowledge and its object is a *necessary* one. In short, what is required is not transcendental phenomenology (exploration of the intentional structure of experience), but transcendental *logic,* a theory of those concepts or "categories" that make objects possible.[30] If a case is to be made for the indispensability of transcendental phenomenology in the theory of meaning, it will be necessary to confront the neo-Kantian position head-on and to show that no merely "logical" position, no position that does not attend to the first-person perspective of concrete experience, can provide a full account, whether of (the possibility of) knowledge, or of its own possibility as *philosophical* knowledge of the space of meaning as such. The chapters in part 1 are devoted to making this case.

PART 1

RECONFIGURING TRANSCENDENTAL LOGIC

1

Neo-Kantianism: Between Science and Worldview

Neo-Kantianism, a movement with roots deep in the nineteenth century, dominated German academic philosophy between 1890 and 1920. Though it carried the impulse of German idealism into the culture of the twentieth century and set the agenda for philosophies which displaced it, the movement is little studied now. One encounters it primarily in liberation narratives constructed by those whose own thinking took shape in the clash between neo-Kantianism and the "rebellious" interwar generation spearheaded by Jaspers and Heidegger. Thus before Heidegger—so Hannah Arendt—"philosophy was not so much communicated as drowned in a sea of boredom." And with Heidegger—so Hans-Georg Gadamer—"the complacent system-building of neo-Kantian methodolgism" gave way; its "calm and confident aloofness . . . suddenly seemed to be mere child's play."[1] Here neo-Kantianism is the terminus a quo of a "liberation from the unbreakable circle of reflection" toward recovery of the "evocative power of conceptual thinking and philosophical language."[2] It thus enters the lore of continental philosophy as the father who had to be slain in order that philosophy might live.

No doubt testimony from those who were there reflects well enough their experience of the matter, even if it leads some (like Gadamer) to stigmatize neo-Kantian motifs in Heidegger's thought as inauthentic. Meanwhile, however, projects such as fundamental ontology or philosophical hermeneutics, which heralded the liberation, have revealed internal aporias which suggest that reassessment of their triumphal claim to have transcended the dead-end questions obsessing their neo-Kantian fathers may be in order. It is a commonplace of contemporary continental philosophy, for example, that epistemology (the neo-Kantian project of ultimate grounding) is dead. Already in 1962 a writer could characterize the time as one in which "epistemology is seen as the ultimate stage of philosophy's degeneration," so pervasive was the ontological (Heideggerian) revolution.[3] Heidegger's claim, however, was not that knowledge needed no grounding, but that it needed *ontological* grounding. Subsequently, Ernst Tugendhat questioned the adequacy of this position, and Karl-Otto Apel began to interrogate the "hermeneutic turn" in light of the neo-Kantian philosopheme "validity" (*Geltung*). Heidegger had been deeply concerned with such questions. His antifoundationalist heirs—the deconstructionists, the pragmatists, the hermeneuticists—find in this concern only residual "philosophy," an incomplete liberation. Rorty rightly ties the rhetoric of the "end of philosophy" to the collapse of the neo-Kantian program which sought, by becoming theory *of* science, to establish an autonomous place for philosophy among the positive (empirical and mathematical) sciences.[4] Depending on one's sympathy for what is announced in that rhetoric, one might well feel that the neo-Kantian paradigm has not been altogether superseded. A balanced assessment of neo-Kantianism might reveal questions with which the onto-hermeneutic turn is burdened by its very nature but which, as transcending all its powers, it is also not able to answer.

The present chapter will neither carry out such an assessment nor pretend to encompass the movement as a whole. In reconsidering the neo-Kantian heritage, one should be aware that continental philosophy defines itself through a largely distortive and reductive reading of the neo-Kantians, but here the aim is simply to indicate something of what is at stake in such readings by situating a few theses characteristic of "classical" neo-Kantianism within the horizon of a particularly contested point, namely, the dispute between the neo-Kantians and their phenomenological critics over the *autonomy* of philosophy. Both movements lay claim to the mantle of "scientific philosophy," but neo-Kantianism differs from phenomenology in maintaining a *continuity* between positive science and philosophy. As theory of science, neo-Kantian epistemology wants to provide grounds for a principled ("scientific") weltanschauung. Phenomenology (here, Husserl and the early Heidegger), on the contrary, establishes the autonomy of philosophy precisely through a *discontinuity* with positive science and the aims of worldview formation.

1. The Neo-Kantian Movement

In 1912 Heidegger, the student of Heinrich Rickert, opened his review of current trends in the philosophy of logic by referring to a long-standing controversy over the meaning of Kant's first *Critique*. The once-dominant "psychological interpretation of Kant," with its "naturalization of consciousness," has now been displaced by the "transcendental-logical conception advocated since the 1870s by Hermann Cohen and his school as well as by Windelband and Rickert," according to which Kant's *Critique of Pure Reason* "did not inquire into the psychological origin of knowledge but into the logical value of its validity" (GA 1:19). Such language indicates that by the turn of the century "Kant" had come to govern a semantic field by no means restricted to a historical figure. The neo-Kantian movement did yield an efflorescence of Kant philology, but the issue dividing psychological and transcendental (aprioristic) readings of Kant was ultimately systematic, not philological: Where does philosophy stand in the economy of the sciences? That Kant, with some justification, had been enlisted on both sides reflects the pluralism of the neo-Kantian movement, its diverse agendas and competing claims jostling throughout a nearly eighty-year period. Some orientation is therefore indispensable if the implications of the debate between "classical" neo-Kantianism and phenomenology are to be seen.

The beginnings of neo-Kantianism have been identified with Otto Liebmann's *Kant und die Epigonen* (1865) in which the phrase, "Thus we must go back to Kant," repeatedly occurs. As Köhnke has shown, however, Liebmann's work is a rather *late* instance of what had been, since 1850 and in step with fluctuating fortunes of philosophy in the academy (and the academy in German politics), a whole series of "programmata" in which Kantian motifs played enormously varied roles.[5] Thus, the earliest neo-Kantian authors (J. B. Meyer, H. Helmholtz, E. Zeller, R. Haym, F. A. Lange, K. Fischer) diversely exploited idealist, realist, critical, skeptical, naturalistic, and metaphysical possibilities contained in Kant's philosophy. Further, as Gerhard Lehmann has shown, the notion that neo-Kantianism arose out of the collapse of German idealism needs to be tempered by the recognition that the Kant to whom these authors "returned" owed much to a "late idealism" (I. H. Fichte, C. H. Weisse, H. Lotze) of the 1830s and 1840s that had not yet succumbed to the divorce between "scientific" (i.e., academic) philosophy and weltanschauung.[6] That impulse would be felt again in the late 1870s when the neo-Kantian "critique of German idealism changed into a new idealism" and "again laid claim to its own systems, to the absolute validity of its foundations, metaphysics, an unassailable apriorism, and theories of ethics and values."[7]

This new idealism is the classical neo-Kantianism identified with the Marburg school (H. Cohen, P. Natorp, E. Cassirer, N. Hartmann), noted for its focus on the logic of the exact sciences, and with the Southwest German (or Baden) school (W. Windelband, H. Rickert, E. Lask, B. Bauch), known for its interest in the historical, cultural sciences and its theory of transcendent value (*Wert*). The views of these schools concerning the relation between philosophy, science, and worldview evolve, in turn, over three distinct periods.

In the first period (1871–78), characterized by an "extremely broad palette of possibilities for the contemporary realization of Kant's theories of apperception and apriority,"[8] there is a certain continuity between a priori and empirical inquiry. The autonomy of philosophy vis-à-vis positive science has not yet become the decisive issue. Cohen, for instance, whose "transcendental" reading of Kant's theory of the ideality of space and time permitted the realistic thesis that scientific knowledge reaches the *thing* and not merely "representations," could contribute to the positivist *Vierteljahresschrift für wissenschaftliche Philosophie;* and Windelband, whom Heidegger later described as rejecting all inquiry into the "origin" of the a priori as irrelevant to the "logical value" of its "validity," could propose a Darwinian evolutionary explanation of categories in terms of ethnopsychology.[9] A version of this realistic or quasi-positivistic strain of neo-Kantianism, developed by A. Riehl at this time, survived into the later idealistic period, though Riehl never established a school.[10] In line with Lange's influential *Geschichte der Materialismus* (1866), "scientific philosophy" is limited in this period to theoretical reason; interest in Kant's ethical philosophy, and the motives toward idealism and weltanschauung stemming from it, emerged only in the second period, from 1878 to the end of the First World War.

During this second period the two schools developed their salient doctrinal differences. Equating Kant's concept of experience with the account of the object given in scientific judgments, Cohen's *Kants Theorie der Erfahrung* (1871) elaborated the characteristic Marburg view of the *Critique of Pure Reason* as a "theory of science." Philosophy has only indirect access to being, mediated by cognitions achieved in first-order scientific theorizing (i.e., "the fact of science"). Unable to deduce truth speculatively from its own principle, as Hegel imagined, philosophy is to reflect upon the principles governing independent sciences. By extending to all reality Kant's thesis concerning the constructed character of mathematics, Cohen's *Das Prinzip der Infinitesimalmethode* (1883) established the Marburg understanding of transcendental logic as a theory of knowledge that (in Natorp's words) brings "ultimate unity" to the system of sciences by uncovering the principles, or categories, according to which the sciences construct being. In E. Cassirer's *Philosophie der symbolischen Formen* (1923–29), this approach undergoes an anthropological extension, from the logical construction of the object of knowledge to the symbological construction of all cultural unities.

In its identification of thought with logical form, Marburg idealism's understanding of Kant's Copernican priority of thought over being recalls both Plato (cf. Natorp's controversial *Platos Ideenlehre* [1903]) and Hegel. The value-philosophical idealism of the Baden school, on the contrary, drew upon the subjectivist, Fichteanized Kant of Windelband's teacher, Kuno Fischer, and advanced a more Aristotelian logic emphasizing the interplay of form and material. Its conception of the relation between philosophy and science reflects Fichte's *Wissenschaftslehre* and the "primacy of practical reason" of Kant's second *Critique.* Both sources are evident in Rickert's theory of judgment.[11] With roots going back to Windelband's idea of logic as the "ethics of thought" and ultimately to Lotze's theory of "validity" (*Geltung*) as a "value," Rickert's view holds that cognitive judgment involves two moments: first, a moment immanent to the subject, in which alogical, irrational material (the "content of consciousness") is combined via categories (logical form); and second, a moment of affirming or denying what is so synthesized, in light of the subject-*transcendent* "value" of cognitive validity, or truth. The "object of knowledge" is thus not a function of thinking alone, as in Marburg formalism, but of interest, position taking, and decision. Being is what "ought" to be affirmed; *Sollen* has priority over *Sein.*

Southwest German idealism's appeal to the primacy of the practical opened it to weltanschauung motives transcending Kant's epistemology, including elements derived from the *Critique of Judgment.* Thus, in a late work Rickert (1934) argued that though for Kant "scientific philosophy must base itself on the theory of knowledge," it would be "the gravest misunderstanding" to think that "Kant intended to substitute a theory of science in place of metaphysics."[12] From the outset the Baden school projected a general philosophy of culture (of cognitive, ethical, and aesthetic validity) grounded in the concept of transcendent *Wert* as philosophy's specific theme, and in its more inclusive epistemology it came to grapple with the question of *historical* knowledge. Developing Windelband's distinction between "nomothetic" and "ideographic" sciences, Rickert's *Die Grenzen der naturwissenschaftlichen Begriffsbildung* (1896, 1902) maintained that the "generalizing" and "homogenizing" concept formation found in natural science (and the Marburg constructivism based on it) encounters an unsurpassable limit in the "heterogeneous continuum," the ultimately "irrational" material, of reality. To approach it, historical concept formation must proceed in an opposed—"individualizing"—direction, its interest being not in general laws but in understanding unique "value-individualities."

The third phase of classical neo-Kantianism begins with the outbreak of war in 1914 and continues through the National Socialist intervention in the German university system in the 1930s. Reflecting the collapse of cultural optimism, this period is characterized by an assault upon academic idealism in the name of *Lebensphilosophie* (a catchall term invoking the theses of philosophical "outsiders" like Nietzsche, Bergson, and Dilthey). In the neo-Kantian schools this appears as a conflict between the epistemological framework of transcendental logic and ontological issues asserting priority over such a framework—for instance, the infinite manifold of particular reality that escapes derivation from the concept, and the concrete or "factic" subject, whose life overflows the transcendental consciousness postulated in logical idealism.

In the Baden school, Lask's *Logik der Philosophie* (1911) and *Die Lehre vom Urteil* (1912) anticipate themes of the third period. Abandoning Rickert's immanentist interpretation of the form/material schema (and so also the primacy of practical reason), Lask adopts the "standpoint of transcendence" to give an ontological interpretation of the object as a unity of categorial form and alogical material.[13] Objects are *themselves* "truths, unities of meaning, not cognitions, judgments, propositions." In contrast to Cohen, for whom the object is constructed in the scientific judgment, Lask argues that "the most basic problems of logic reveal themselves only if pretheoretical cognition is included in the investigation."[14] In Marburg, N. Hartmann offered the *Grundzüge einer Metaphysik der Erkenntnis* (1921), a quasi-phenomenological "realistic" theory of the subject-object relation intended to account ontologically for what is merely presupposed in Natorp's logical idealism, namely, the subject's ability to "transcend" its own sphere. In Kant philology, H. Heimsoeth began to uncover the "metaphysical motives" of Kant's critical philosophy, an interpretation pursued in Heidegger's 1927–28 lecture course on Kant and in *Kant und das Problem der Metaphysik.*[15]

Thus, in the third period the neo-Kantianism that had begun as a "theory of science" continuous with the positive sciences and hostile to "antiscientific" philosophy (i.e., metaphysics understood positivistically as mere weltanschauung), and that had grown into an idealistic worldview based on an *incomplete* autonomization of philosophy (transcendental reflection on the constructions of natural or historical science), is challenged by a resurgent metaphysics laying claim to sources more "primordial" than what has already been elaborated scientifically. But how are such sources accessed, and with what right are claims about them advanced? Are such claims anything more than uncritical speculation, rhetoric, personal effulgences, or mysticism? Rickert, for example, rejected phenomenology's appeal to intuition because it lacked any *principle* for the systematic ordering of *Erlebnisse,* which alone could render "scientific" an approach to them. The concern of philosophy "is not life, but *thought* about life."[16] Can philosophy go back behind the critical, epistemological starting point—in this sense abandon neo-Kantianism—without losing its identity as a principled claim to truth, an autonomous "science"? The debate between Natorp's critical idealism and phenomenology, at whose heart lies the issue of what constitutes scientific philosophy, exemplifies what is involved in trying to answer this question positively.

2. Natorp's Critical Idealism

In 1911—the same year Husserl published his "Philosophie als strenge Wissenschaft" in Rickert's *Logos* journal—Natorp opened his *Philosophie, Ihr Problem und ihre Probleme* by observing that the younger generation, schooled in skepticism vis-à-vis all "merely traditional wisdom," yearns after a "truth armored with the impenetrable steel of genuine science," one able "to satisfy not only the calculating intellect but also to answer the secret, innermost doubts and questions of the soul." *Critical* idealism is to address this yearning by exploiting the "close unity between science and philosophy," whose differences are but "opposite directions of one and the same path." Progressing systematically from logical through ethical, aesthetic, and religious principles, Natorp abjures any move into "the suspicious land of metaphysics"; nevertheless, the goal is a "reconciliation between experience and idea" that will fulfill "the demands of a *Weltanschauung*."[17] In continuity with the positive sciences, philosophy can satisfy both intellect and soul.

To "reduce the manifold to law" is the "inner law of knowledge itself"; hence philosophy and science, as modes of knowing, have this in common.[18] In philosophy, however, the manifold consists of sciences themselves, and its laws are logical, not natural. Philosophy seeks the "unity and ground" of science, but it does not propose an explanatory theory of the fact of knowledge (*questio facti*) as might be found, say, in psychology or anthropology. Its distinctive task is the *critique* of knowledge (*questio juris*), a reflection on the principles that, as necessary conditions of any knowledge of objects at all, make science possible and provide the "justification" of its claim to truth.

The first condition of scientific validity is the priority of *methodological thinking* over being (where "thinking" does not refer to individual subjectivity but to thought, logical form, as such); and because the factic subject is not at issue, the resulting idealism is "critical," not "subjective."[19] If "by thinking one understands the infinite process in which being is posited as object and first of all receives its concrete determination," then "being becomes a function of thinking." To ask for a "being in itself" apart from the process of scientific knowing is to ask for something "internally contradictory." Being "resolves itself into becoming" as the correlate of the *process* of "objectification," the "construction" of being as object through conceptual determination.[20] The "fact of science" is the fact of objectification at its most developed stage, and philosophy's task is to grasp the categories of objectification governing scientific development. The logic of science is thus transcendental since it concerns conditions under which objects can be known and since logical principles are simultaneously principles of *being*. It is in the (diachronic) coherence of this system of categories, not in any single principle, that the answer to the *questio juris* is demonstrated.[21]

Natorp's projection of a transcendental logic contrasts, in important respects, with Kant's. First, by jettisoning the so-called subjective deduction of the first edition of the *Critique of Pure Reason* in favor of the second-edition version, psychological and anthropological elements of the doctrine of synthesis are purged from logic such that the concept of the thing-in-itself loses its skeptical implications. The thing- (or object-) in-itself is simply the limit of the infinite process of objectification. Subjectivist elements are further eliminated by incorporating the transcendental aesthetic into logic. On Natorp's reading, Kant makes the space-time order depend not merely on "pure intuition" but on "the entire system of synthetic functions of thought."[22] Because intuition is not an *independent* cognitive faculty, there is no independently given realm of "phenomena" which would have its own laws. The wholly indeterminate, intuitively "given" is, in Natorp's phrase, only *aufgegeben,* presented as a *task.*[23] There is, then, no ultimate hiatus between the "form" (universal) and the "material" (particular) of knowledge: "Particularity" signifies nothing but "completed determination . . . in which nothing remains to be determined."[24] This Panlogism, the effacement of all dualistic elements in Kant's theory of knowledge, invites the thesis that neo-Kantianism is often equally a neo-Hegelianism. It also indicates the primary point of disagreement between Natorp and phenomenology.

This is most clearly seen in the way Natorp reworks Kant's concept of apperception into his doctrine of transcendental psychology. Natorp accepts the "Kantian" view that "it is from the inner life that all things must spring" but argues that inner life is "in itself formless" and hence cannot be grasped in immediate reflection. Nor can it be approached (as the "leading psychology currently does") as a field to be objectified, reduced to law, since this destroys its character precisely as the (flowing) subjective. Mental life can only be reconstructed, via a process of "subjectification." Only by a "regress from an objectification accomplished from its sources in the subject and its mental life [*Erlebnis*] can these latter be brought to cognition."[25] Like Kant's unity of apperception but unlike Husserl's transcendental consciousness, the "ego of *Bewußtheit*" is "neither a fact nor something existing nor a phenomenon"; it is, rather, "the *ground* of all fact, the ground of all existence, all givenness, all appearance."[26]

The formal structure of *Bewußtheit* (ego, formless content [task], object) can be traced in two directions, one of which has teleological, the other foundational, priority.[27] Object determination has teleological priority: I objectify my experience by attributing the red I see to the apple. But as knowledge progresses I come to see that what is objective at one stage is in fact only subjective, that the redness of the apple is a function of my subjective life. Though it has foundational (transcendental) priority, this subjective life cannot be described; it is accessible only by working back from a given stage of objectification (abstraction) to *reconstruct* a previous, richer, more "subjective" stage. The subjective is not a distinct region of being; there is only being itself, which can be grasped in two cognitive directions.

Critical idealism thus fulfills the yearning for philosophical wisdom, for weltanschauung, by demonstrating a systematic, progressive constructivism as the "methodology" of science, grounded in a reconstructive transcendental psychology as the source of "the living mutual relations of the logical, ethical and aesthetic."[28] Rather than basing its approach to practical orientation in the world (worldview) on the dictates of conscience or upon vague intimations of the subject's sense of itself as a natural or a social being, critical idealism thus promised access to a scientifically established worldview grounded in the recovery of that universal transcendental subjectivity from which science itself, and all other objectifications of the spirit, had sprung. In both form and aim, this neo-Kantian version of scientific philosophy contrasts sharply with that developed in the phenomenological movement.

3. Critical Idealism and Phenomenology

In *Ideen I* (1913) Husserl claims, with only slight irony, that "we are the genuine positivists" (Hua III:46/39). Under Brentano's tutelage Husserl's initial attitude toward Kantian apriorism had been altogether negative, and in harmony with neo-Kantianism's own early positivist period, he instead proposed a psychological account of the a priori (e.g., in *Philosophie der Arithmetik* [1891]). By the 1890s this kind of continuity between philosophy and positive science had been abandoned in Marburg for transcendental idealism. Husserl nevertheless established close ties with Natorp, who was instrumental in steering him away from psychologism and would later inspire Husserl's move from static to genetic phenomenology. By 1913 Husserl had developed his own phenomenological "transcendental idealism," but it remained distinct in principle from Marburg neo-Kantianism. While the latter defined the scientific character of philosophy in terms of a transcendental *logic,* a systematic presentation of the a priori principles ("method") of empirical science, the former retained the antisystematic, empirical cast of its founder's early period, grounding its theory of the a priori on a philosophical appeal to *intuition.*

In his treatment of Natorp's psychology in the first edition of the *Logical Investigations* (1900, 1901), for example, Husserl rejects Natorp's doctrine of the pure ego of apperception. In the second edition (1913), however, he claims that he has "since managed to find it," having learned "not to be led astray from a pure grasp of the given through corrupt forms of ego-metaphysic" (Hua XIX/1:374/549). If the more idealistic Husserl no longer associates the Kantian ego with the "corrupt ego-metaphysic" of speculative idealism, his note also advances the very *un*-Natorpian claim to have *found* the pure ego in a "pure grasp of the given," that is, in intuitive evidence. Another note states that the pure ego is "apprehended in *carrying out* a self-evident *cogito*" (Hua XIX/1:368/544). Natorp had denied the phenomenality of the ego; it can neither be objectified, nor present itself at all, without ceasing to be genuinely "subject." For Husserl, however, this argument is merely verbal: The ego is there as a fact, an object, in its own appropriate manner. To claim otherwise is tantamount to consigning the ego to the realm of myth (Hua XIX/1:373–76/549–51).

This episode indicates how Husserl remains a "positivist" by insisting on a *philosophy of evidence.* Whether as a correlate of empirical intuition or of phenomenological reflection, givenness is no mere "task" but the ultimate source of justification. If so, then the point on which the neo-Kantian account of philosophy's scientific character turns—a distinction between a priori and empirical dimensions of positive science according to which intuition should play no role in philosophy—proves to be a mere prejudice. For Husserl, in contrast, only the phenomenological reduction can establish a truly presuppositionless scientific philosophy by bracketing questions of *being* to disclose the field of phenomenological *experience.* Phenomenology reflects on the intentional (neither simply logical nor causal) interconnections wherein the intelligibility (*Sinn,* meaning) of things is constituted; it is, therefore, able to clarify the meaning-structure of scientific validity claims. But can it also provide a theory that *justifies* the claim of positive science to a progressive grasp of being? While phenomenology censures neo-Kantianism for presupposing too much, the latter objects that phenomenology does not really ground the *validity* of knowledge at all.

Because Husserl does not identify the task of scientific philosophy with the *questio juris,* transcendental phenomenology, unlike critical idealism, introduces a radical *discontinuity* between philosophy and positive science. It is the world horizon as such—the space of meaning and not the fact of science—that phenomenology, as a reflection on evidence (*Evidenz*), claims for itself. If, as Husserl writes to Natorp in 1909, the Marburg school operates with "fixed formulas" that serve as first principles governing all investigation, "we in Göttingen work from an entirely different attitude and, though we are genuine idealists, it is an idealism from below"—not the "false empiricistic and psychologistic" ground but "a genuinely idealistic one from which one may ascend, step by step, to the heights."[29] Natorp, however, like Rickert, doubts that Husserl's idealism "from below," based on intuitive givenness, is in a position to claim scientific—that is, ultimately grounded—status for its own assertions. According to Natorp, phenomenological empiricism cannot provide the necessity and universality demanded of any philosophical cognition worthy of the name. The question of whether philosophical cognition is grounded in concepts (logic) or intuitions (evidence) remains a crucial point of contention between phenomenological and neo-Kantian modes of thought.

If the foundations of neo-Kantian and phenomenological conceptions of scientific philosophy are different, so are the motivations and aims. In the tradition of German idealism, Natorp seeks a scientific philosophy that will satisfy the soul as well as the intellect, whereas Husserl's idealism retains, somewhat reluctantly, its positivist character. As he writes in "Philosophy as Rigorous Science," ethical, social, and existential situations demand a weltanschauung—"we cannot wait . . . we have to take a position"—but it is illusory to think that this goal, "set in the finite," can be attained by scientific philosophy. To seek a scientific philosophy that will "satisfy both intellect and feeling," to hope "to have [a] system . . . soon enough to be able to live by it," is to conflate two distinct goals. The first, the aim of weltanschauung philosophy, is *wisdom;* the second, the only legitimate motivation of scientific philosophy, is "*responsibility* . . . in regard to humanity." Hence, Natorp's position must be rejected. As Husserl writes, "To the extent that this is intended as a reconciliation calculated to erase the line of demarcation between *Weltanschauung* philosophy and scientific philosophy, we must throw up our defense against it" (Hua XXV:56–59/141–44).

Husserl's refusal to subordinate scientific responsibility to individual wisdom had its origin in a positivist, empiricist apprenticeship which Heidegger, trained in Southwest German neo-Kantianism at Freiburg, did not share. It might be expected, then, that as he began to develop his own postwar theory of "concrete subjectivity," Heidegger would retain the sympathy for neo-Kantian weltanschauung tendencies which he expressed in the 1916 conclusion to his *Habilitation*, referring to "the deeper, worldview essence of philosophy" (GA 1:410). Instead, the lecture courses of 1919–23 introduce the "hermeneutics of facticity" as an extension of the phenomenological principle of evidence, and they cultivate Husserl's radical distinction between scientific philosophy and weltanschauung. At least rhetorically, Heidegger resists the spirit of the age. He proposes to reform the university by recovering the roots of genuine "science" and in this context offers detailed criticisms of both Marburg critical idealism and Baden *Wertphilosophie*.[30]

Both schools "exhibit a nonscientific tendency toward *Weltanschauung*" and an "overhasty striving toward systematic closure" (GA 58:9). Without the "phenomenological criterion" of "understanding evidence and evident understanding," neo-Kantianism "lacks a genuine scientific problematic" (GA 56/57:125, 126). It is a "standpoint philosophy" that confuses reflection on science with scientific philosophy (GA 59:142). It mistakenly restricts "the transcendental problem to the constitution-form 'science' " and sees "all domains of life through this filter" (GA 58:23). Natorp's method is merely the uncritical "radicalization of the theoretical"; defining itself by the *questio juris*, it does not permit anything "outside the theoretical attitude" to be seen as a philosophical problem (GA 59:143).

Husserl's nonformal concept of transcendental consciousness represented an initial break with the "theoretical" in this sense, but it shared with the neo-Kantian formal-logical subject the status of being "a priori," related to the world as an intentional ground, not as a natural, empirical item. Can this discontinuity—which defines phenomenology as an autonomous science and distinguishes it from mere worldview—be maintained when phenomenology becomes the *Urwissenschaft* of *factic* (historical, finite, situated) "life"? Early Heidegger thought so, and in his lecture from summer semester (SS) 1920, *Phänomenologie der Anschauung und des Ausdrucks*, he recognizes the "methodological" demand that one show how "life as *Erleben* becomes *rationally* accessible for philosophy" (GA 59:88).

In this regard, Natorp's method of subjectification represents the "antipode" (GA 59:96) to Heidegger's own phenomenological approach. The argument that phenomenological description objectifies, and hence destroys, the subjective character of the life flux "is correct from the constitutive [sc. Natorp's constructive] perspective," but phenomenological description—initially defined only negatively, against natural-scientific causal and genetic methods—is not equivalent to constructive objectification (GA 59:194). No doubt Natorp is right that "the ego cannot become an object of thought" (i.e., in Natorp's terms, an object of logical construction), but "the question is whether it must become an object of thought, whether what it 'is' is determined in thought." This is not, however, to "resign" the ego, with the Baden school, to the conceptual limbo of being an "irrational remainder," for such resignation arises from the same constructive, theoretical standpoint. Phenomenology does not ask that one "abandon thinking" in favor of "enthusing and intuiting" in some irrational immediacy; it invites one to explore "a more original form" of "theory" or thinking, one not driven by the "standpoint" of "neo-Kantian logical methodology" (GA 59:143–44).[31]

In chapter 7 I shall explain how early Heidegger conceives this "more original" thinking in terms of "formal-indicating concepts" that arise from within life itself and adumbrate an "evidence situation" where *philosophical* interpretation of factic life becomes possible, a cognitively responsible re-collection (*Wieder-holung*) of the meaning (*Sinn/Sein*) presupposed in any encounter with entities. With respect to the contrast between phenomenology and neo-Kantianism, however, the salient point is that even Heidegger's hermeneutics of facticity remains a form of *categorial* research into an existential a priori, and, like Husserl, Heidegger continues to see the demand for weltanschauung as a corruption of the genuine motive of philosophy (GA 59:170). His appeal to an ontological ground for philosophical science thus also faces the neo-Kantian *questio juris:* Upon what is grounded the validity of those categories factic life employs in understanding itself philosophically? By winter semester (hereafter WS) 1927–28 Heidegger will argue that a phenomenological account of the *origin* of categories renders the question of their *validity* otiose (GA 25:314 ff.). But if that origin is finite, factical, and situational, can it possibly suffice to ground those judgments that, in science and philosophy, lay claim precisely to trans-situational truth? At their famed 1929 Davos "dispute," Cassirer posed this question to Heidegger: If truth is ontologically relative to finite Dasein, must we not give up the idea of necessary truth? How can a finite being be the ontological ground of a priori validity, a validity claimed by all ontological theories, including Heidegger's (GA 3:278/195)? Heidegger replied that his thesis of ontological relativity meant nothing more than that "truth only has meaning [*Sinn*] when Dasein exists" (GA 3:281/198). Unhappily, he did not go on to say how the distinction between the "scientific" validity claimed by his own categorial analysis of "life" and those interpretations which belong merely to weltanschauung could be preserved in light of his emphasis on the "finitude" of the ontological ground of truth.

It is to provoke further inquiry into questions such as these that the following chapters begin to stage the encounter between phenomenology and neo-Kantianism as a reconfiguration of transcendental logic. In the 1920s Heidegger did not wish to substitute weltanschauung wisdom for scientific philosophy, but to *expand* the reach of reason beyond the limits of a logic of science to encompass the space of meaning as a whole. This still seems to be a pressing task in philosophy, at least among those philosophers—whether of hermeneutic or analytic persuasion—who do not yet embrace the thesis that questions of validity are exclusively the effect of a superannuated mode of writing. That Heidegger later abandoned the terrain of philosophy (scientific or otherwise), though without ever ceding his claim to a certain rigor, does not demonstrate that the neo-Kantian problematic is either degenerate or irrelevant. It signals, instead, the truculence of issues that must reappear whenever phenomenology seeks to maintain contact with philosophy.

2

Emil Lask: Aletheiology as Ontology

Our predominantly whiggish tendency in writing the history of philosophy occasionally has the consequence of effacing from view a thinker whose influence in his own time was significant and whose philosophical ideas may still be of some interest. This is the case with Emil Lask. The general eclipse of neo-Kantian philosophy in the 1920s by phenomenology and existentialism buried in nullity the name of a thinker who, at the height of his powers, importantly influenced philosophers as diverse as Heidegger and Lukács and was "certainly one of the best" according to many of his currently better known contemporaries.[1] Lask's death in 1915 at the age of thirty-nine contributed to his subsequent obscurity; but as others concerned with the question of philosophical or transcendental logic discovered, philosophers simply changed the subject.

Under such circumstances it can be revealing to explore the particular influence which a thinker like Lask had upon those who are currently more in vogue. Recently, a few such studies have begun to appear, and in time they may help to modify the prevailing judgment on neo-Kantianism as a sterile academicism.[2] The aim of this chapter, however, is different: to present an aspect of Lask's thought that did survive the change of subject, namely, his attempt, on the basis of a theory of meaning, to determine a concept of autonomous philosophy distinct from both empirical science and metaphysics.[3] Heinrich Rickert described Lask's thought as an attempt "to generate a synthesis between Platonic-Aristotelian philosophy and modern Kantianism."[4] This yields an *aletheiology*—an ontological (nonmetaphysical, nonrepresentational) theory of meaning grounded in the concept of truth. The first four sections of this chapter discuss issues central to the development of such a theory of meaning as they appear in Lask's first major work, *Die Logik der Philosophie und die Kategorienlehre* (1911). A final section evaluates two opposing views as to the success of Lask's synthesis and introduces some topics to be pursued in later chapters.

1. The Copernican Turn

Lask's theory of meaning is the cornerstone of his effort to establish a transcendental philosophy against contemporary positivism and psychologism on the one hand and Hegelian "Panlogism" (a code word for Marburg neo-Kantianism) on the other (*LP* 26).[5] The immediate problem was to articulate a doctrine of categories which could navigate between the Aristotelian conception of categories as predicates of being and the skeptical-psychologistic conception of categories as mental forms of representation. Thus, the doctrine of categories belongs to transcendental logic, which Lask considers to be the genuine *prote philosophia,* the "self-reflection and 'self-consciousness' of philosophy itself" (*LP* 210). What, then, is thematized in a specifically transcendental philosophy, and particularly in a transcendental logic? The theory of meaning is designed to address this question.

To understand how Lask sees the problem of transcendental logic—which Kant had called the "logic of truth"—one must appreciate those points where Lask is constrained not only to revive Kant but also to revise him.[6] To renew the Kantian project of a logic which goes beyond the syntactic structures investigated by the traditional formal consequence logic toward a semantics of object-constituting categories it is necessary to recover Kant's "Copernican achievement" (*Kopernikanische Tat*). Lask sees as his primary debt to Kant this founding insight of transcendental philosophy, interpreted as "the conversion of the concept of being into a transcendental-logical concept" (*LP* 28). It thus expresses the hegemony of the logos over all extralogical philosophical starting points, the rapprochement of logic and ontology.

With this, Lask hopes to overcome the gulf opened up by the traditional two-world theory, according to which the realm of knowledge (reason or logos) is confronted by a thoroughly "metalogical" transcendent object. On this theory, categories such as causality are either asserted of objects dogmatically, or the a priori status of such categories is skeptically denied in favor of nonphilosophical empiricism or positivism. The Copernican achievement, however, is to see such categories, or "logical content" (*logischen Gehalt*), as "determining or constituting objectivity"

(*LP* 29). The objectivity of objects, the being of beings, the thinghood of things, the causality of causes, and so on, is not a real (physical or metaphysical) element, but a logical moment. Still, if Lask accepts the role in general assigned to logic by Kant's Copernican turn, he finds the details of Kant's own conception of transcendental logic to be in need of revision. In Lask's terms, transcendental logic is not primarily gnoseology but aletheiology, not a reflection on the conditions for the possibility of *knowledge,* but a reflection on the formal-ontological structure of *truth.*[7] In what sense is this to be understood as a revision of Kant?

Lask's aletheiology turns on denying any role to subjectivity (the transcendental unity of apperception) in grounding the theory of categories. Where Kant holds that categories arise from the spontaneity of understanding as subjective forms for synthesizing a given manifold of sense, and then deduces or justifies their objective validity by arguing from the unity of experience in a single consciousness, Lask drops all reference to subjective unity and synthesis in specifying the nature and function of categories.[8] For Lask, Kant's whole attempt to argue from subjective origin to objective validity is based on a misinterpretation of the nature of "the logical," a misinterpretation reflected in Kant's failure to clarify adequately the difference between the transcendental level of analysis, on the one hand, and both the metaphysical and the psychological levels, on the other. Lask understood that the psychologistic interpretation of Kant, leading to a naturalizing and psychologizing of logical categories, had been a misreading (*LP* 250).[9] Such misreading is understandable, however, since Kant had defined the object of knowledge phenomenalistically—by appeal to the concept of experience—and had taken up the transcendental problem of truth only at the level of the judgment, the "representation of a representation."

For Lask, neither experience nor judgment may play a role in determining the field of transcendental logic. To the extent that both experience (scientific as well as prescientific) and judgment (the act as well as the ideal content) make essential reference to the "subject," they have their foundation in a theory of truth that makes no such reference. Although transcendental logic does involve a gnoseology or theory of cognition, it is merely "secondary, supplementary" to aletheiology, the theory of being in the sense of truth.[10] Here Lask seeks to recover the ontological significance of the Aristotelian conception of categories while retaining the decisive Kantian insight into their purely "logical" character. Transcendental reflection is not "a one-sided epistemological 'standpoint' " but rather, through it, "*the* essence of being, objectivity, actuality is revealed, and there is no standpoint at all from which it could appear otherwise" (*LP* 31). The doctrine of categories is not a theory of representation, a theory of objects "for us," but an ontology, a nonmetaphysical theory of the being of objects "prior to all contact with subjectivity" (*LvU* 425).

2. Validity and Its Consequences

Lask's ontological attempt to maintain Kant's Copernican distinction between transcendental logic and metaphysics, while bracketing the issue of transcendental subjectivity, was bound to expose him to the objection that he had fallen back into a precritical position.[11] Far from signifying a synthesis of Aristotle and Kant, does not the very idea of a logic of the object "untouched by all subjectivity" represent merely a return to Aristotelian realism? Lask does push transcendental logic very far in the direction of Aristotelianism; only the barest nuance distinguishes his position from that of Aristotle.[12] But it is just this nuance, according to Lask, that has eluded the tradition from Plato to Kant, thus concealing the genuinely transcendental character of logos (*LP* 62). The root of the tradition's blindness lies in its commitment to the two-world theory. Since Plato it had been assumed that the fundamental philosophical distinction between the "sensible" and the "nonsensible" was equivalent to a distinction between sensible being and supersensible (metaphysical) being. With his discovery of transcendental reflection as a third way between rationalist and empiricist efforts to fit logical categoriality into one or the other of these worlds, Kant represents a turning point in the tradition (*LP* 28). Nevertheless, because Kant himself was finally committed to the same two-world theory, he could not adequately distinguish categories from psychological functions on the one hand and from metaphysical elements on the other (*LP* 234); hence "the logical" (the theme of transcendental logic) remained completely "homeless" in his thought (*LP* 260). Precise delimitation of the nature of logical categories calls for a distinction that cuts across the traditional distinction between the sensible and the metaphysical. Hermann Lotze had first proposed the necessary distinction. Within the traditional world of the nonsensible there are the "supersensible" beings of metaphysics and the nonsensible *validities* of logic.[13] With this the metaphysical two-world theory gives way to a more fundamental, transcendental duality. Lotze's "liberating and clarifying achievement" is "once again to have conceived the totality of what is at all thinkable in terms of an ultimate duality; in terms, namely, of a gulf between that which is [*Seiendem*] and that which holds [*Geltendem*], the realm of beings and the realm of validities . . . between that which *is* and *occurs,* and that which *is valid* without having to *be*" (*LP* 6). The distinction essential for transcendental philosophy is not that between physical and metaphysical *existents* (for both are still existents, entities), but that between existents and *validities.*

This is the nuance which distinguishes Lask's position from that of both Aristotle and Kant. Logical categories have their locus neither in the thing nor in consciousness because they "are" not at all. The category "being" does not apply to them. They instead hold or are valid. Transcendentality is a specific function neither of the subject nor of the object but of the logos as such. In its "uniqueness" with respect to both sensible and supersensible being, this "domain of validity" represents "a new precinct for philosophical reflection" (*LP* 15). Thus the basic principles of *Geltungslogik* enable Lask to address a significant aporia in Kant's transcendental philosophy. The Critical Philosophy preserves the possibility of a priori knowledge by restricting the concept of knowledge to cognition of the intuitively given sensible realm. This entails the rejection of transcendent metaphysics, but it also yields a situation where it is difficult to determine the cognitive status of transcendental reflection itself. Because transcendental reflection proceeds neither on the basis of sensible intuition nor by employing the categories constitutive of the realm of nature, it is not clear how it can count as a species of knowledge at all. For Lask, however, this is not an argument against the possibility of transcendental knowledge but an indication of Kant's failure to distinguish positively between supersensible being (metaphysics) and nonsensible validity (logic). Because Kant held the totality of possible objects (*Inbegriff des Etwas*) to be exhaustively circumscribed by the "duality of the sensible and the supersensible," he managed to "ignore in his theory of knowledge his own critique of reason, his own knowledge of the non-sensible transcendental forms. . . . The sphere of validity as the object of his own transcendental philosophy did not yet count for him, so to speak" (*LP* 131). But since "logic plays the same role with respect to philosophical knowledge as it does to all other knowledge" (*LP* 23), a corresponding widening of the task of transcendental reflection is required. Reflection must turn, in Kantian fashion, toward the conditions of possibility for transcendental knowledge itself; the enabling categories of transcendental reflection must themselves be "uncovered" (*LP* 195). "Only one who gainsays to philosophy the character of knowledge . . . may abjure the logic of philosophy" (*LP* 23).

The demand for a logic of philosophy is one consequence of recognizing the realm of validity. Another consequence—equally important for understanding how Lask transforms transcendental logic into aletheiology—radically alters the sense of Kant's critical project. If the objective validity of categories is no longer established by reference to an argument from the interplay of subjective (sensible and intellectual) faculties—that is, if the nature of categorial "form" is not understood in terms of a synthesis of the manifold of sensibility but solely in terms of its validity character[14]—then a pillar supporting Kant's rejection of the very possibility of metaphysical knowledge is undermined. The metaphysical realm of supersensible entities "may prove to be nothing at all," but transcendental logic cannot show this to be so; the argument of *Die Logik der Philosophie* implies that "the sole conceivable possibility for a destruction of metaphysics—namely, banishing it through the 'epistemological' considerations of the doctrine of categories"—is "futile" (*LP* 9). The distinction between nonsensible validity and supersensible being implies nothing concerning the possibility of metaphysical knowledge of the latter; it does, however, enable Lask to criticize those metaphysicians (in particular Aristotle and Hegel) who "usurp" logical validity problems by "hypostatizing" logical forms (*LP* 128). Lask's aletheiology—his genuinely "a-metaphysical" (*LP* 8) form of transcendental logic—places no a priori restriction on what can be known (*LP* 126).

This point also has consequences for Lask's approach to Kant's transcendental aesthetic; indeed, the whole issue of a transcendental aesthetic (the theory of intuition) is absent from his work. Categorial validity is still thought in relation to a "nonlogical" material (it need not be sensible) with which it is bound up in the unity of "truth *in concreto*" (*LP* 39),[15] but Lask develops this aspect of his doctrine, like all others, without reference to what he sees as anthropological or psychological appeals to the knowing subject. At the same time, Lask does not abandon the limits set in Kant's transcendental aesthetic by arguing for an intellectual intuition which would provide access to metaphysical entities. His sole aim is to establish the independence of a transcendental concept of truth from any a priori concept of what "we" can know. Thus "the domain in which the logical is sovereign is in itself without restriction; the domain of the logical which discloses itself in knowledge is perhaps restricted" (*LP* 129). A consistent transcendental logic concerns itself with the universal, objective-logical *structure* of truth, the intelligibility of any discoverable object.[16] The limits of knowledge can only be approached empirically, historically; they are matters for the development of the concrete sciences themselves (*LP* 271).[17]

3. Meaning: The Boundlessness of Truth

In distinguishing between truth and knowledge, Lask seeks to account for the possibility not only of transcendental knowledge, but also of knowledge in those domains excluded by the sensualism of Kant's transcendental aesthetic. An heir of Windelband and Rickert in this regard, Lask holds that transcendental logic—as the foundation of a theory of science—should not be limited to laying out the categories appropriate to the realm of nature but should reflect on the categorial structure of the objects with which history, for example, and the related cultural sciences have to do.[18] Historical or aesthetic objects are not reducible to the categories of physics, yet scientific investigation into them is possible. They have their own intelligibility (truth) and thus demand independent categorial investigation. By divorcing the transcendental theory of truth from all verificationist elements, Lask projects a "functional" concept of the object as the basis for a pluralistic doctrine of categories, which he terms "the boundlessness of truth" (*Schrankenlosigkeit der Wahrheit*)—the conviction that "everything, to the extent that it truly is at all and is not nothing, is encountered by categorial form, stands in logical form" (*LP* 125). Here the path from aletheiology to an ontology of meaning is adumbrated. After this path is briefly sketched, it will be necessary to examine more closely its pivotal principle, the functional relation between categorial form and categorial material.

The doctrine of the boundlessness of truth follows from Lask's disassociation of transcendental-logical reflection on categories from Kant's orientation toward the synthesis of representations in a judgment, together with the idea of categories as Lotzean "validities." If transcendental logic is a "logic of truth," the truth at issue cannot originally be a predicate of the judgment, that is, of something whose very being refers to the subject. As a product of the subjective-cognitive project of knowing (gnoseology), judgment itself refers back to a "nonartificial" (*ungekünstelt*), nonrepresentational truth which can serve as its measure. Judgment is a "breaking into pieces," an "atomization" of what Lask calls the "paradigmatic object" (*gegenständlicher Urbild*), by which he means the categorially structured thing itself (*LvU* 287, 418). Thus, Kant's Copernican turn does not mean that objects are made possible by our cognitive faculties; it means that they are constituted as objects by categorial validity:

> When seen as an achievement of transcendental logic the Copernican turn signifies not that logical validity content turns on the objects, standing in functional dependence on them like some accompanying shadow . . . but

> just the reverse: the objects turn on logical validity . . . their objectivity is valid truth [*geltende Wahrheit*]. (LP 30)

It must be emphasized that Lask is interested not in what it is to *know* an object but in what it is to *be* an object:

> Here too one must not permit the sundering into two domains—that of the object and that of "truth about" it—but rather [see that] truth reaches into the object itself, is *identical* to it . . . Here too the thing itself and truth about it are one and the same. (LP 109)

Categorial validity *is* the objectivity of objects, the being of beings, the thinghood of things—not merely as such objects are known through the subject's representing (judging) activity, but "in themselves."

The boundlessness of truth (the rejection of Kantian skepticism regarding things-in-themselves and the pluralization of the table of categories) thus follows from a distinction that, according to Lask, Kant failed to make between a "derivative" and a "paradigmatic" sense of truth—between the *nachbildlich* truth of judgments and the *urbildlich* truth identical to the (transcendentally grasped) object itself. Lask thus removes all verificationist elements from the transcendental theory of truth. The truth of a scientific statement, "correctness," is a subjective, "artificial" construct which for that reason necessarily stands in opposition to possible falsehood. Paradigmatic truth, defined solely in terms of the *Urverhältnis* between categorial form and material (*LP* 174), is "beyond the oppositions" generated by the incursion of subjectivity:

> Individual objects are individual unities of meaning, individual "truths." For truths as unities of theoretical meaning include the nonvalid material in addition to atemporal validity moments. Thus one may simply say: space-time objects *are* truths, physical objects are physicalistic truths, astral objects are astronomical, psychical objects are psychological truths, etc. To be sure, truths, unities of meaning—*not* cognitions, judgments, propositions; and further, truths in the paradigmatic sense, not in the sense of being abstracted from scientific statements. (*LP* 41)

Truth is in a unique Copernican sense "transcendent"; it is neither merely phenomenal nor altogether metalogical.[19]

Truth ("unity of meaning") is here conceived ontologically, not epistemologically. But because such an ontology begins with the concept of (paradigmatic) *truth,* it is a *transcendental* ontology distinct from traditional metaphysical realism and idealism.[20] Metaphysical (pre-Copernican) theories, whether realist or idealist, treat truth as a derivative relation of *Abbildlichkeit.* Realism dogmatically asserts a conformity between the logical structure of thought and the metalogical structure of being, while idealism guarantees agreement between thought and being by altogether reducing metalogical being to logical content. Against these alternatives Lask proposes his aletheiological concept of meaning. Meaning (*Sinn*) is the "interpenetration, the clasping, of form and material, i.e., the form (in itself empty and demanding fulfillment) together with its fulfilling content" (*LP* 34); thus meaning *is* the object "in truth," the essence of what it is to be an object (*Inbegriff der Gegenstände*) (*LP* 40).[21]

Meaning is here understood in an absolute sense, prior to the relational "meaning of" a word or proposition (*LP* 34). This absolute sense is finally intelligible only within transcendental reflection; it is a specifically "philosophical categorial epithet" (*LP* 123), namely, what the object is when the "truth" of its truth, its structure, is explicitly uncovered by transcendental reflection. Lask insists that this does not replace the robust reality of (say) a tree by some kind of representation, something merely "meant." The term "meaning" expresses only the difference between the tree as it is taken in nonphilosophical contexts (both everyday and scientific) and the same object as it is known through the transcendental reflection which clarifies its truth structure, the *Urverhältnis* of categorial form and material. The natural-scientific investigation of the tree, for example, is concerned exclusively with the *material* which "stands in" the category "being" or "causality"; it is not concerned with the category at all: "Such knowing consists in submission to the physical thing, to categorially organized material, whereby however the validity character of the form and correspondingly the meaning-character of the total object remains unknown. In such knowledge only the object material and not the object is known" (*LP* 122). Philosophical reflection, then, is itself a mode of knowing which uncovers what lies concealed in prephilosophical experience and knowing. By thematizing the categorial form of the object, the being of a being, it alone gets the object "in its truth" into view. This philosophically grasped whole constitutes the ontological concept of meaning.

Lask's theory of the object as meaning, as a reflection on structures and not a direct investigation of object material, is *autonomous* with respect to nonreflective sciences, whether empirical or metaphysical. For a reflective philosophy the philosophical first principle is not a sort of entity—whether subject or substance—but that which "logically" precedes both: meaning, being in the sense of truth, intelligibility as such. In its deepest impulse, then, though not in its actual execution, Lask's transcendental philosophy cannot be a science of entities at all. The specific theme of transcendental logic, categorial form, would be nothing but the reflectively grasped difference between the material of a robust reality and the intelligibility of that material.[22]

4. Form and Material: The *Urverhältnis*

To be at all plausible Lask's ontologization of transcendental logic, the identification of object and truth in the absolute concept of meaning, must succeed in giving an account of the *Urverhältnis* between categorial form and material that, unlike Kant's, makes no appeal to subjective—and hence at best verificationist or epistemological—functions of synthesis (*LP* 119).[23] To do this Lask develops some implications of the concept of validity. To speak of the category as a "form," for example, is merely to acknowledge that, as belonging to the realm of validity, it must be "valid *of*" something: "There is no validity that would not be a validity-with-regard-to, a validity-in-respect-of, a validity-of [*Hingelten*]." This "dependence, this unavoidability of being toward an other and for an other, can be called the form character of validity" (*LP* 32–33). Categorial form is valid with respect to its "material"; it holds *of* its material. Because validity carries this sense of being "toward" its material within itself, there need be no deduction of how such holding is possible. In itself, valid form is meaningless; it constitutes meaning only with respect to *X*. Similarly, the concept of material makes sense only with reference to its place in the *Urverhältnis;* there is no material that would await a form, nor is material to be defined with reference to some sort of subjective "receptivity." The category that holds of some specific material may be unknown, as in the case of the prescientific, groping stages of a developing science. In itself, however, the material is already "involved" in the *Urverhältnis;* it is simply, as Lask says, "logically naked" (*logisch nackt*), in need of the categorial clothing that comes through explicit discovery of the form in which it stands.

In Lask's sense, form signifies only this fulfillment-requiring character of validity and is not to be associated with any forming activity. The subject does not bring the category to the material, nor is the material formed by knowledge. "The material receives its categorial stamp not from a legitimizing thinking subject, but from the impersonal logical truth content" (*LP* 70). How, then, does this impersonal form differ from an Aristotelian metaphysical energeia or indwelling element "in" things?[24] The *Urverhältnis,* the simple interpenetration (*schlichtes Ineinander*) of form and material, is in fact not a relation at all, if a relation presupposes the coordination of distinct entities.[25] As a transcendental-logical notion, it is instead a functional distinction within the one "existing" object-as-meaning. This functional distinction, or "relation," permeates our experience of meaningful objects in everyday and scientific life, but it remains logically naked, not recognized as such until it is categorially grasped in a transcendental-logical reflection on meaning that clarifies the (ontological) nature of logical form itself. Without the concept of validity, Aristotle was unable to distinguish such logical form from supersensible (metaphysical) entities.

Lask analyzes the sense in which valid form is always valid "of" (its *Hingeltungs* character) by means of two further notions: "involvement" (*Bewandtnis*) and "clarity." With the first, *Bewandtnis,* Lask seeks to indicate how form is bound up with material if it is not to be seen as a cognitive synthesizing of material. Categories do not synthesize material since they are nothing but a certain way of being *of* material, a certain objective *Bewandtnis* (*LP* 66).[26] Categories reflect or indicate the "condition" of their material, the "circumstances" or "involvement" of the material itself. "Objectivity, being, objective subsistence, actuality, reality, existence" are nothing "other than a particular objective involvement [*Bewandtnis*] which pertains to sensible alogical material" (*LP* 69). Transcendental reflection on categories only registers as "form character" what the material "is in itself" (*LP* 69) and so brings out the meaning-character of the object as a whole.

To say that the category reflects or indicates the objective involvements of the material is to invoke the second, and decisive, characteristic of form in Lask's sense. For while the involvement belongs to the material qua material, the form as such is identified as a "moment of clarity" (*LP* 75), the intelligibility of the object qua meaningful whole. It is as it were the light by means of which the material not only *has* an involvement but is made intelligible, accessible, to the subject. Form as such is that clarity whereby the involvement becomes available *as* involvement. Wherever we are occupied or absorbed in a world of intelligible (familiar) things we are already in the presence of the category, though it is not grasped conceptually. Transcendental philosophy must therefore abandon its exclusive orientation toward the conceptual frameworks of the developed sciences. The transcendental logician who seeks to become clear about form *as* form (and not to become clear about the material *through* the form) cannot ignore the categoriality embedded in the lifeworld. Indeed, "the most elementary logical problems only reveal themselves to the logician who also includes 'prescientific' life in the purview of his investigation" (*LP* 185). Categorial clarity pervades scientific and nonscientific experience alike, though in both cases it is, prior to transcendental reflection, simply "lived through" and not itself "known." Lask speaks of "living *in* the truth" (*LP* 86, 191)—the prereflective experience of categorial clarity subtending everyday and scientific dealings with the world.[27]

In characterizing logos as a moment of clarity, Lask once again emphasizes the dependent, or empty, character of logical form. The Copernican achievement posits the identity of the object and truth but does not reduce the object to logical content as such: "That clarity pervades something means that something has been encountered in its categorial aspect, merely surrounded by clarity; it has not been flooded [*durchleuchtet*] with clarity but only illuminated [*umleuchtet*]. . . . One must not think fuzzily about truth as some simple mass of clarity" (*LP* 76). In opposition to the Hegelian dialectic of thought and being, Lask argues that to clarify the material is not to resolve material into pure logicality. The object material is intelligible, but not transparent. Lask thus rejects the Hegelian route to ontology (Panlogism) and returns to a version of Kantian dualistic formalism in his theory of the object (*LP* 110). "Not panlogism, but indeed the hegemony [*Panarchie*] of the *logos* must once again be brought into repute" (*LP* 133). Lask insists that the object consists of both rational (logical form) and irrational (the form's material) moments (*LP* 76). The material "is" its intelligibility by "standing within" the clarity of logical form, and thus Lask calls the object "logos-immanent"—immanent to, but not identical with, its logical clarity, its objective involvements. This nonidentity precludes absorption of the material into the realm of the logos; at the same time, Lask's formalism is distinguished from Kant's by a new account of the material moment of the meaningful object.

Lask is not worried that the "irrationality" of the material (which the science of philosophy, no less than physics, must acknowledge) will threaten the Copernican hegemony of logic since, as transcendental concepts, form and material have meaning only in relation to each other. Unlike Kant, who defines "material" in terms of a receptive faculty of sensibility, Lask conceives material purely functionally, as that which is clarifi*able* by way of logical form. Material is thus not defined by a certain way of being given, but by its functional relation to the category; it is that in the full object which is clarified, made intelligible. This material may be thoroughly "alogical," as in the case of the *Urmaterie* for the category "being" (*LP* 50). On the other hand, something that is itself already categorially formed may occupy the material position in an object of a higher order, as is the case with all cultural objects. As material, these are clarifiable by means of categories appropriate to them, ones indicating their objective involvements, and they are not reducible to the naturalistic material with which such objects may indeed be bound up (e.g., the physicality of works of art). Finally, logical form itself can occupy the material position, as when, in transcendental-logical knowledge, categories are cognized in terms of the categorial *Urform* "validity."[28]

An important feature of this functional concept of material is seen in Lask's discussion of how there can be a plurality of logical forms (categories), given their common (and empty) character of being "valid form" as such: "Just as form character in general is a symptom of being valid 'of' [*Hingelten*] in general, so the determinateness of individual forms is nothing other than a symptom and expression of the reference of valid form to a definite particular material" (*LP* 58). Lask here targets Hegel, against whom he argues that categorial differences cannot be generated dialectically from the realm of logos itself, and Kant, who acknowledged an independent material but inappropriately deduced a plurality of categories from the logical table of judgment. In contrast, Lask views the theory of categories as a quasi-empirical reflection on the way individual categories exhibit their "dependence" on a *specific range* of material, one that "investigates the particular aspect which determines the significance of 'thinghood,' 'causality,' etc." (*LP* 60). Individual categories—Lask calls them *Bedeutungen* (significations)—are all validities, but each, in addition to its form quality, exhibits a certain "excess of significance" which must therefore originate outside the domain of validity, in the irrational or alogical sphere of material (*LP* 60). This constitutes a moment of "impenetrability" (*LP* 77) within the logical itself, for which reason neither deduction nor dialectic can be the method of categorial investigation. Categories have a specific intension which signifies their appropriateness for, their being "cut to the measure of," something outside the sphere of logic; they are "materially determined" (*LP* 59). More precisely, if material is conceived in its full functional generality, only certain *aspects* of the material are determinative for specific categories. This, for Lask, is the "moment which determines significance" (*LP* 59), the "*principium individuationis* . . . in the sphere of validity" (LP 61), that which explains why not every category is valid of all material—why the category of being, for example, does not apply to the material of transcendental logic, the valid forms themselves.

Unfortunately, Lask is very sketchy on what an investigation into this "moment which determines significance" would involve. This is understandable, since it is hard to see how he could explain it without entering into an extensive revision of Kant's transcendental aesthetic—a project he avoids out of fear of psychologism. This fear is evident in the one example he does discuss in any detail, that of the material that determines the significance of the category "being." The discussion is important because the material specific to this category is, from the functional perspective, the limiting case of alogicality, the irrational par excellence.[29] It also provides the foundation (presupposition) for other categories which are more specific—those whose significance-determining material is more restricted—within the realm of being itself, such as causality. Being is thus what Lask calls a "domain category" (*Gebietskategorie*). Like validity (the domain category of the logical), it defines an autonomous object domain of inquiry and is presupposed by all other categories which hold in that domain.

When Lask inquires into the material determination of the category of being, he encounters a telling difficulty. On the one hand, since the material appropriate to this category is such as contains no further categorial formation (unlike the material for causality, which can be identified further in terms of the category of being itself), it can be characterized only negatively—it is thoroughly impenetrable (*LP* 49). On the other hand, when Lask nevertheless offers a quasi-positive characterization of it as "sensible-intuitable" or "perceivable" material, he immediately admits that these terms, in spite of their positivity, are "mere names which tell us just as little of philosophical value as 'blue' or 'sweet.' . . . They are mere references to psycho-physical experience-events and organs of experience, to the 'senses,' sensibility, intuition" (*LP* 52). At its lowest level, then, Lask's specification of a transcendental-logical ontology runs up against an unavoidable reference to the "subject." By consigning it to the philosophically irrelevant sphere of the psycho-physical, the very foundation of the doctrine of material determination of form is left transcendentally unclarified.[30]

The lack of a transcendental aesthetic and the failure to explore the whole problem of "givenness" thus indicates a major aporia in Lask's thought. Occasionally, Lask suggests the need for an "extended sense of intuition" (*LP* 217), which would presumably address the issue raised here. But since he radically separates aletheiology from gnoseology, Lask does not consider that an investigation into intuition could contribute positively to grounding the doctrine of categories. His gestures in that direction remain gestures only; his contribution to transcendental philosophy thus lies primarily in his idea of the object-as-meaning (truth), grounded in the functional form-material *Urverhältnis*. To complete the theory Lask would have had to get over what Husserl called the "bogy of psychologism" and incorporate the theory of the object into a functional theory of *intuition* and evidence (Hua XVII:159/151). Husserl argued that such problems are accessible only in a genuinely nonpsychologistic, transcendental way, on the basis of a phenomenological reduction. Though Lask knew Husserl's *Logische Untersuchungen* well, the concept of the reduction appeared in print too late for him to become aware of its significance.[31] His doctrine of categories remains objective-logical, and thus one-sided.

5. The Limits of Logical Ontology

How successful, finally, is Lask's attempt to move transcendental philosophy toward an ontological, nonrepresentational theory of meaning? Though a complete evaluation would call for a more detailed investigation than has been given here, it is clear that the question largely turns on the legitimacy of severing aletheiology from the Kantian orientation toward the synthetic activity of the judging subject. Only if such a move is defensible will Lask's absolute concept of meaning (what the object "is" for transcendental reflection) be a plausible development of Kantian transcendental logic, and not a renunciation of it.

Lask's theory of meaning is designed to express the difference between transcendental and positive (whether empirical or metaphysical) inquiry—the difference between a straightforward thematization of entities that aims to uncover their material properties and a reflective thematization of the truth structure (the intelligibility or the "being") of entities. His claim for the ontological significance of logical categories depends on keeping this difference between philosophical reflection and positive inquiry in mind; otherwise, the prejudicative concept of the object as meaning necessarily collapses into a quasi-Aristotelian dogmatic realism. But can a reflective philosophy that lays claim to the Copernican difference between metaphysics and aletheiology really be executed, as Lask tries to do, by bracketing all those issues that Kant addresses in his theory of transcendental synthesis? Clearly, a nonrepresentational theory of meaning must avoid any concept of the object as in some sense a construct of the subject, but does this mean that transcendental subjectivity is to be reduced (as in Lask) to being a kind of receptacle for original meaning?[32]

On this issue commentators differ as to the implications of Lask's position. In his essay "Emil Lasks Kategorienlehre vor dem Hintergrund der Kopernikanischen Wende Kants," Michael Schweitz argues that Lask's conception of the relation between form and material, posited as "independent of all synthesizing activity of the subject," effectively abandons the transcendental dimension altogether and "allows the dogmatic sense of being-in-itself to celebrate its return." For Schweitz, Lask's form-material *Urverhältnis* lacks a "principle [*Instanz*] which establishes the relation"—a transcendental synthesis—without which Lask has no right to don the mantle of Kantian *transcendental* philosophy at all and instead falls back on "a bit of metaphysics, long overcome, and within neo-Kantianism entirely untenable."[33] Schweitz argues that if the subject is not, as it is for Kant, the "source [*Inbegriff*] of theoretical principles," then the domain of "truth in itself" (the object) and the domain of judgment (knowledge) are once again separated by an unbridgeable gulf. Compatibility between the two could be assured only if the object-in-itself was "already known in its complete determinateness"—a possibility that Lask apparently denies.[34]

While there is much validity in such criticisms, it may be that the emphasis is misplaced. It is true that Lask cannot be called a Kantian in any strict sense, but it is not clear that his theory of the paradigmatic object as meaning abandons the transcendental dimension and relapses into metaphysics. If it is true that the transcendental subject does not *constitute* the object for Lask, such a subject is still thought of in some sense as a prejudicative *correlate* of that object. One may well admit that Lask's reference here is inadequate, finally, as an account of transcendental subjectivity; but to deny that the transcendental subject is the "source" (*Inbegriff*) of categories does not by itself entail that their transcendental character has been left unclarified. Indeed, it is a virtue of Lask's concept of categories as nonexisting validities that it becomes meaningless to seek a locus for them—whether in the thing (as Aristotelian elements) or in the subject (as Kantian functions).

Lask was certainly not alone in trying to preserve the ideal validity of categories while refusing to derive them, whether in the fashion of Kant or Fichte, from subjectivity. In the *Logische Untersuchungen,* for example, Husserl holds that only the *evidence* for categorial meaning is a function of the subject; categories as such are not products of the subject but ideal objects in themselves. Like Lask, Husserl objects to Kant's conception of categories as subjective forms of synthesis. Even in Husserl's later thought, where he moves closer to a certain Kantianism, transcendental subjectivity is never conceived as the source of self-generated categories subsequently imposed on world material. Continuing in that direction, Heidegger's position has an even greater affinity with Lask's view of the nonsubjective origin of categories. His most explicit statement on the issue, in his lecture course from the 1925 summer semester, characterizes the ideal (a priori) validity of categories in terms that could have been Lask's own: "This already suggests that the apriori phenomenologically understood is not a title for comportment but a *title for being.* The apriori is not only nothing immanent, belonging primarily to the sphere of the subject, it is also nothing transcendent, specifically bound up with reality" (GA 20:101/74). Like Lask, Heidegger speaks of the "specific indifference of the apriori to subjectivity." Is Lask thus correct in thinking that a transcendental ontology, which would not be dogmatic metaphysics in Schweitz's sense, can be articulated without a legitimating appeal to transcendental subjectivity?

This seems to be the view of Konrad Hobe, who sees Lask's theory of the "logos-immanent object" as a precursor to Heidegger's view of ontological truth as "disclosedness" (*Erschlossenheit*). According to Hobe, Lask does not abandon transcendental philosophy when he conceives the paradigmatic object independently of all reference to subjectivity and synthesis. Dogmatic "epistemological realism" can be avoided so long as "the object itself stands before judging cognition in an 'openness,' i.e., in a relation of knowability to the subject."[35] In other words, transcendental logic need not guarantee that the object that stands in this openness be already fully determined, known; the theory need only guarantee that it be know*able*. Lask's doctrine of categorial clarity is said to provide just such a condition for the possibility of the prejudicative open availability of objects. It is not, then, the subjective origin of the categories that transcendentally grounds propositional truth, but their function as the clarity that first makes any relation to objects "in truth" possible.

Hobe's emphasis on the kinship between Lask's doctrine of categories and Heidegger's transcendental-ontological project in *Sein und Zeit* has much merit. Lask's idea of transcendental logic depends on recognizing a kind of "ontological difference" between the realm of entities on the one hand and the categorial realm of validity—the truth, clarity, or intelligibility *of* entities—on the other, and his transcendental concept of meaning marks this "difference" well. But even if one accepts the argument that Heideggerian fundamental ontology involves something like Lask's concept of meaning, Hobe's judgment that Heidegger's concept of disclosedness as "ontological truth" is "already the position of Lask's logos-immanence" still appears questionable.[36] The reason hints at a deeper inadequacy of Lask's position taken as a whole, namely, that a transcendental-ontological theory of meaning cannot take the form of a transcendental *logic*. Meaning in the absolute sense cannot be thought as an *object;* the space of meaning is not, strictly speaking, logical space.

When discussing Heidegger's theory of truth Hobe fails to make a distinction that is essential for understanding the point at which Heidegger criticizes Lask, a criticism that makes contact with what is important in Schweitz's doubts about the neglect of transcendental subjectivity. For Hobe identifies "disclosedness" with the prejudicative manifestation of the object of knowledge. By equating this with Lask's logos-immanence (the standing of material in categorial clarity), Hobe can assert that "with logos-immanence Lask has already reached the dimension out of which Heidegger can dispense with intentionality in Husserl's sense."[37] However, if logos-immanence signifies the dimension in which *objects* are originally made manifest, this corresponds in Heidegger *not* to disclosedness as such, but to the "uncoveredness" (*Entdecktheit*) of objects through "circumspective concern" (*umsichtiges Besorgen*). Disclosedness, on the contrary, is characterized as the disclosure not of objects in the world, but of being-in-the-world as such.[38] What may appear to be simply a terminological issue involves a crucial difference between Lask and Heidegger.

First, as I will argue in detail in later chapters, it should be acknowledged that the concept of ontological truth (disclosedness) does not so much dispense with, as reinterpret, Husserl's notion of intentionality. Within the limits of the present chapter this means that Heidegger develops a transcendental theory of ontological truth not, as does Lask, by abandoning inquiry into the subjective dimension of the disclosure of meaning, but by deepening it.[39] Heidegger does not believe that a transcendental theory of the meaning (being) of objects can be carried through without a simultaneous reinterpretation of the subjectivity of the subject, a *fundamental* ontology. The ontological status of the object as meaning remains dogmatic so long as the transcendental subject is conceived as a featureless correlate for the emergence of Laskian paradigmatic objects. Lask is right to reject the concept of subjectivity as synthesizing representations, but Schweitz is right to insist that the role of transcendental subjectivity cannot be treated simply as a formal placeholder.[40] Heidegger's analysis of disclosedness (truth) in terms of the Da of Dasein is by no means a dismissal of this question (GA 2:174–239/169–224). On the contrary, his view culminates in a version of subjectivity as ek-static thrown project which simultaneously grounds intentionality in Husserl's sense *and* the emergence of the paradigmatic objects as Lask sees it. Only with this is the transcendental theory of the object as meaning-unity sufficiently distinguished from the dogmatic assertion of a metaphysical "in itself." For Heidegger, Lask is not so much wrong as naive.

This was the point of Heidegger's earliest criticism of Lask. In his *Habilitationsschrift* (1915), an essay owing much to Lask and full of praise for his work, Heidegger remarks that "a *merely* 'objective' general theory of objects necessarily remains incomplete without putting it into relation with the 'subjective side'" (GA 1:404). Heidegger refers specifically to the problem of the "form/material relation," to the question of how the determination of form by material can be conceived if one brackets out the role of subjectivity. With Lask clearly in mind, Heidegger insists that "final illumination of this question is not to be won by remaining within the sphere of meaning and of the meaning-structure" (GA 1:405). Earlier Heidegger had suggested how a theory like Lask's could be enriched by grounding the "being valid of" (*Hingeltungs*) character of logical form not in a Kantian transcendental synthesis but in "intentionality" (GA 1:283). Whether this sort of ground would satisfy a critic like Schweitz must be left open, for the question concerns not only whether Lask has a right to the term "transcendental" but also whether phenomenology does.

Nevertheless Heidegger's subsequent work suggests that a post-Kantian reflection on the subject undermines the primacy of transcendental *logic* for the theory of meaning. Meaning can no longer be identified with the object, with the form/material unity as such. Instead, the meaning of objects must be seen as a function of that in which all entities are located while not itself being an entity—the *world* of being-in-the-world. A fair evaluation of Lask's proposal for a transcendental-ontological concept of meaning, then, would seem to lie somewhere between the extremes of total rejection (Schweitz) and full defense (Hobe). Although the problem of a "synthesis of Aristotle and Kant" is considerably more complicated than Lask was prepared to recognize, his aletheiology points unambiguously in the right direction: toward the correlation between transcendental reflection and the philosophically primary space of meaning.

3

Husserl, Lask, and the Idea of Transcendental Logic

The question of a transcendental logic was one of the two great issues to which Husserl devoted himself in the last ten years of his life. Together with the theme of the lifeworld, transcendental logic seemed to provide a way of articulating what he saw as the universal mission of phenomenology: to reanimate the tradition of Western rationality by establishing philosophy in its historically mandated role as foundational science. Of these two issues, inseparable though they were in Husserl's mind, the problem of the lifeworld continues to enjoy a currency which that of transcendental logic seems to lack. Yet contemporary debates within epistemology and metaphysics, such as that concerning the nature of realism, come increasingly into the orbit of problems Husserl addressed under the heading of transcendental logic: what it is to be an object, the relation between objectivity and evidence, "categorial frameworks," and the ground of propositional truth. But to appreciate Husserl's contribution to this debate it is first necessary to become clear about the sense in which they are *transcendental* problems, and that means to become clear about what a transcendental problem is.

In this chapter I hope to contribute something to such clarification by contrasting Husserl's conception of transcendental logic with that of Emil Lask, whose major writings on the subject were published just prior to the development of Husserl's transcendental version of phenomenology.[1] Lask's work involves a criticism of Husserl's pretranscendental approach to the philosophical problems of logic. At the same time, the shortcomings of Lask's own conception of the transcendental point toward issues which were even then leading Husserl to the phenomenological reduction, his path into transcendental thematics. In specifying certain points of convergence and divergence in their views, we will be tracing a moment in the archaeology of transcendental philosophy.[2]

1. Transcendental Logic as a Theory of Meaning

The origin of the contrast between Husserl and Lask is to be found already in Kant's transcendental analytic, or "logic of truth." Whereas general logic abstracts from all content and thematizes the purely syntactical rules to which knowledge must adhere lest it contradict *itself,* the logic of truth has the task of providing an a priori semantics, or rules without which the formal laws of thought can have no content, "without which no object can be thought."[3] Transcendental logic thus deals with categories and principles valid of objects a priori, those that truly refer to objects but whose reference cannot be established empirically. How is such a logic possible?

Kant answers with his famous "Copernican revolution": The categories are valid of objects a priori because they *constitute* objects. Here transcendental logic faces a twofold task, and subsequent transcendental philosophy inherits a twofold problem. On the one hand, transcendental logic involves the "objective-logical" question of which concepts are "forms of an object in general." Which concepts have objective validity a priori? On the other hand, it involves the "subjective-logical" question of the "origin" of such nonempirical concepts.[4] Under the Copernican hypothesis the two questions are related. Certain nonempirical concepts have objective validity because, as originating in the subject, they first of all make objects possible *for* the subject. As subjective forms for the synthesis of a space-time manifold, the categories are rules for what it means to be an object at all. But just because the object is seen as a function of subjective synthesis, its transcendental status cannot be that of a metaphysical "in itself," but only that of an objective representation.

In the wake of the Hegelian criticism of Kant and the emergence of positivism, various neo-Kantian philosophers sought to renew the project of transcendental logic. But even those who turned "back to Kant" acknowledged significant limitations in Kant's original idea. On the objective-logical side, Kant's deduction of the categories from the table of logical judgments was felt to be both artificial and too restrictive. Not only did the emergence of logistics make the table itself obsolete, the categories seemed to provide a foundation only for the knowledge of nature. If the Kantian project was at all tenable, would there not be categories specific to knowledge in the domain of history and the related cultural sciences as well? On the subjective-logical side, the idea that categories were subjective forms of synthesis seemed all too reminiscent of the then-current psychologism. What were these syntheses, if not part of a specifically human (and therefore evolving, changing) psychological apparatus? Finally, when taken together, these problems indicated perhaps the most troubling difficulty of all: the failure of Kant's transcendental reflection to account for *itself* as a legitimate mode of knowledge.

Against the background of such problems, Husserl and Lask, each in his own way, seek to reinterpret the idea of transcendental logic. Such a reinterpretation demands a thorough recasting of both the objective-logical and the subjective-logical dimensions of Kant's project. For present purposes it is essential to note that both Husserl and Lask do so by appeal to the concept of meaning (*Sinn*). For both, this concept comes to supplant the Kantian notion of representation as the term for the transcendental status of the object. But though both provide a nonrepresentational theory of meaning, their views on what constitutes the transcendentality of meaning present us with a study in contrast, a case of diametrically opposed emphasis. For Lask, transcendental logic as a theory of meaning is first of all *ontology;* for Husserl, it is *phenomenology.*

Lask emphasizes the objective-logical side of Kant's project by identifying meaning with the transcendental truth structure of the object "prior to all contact with subjectivity" (*LvU* 425). By this he does not mean that the object lies in a "metalogical" region beyond the reach of knowledge. Rather, his point is that knowledge, as the properly subjective activity of making judgments, must be grounded in a transcendental truth concept that serves as its measure, namely, "meaning" as the objective unity of categorial form and material. Thus, Lask's revision of Kant minimizes the role of the transcendental synthesis, according to which objects are constituted "in" the subject, and moves toward a nonmetaphysical Aristotelianism, an ontology of the transcendental object as meaning.[5]

Husserl, on the other hand, revises the Kantian project by an ever-deepening concern with its subjective-logical dimension. Husserl's earliest logical works are not works of transcendental philosophy and exhibit a deep distrust of Kantianism. But the subsequent development of his phenomenology comes increasingly under the sign of a Kant mediated by Descartes, the true father of the "transcendental turn."[6] Though Husserl, too, is concerned with ontological problems, the genuinely transcendental issues of logic are for him contained in the Kantian idea of synthesis, which Husserl makes his own by enriching it with a "Cartesian" theory of evidence, the backbone of his account of phenomenological constitution.

As important as these differences are, they must not be allowed to obscure the fact that both Husserl and Lask have in view the same (transcendental) space of meaning. At bottom their theories of meaning are distinguished by a nuance, albeit one that spells the "life and death" of genuine transcendental philosophy—the phenomenological reduction. Lask's ontology of meaning already in some sense occupies the field of evidence opened up by the reduction, though it does so naively and therefore inconsistently. In contrast to the position of the *Logical Investigations* (the only work of Husserl's with which Lask was familiar), Lask's ontology already sights the problem of *transcendence,* and does so in a nonmetaphysical way. Yet his elision of the transcendental subject, motivated by antipsychologistic insights he shared with Husserl, involves his account of transcendence in certain naturalistic inconsistencies that only an explicit application of the reduction can resolve. Just such inconsistencies led Husserl to propose the reduction as a sine qua non of transcendental logic in the first place, as his 1906–7 lecture course, *Einleitung in die Logik und Erkenntnistheorie,* testifies. In bringing this text to bear on the aporias of Lask's position, therefore, we shall illustrate what Iso Kern has called "the way from ontology" to the phenomenological reduction,[7] and so illuminate a central aspect of the transcendental theory of meaning.

2. Judgment and the Paradigmatic Object

Both Lask and Husserl hold transcendental logic to be a theory of the conditions for the possibility of knowledge. Thus, the conditions for the truth of the judgment make up an important theme for investigation. But again for both, the judgment as such is not the most primordial level of the logical problematic. As Lask puts it, the judgment is merely the *proteron pros hemas,* the first with respect to us (*LvU* 287). It must be clarified by recourse to a level which is first in itself. In specifying what this more primordial level is, however, Husserl and Lask part company. For the former it is the evidence of prepredicative *experience;* for the latter it is what he calls the "paradigmatic" (*urbildlich*) region of the transcendental *object* itself. Lask's arguments for this position, and the resulting account of judgment-meaning, thus provide a frame of reference for our contrast with Husserl.

Lask takes the significance of Kant's transcendental turn to lie in the insight that the phenomenon of judgment (judgment form) does not exhaust the scope of purely logical nonmetaphysical inquiry. Indeed, judgment is a "derivative" or secondary theme presupposing what Lask calls a "doctrine of categories," an objective-logical theory of how "the logical reaches to the level of objects themselves as a constituting moment" (*LvU* 286). The judgment takes on secondary status within transcendental logic because it is merely a "means for taking possession of the object" on the part of the subject, and thus presupposes an investigation into the logical status of this object itself "wholly untouched by subjectivity" (*LvU*

287). The transcendental object, or what Lask calls the "paradigmatic object," is thus the original theme of transcendental logic.

But if it is not constituted by the subject, in what sense is such a prejudicative paradigmatic object still a *transcendental* concept? Here Lask gives an Aristotelian accent to what he calls Kant's "Copernican achievement": It is not that the object is constituted by the subject qua representation, but that "the concept of being is transformed into a transcendental-logical concept" (*LP* 28). In other words, Kant saw that "being" (and eo ipso any a priori concept, any category) is neither a nominalist flatus vocis, nor the name of a metaphysical element or entity, but "logical content" (*logischen Gehalt*) which constitutes the "objectivity" of an object, the "being" of a being (*LP* 30). The doctrine of categories is a study of the logical content that belongs to the transcendental structure, the objectivity, of the object.

Thus, Lask's paradigmatic object, as the goal and measure of cognition, is not something "metalogically" transcendent—something whose structure "in itself" would be thoroughly extralogical—but is something in which logical content is already found. Lask argues that this is sufficient to distinguish his transcendental position from the Aristotelian metaphysics with which it shares many features. Both Lask and Aristotle conceive the paradigmatic object as an original (not subjectively synthesized) unity of categorial form and material. Where Aristotle's forms are metaphysical (metalogical) "actualities" existing in things, however, Lask's categorial form is not a real part of the object, but its "objectivity."

To understand the transcendentality of the object here one needs to know how logical form is to be distinguished from metaphysical form. According to Lask, all pre-Kantian theories of logical categoriality were blinded by their commitment to the metaphysical two-world theory, a fundamental duality within the totality of what is thinkable (*All des Denkbaren*) between the world of "sensible being" and the world of "supersensible being" (*LP* 5). On such a schema logical form can only remain homeless, for it is neither a sensible entity nor a supersensible entity. Even Kant's doctrine of categories did not entirely break free of this two-world picture. According to Lask it was Hermann Lotze who first saw clearly the proper *transcendental* distinction within the totality of the thinkable, between beings (physical and metaphysical) on the one hand and validities on the other, between "that which *is* and occurs, and that which *holds* [*gilt*] without having to be [*ohne sein zu müssen*]" (*LP* 6). Logical form is neither a metaphysical element nor a subjective function of synthesis because it "is" not at all; it is "valid," or "holds." To say that the object is constituted by logical form is thus simply to have in view the object as a primordial unity of valid form and the material of which it is valid.

To this primordial unity, the *Urverhältnis* of categorial form and material, Lask gives the name "meaning" (*Sinn*), the object in its "truth." Meaning, as Lask notes, is a specifically transcendental-philosophical predicate, since it denotes what the object shows itself to be from the perspective of transcendental reflection (*LP* 122–23). Thus, meaning does not signify a realm of entities *in addition* to the entities of physics and metaphysics but is just these very entities themselves "in truth." To be "something" (*Etwas*) at all is to be material which "stands in" categorial form: "Particular objects are particular unities of theoretical meaning, particular truths" (*LP* 41). Precisely because Lask defines categorial form in terms of the Lotzean concept of validity, and not in terms of a subjective function of synthesis, the object as meaning cannot be seen as a mere representation. The subject does indeed constitute "representations" (*Nachbilder*) in the act of judging, but transcendental logic is concerned first of all with the truth structure (meaning-structure) of the object itself, the *ground* of such representing activity.

Meaning is thus a purely transcendental concept whose extension coincides with that of "object in general." The domain of objects, however, is not a uniform field restricted to the sensibly given manifold. It is differentiated into regions on the basis of a functional conception of the form/material relation. To be a category is to be functionally related to a certain range of material as that which provides the "*Klarheitsmoment*" (*LP* 75), or moment of intelligibility, in the object, and to be material is simply to be that which is clarified or objectified by categorial form. Thus, while it is true that all categorial form is valid, it is not necessary that all material be nonvalid or thoroughly alogical (*LP* 49).

With its functional definition of the form/material relation, Lask's doctrine of categories provides what Husserl called "regional ontologies," a theory of the "material logical" forms that ground the object domains of individual sciences. There is, further, an analogue to Husserl's doctrine of *Fundierung* in Lask's notion of "tiers" (*Stockwerke*) within the domain of objects in general. At the lowest level lies the thoroughly alogical material that pertains to the category "sensible being" (*LP* 50), but this "limiting case of alogicity" does not define materiality as such. The unity that is constituted by the relation between "being" and its specific material ("sensibly intuitable" material strictly as such) can itself occupy the material position for higher-order categories, for example, that of "life." The category "life" presupposes, but is not reducible to, the material of the lower level. Just as the category "being" includes in a logically ordered way the plurality of a priori concepts of physics (thinghood, causality, etc.), so the category "life" indicates a *further* "objective involvement" (*objektive Bewandtnis*) in the material which displays itself in the a priori concepts of biology (organism, development, etc.). And at still higher levels the material for psychology, history, and the other human sciences makes its appearance within the more specific categories of "psychic life," "value individuality," "cultural achievement," "historical event," and so on (*LP* 60 f.). At each level the founded science takes as its material not the material of the previous level, but the categorially formed unity (object) as such, in which the founding material is no longer thematic.

This functional, or founded, concept of an object accounts for why it is that the object as such is "meaning" only at the level of transcendental logic. For only in transcendental reflection is the category itself (logical form) the specific *material* of investigation. Only in making explicit the logical content itself (as material) by grasping its character as valid form does the meaning-character of the object at each lower level show itself. At these lower levels, in contrast, the levels of positive or nonphilosophical sciences, knowing consists in "being given over to the object, to categorially formed material, whereby however the validity character of the form and correspondingly the meaning-character of the whole object remains unknown. In such knowledge it is never the object, but always the object material which is known" (*LP* 122). Because the categories are simply the clarity of the material itself, a transcendental reflection that thematizes them postulates no new entities. It merely recognizes explicitly the logical structure that always already makes up the objecthood of the objects belonging to the domains of the particular sciences. In these sciences (and ultimately in prescientific life as well), there is a certain prethematic, prepredicative familiarity with the categories sustaining the thematic concern with object material. Positive cognition "experiences" categorial clarity without "knowing" it. Thus, as Lask puts it, we "live in the truth" (*LP* 86–87).

Upon this prepredicative domain of truth Lask grounds the structure of the judgment and addresses the question of propositional truth. Here again his concern is not with prepredicative experiencing as such, but with the object as it becomes available in transcendental reflection, as an ontological unity of meaning, as "truth" in the paradigmatic sense. The structure of this object must serve to clarify the structure of the judgment and so account for the possibility of a correspondence between the judgment and the object. Only because the object itself is meaning (and not, e.g., a metalogical substance) can meaning in the judgment correspond to it: "The separation between [judgment] meaning and the object amounts to a distance between meaning and meaning" (*LP* 43).

But if judgment-meaning in some sense corresponds to object-meaning, or truth in the paradigmatic sense, it cannot do so by "picturing" it.[8] The "separation" referred to here indicates that the form of the judgment is not the same as the structure of the object, but is a "complication" of the latter arising through "decomposition" and "reconstruction" of the object (*LP* 291). This introduces a moment of "compositeness" (*Zusammengesetztheit*) in the structure of the judgment (represented by the copula) not to be found in the object itself. This renders the grammatical form of judgment unreliable as a clue to the categorial structure of objects. Thus, if the transcendental object is nevertheless to serve as the "measure" (*Lv*U 357) of truth in the judgment, Lask must show how the grammatical form of the judgment conceals within itself a logical form that *does* reflect the structure of the object. Like Husserl in the *Logical Investigations,* Lask seeks to divorce the logical structure of judgment-meaning from the grammatical structure of the expressions in which it is articulated. But Lask believes that this can be done in a way that explains the possibility of propositional truth (*LvU* 321) only by deriving the logical elements of the judgment from the elements of the paradigmatic object. To this end he offers his "metagrammatical subject-predicate theory."

In judgment a predicate is asserted of a subject. Thus, to use Lask's example, in "*a* is the cause of *b,*" "being the cause of *b*" is asserted of the subject "*a.*" But this grammatical form conceals the logical achievement of judgment, the act of knowing itself, which is "to place the material in the categorial determinations in which it stands *an sich*" (*LvU* 333). The genuine *logical* elements of judgment-meaning are thus the category and the material: The genuine subject of which something is asserted is not "*a*" but the material <*a,b*>, and that which is asserted of this material, the predicate, is the category "causality." The logical meaning of the causal judgment, then, is that certain material <*a,b*> "stands in" the category "causality" (*LvU* 333).

The logical structure of judgment-meaning thus consists of the same elements as the paradigmatic meaning of the object, though it contains them only in the alienated form of individual "pieces" or concepts (*LvU* 362) between which a relation needs to be *established.* From the point of view of cognitive inquiry, the material (which in itself stands in the clarity of logical form and manifests itself as such in pretheoretical experience) is not yet recognized *as* standing in some *specific* logical form. It faces us as "logically naked." Revising the Kantian formula to correspond to the functional form/material concept, Lask writes: "Form without content is empty, content without form is naked" (*LP* 74). The task of cognition is to "clothe" the material with the category that pertains to it. Thus the problem of knowledge appears as a problem of choosing (or discovering) the proper category for given material (*LvU* 418). Error, on this view, consists in predicating of some material a category in which it does not stand. At the highest level this would even account for Kant's error in conceiving the transcendental object as representation. For the material cognized in Kant's transcendental reflection on knowledge is the pair <form, manifold>, and Kant asserts a relation between this material and the category <subjective synthesis>, thus producing the concept "representation." However, he has misidentified the category in which the material actually stands, since what governs the form/manifold connection is not synthesis but <validity> as the *Bewandtnis* or involvement of categorial form as such. With that, however, there is no need to conceive the result as a representation.

So far in Lask's theory of the judgment no explicit reference has been made to the role of subjectivity or the transcendental subject. This results from two deep commitments in Lask's objective-logical approach to transcendental logic. The first is that only by tracing propositional truth back to the paradigmatic object, or truth in the transcendental sense, can the "positivist" prejudice (*LvU* 390) of remaining fixed on secondary or "artificial" (*gekünstelt*) judgment-meaning in the account of knowledge be decisively refuted. The second is that any account of the paradigmatic object in terms of a Kantian synthesis must lead to psychologism. Lask's claim is that the Kantian synthesis can itself be explained only in terms of the objective *Urbild* and so can contribute nothing to clarifying the latter (*LvU* 406–7). Nevertheless, though the subjective-logical aspect of transcendental logic remains undeveloped in Lask's work, it cannot be altogether ignored. In the following section I approach this issue by contrasting Lask's theory of judgment with Husserl's position in the *Logical Investigations,* a work in which it is precisely the subjective dimension that holds the key to clarifying the problem of knowledge.

3. Subjectivity and Transcendence

Lask had studied the *Logical Investigations* carefully and makes several references to it in his writings, but from the outset there is a critical tone. It is true that Lask applauds the antipsychologistic direction Husserl gives to philosophical logic, and especially the theory of judgment. Husserl's "historical significance" consists in having "pushed through to the separability of meaning—the proposition in itself—from its real substrate" (*LvU* 425), namely, from the psychically occurring, "nonvalid" acts that are, for Lask, merely the "bearers" of logical meaning (*LvU* 292). Lask goes so far as to say that this "separability" thesis lies at the foundation of his own theory of judgment (*LvU* 292). And in one sense it does. However, the real foundation of his theory lies in the paradigmatic object as measure of judgment-meaning, while for Husserl the separability of judgment-meaning consists in its being a "species" *of* acts, or "intentional experiences," that can be clarified only by recourse to such acts in their eidetic descriptive character.[9] Like many others who could not see a continuity between the *Logical Investigations*' introduction, "Prolegomena to Pure Logic," and the "phenomenological clarifications" that followed it, Lask had deep suspicions about the relevance of this inquiry into acts.

This is not because Lask denies the subject any role in the formation of judgment-meaning but because he asserts that the separability of meaning is alone of significance for logic. The subject is active not in creating the meaning of the judgment (this is what it is no matter in what language, or under what circumstances, it is uttered), but only in "breaking up" the undivided unity of the prepredicatively experienced object into "pieces" or concepts. And although this would seem to be an important problem for transcendental scrutiny, Lask sees it as a psychological issue. He is not concerned with the "origin" (*entstehen*) of the judgment, but only with its "structure" (*LvU* 309).

As we have seen, this structure gets explained as a complication of the more primordial structure of the paradigmatic object. Thus it is not enough for transcendental logic merely to recognize the separability of judgment-meaning, as Lask claims Husserl does (*LvU* 425). This is still only a "quasi transcendence"; although it is structurally separable from subjective acts, it nevertheless *points back* to an involvement with subjectivity. Only a theory of *genuine* transcendence, completely free from all reference to the subject, can account for the possible truth of the judgment. Only ontology can ground apophantics.

It is here that we locate Lask's main quarrel with the Husserl of the *Logical Investigations.* Their differences concerning the structure of the judgment, though significant, are less important than their fundamental disagreement on what the genuine philosophical task is with regard to the question of truth. Husserl could not approach the problem of truth ontologically since the paradigmatic object in Lask's sense seemed to lie quite beyond the apodictic evidence available within the sphere of intentional experiences. As Theodore de Boer has argued, the *Logical Investigations* is methodologically structured on the basis of an ontological dualism that has not yet entirely freed itself from naturalism.[10] The realm of intentional experiences was an island of descriptive certainty, so to speak, within a sea of nonintentional nature. Thus the "thing of physics" (as de Boer calls it) does not figure in this work at all. Husserl's sole recourse for treating the problem of truth in the judgment is to carry out a phenomenology of truth *claims,* of the intentional experiences pertaining to the phenomenon of judgment itself.

Thus, Husserl's sixth investigation yields an interpretation of the correspondence theory of truth by way of a description of the interplay between "assertive acts" and "fullfilling acts," a "synthesis of identification" in which the emptily intended judgment-meaning is taken together with the "fullness" present in a fulfilling act of the same intentional sense (Hua XIX/2:650–51/764–65). On the question of the object itself that imparts such fullness, however, Husserl had to remain silent. From the methodological standpoint of a reduction to intentional experiences, all discussion of such "transcendent" objects must be bracketed. At best, the object can be characterized as *wahrmachender,* that is, "as the ideal fulness for an intention, as that which makes an intention true" (Hua XIX/2:652/766).[11] Lask is therefore correct in noting that Husserl's account of truth remains within the sphere of "quasi transcendence," hence that Husserl's position is not a *transcendental* one at all. It does not account for the *possibility* of knowledge, but only analyzes the descriptive psychology of knowledge claims. Of course, Husserl did not consider his phenomenology to be transcendental at this stage. Nevertheless, even as a clarification of knowledge claims, "This theory of knowledge is caught in an impasse." As de Boer notes, "It was only later that Husserl saw that a theory of knowledge on a psychological basis is a 'transcendental circle': it seeks to clarify the relation to the world despite the fact that the world is itself presupposed as the surrounding ground of consciousness."[12]

As we shall see, Lask too is guilty of "presupposing the world." Yet with respect to the question of a transcendental theory of judgment, he is correct to argue, against Husserl's early phenomenological conception, that the problem of truth can be clarified only by drawing into the analysis the transcendent object as such, which is not merely a meaning separable from the judging subject, but altogether separate: "Genuine transcendence is the condition of meaning prior to all contact with subjectivity, while behind the independence of the quasi-transcendent meaning stands the mere separability of meaning *after* its contact with subjectivity" (*LvU* 425). Thus, even if transcendental logic could thematize the subjective origin of the judgment without becoming psychologistic, the transcendental problem of truth would still require a radically different sort of investigation of "transcendent"object-meaning itself.

In the next section we will explore the sense in which Husserl came to agree with this point.[13] But first an obvious question about Lask's own transcendental position needs to be addressed. For it is one thing to recognize the need for such a paradigmatic object, and it is quite another to give a philosophical account of how it is accessible as something other than a dogmatic postulate.

Here Lask's position is at its weakest. On the one hand, the paradigmatic object (meaning) is to be considered prior to all contact with subjectivity. On the other hand, the transcendence of this object is not to be construed metaphysically as a Kantian thing-in-itself. Lask tries to navigate these treacherous waters by claiming that the subject, in addition to being the source of the "structural complication" into which the object falls in the act of judging, is also a passive "receiver [*Empfängerin*] . . . of the transcendent object," able "to offer a site [*Stätte*] for meaning" (*LvU* 415). This is what Lask calls the "becoming immanent" of the transcendent object:

> The condition of being there in subjective acts, of hovering before or being contained within experience, may be termed becoming an object or becoming immanent; the condition independent of this situation of becoming experienced may be termed transcendence. Becoming immanent . . . shows itself to be merely an external destiny, a chance situation into which the transcendent object or paradigmatic meaning falls. The becoming immanent of what is transcendent in this sense therefore involves no contradiction. It means merely a transposition into another situation. (*LvU* 414)

Given the fact that Lask occasionally mentions Husserl's concept of intentionality with favor, and indeed in a letter to Husserl claims that the "von ihr entworfenen Typ des Subjekt-Objekt Verhältnis als Intentionalität" supersedes all theories of "Bewußtsein überhaupt," one might expect him to clarify "becoming immanent" in ways that would resemble Husserl's later transcendental phenomenology of prepredicative experience.[14] But Lask's interests lie in an entirely different direction. In the same passage from which we just quoted, Lask is quick to point out that the "standpoint" for his definition of "transcendent" and "immanent" is precisely *not* that of "immanence within experience or consciousness," but that of transcendence itself. Transcendence does not mean "going beyond," but "independence" from the subject (*LvU* 414); hence Lask shows no concern for the *way* that the paradigmatic object shows itself *as* transcendence in immanence. An analysis of the intentionality of sensibility or perception could provide nothing of philosophical significance. In spite of his appeal to Husserl's notion of intentionality, there are indications in Lask's text (though never a direct discussion) that an account of such becoming immanent could only belong to a nontranscendental "psycho-physiology" (*LP* 52).

Thus, even though Lask acknowledges a prepredicative concept of experience as the correlate of paradigmatic meaning, his fear of psychologism keeps him from recognizing the kind of subjective "achievements" that Husserl investigates in his later transcendental phenomenology of meaning constitution. The genuine problems seem to him to lie at the level of transcendence itself, at the level of the ontological concept of validity. But just for this reason Lask's notion of prepredicative experience, of the pretheoretical subject-object relation as "simple submission to categorially formed material, . . . to the paradigmatic structural whole which coincides with the object itself as truth" (*LvU* 396), remains deeply ambiguous. Without support from a functional notion of *intuition* such as Husserl proposes in his phenomenology of evidence, the ontological status of Lask's functional concept of the (transcendent) object remains transcendentally unclarified. For it is impossible to say how the transcendental object is accessible, impossible to specify the *modes* in which it is given. Thus, Lask claims, on the one hand, that prior to judgment the subject simply "receives" the transcendent object. On the other hand, he also claims that we "never" have the object as such, that we "always" operate with pieces (*LvU* 417). We are "ignorant" of the "simple interpenetration of the transcendental structural elements" of the object, which remains for us a "lost paradise": "After the original sin of knowledge, it is no longer ours to possess the transcendent meaning, but only the immanent [judgment] meaning" (*LvU* 426).

What Lask points to here is of course correct: The transcendent object is never *adequately* given in experience. But if that is so, then it will not do, as Husserl says in *Formal and Transcendental Logic,* to "stop short with the empty generality of the word consciousness, nor with the empty word experience, judgment, and so forth, treating the rest as though it were philosophically irrelevant and leaving it to psychology" (Hua XVII:251/244). The transcendental concept of meaning remains homeless if not fleshed out in terms of its own "noetics," in terms of the evidence with which it presents itself. But when this is recognized, the whole ontology of transcendent meaning that Lask saw as the *sole* concern of transcendental logic is transformed into a "transcendental clue" (*Leitfaden*) for tracing intentional implications, or modes of givenness, within a phenomenology of prepredicative object constitution (Hua XVII:251/244). The doctrine of categories as an ontology of meaning must become a transcendental phenomenology. In the final section of this chapter I shall suggest how such considerations inform Husserl's own conception of transcendental logic after he, too, had found a way to include the transcendent object in a specifically phenomenological investigation.

4. Transcendental Logic and the Phenomenological Reduction

For both Lask and the Husserl of the *Logical Investigations,* an account of the truth of judgment requires an inquiry that goes beyond the level of judgment as such. For Husserl, however, such an inquiry goes back to the intentional experiences in which signifying and intuiting acts come to a synthesis of identification. The question of the transcendent object of the intuitive act is, at this stage of Husserl's thinking, explicitly ignored as lying outside the sphere of adequate phenomenological evidence. Lask, on the other hand, sees in just this transcendent object the genuine theme of transcendental logic; it is that meaning-structure whose elements reappear in atomized form in the judgment, thus accounting for the possibility of knowledge of what is in truth. With regard to the question of the object of knowledge, then, Lask's position is genuinely transcendental, while Husserl's is still "descriptive psychology."

At the same time, neither thinker can give an adequate account of transcendental *subjectivity.* This is clear for Husserl, whose eidetic psychology makes no pretense of explaining the possibility of knowledge. But Lask's conception of the subject is at bottom a psychological one as well, for which reason he excludes it in all but name from the scope of transcendental logic. As the "real bearer" of judgment-meaning, the subject is simply discounted as irrelevant; the question of the origin of such meaning in the breaking apart of the paradigmatic object is a psychological one, entirely subordinate to the question of the structure of judgment-meaning itself. And as the prejudicative "site" in which paradigmatic meaning is originally given, subjective immanence is a mere "chance situation" into which transcendent meaning falls. Lask nowhere gives an account of this "transcendence in immanence," the condition of the transcendent object as correlate of the nonactive subject. To the extent that any nonpsychological sense can be given to the subject here, it is simply an abstract "subject pole" of paradigmatic meaning, while the actual givenness of the object seems to be a question for psycho-physiology.

In writings subsequent to the *Logical Investigations,* Husserl came to recognize the need to include this transcendent object in the purview of phenomenology, and precisely as a structure of *meaning.* Thus, in the first major work that he published after the *Logical Investigations,* the first volume of *Ideas* (1913), we read: "In a certain sense and with the proper care in the use of words we may even say that all real unities are unities of meaning" (Hua III:134/128). But as the passage continues it appears that while Husserl now stands within the horizon of the Laskian transcendent object, it is not Lask's "perspective of transcendence" that he has adopted, but rather that of a "transcendence in immanence" made possible by the phenomenological reduction: "Unities of meaning presuppose . . . a sense-giving consciousness which, on its side, is absolute and not dependent in its turn on sense bestowed on it from another source" (Hua III:134/128–29). The transcendental space of meaning "presupposes" consciousness; but then in what sense is meaning transcendent? *How* is the transcendent object to be included in a phenomenology of consciousness without falling back into psychological representationalism?

Husserl's answer to this question is bound up with the theory of the phenomenological reduction, a concept that emerges in Husserl's lectures during the Göttingen period. A series of these lectures, given during the summer semester of 1907, was published as *The Idea of Phenomenology.* In this text, as Kern has shown, the reduction is motivated primarily through "Cartesian" considerations in the search for apodictic evidence.[15] However, in the lectures of the previous winter semester (1906–7), published as *Einleitung in die Logik und Erkenntnistheorie,* the reduction is introduced in the context of ontological considerations deriving from the idea of transcendental logic.

In this text Husserl explicitly proposes a doctrine of categories, a logic of the object or "ontology" in the transcendental sense, but in such a way as to bring out the one-sided character of any theory of knowledge, like Lask's, that remains at the objective-logical level of categorial validity. Ultimate transcendental clarification of transcendent meaning is seen to require a radical "change of attitude"; the transcendent space of meaning is not adequately characterized simply by noting the "validity character" of categorial form but requires a reflective modification of the objective ("positivistic," "naturalistic") attitude of thought itself. In what follows, then, I briefly chart the emergence of this demand for an *Einstellungsänderung* as the condition for the possibility of transcendental logic.[16]

Husserl begins by considering the role of logic in the context of a theory of science where it appears, first of all, as "apophantics," the theory of the formal structure of propositions. Now it belongs to the essence of any proposition that it "raises a claim to validity," or truth (Hua XXIV:70). Thus, a complete theory of science will not be able to remain within apophantics, which studies the forms of the proposition in abstraction from this implicit truth claim, but will have to investigate "that which in the essence of the proposition grounds it as a unity of validity [*Geltungseinheit*]. In a certain sense," Husserl continues, "the concern here is a logic of truth" (Hua XXIV:74).

The logic of truth, which Husserl calls "ontology," is not restricted to a consideration of "objects of a higher order," a purely formal ontology which still abstracts from the "underlying objects" that are bound up in (possible) states of affairs, "categorially formed objects" in the sense of the *Logical Investigations.* Rather, logic includes "the idea of an a priori ontology, and further not a formal-logical one, but a metaphysical one."[17] This latter has the task of investigating "the fundamental categories in which the Real as such is to be conceived according to its essence" (Hua XXIV:101).

Such an a priori ontology of the real provides the basis for "empirically founded metaphysics," or ontologies of the "regions" of the individual sciences. It can do so without becoming metalogical in Lask's sense because "logical form points a priori toward material [*Stoff*] which is to be . . . rationalized," toward "something extralogical, a world of hyle" (Hua XXIV:104). Thus, we find here a widening of the concept of logical form that appeared in the *Logical Investigations,* such that now "one can count within logic all that which belongs a priori to the possibility of knowledge of the real. . . . On this view logic includes a twofold a priori, one of pure form and one of the formally determined material" (Hua XXIV:111).

With the transition from formal apophantics to formal and material ontology, Husserl for the first time speaks specifically of a "transcendental logic." Logical categoriality includes not only formal determinations, but also the "essential categories of reality"—for instance, "thing, quality, real connection, real whole, real part, cause and effect, real genus and species, etc." (Hua XXIV:112, 111).

At this stage, then, Husserl has in view a doctrine of categories along the lines suggested by Lask—a theory of the "objectivity of objects" as an ontology of what is as such. The same view, more explicitly articulated, is found in *Formal and Transcendental Logic* (1929). There Husserl begins by marking the specific difference between a logic of judgment and a logic of the object: "Categorially formed objectivity is not an apophantical concept; rather it is an ontological concept" (Hua XVII:151/145). He then reiterates the theory of truth as a "synthesis of identification" found in the *Logical Investigations,* except that now the objects of the fulfilling acts are not simply "true-making," but the things themselves: "If the fulfillments are ideally perfect then the substrate-objectivities with all their categorial formings are themselves given in the strict sense; the evidence actualizes and seizes upon them themselves as they are in truth" (Hua XVII:151/145). This, finally, indicates that there can be no metaphysical problem of "application" in logic; the objects *themselves* are not, as Lask would say, metalogical: "Truly existing nature, truly existing sociality or culture, and the like—these have absolutely no sense other than that of being certain categorial objectivities" (Hua XVII:152/146).

Thus, a genuinely transcendental ontology is now part of Husserl's conception of logic.[18] It is necessary (as Lask saw) because the question of possible truth in a judgment implies reference to a concept of the "truly existing" categorially constituted object, *being* in the sense of truth, as the measure of "mere judicial meaning" (Hua XVII:152/146). But if Husserl has now come to see the need for a transcendental ontology it is by no means the case that this is *sufficient* for a transcendental theory of knowledge as Lask believed. For the possibility of such a "way out" of the problem of truth remains merely dogmatic without a corresponding account of the *Evidenz* in which this paradigmatic object is given. If a doctrine of categories is to provide the a priori structure of "logically formed material," then the accessibility of logically formed material must allow for a reflective clarification that is itself transcendental. There remains the problem of subjective logic, or what Husserl, in 1906–7, calls "noetics."

This, as we saw, is precisely where Lask's transcendental logic pulled up short. The question of the evidence in which the object is prepredicatively given was left unclarified: How can an investigation into the modes of givenness of the object be anything other than a psychological one? The phenomenology of the *Logical Investigations* tendered no definitive answer to this question. Now, however, Husserl believes that phenomenology can provide the foundations for an ontology by way of a differentiated theory of evidence based on a conception of intentionality purified of all psychological elements, a sphere of transcendental "immanence" in terms of which alone the *meaning* of transcendence can be concretely articulated.

The issue of a noetics or subjective logic is, for Husserl, the issue of the *legitimacy* of the claim to justification which any mode of knowledge raises. Any theory of knowledge must concern itself with this problem, which includes the legitimacy of Lask's claim that the transcendent object is given in prejudicative experience (Hua XXIV:120). This in turn means that transcendental logic must investigate the subjective dimension: "All knowledge comes to pass as subjective act, and the subjective act must harbor in itself that which represents and grounds its claim to justification [*Rechtsanspruch*]" (Hua XXIV:130). Only by considering how an act of knowledge, or object consciousness in general, "harbours in itself" its source of validity can "the problems of transcendental philosophy, these most difficult of all scientific problems generally," be addressed (Hua XXIV:139).

Thus, on Husserl's view Lask simply presupposes the deepest issues of transcendental logic. What Lask from his "standpoint of transcendence" takes as a simple given, namely, that we have a prejudicative familiarity with the transcendent object, a precognitive experience of ontological meaning, is for Husserl a mystery that must be cleared up if philosophical logic is to have a "good noetic conscience." If the "trivially obvious fact that things-in-themselves are and we merely come to them, apprehend them, consider them, make assertions about them, etc., has become a mystery" (Hua XXIV:153), then the question to be raised is "*how* objective being can become conscious and known in subjectivity." It is a question of *Evidenz*, for "evidence too belongs to the subjective dimension" (Hua XXIV:156).

Husserl's view of evidence overlaps with Lask's concept of experience in one important respect. Evidence, as "givenness," is *never* the thematic concern of nonphilosophical sciences: "One *lives* in evidence, but does not reflect on evidence. One simply encounters objects, objects are given, one does not however reflect upon, or investigate in reflection, what givenness means or how it is possible" (Hua XXIV:164). But how is this level of evidence in which we "live" to be thematized in a nonpsychological way? It is here, motivated by ontological considerations, that Husserl introduces the notion of the phenomenological reduction, which "seems at first to be an overrefined subtlety" though "here lies the genuine Archimedean point of philosophy" (Hua XXIV:211).

The reduction opens up the sphere of transcendental subjectivity, the descriptive domain of the intentional correlation between noesis and noema. In the 1906–7 text this move to subjectivity is motivated neither by the demand for absolute certainty, nor by the demand for a grounding of psychology, but precisely by the recognition that ontology, as an aspect of the transcendental theory of knowledge, rests upon a "field" of evidence that is presupposed, but not investigated, by the sciences themselves. Thus, the method for making such a field of evidence accessible must belong to an inquiry that "lies prior to all natural knowledge and science and has an entirely different direction from natural science" (Hua XXIV:176).

The reduction, as it appears here, is simply the expression of the radical difference between philosophical reflection and all other modes of thought. It is meant to overcome the naïveté of the "naturalistic" attitude, which presupposes the "world" as a pregiven source of validities. The reduction inaugurates an "unnatural direction of thought" (Hua XXIV:165) that does not lose itself in "positive" investigation on the basis of worldly evidence, but rather reflects on this evidence structure itself. Thus, the reduction involves the "detachment of all naturalistic theories," not in the sense of denying their validity but in the sense of refusing to use them as premises, or modes of explanation, in philosophical reflection (Hua XXIV:165). Such "detachment" is merely to remind us, as it were, that no naturalistic or worldly theory (including psychology) can account, without vicious circularity, for the correlation between knowledge and the world that constitutes the "unnatural" theme of philosophical reflection, since all such theories presuppose that correlation itself.

Thus this unnatural direction of thought, the critical direction that investigates *Rechtsansprüche,* does not exclude the domain of transcendence from consideration, but includes it under a change of signature. Reflection investigates "particular sciences, particular theories, particular cognitions not as validities, but as validity claims, validity phenomena" (Hua XXIV:199). A reduction to the sphere of immanence, to transcendental subjectivity in Husserl's sense, thus in no way brackets the transcendent object itself. Instead, it is what Husserl calls here the "empirical apperception" of it, the doxic positing of the object in the straightforward attitude of simple experience, that is reduced or that is not allowed to dominate reflection in its presumed self-evidence (Hua XXIV:211).

Such a reduction of transcendence to the status of transcendence phenomenon alters nothing of its objectivity but only clears a space for a nonpsychological investigation into the noetic acts in which alone the question of "how such a relation to objectivity is possible" can be explored concretely: "From the very beginning it is therefore to be noted that not merely perceptions or other kinds of objectifying acts belong in the sphere of immanence, but also in a certain sense every object, in spite of its transcendence" (Hua XXIV:212, 213). In the context of the reduction, therefore, immanence is itself a purely transcendental concept, one that is absolutely necessary for grounding the transcendental concept of the object as meaning. Immanence means neither the real containment of the object within psychological consciousness (as "representation"), nor the "*reell*" parts of intentional experiences themselves (noesis, hyle), but simply the givenness of the object, the presence of the transcendent to the (reduced, "transcendental") subject *as* it presents itself, *as* a "unity of meaning."[19]

In conclusion, it is possible to see that the ambiguities in Lask's account of the transcendent object result from his failure to recognize explicitly the function of a reduction, of a change of attitude, for transcendental philosophy. On the objective-logical side Lask does recognize that transcendental philosophy concerns itself with the object as a unity of meaning. Philosophy deals with the same objects as do the sciences and daily life, but in such a way as to recognize the "logical structure" of the object that is merely presupposed in nonphilosophical modes of thought. But because this approach to the difference between philosophy and natural inquiry remains naive—that is, because in Lask's appeal to our experience of the object in prepredicative life the "empirical apperception" of this object is not explicitly reduced—his concept of meaning remains homeless. The concept of meaning is not, as Lask assumes, a "worldly" concept that emerges as one ascends *in a direct line* from everyday life to positive science to the theory of knowledge. His error here simply reflects the thesis of a *continuity* between positive science and philosophy that we have previously seen to characterize neo-Kantianism in general. Husserl's implied criticisms of Lask's "Ungründlichkeit und Belastetheit mit Äquivokationen" show the extent to which Lask, for all that he breaks with neo-Kantian constructivism, did not decisively break with the continuity thesis. The philosophical significance of the space of meaning, however, can be appreciated only by bracketing the naturalistic assumptions underpinning the idea of such a continuity.

Thus, on the subjective-logical side, Lask's implicit naturalism, his presupposition of the world as the ultimate ground of validities, shows itself clearly in his demotion of all questions of the subject, and thus all questions of evidence, to the status of philosophically irrelevant psychological ones. Lask's concept of the subject as a passive receiver of the transcendent object forces him to see the transcendent object as a "lost paradise," so far as investigation into its modes of givenness is concerned. But a reduction of the naturalistic assumption that transcendence constitutes an autonomous sphere of validity would have allowed Lask to recognize that the very inadequacy with which the transcendent object is given is precisely the clue to how the meaning of transcendence is constituted *within* immanence. Such constitution is in danger of falling back into a psychologistic "creation" of representations only if one still thinks of both transcendence and immanence in essentially naturalistic ways. But in that case the transcendental explication of the object as a unity of *logical* form and material can only appear as a strange perversion, for to natural thought the idea that the object "in truth" is meaning must seem no more than a deus ex machina.

What it means to practice the reduction in Husserl's sense will always be difficult to grasp, for it is the way to a cultivation of that "nonnatural," nonworldly mode of reflection in which philosophy first discovers its own genuine problems. But without it, as our discussion of Lask has begun to indicate, the attempt of natural thinking to become clear about its own achievements and possibility remains condemned to equivocation. Of course, having carried out such a bracketing of naturalistic ways of thinking, everything depends on an appropriate characterization of what then comes into view. Husserl had no hesitation about designating the space of meaning, of phenomenological immanence and givenness, as transcendental *subjectivity,* or consciousness. But is it not equally "world," where world is no longer equated with the naturalistically construed *kosmos?* In the next chapter we begin to trace the trajectory of Heidegger's thought as a response to just this question.

4

Lask, Heidegger, and the Homelessness of Logic

What is it, exactly, that philosophers study, investigate, inquire into? If (to adopt the familiar Quinean account as an example) the sciences divide up "what there is," each taking a particular "object domain" as its field defined by the interpretation which assigns values to the variables over which its theory quantifies,[1] and if philosophy proposes to contribute to this scientific enterprise, what remains as the object domain of philosophy? What, if anything, escapes the grid of the logico-empirical sciences?

Much twentieth-century philosophy can be understood as an attempt to answer this question. One may trace a path from the militant austerity of logical positivism and its revival of Locke's "underlaborer" conception of philosophy to the recent attempts at linking conceptual analysis, linguistics, artificial intelligence, and experimental psychology into the master discipline of "cognitive science." Or one may follow the road which leads from Husserl's heroic plan for a rigorous science of phenomenology to the various forms of antifoundationalism, pragmatism, deconstruction, and the postmodern "performativity criterion." In either case it appears that though the inn of theory has many rooms, the NO VACANCY sign is brightly lit when philosophers come calling. The specific theme of philosophical inquiry has become an enigma.

The problem posed by the enigmatic character of the philosophical topos provides the context for Heidegger's lifelong effort to reawaken a sense for the question of being through a recollection of the ontological difference. Theodore Kisiel rightly maintains that "Heidegger launched his career in 1919 not as a philosopher of being, existentialist, and so on, but as a philosopher of philosophy, a metaphilosopher, and not only maintained but magnified that discourse from outside of philosophy to the very end."[2] Though the sense of "outside" here may be problematic (what is outside philosophy in Heidegger's sense is still—or better, is just—philosophy), it is true that "philosopher of philosophy" accurately describes Heidegger's itinerary.

What brought Heidegger onto this metaphilosophical path? It was not (as the familiar story goes) his fascination with Brentano's book *On the Several Senses of Being in Aristotle* and the question of the unity of these senses, though the importance of the book cannot be denied. It was rather a reflection on *logic* and, specifically, on the homelessness of logic in the geography of the sciences Heidegger inherited from his neo-Kantian and neo-Scholastic teachers. The publications from Heidegger's apprentice years show that the way to the question of being and, in particular, to the central thought of the ontological difference between being and entities passes through the theory of logic, through a reflection on what logic itself is and how cognition of the "object of logic" is possible. These writings also document Heidegger's debt—frequently acknowledged but infrequently studied—to the neo-Kantian philosopher and fellow student of Heinrich Rickert, Emil Lask. As the present chapter will illustrate, it was Lask's conception of transcendental logic as "the self-reflection and the self-consciousness of philosophy itself" that provided the early Heidegger with both the initial set of problems and with many of the conceptual tools that would later serve him in formulating the ontological difference as the specific theme of philosophical inquiry (*LP* 210).

The thread that leads from Heidegger's early metaphilosophical reflections up to *Sein und Zeit* is provided by the concept of meaning (*Sinn*), and its evolution can be summarized briefly. Heidegger began by appropriating specific elements of Lask's conception of logic as a theory of meaning whose object domain is not a domain of "what is," but of "what holds" (is valid). He then came to recognize that meaning is not a realm of "obscure intermediary entities,"[3] is not a realm of *entities* at all, and so developed the metaphilosophical argument that philosophy has to do not with entities, but with the (reflective) *difference* between entities and their meaning (being). For this reason, as we learn in *Sein und Zeit,* the "logic" of philosophy is hermeneutics. The origin of this line of questioning lies in what I have called the "homelessness" of logic. The term is borrowed from Lask, and to understand the problem it names one must understand something of Lask's work and the way it was taken up into Heidegger's early conception of logic.[4]

1. Heidegger's Proximity to Lask

As Heidegger remarks in the 1972 "Vorwort" to *Frühe Schriften,* while he "mediated" between Rickert and Husserl, Lask "also tried to listen to the Greek thinkers" (GA 1:56). Setting aside the reference to Husserl for the moment, it is important to note that mention of Rickert and the Greek thinkers in the economy of Heidegger's early thought signifies something quite specific, namely "the attempt," as Karl Lehmann put it, "finally to inaugurate the long postponed dialogue between modern transcendental philosophy and classical metaphysics."[5] The early Heidegger finds his point of departure in the attempt to reconcile Aristotle and Kant on the nature and systematic-scientific "place" of logic. As attentive to both Rickert and the Greeks, Lask is a catalyst for this reconciliation. Heidegger's early views on logic, centering on the theory of categories, draw heavily upon Lask's interpretation of Kant and Aristotle, an interpretation highlighting the presumed inability of either thinker to distinguish adequately between logic and metaphysics. Lask argues that since Kant and Aristotle both subscribe to a two-world theory—an ontological dualism of sensible (physical/psychical) and supersensible (metaphysical) entities—the object of logic is left ontologically underdetermined. It is homeless.

According to Lask, the homelessness of logic arises already with Aristotle's use of the term "form" to refer both to logical categories and to metaphysical essences. "In this sense substantial essence and concept, the relation of inherence and the structure of the judgment, are said by Aristotle to correspond to one another" (*LP* 379). From this, ambiguities arise that will haunt the metaphysical tradition through Kant. Logical or syntactic structures can be mistaken for elements of sensible existents, "entities" that are (in some cases at least) "separable" or capable of existing apart from the entities they help to constitute. They take on, as Heidegger comments, "metaphysical significance as formative principles of physical, psychical, and metaphysical realities" (GA 1:223). Further, because sensible existents exhibit a contingent and dependent character incompatible with the universal and necessary character of logico-deductive knowledge, the ground of knowledge comes to be sought in supersensible or "changeless" entities that often turn out to be nothing but hypostatized logical form.[6] Lask argues that Aristotle's commitment to the two-world theory carries with it a failure to recognize the peculiar character of logical form, the "object of logic" (*LP* 230).

Kant is said to improve the situation, though at bottom he too subscribed to the two-world theory. On the positive side, Lask praises Kant's

"Copernican achievement"—the "transformation of the concept of being into a concept of transcendental logic" (*LP* 28), or more generally, the recognition that categories, a priori concepts, belong not to metaphysics but to logic. Thus, a distinction between logic and metaphysics represents the heart of Kant's critical project. Because a priori concepts (exhaustively represented by the logical forms of judgment) have their seat or origin in the understanding, which in turn depends upon material from the faculty of sensibility on which to exercise its cognitive functions, all knowledge of supersensible entities is excluded. Logical forms have semantic import solely for the realm of appearances, and (though Kant never doubted their existence) supersensible entities lie forever beyond our cognitive capacities.

Given the decisive demarcation between the logical and the metaphysical resulting from Kant's "experiment of reason," one might expect Lask to celebrate the homecoming of logic. Surprisingly, he does the opposite. Lask insists that Kant "is not fully serious about the nonsensuous, rational character of the logical. He does not really house the world of the logical in a third realm beyond the sensible and the supersensible, but rather makes it entirely homeless in his two-world metaphysics" (*LP* 260). Thus, on the negative side, Lask argues that Kant's adherence to the two-world theory makes it impossible for him to give a nonpsychological characterization of logic. Identifying logic with transcendental apperception—"which is neither the I 'as I appear to myself' nor the I 'as I am in myself' " (*LP* 261)—Kant could determine the logical only along a *via negativa,* inaugurating "the homelessness that it has retained in all the transcendental philosophical Kantianism of the nineteenth century" (*LP* 261). Had Kant been able to determine the place of logic positively, however, he would have had no grounds to restrict its validity by way of a dogmatic-psychologistic concept of intuition as "sensibility," and thus he would have had no grounds for his critical skepticism toward metaphysical knowledge. According to Lask, Kant should have seen that "[e]ven if all metaphysics is indeed deception and fantasy, no epistemological, logical reflection has the power to convince us of this. Epistemology, logic, the theory of categories, is not the place where this question could be decided" (*LP* 128). Acceptance of Kant's Copernican achievement is thus compatible, for Lask, with rejection of his critical resignation. Opening the door to ontology, Lask asserts the "boundlessness of truth" (*LP* 125 f.), the pertinence of logical form to any entity, whether sensible or supersensible. Lask's rehabilitation of the unbounded reach of "truth," the universality of (transcendental) logic, provides the logical space for the incubation of the ontological difference in Heidegger's earliest writings. Transcendental reflection on the nature of "logical form"—neither a sensible nor a supersensible entity, though it pertains to all entities—is the immediate precursor of that inquiry in which Heidegger identifies the nonentitative being of entities as the genuine transcendental-philosophical theme.

Lask's transformation of Kant's transcendental philosophy by way of a universalization of transcendental logic, which Heidegger deepens and extends, rests upon two major criticisms of Kant's position as a theory of knowledge. The first was shared by many philosophers at the turn of the century: Kant, like Aristotle, restricts his logical investigations to those categories that pertain to the cognition of nature, ignoring the a priori concepts which make knowledge possible in history, the human sciences, and so on. Echoing the wider perspective of a universal transcendental logic sought by Rickert, Dilthey, and others, Heidegger argues that "the Aristotelian categories appear as a particular set [drawn from] a particular realm [of reality], and not *the* categories *simpliciter*" (GA 1:211). This may be called the criticism from "categorial pluralism." The second, which may be called the "metaphilosophical" criticism, is closely related to the first, though only Lask (among neo-Kantians) made it the centerpiece of his interpretation of Kant. Lask argues that Kant's transcendental schema not only leaves out the conditions for the possibility of many forms of empirical knowledge, but, fatally, it overlooks the conditions for the possibility of transcendental critique itself. Kant's theory of cognition cannot account for its own cognitive validity. For Lask, the homelessness of logic in Kant leads to the homelessness of transcendental critique as a form of knowledge: "In Kant's theory of categories there is no place for the categorial forms of his own speculation, and thus the critic of theoretical reason denies the logical conditions of his own critique of reason" (*LP* 263). In the title of his first book Lask therefore called for a "Logic of Philosophy," an "uncovering" (*Entdecken*) of those categories that make philosophical knowledge itself possible. Heidegger echoes this view in his *Habilitationsschrift:* "Logic itself requires categories of its own. There must be a logic of logic" (GA 1:288).

How does Lask solve the topographical problem of the homelessness of logic and so address the metaphilosophical issue of how philosophical (transcendental) cognition is possible? The answer involves a series of distinctions that Heidegger, too, adopts in his earliest publications. Focusing on the nature of categories as the conditions for the possibility of objects, Lask proposes to substitute for the *metaphysical* two-world distinction (between the domains of sensible and supersensible objects) a *transcendental* two-world distinction (between objects of any kind and the logical forms that render such objects intelligible). To designate the distinctive character of logical form Lask helps himself to an expression—*Geltung* (validity)—then current in the logic deriving from Hermann Lotze.[7] In Lask's view it is precisely the "liberating and clarifying act" of contemporary logical theory to have identified a new "ultimate duality . . . between that which is or occurs and that which holds without having to be" (*LP* 6). *Seiendes* and *Geltendes:* This is the basic duality within the "universe of the thinkable."

Heidegger's dissertation, *Die Lehre vom Urteil im Psychologismus* (1914), provides ample evidence of his proximity to Lask. For example, in a context where he is inquiring into the object of logic, trying to specify what it is that logic as a science thematizes, Heidegger argues that "there must accordingly be yet another mode of existing in addition to the psychical, the physical, and the metaphysical. For this Lotze has found in the treasury of our German language the decisive designation: Beside a 'this is,' there is a 'this holds' " (GA 1:170). The "form of reality" of the object of logic "can only be validity" (GA 1:170). Logical form, the categories, *are* not, but hold. Thus, there is a fundamental difference between the object of philosophy—as transcendental logic—and the object of those sciences that study "existents." This "logical" difference is already ontological, already concerns the *being* of entities: In his *Habilitationsschrift* Heidegger writes that "it is the function of form to give an entity its being" (GA 1:325). The idea had been explicitly formulated by Lask: "The being of entities [*Sein des Seienden*] belongs to the realm of validity, and thus to the non-entitative [*Nicht-Seienden*]" (*LP* 46).

Setting aside the complications of what Heidegger means by "being" in his early writings, the important point is that it is in the context of transcendental logic—an account of logical form as "a moment of the object that conditions its objecthood" (GA 1:222)—that Heidegger encounters a basic difference between entities and nonentitative "conditions" of entities. "In the entire history of philosophy [this difference] has never received its due," wrote Heidegger already in his 1912 "Neuere Forschungen über Logik" (GA 1:24). Kant's own gloss on forms as syntheses or as functions of combination remains ambiguous since he locates such syntheses "in" the subject and thus views them as (quasi) entities interacting with or doing something to other entities (the data of sensation). Against this, Heidegger, following Lask, sees that logic as a theory of form is at home not in a realm of beings, but in a realm of "validities." Transcendental logic, as a theory of how logical form makes objects possible, must specify the character of the relation between nonentitative validity and the objects (or entities) themselves. Both Heidegger and Lask accomplish this specification through a theory of *meaning*. Meaning emerges as the basic theme of a philosophy of logic that attempts to avoid Kantian representationalism without falling into metaphysics.

Lask rejects Aristotle's metaphysical construal of logical categories and adopts the Kantian position, but this does not prevent him from describing objects of knowledge in a quasi-Aristotelian, "realistic" way. This is because Kant's transcendental logic is interpreted to mean the overcoming of the duality between "object and truth," the "destruction of the ancient opposition between object and truth content" (*LP* 29). The Copernican turn is taken to mean that there is no "metalogical" (and so no skeptical) abyss between the thing and the "truth" of the thing, that "truth extends to the object itself, is identical to it" (*LP* 109). Concepts like reality, factuality, existence, and being testify to this when heard with Kantian ears: "Something is in fact so, something is actually so: This means nothing else but that it is *in truth* so" (*LP* 29). The concept of the object, on Lask's reading of Kant, is to be understood simply as "what something is *in truth.*" But this reference to truth does not mean that the object is a judgment about the thing. Judgment is an "artificial" or secondary construct whose own truth depends on reproducing in a derivative way the "original" truth which is identical to the thing itself, "untouched by all subjectivity" (*LvU* 287). In the clearest expression of this aletheiological realism, then, Lask goes so far as to claim that "spatiotemporal objects *are* truths, physical objects are physical truths, astral objects are astronomical truths, psychical objects are psychological truths, etc." (*LP* 41).

In his Scotus book Heidegger expresses the same view while commenting on the medieval *ens/verum* convertibility thesis: "Every object is *an* object. Every object is a *true* object." But he follows it with a question that will lead him beyond Lask: "What pertains to it such that it may be called 'true' " (GA 1:265)? To locate the difference, let us recall some of the features of Lask's theory which we encountered in chapter 3.

Lask's theory of the object is the centerpiece of his transcendental philosophy of meaning. From the unreflective (prephilosophical) standpoint, a plurality of domains of entities can be identified (astral, psychological, physical, etc.) whose empirical features are investigated by the relevant positive sciences. But transcendental philosophy, which raises the question of the conditions for the possibility of such sciences, thematizes *all* objects in terms of their validity structure or intelligibility (truth). Such investigation reveals in empirical objects a transcendental predicate (*LP* 123)—"meaning"—that is not found in any empirical catalog of what there is. Thus, as Lask continues, "the objects are identical to theoretical meaning." As truths, that is, they are "unities of meaning"—to be sure, "not cognitions, judgments, propositions, but truths in the original [*ungekünstelten*] sphere" (*LP* 41). For philosophy, objects are "in truth" *meanings*.

This is no doubt a curious claim, but certainly no more curious than the claim it is meant to displace, namely, that objects are representations. Lask's departure from mentalism and representationalism toward meaning, a move Heidegger follows, depends on characterizing logical form as validity, since Lask analyzes the concept of meaning as a relation between valid logical form and the material *of which* it is valid. Such a relation is governed by Lask's principle of the "material determination of form" according to which "the moment that differentiates form does not lie within the realm of validity itself but must be chalked up to that which is engaged by the form, . . . to the material" (*LP* 58). This principle asserts that since forms are validities rather than entities they must be thought of as relative to (a specific range) of material. Only this relativity can account for differences within the formal realm of validity. Against Hegel's "Panlogism," where categorial differentiation is supposedly the result of dialectical relations between forms themselves, Lask argues that validity is an *intentional* concept, a "*Hingelten*" (*LP* 32). Validity can only be validity *for* something, a holding or being valid *of* something. Indeed, this alone constitutes its "formal" quality: "According to an honorable terminology one can designate this nonindependence, this unavoidability of being in and for something else, as the form character of validity" (*LP* 33).

The principle of material determination of form is designed to avoid the notion that form does something to its material, that it "forms" it either as a Kantian synthesis or as an Aristotelian indwelling essence or entelechy. "The material is not formed . . . by cognition, rather *in itself* it is engaged by logical form" (*LP* 69). In describing how one is to think of such non-Aristotelian, non-Kantian "engagement" of form and material, Lask employs a term familiar to readers of *Sein und Zeit*—*Bewandtnis*—which is as difficult to translate as it is important for both Lask and Heidegger in their attempt to develop a nonmetaphysical and a nonrepresentational theory of meaning.[8] Logical form is nothing other than a certain "involvement" (*Bewandtnis*) of the material itself. For Lask the categories of "objectivity, being, subsistence, actuality, reality, existence" are nothing but "those particular objective involvements that obtain within the sensible alogical mass of material" (*LP* 69). Specifying further the peculiar nature of the logical moment pertaining to the material, Lask suggests that categorial involvement is a kind of *clarity:* "To stand within a category is synonymous with standing in clarity." Form is the clarity in which the material always already stands. Material here is not reduced in Hegelian fashion to "pure *Klarheitsmasse,*" it is not made logically "transparent," but rather "surrounded or touched" by clarity, "lit up" or "clarified" (*LP* 76).

Heidegger uses these same terms to describe logical form: "To be an object is to stand in clarity," while "through the *unum* [Heidegger's example here of logical form] a specific relevance of the object is present [*es hat durch das Unum eine gewisse Bewandtnis mit dem Gegenstand*]" (GA 1:224). Because both Heidegger and Lask see forms as validities, and because validity is always dependent, validity for something, there can be no call for establishing a causal or synthetically imposed connection between form and material. This means that the difference between form and material is not a "real," but a purely *reflective,* difference; form is nothing but the clarity, the intelligibility, the "truth moment" of the material itself.

The reflective character of this difference supports Lask's peculiar "meaning realism," which amounts to the claim that all objects, whether physical, metaphysical, or psychical, are, from the philosophical point of view, meanings—that is, truths, combinations of form and material: "The intertwining, the combination of form and material—the totality in which the form, in itself empty and requiring supplementation, together with its material fulfillment, emerges—is to be designated *meaning* [*Sinn*]. The objective realm, therefore also the realm of truth . . . is a realm of 'meaning' " (*LP* 34). Ordinarily, we remain unaware of the meaning-character of objects since in daily practical and scientific contexts we are rightly concerned not with the object as such but only with the object *material:* "Every knowing consists in the directedness toward the existing object, toward categorially engaged material, whereby however the validity character of the form and correspondingly the meaning-character of the entire object remains unrecognized" (*LP* 122). Such material is in varying ways intelligible to us only because we are immersed in the space of meaning without thematizing it. We can be engaged with the object material only because it *already* stands in a certain clarity, within a certain involvement (or relevance), in short, in logical form. Thus, as Lask formulates it, we "live in the truth" (*LP* 86–87, 124–25, 191 f.).

In practical or pretheoretical life, where we manipulate objects without thematizing them, the object material is "logically naked" (*LP* 74). With the emergence of the theoretical attitude (e.g., in a situation of perplexity) this logical nudity becomes an *issue.* The task of empirical science is to "clothe" the material by making explicit the form or category that constitutes the clarity or intelligibility of our previously pretheoretical experience.[9] At the level of "positive" theory, however, the specific character of the object as meaning does not show itself. Such an understanding is reserved for a philosophical, or reflective, investigation that seeks the categories not of this or that realm of objects, but those that make *intelligibility itself* possible. Thus, the theme of philosophy as transcendental logic is truth *as such;* it attempts to thematize the categories themselves, to clothe them with the theoretical predicates (for instance, "validity") that clarify them *as categories,* to find the specific relevances or *Bewandtnisse* that articulate the space of meaning itself. This higher-order theorizing reveals the structure of the object at the previous level to be "meaning" or "being in the sense of truth."[10]

In his *Habilitationsschrift* Heidegger follows Lask's conception of a pretheoretical, prereflective absorption in the space of intelligibility that sustains everyday and scientific being-towards entities: "Whatever is cognized, whatever gets judged, must belong to a world of meaning, for only therein are cognition and judgment possible. Only because I live in the realm of validity do I know anything of what exists" (GA 1:280). To live in the realm of validity is, in the language of *Sein und Zeit,* to possess a "preontological" understanding of being. In the Scotus book it is said that entities of any sort "can be given in turn only in and through a context of meaning having the character of validity" (GA 1:279). For Heidegger, as for Lask, the ontological difference between an entity and its meaning is not a difference between two entities but a difference between a straightforward and a reflective grasp of any entity. A reversal of Aristotelianism: Logic is not in things; things are immanent to the clarity of the logos. The object is what Lask calls "logos-immanent" (*LP* 245).

2. Heidegger's Criticism of Lask

Heidegger's early reflections on logic are indelibly marked by Lask's thinking, both in vocabulary and conception. This, as has been suggested above, is because Lask's conception of categories provides a way for "bringing Aristotle and Kant as close together as possible" (GA 1:33). Lask's conception of the logos-immanent object as meaning would combine the realism of Aristotelian metaphysics with the idealism of Kantian transcendental philosophy by designating logical categoriality as nonentitative validity that is nothing other than the "involvement" of the alogical material. Yet though he approves of this basic position, Heidegger does not think that Lask's theory of the logos-immanent object is *sufficient* as a philosophical account of the place of logic. Heidegger expresses a crucial reservation that suggests why he holds logic to be homeless even in Lask's theory and thus why he will seek to move away from a quasi-realistic transcendental logic toward a fundamental ontology, toward an *account* of clarity, meaning, and intelligibility in terms of Dasein's "understanding" of being. As he remarks in the Scotus book: "Through pure givenness consciousness may be oriented toward 'truth,' but only through judgment does it become aware of it *as* true, valid meaning" (GA 1:285). Hence, "objecthood has meaning only for a judging subject, a subject without consideration of which it will never be possible to elucidate what one designates as 'validity' " (GA 1:405). In the end Lask's account of logic falls short since it remains objectively oriented and does not sufficiently take into account the Kantian side of the equation. Because transcendental determinations such as meaning and validity are *reflective* determinations, they require treatment of the "subjective logical" problems involved in any claim to respect the difference between logical form and entities, meaning and things (GA 1:404). Nowhere does Lask supply such a treatment. By adopting insights from Husserl's phenomenology, however, Heidegger thinks he can overcome this tendency toward dogmatism in Lask's meaning-realism without sacrificing the concreteness, the non-representationalism, of Lask's transcendental theory of meaning as "the object in truth."

The point can be made in the language of *Sein und Zeit* this way: Though both Heidegger and Lask appeal to a concept of meaning as "ontological truth"—neither one of them reduces the logical object to a mental representation, and both of them describe it as a kind of truth prior to the theory of judgment—Lask remains uncritical since he simply *posits* such an object as the ground of logical reflection, whereas Heidegger faces up to the question of how such an object is "there" for reflection, what it means to say that ontological truth is "given." Husserl's theory of evidence as the "subjective correlate" of truth had made this a central problem of logic, and on this matter Heidegger follows Husserl against Lask. Thus, whereas Lask's conception of logical investigation is *nominally* phenomenological, Heidegger, with Husserl, demands phenomenological work—and that means working out a conception of subjectivity that will make intelligible how the object, as ontological truth, is *accessible* as the measure of propositional truth.[11]

Heidegger's *Habilitation* thesis documents this move. Whereas Lask took the concept of validity to be ultimate—the "category of categories" that renders the logical space of meaning intelligible—Heidegger holds validity to be capable of further analysis because of its very intentionality. "Intentionality," and not validity, "is the defining category [*Gebietskategorie*] of the logical realm" (GA 1:283). Thus, "the moment that defines the order within the logical realm is intentionality" (GA 1:281), a moment that must be taken explicitly into account if Lask's theory of material determination of form is itself to be clarified, to be logically self-grounding. Lask correctly sees that the fundamental logical problems reveal themselves at the pretheoretical level of living (*Erleben*), but without an explicit theory of intentionality he can only stand mutely before these lifeworld issues. Lask simply has no conception of a reflective investigation of what Husserl calls "passive genesis" or what Heidegger, in *Sein und Zeit,* will identify with the meaning-constituting function of "circumspective concern."[12]

It is true that Lask nominally adopts Husserl's conception of intentionality. His analysis of the judgment in *Die Lehre vom Urteil* operates explicitly with the language of "act" and "object" that Husserl had developed in the *Logical Investigations* (the only book of Husserl's with which Lask was familiar), and we have already noted his comment to Husserl that "the concept of intentionality projected by you supersedes all theories of 'consciousness in general.' "[13] However, Lask rejected the revolutionary critical implications of Husserl's phenomenology. For him phenomenology may be a "beginning," but it is "not the whole of scientific philosophy" since the theory of meaning must be grounded in the object itself untouched by all subjectivity. Philosophy must move from phenomenological quasi transcendence to genuine transcendence. For Lask, "the ideal meaning of the assertion in Husserl's sense remains wholly within the limits of quasi transcendence." In contrast, "genuine transcendence is the condition of meaning prior to all contact with subjectivity, while behind the independence of quasi-transcendent meaning stands merely the separability of meaning *after* its contact with subjectivity" (*LvU* 425). Beyond intentionality, Lask purports to grasp a realm of logos-immanent objects in themselves that, as "untouched by all subjectivity," cannot be described or investigated but only posited as logically necessary for a theory of knowledge.

Thus, though Lask claims to be following Husserl's theory of categorial intuition, and though Heidegger actually praises him for doing so in *Sein und Zeit* (GA 2:289/494), a close examination of his position reveals that this notion neither does, nor can, do any work. With his theory of intentional constitution, of passive and active genesis of meaning, Husserl can reflectively trace the origin of logical forms, the specific *Bewandtnisse,* to those primordial "styles" of our intentional experience or engagement in the world that provide intuitive evidence or givenness of what grounds subsequent judgment.[14] For Lask, on the other hand, such investigations remain psychologistic. Though he pays lip service to Husserl's theory of intentionality, he gives the game away when he suggests that an investigation into the subjective correlate of original meaning could only be a matter for "psycho-physiology" (*LP* 52). In spite of his claim to be doing *transcendental* logic, his overall conception remains *naturalistic.* And, as Husserl had already argued in "Philosophy as Rigorous Science" (a 1911 essay that Lask knew), such psychological naturalism will inevitably overlook the specificity of logic, rendering it homeless once more (Hua XXV:9/80).

Since Heidegger takes Husserl's critique of naturalism seriously, he is able to follow Husserl into the subjective problems of logic without fearing the "bogey of psychologism."[15] By arguing that the *Hingeltung* character of logical form is not an inexplicable primitive but a function of the intentional structure of consciousness, Heidegger can project a program for categorially investigating the key concept in Lask's approach to the space of meaning, namely, the "material determination of form." Rather than merely assert that specific logical forms derive their sense from a specific range of material, Heidegger can demonstrate it by thematizing the *modes of givenness* (as Husserl would say) of such material. Thus, Heidegger suggests that logical significations "must be grasped as intentional contents, as achievements of intentional acts" (GA 1:308). And in a comment on Lask's principle of *Materialbestimmtheit,* the objective character of the form/matter dichotomy is said to "express the necessary correlation between act-quality and act-material of noesis and noema" (GA 1:311). In the idiom of his Scotus book, Heidegger goes beyond Lask to recover for logic the medieval *modus essendi activus*—"givenness as achievement of consciousness" (GA 1:309): "Forms are nothing but the objective expression of the ways in which consciousness is intentionally directed toward what is objective" (GA 1:319), the way the object "is given" (GA 1:316).

To summarize: Heidegger overcomes the traditional homelessness of logic by following Lask in his recognition of the limits of the traditional two-world theory. Logical form belongs neither to a realm of metaphysical entities nor to a realm of physical entities; nor is it a denizen of the psychological realm of subjective entities. It is its "own world" (GA 1:303), a world of validities that do not exist, but hold. In opposition to Lask's view, however, this logical world must be grounded in the theory of intentionality, since intentionality provides a concept of givenness or evidence that allows us to see how logical meaning is present in pretheoretical experience and so allows for developing a *critical* theory of the original intelligibility or truth of the "thing itself." Lask attained the stage of recognizing the logos-immanent object and so could see that the place of the logical was neither beyond the things themselves nor located in subjective psychological functions imposed on indeterminate material manifolds. But Heidegger goes one step further in recognizing that the logos-immanent object implied the principle of immanence (*Satz der Immanenz*), a nonnaturalistic, intentional concept of the subject: "Properly understood, the principle of immanence does not dismiss reality or transform the external world into a dream; rather, precisely through the absolute primacy of valid meaning the lance is broken over all physiological and psychological and economic-pragmatic theories of knowledge, thus founding the absolute validity of truth, genuine objectivity, in a decisive way" (GA 1:273).

Determining the "logical place" of logic thus leads both to an incipient ontological difference between entities and the being (meaning) of entities and to the call for a theory of intentional immanence. That this difference does not multiply entities or reduplicate the world of things with a mirroring world of forms depends, indeed, upon its connection with the principle of immanence; for it arises with the practice of transcendental reflection. The difference between entities and validities, the difference between what is and what holds, implies a difference between the thing and its meaning. This in turn is no empirical or "ontic" distinction, but rather a difference in the way one and the same thing is "taken"—first in straightforward experience, and then again in the reflective inquiry that grasps the conditions of possibility for the first. Meaning *is* the thing as it presents itself to phenomenological reflection. And because Heidegger, unlike Lask, explicitly traces this difference to the "immanence" of phenomenological (intentional) consciousness, new prospects open up for *Sein und Zeit*'s "genuine *philosophical* empiricism" (GA 2:67/490) as the exploration of how the intelligibility of things is constituted in pretheoretical life.

3. Does Heidegger Leave Logic Homeless?

Of course, Heidegger's own articulation of the ontological difference in *Sein und Zeit* involves radical departures from Husserl's theory of intentionality. Yet this is not because, as some would have it, he uses Lask's realism against Husserl's idealism of consciousness.[16] On the contrary, because Heidegger takes the problems of "subjective logic" seriously he can demand, in 1925, that "the being of the intentional" be investigated more radically than in Husserl's theoretically oriented conception of consciousness, laden with "traditional [Cartesian] prejudices" (GA 20:147–57/107–14). This investigation, in turn, occasions important revisions of the theory of meaning found in Heidegger's earlier thinking. Above all, meaning comes to be seen not as the object of a transcendental logic, but the topic/topos of transcendental *ontology*.[17] Already in his 1915 thesis Heidegger had cautioned that "one cannot see logic and its problems in a true light if the context in terms of which they are interpreted does not become a translogical one" (GA 1:405). Only if "logical meaning becomes a problem with respect to its ontic significance" will it be possible to answer the question of how the "'unreal' 'transcendent' meaning guarantees for us true reality and objectivity" (GA 1:406).

The most important implication of this revision is that, having broken with the theoretical bias in the reflection on subjectivity, the space of meaning is no longer to be conceived "logically" as a realm of *objects,* but as the nonobjective "horizon" of intelligibility *in* which any object can be encountered as what it truly is. Meaning in *Sein und Zeit* is "that wherein the intelligibility of something maintains itself"; the "formal-existential framework of the disclosedness which belongs to understanding" (GA 2:201/193). Meaning is not an object domain of validities, but now, simply, the world of being-in-the-world. Even so, significant as such revisions are, the characterization of meaning in *Sein und Zeit* retains deep affinities with its ancestor in the early work. Heidegger continues to speak of meaning as the "clarity of" the thing, as that *Bewandtnis* of the material that comes to light as Dasein's projects "let" entities "be," allowing them to show themselves in themselves (GA 2:111–17/115–20). And even though the form/matter schema is abandoned, the "material determination of form" is present (as modified through Husserl's views on evidence) in the conception of Dasein as "having meaning" only "so far as the disclosedness of being-in-the-world can be 'filled in' by the entities discoverable in that disclosedness" (GA 2:201/193).

In spite of such affinities, however, it might seem that Heidegger's approach to meaning in *Sein und Zeit* once again loses sight of the specificity of logic—that logic is homeless in Heidegger's fundamental ontology. Heidegger's break with the theoretical attitude in his reflection on meaning, and his path to the question of the meaning of being through an existential analytic of everyday and authentic being-in-the-world, yield a conception of the logos far removed from the traditional interpretation of logos as reason, ratio, or logic as the laws of valid argument. Logos as discourse, as "letting be seen," is freed from its restriction to the *logos apophantikos,* the logic of judgments or propositions, and is traced to the hermeneutic structure of Dasein's factic understanding. For Heidegger, the intelligibility of the world, the "as-structure" of all experience, is no longer explicable in terms of formal-logical categories but rather originates in the historically situated projects by means of which we make our way in the world. When Heidegger begins to articulate the original level of logos, of the disclosedness of the "totality of involvements" that is the successor to the "logical space" of the earlier works,[18] he does so in terms of the traditionally nontheoretical domains of techne (disclosure of the ready-to-hand), phronesis (the complex of conscience, resolve, and decision in the "moment"), and (in the later work) poiesis. Thus, Heidegger's position has been compared to a sort of pragmatism, and rightly so, to the extent that in it meaning is traced to the practical, engaged attitude of human beings in the concrete historical world.[19] Yet Heidegger consistently rejected pragmatism. Was this a case of mere ignorance, or of German chauvinistic anti-Americanism? A more philosophical hypothesis is that it was a consequence of his *continued adherence* to Husserl's critique of naturalism, to the phenomenological "principle of immanence," and so to the rejection of "economic-pragmatic theories of knowledge" that undermine "the absolute validity of truth, genuine objectivity" (GA 1:273). In any case, only if something like this is so can logic, conceived as it was in the early work as the "theory of theory," find a home in fundamental ontology. This strong claim can be illustrated, though by no means adequately supported, by a few concluding reflections.

Heidegger's concern with the homelessness of logic was a concern with understanding the nature of logical *ideality*. This led him from the theory of logical validity to an ontology based on a reinterpretation of Husserl's conception of intentional consciousness. But a glance at *Sein und Zeit* might well suggest that there is no place for logical ideality in Heidegger's ontology, for very little is said of logic in that text except that it is "derivative," a product of "formalizing" the reduction of the ready-to-hand to the present-at-hand, and so forth.[20] Now if Heidegger were indeed advocating a pragmatic or a naturalistic position—for example, if his emphasis on temporality and finitude finally forced one to view the supposed ideality of logical forms as a function of the relative unlikelihood of our giving them up "in the event of recalcitrant experience"[21]—then in the terms of Heidegger's early work logic would indeed be homeless once again and Husserl's transcendental project would not have been modified, but simply abandoned. But if this is not the proper way to understand Heidegger's development, what *is* the status of logical ideality in *Sein und Zeit?* And why does Heidegger have so little to say about it?

A conclusion is no place to answer the first question, but an answer to the second may be suggested here. Heidegger paid little attention to the phenomenology of logic in *Sein und Zeit* because, rightly or wrongly, he believed that most of what Husserl had written on the subject was correct and that it could be made compatible with the new "ontological foundations" that the existential analytic provided. Logical and epistemological analyses play little role in the 1927 text because, in the main, Heidegger agrees with Husserl on the basic phenomenological structure of (positive or nonphilosophical) knowledge. For example, Heidegger's remark that formal-logical concepts arise through a process of "formalization" whereby the "context of assignments" is formalized into a "system of relations" (GA 3:118/121) is an allusion to an important distinction Husserl drew between "formal" and "general" concepts. Far from rejecting such an account, therefore, Heidegger adopts it. What he rejects is that formal concepts can tell us anything of *ontological* significance. Or again, Heidegger's emphasis on the radical temporality of Dasein—indeed, of being itself—does not exclude the timeless validity of logical idealities in Husserl's sense. Such references to temporality cannot support inferences to temporal contingency in the sense that this is commonly taken to undermine what is designated by the (somewhat misleading) term "timeless validity." Rather, Heidegger's conception of temporality as the horizon of all understanding of being is fully consistent with the mature Husserl's claim that the "supertemporality" of "ideal objectivities" such as the laws of logic and mathematics "turns out to be *omnitemporality* as a correlate of free producibility and reproducibility at all times" (Hua I:155/127). A phenomenology of time—whether Husserlian or Heideggerian—does not imply the naturalization of epistemology or logic.

If these suggestions were to be fleshed out it would become apparent that Heidegger did not in fact leave logic homeless in fundamental ontology. Husserl had built the house; Heidegger was concerned with the zoning laws.

5

Making Logic Philosophical Again

1. Toward a Philosophical Logic

Between 1912 and 1916 Heidegger published a series of writings in which he confronts the major logical theories of the time, including the metaphysical logic of neo-Scholasticism, neo-Kantian "critical idealism" (transcendental logic, epistemology as first philosophy), O. Külpe's "critical realism," and Husserl's phenomenology. In each of these positions a central issue is the theory of categories. Whether inspired by Aristotle or Kant, logical theory sought to account for the concepts that make empirical scientific knowledge possible, the ground of the "objective validity" of knowledge. Logic in this sense does not merely elaborate formal properties of argument; as transcendental logic or "logic of truth" it embraces fundamental questions of the theory of knowledge and science. Even neo-Scholastic positions subordinating logic to metaphysics were formulated in terms of the transcendental question of the conditions of possibility for knowledge, though they would restore to the term "transcendental" the pre-Kantian connotation of the medieval *transcendentia* to retrieve the ontological sense of categories as determinations of being.[1] Heidegger's most original contribution to this debate, his 1915 *Habilitationsschrift* and its 1916 *Schluss,* shows the strain of trying to find an independent path between neo-Kantian and neo-Scholastic logics.

The main text revisits an issue left hanging in Heidegger's dissertation, that of determining the relation between logic and grammar. Heidegger had argued that "the true preparatory work for logic . . . is not accomplished by psychological investigations into the genesis and composition of representations, but by unambiguous definition and clarification of the significations of words" (GA 1:186).[2] But what *are* significations? Philosophical incorporation of this preparatory work requires that significations be distinguished categorially from the spoken, written, or mental sign token, which in turn requires a general theory of categories. Heidegger's reconstruction of Duns Scotus's theory of categories and signification, guided explicitly by "the perspective of modern [logical] research" (GA 1:202), aims to address both issues.[3] Scotus's theory of categories allows Heidegger to argue that "the guiding value for the investigation of significations is . . . *truth* as valid meaning" (GA 1:307). Since the orientation toward truth "unavoidably requires a decision on the relation between the region of significations and the being of object" (GA 1:307), Heidegger manages to retain the ontological character of Scotus's categories. But the reconstruction in the main text is informed far less by ontological perspectives than by neo-Kantian critical idealism. Because (as Heidegger puts it in 1912) logic is a "theory of theory," it has (as he says in 1915) "absolute hegemony over all cognizable or cognized object worlds" (GA 1:23, 279). Logic is first philosophy.

But another note is struck in *Das Kategorienproblem,* a short conclusion appended to the Scotus book upon its publication in 1916. Here Heidegger offers a limited, "preliminary look at the *systematic* structure of the category problem" that draws out "the essential *Potenzen* of the problem and its context" (GA 1:300). The account in the main text has been "strictly conceptual" and "to a certain extent one-sided"; it has "self-consciously excluded deeper-reaching sets of metaphysical problems" (GA 1:400). There is need for a "metaphysical resolution to the problem of knowledge" (GA 1:403). "In the long run," philosophy, including logic, cannot "avoid its genuine optic, metaphysics" (GA 1:406). The "absolute hegemony" of logic thus appears compromised here by the need for "metaphysical" resolution; transcendental logic must be seen within a "translogical context" (GA 1:405). Hence *Das Kategorienproblem* identifies three problem areas that adumbrate the metaphysics which Heidegger—having dispatched psychologism and grammaticism—believes is necessary to restore philosophical significance to logic, to make logic philosophical again.

The project of making logic philosophical again is not limited to Heidegger's student years. In his 1912 review of logical theory, Heidegger asked "What is logic?" and answered that "here we already stand before a problem whose solution is reserved for the future" (GA 1:18). Fifteen years later, in his lecture course on the *Grundprobleme der Phänomenologie,* Heidegger still calls for a "radical conception of the problems of logic as such" (GA 24:252/177). Alluding to two dominant influences on his early work, Heidegger argues that neither Husserl's phenomenology nor Lask's theory of categories does justice to the "ontological problems" that emerge, under pressure of the "things themselves," in a philosophical inquiry into logic (GA 24:253/178). If one is ever to succeed in "making logic again into philosophy," one must first overcome Hegel's "reduction of ontology to logic" and ask what logic, the being of the logos, *is* (GA 24:254/178).

This problem had been suggested two years earlier, when Heidegger opened his lecture course on *Logik: Die Frage nach der Wahrheit,* by criticizing contemporary "school logic" for leaving "all philosophy, i.e., all questioning and investigating, behind" (GA 21:12). A cozy discipline within the philosophical *Fach,* the "science" of logic is in fact rootless, confused about its own object, its scientific domain. Defining it as the science of logos—as argument, discourse, sentence, proposition—does not distinguish it from other sciences investigating these things, unless one adds that logic is specifically concerned with logos "in respect to truth." Other sciences seek "what is true" by inquiring methodically into their objects; logic alone, "strictly speaking," is the science of "truth" as such (GA 21:7). Thus, if logic "wants to be a form of scientific research, a philosophizing logic," then what "should most concern it" is not further technical development, but the question of "the primary being of truth," what it means to be true (GA 21:12). To make logic philosophical again is to reestablish the connection—posited by Aristotle and renewed by Kant—between logic and the question of being, by determining the being of truth.

The concept of truth already governs Heidegger's perspective when, in 1916, he identifies the *Potenzen* of the category problem. But his call for a "metaphysics of the truth problem" (GA 1:402) only gives a name to the basic tension between the *Habilitation* thesis and its *Schluss.* On the one hand, Heidegger's appeal to metaphysics signals his proximity to the neo-Scholastic project, but the argument in the main text rules out a metaphysical solution in the neo-Scholastic sense. And on the other, focusing metaphysics on the problem of *truth* preserves the main text's critical insistence on the priority of truth as "logically valid meaning," but without the neo-Kantian willingness to subordinate metaphysics wholly to logic.[4] The transcendental logical theory of truth thus sets the terms for Heidegger's projected move into metaphysics, but the uneasy compromise he suggests cannot hold. Making logic philosophical again ultimately calls for something other than metaphysics, namely, the transcendental ontology of *Sein und Zeit.* In this chapter I uncover the reasons for this that lie immanent in the three issues Heidegger identifies as problem horizons for the theory of categories. First, however, it is necessary to show how these problem horizons themselves emerge from the transcendental logical approach to truth.

2. The Problem of Truth

Kant had distinguished formal from transcendental logic by arguing that while the former provides a "negative condition" of truth (without which our thinking cannot be consistent with itself), the latter is a "logic of truth" since it provides the conditions without which our thinking can have no "relation to any object."[5] If the former concerns the a priori syntax of thought, the latter concerns its a priori semantics. Granting "the nominal definition of truth, that it is the agreement of knowledge with its object,"[6] Kantian categories become conditions of possibility for truth as agreement or correspondence. Within this framework, the issue between neo-Kantians and neo-Scholastics turned on whether or not the logic of truth requires grounding in "ontological truth" (*ens tanquam verum*), hence in a metaphysical concept of the object as the measure of judgment. Can a purely logical account of correspondence be given? Both sides agree that merely analyzing the structure of truth is not enough; it is further necessary to show how a cognitive grasp of truth—the *knowing* of the known—is possible. But if to know is to grasp the correspondence between thought and thing, judgment and object, a problem arises, cited by Heidegger in his 1914 review of Charles Sentroul's *Kant und Aristoteles* as the "antinomy in the problem of truth": "Either one has both elements of the comparison requisite for truth, namely, the thought and the thing, yet without the possibility of comparing them, or else one has an actual comparison, but not between the desired elements" (GA 1:51). The first case takes judgment or thought as a real existent, an individual subjective act, and the object as an equally real existent, independent of the process of knowing. But then, since comparison itself is simply another subjective act, even where truth as correspondence obtains it is impossible to *know* that it does. The second case assumes that a comparison obtains—for example between the judgment and the thing as given to perception—but since what is given cannot a priori be identified with the real thing, the comparison is not "between the desired elements."

The neo-Scholastic solution advocated by Sentroul invokes the idea of ontological truth, the metaphysical "relation of identity between the 'thing which is' and 'what it is' " (GA 1:52). Here the judgment is supposed to correspond to an "objective counterpart" that "in some sort of way is necessarily the thing itself." For Heidegger this is no solution: "What is this objective counterpart? Wherein consists its objectivity?" (GA 1:52) Heidegger thus poses the classic neo-Kantian questions. Though he too will move toward a theory of ontological truth, he finds precritical neo-Aristotelian realism epistemologically inadequate. Its concept of the "object of knowledge" remains "metaphysically encumbered" (GA 1:50), nor can it do justice to actual science: "The orientation toward the theory of science is lacking even now in Aristotelian-Scholastic philosophy" (GA 1:53). Heidegger will not try to resolve the antinomy by a return to Aristotelian realism.

There remain, then, two possibilities: skepticism, or else a purely "logical" account of correspondence that preserves the real transcendence of the object while showing how it can possibly be known. In his dissertation Heidegger suggests such an account: "Insofar as the significative content [of a judgment] is valid as a determination of the object of judgment, the judgment is true or false. The old concept of truth—*adaequatio rei et intellectus*—can thus be rendered purely logically, if *res* is conceived as object and *intellectus* as determining significative content" (GA 1:176). How does this avoid the antinomy? Clearly, the main question is how one is to understand "object." If it is conceived metaphysically, dogmatism results; if it is conceived as subjective representation, skepticism. If knowledge is possible, the logical object must be the thing itself, though with an essential (a priori) relation to knowing.

The logical character of the object becomes a dominant theme in Heidegger's *Habilitationsschrift*. The theory of categories is a theory of the objecthood of the object (GA 1:216); it thus assumes such importance because, in the context of the truth problem, it must provide the principles for understanding what objects are such that they can serve to measure knowledge. Anticipating later discussion, two aspects of Heidegger's view should be noted early on.

First, part of the solution to the antinomy involves replacing the misleading metaphor of "comparison" with the phenomenological notion of *Erfüllung*, as when, in 1912, Heidegger suggests that truth is a matter of whether or not "the 'intentional thought' [is] fulfilled by the object" (GA 1:35–36). But this says nothing about what the object must be in order to fulfill the judgment. What is the cognitive relation? Heidegger starts with the antipsychologistic thesis that the judgment is "significative content," neither the psychical act nor the grammatical structure but "valid meaning" (GA 1:31). Significative content can be true or false. By 1915 Heidegger argues that what determines it to be one or the other, the object, is "the significative content of what is given, the intuited state of affairs *simpliciter*" (GA 1:273).

The second point thus concerns this significative content of the given. Appeal to givenness distinguishes Heidegger's position from dogmatic metaphysical realism, but it also invites the opposite charge—skepticism—if the given is merely "subjective." The logical object cannot be the mere thing, but neither can it be a subjective, psychically real representation. For Heidegger, it is the *meaning* of the thing as given.

The antinomy of truth demands a transcendental theory of that meaning-full object presupposed in both metaphysical and physical-psychologistic theories of knowledge. The "metaphysics of the truth problem" projected in the *Schluss* should thus be a metaphysics of meaning. But how can a metaphysics of meaning resolve the problem of knowledge (truth) if metaphysics already presupposes the transcendental logical concept of the object? This is an aporia in Heidegger's early work; its parameters are reflected in the three issues Heidegger identifies as problem horizons of the theory of categories.

3. The Object and Object Domains

The first—"the basic requirement of the theory of categories"—is the "delimitation of the various object domains into categorially irreducible regions" (GA 1:400). An object domain is roughly that set over which a scientific theory quantifies, an "interpretation" in the sense of contemporary logic. Heidegger's transcendental logical interest lies above all in determining the categorial relations in and among such domains, in locating objects within "regional ontologies" (Husserl) or "realms of reality" whose "particular structure and constitution" is governed by a specific category (GA 1:210–11).[7]

Categories determine the "logical place" of any object. "Place" makes sense only in terms of a certain "order," and thus "whatever has its logical place fits in a particular way into a particular totality of relations" (GA 1:212). Any phenomenon "within the realm of the thinkable" occupies a place in logical space. A particular event is cognized in chemistry as an instance of an alkali-base reaction. It thus becomes part of the object domain of chemistry by being given—being shown to have—a place in the logical space (or realm of reality) governed by the categories of nature.[8] Categories belong to the rational structure of science and provide the object-constituting principles that make science a "theoretical elaboration of what is objective" (GA 1:208). Given this view, why does Heidegger find it so important to delimit logical space into irreducible categorial regions?

In part, this is a function of his relation to a debate within neo-Kantianism. Focusing upon mathematical natural science, Natorp's Marburg school developed a theory of categories roughly adhering to Kant's own, in which to be an object of a science is to be capable of being brought under categories that have formal validity irrespective of the *kind* of object.[9] But Rickert's Southwest German school, with whom Heidegger sides here, proposed a more pluralistic approach to categories which recognizes that concepts grounding historical knowledge, for instance, are not identical to those holding for physics. Dilthey's call for a critique of historical reason and Husserl's demand for nonnaturalistic categories in psychology also reflect this trend. Heidegger argues that logic, as a theory of science, must recognize that "the Aristotelian categories" (and so also the Kantian) "appear as merely a particular class of a particular region and not *the* categories *simpliciter*" (GA 1:211). Further, categories can neither be "deduced" from thought in abstraction from the sort of object considered, nor established "analogically" by reference to an ultimate metaphysical instance, but only uncovered *phenomenologically.* In reflection upon the ground of the various sciences, the "irreducible" regions of reality show themselves and so are "demonstrated" (GA 1:213).

But beyond this internal debate, there is a more pressing reason to delimit categorial regions. If logic is a science, a "theoretical elaboration of the object," to which realm of reality does the object of logic belong? The problem of truth requires a logical theory of the object, and if that theory is to be a *true* theory, its principles must apply to itself: "Logic itself therefore requires its own categories" (GA 1:288); "there must be a logic of logic" if logic is to clarify how knowledge of objects—including its own—is possible. This issue informs the first problem horizon, as well as Heidegger's early thinking generally.

What is the "object" of logic? Immediate background for this question is the critique of psychologism which purported to show the absurdity of identifying the logical judgment—where we "most easily and immediately encounter the object peculiar to logic" (GA 1:166)—with the psychical act of judging.[10] In his 1914 dissertation, *Die Lehre von Urteil im Psychologismus,* Heidegger had further argued against identifying it with the sentence ("grammatical form"), and for the same reason: Act and word belong to the categorial region of changing, sensibly existing being, while the judgment shows itself to involve something "identical" that "makes itself felt with an insistence and irrevocability" in contrast to which "psychical reality can be termed merely fleeting and insubstantial" (GA 1:170). Heidegger terms this object of logic, the identical factor in the judgment, "meaning" (*Sinn*). But to what realm of reality does meaning belong? What are the categories of meaning (GA 1:171)?

The question of meaning "has, in the entire course of the history of philosophy, never been given its due in a fully conscious and consequential way" (GA 1:24). If Heidegger will later address it within the ontological framework of *Sein und Zeit,* here he does not ask about the meaning of being, but about the "being" of meaning, its place in logical space. Phenomenological grasp of meaning as the object of logic implies recognition of a third sort of reality in addition to sensible (psychophysical) and supersensible (metaphysical) being, for which "Lotze has found the decisive expression in the treasury of our German language," namely, that "in addition to an 'it *is*' there is an 'it *holds* [*gilt*]'"(GA 1:170). Meaning, the object of logic, is neither sensible nor supersensible, but "nonsensible." An ontological difference obtains between meaning and everything that is or occurs. Meaning "holds without having to be" (*LP* 6).[11]

This phrase is Lask's, and though the concept of *Geltung* was initially introduced by Lotze (and was accepted in some form by virtually all antipsychologistic logicians), it is primarily Lask's elaboration of the term that stamps Heidegger's views. Lask replaces the traditional Platonic theory of two worlds—the physical and the metaphysical—by a new two-world theory: The "universe of the thinkable" is divided into what exists and what is valid. The consequences for the theory of categories are two. First, this two-world theory resolves the question of whether logical categories are metaphysical entities (Aristotle) or psychic *Denkformen* (Kant). Categories are neither; they belong to the region of validity.[12] Second—and decisive for Heidegger—this two-world theory establishes what may be called a "transcendental" priority of meaning over any and every object domain. Since categories are not forms of thought but forms of meaning, the realm of logic is unlimited; there can be no domain of "what is" (including metaphysics) that would be "metalogical," beyond the reach of categorial validity (*LP* 128). Lask's logic thus undoes Kant's "critical" resignation and restores the "boundlessness of truth" (*LP* 125), a notion echoed in Heidegger's talk of logic's "absolute hegemony over all object worlds." The relation between meaning and the object thus becomes the central issue of Lask's (and Heidegger's) logical investigations.

The term *Sinn* was initially introduced to designate the logical judgment, but the antinomy of truth already points toward a widening of the concept, one Lask undertakes in his *Logik der Philosophie.* On Lask's view logical categoriality pertains to the objecthood of the object itself (*LP* 29), and thus it is to this latter, the object of transcendental logic, that the term "meaning" ought to apply. Judgment-meaning is a "derivative," secondary, artificial construct. Meaning "in an absolute sense" is "the unity or clasp of form and material" (*LP* 34). Such unity is not a relation between existing parts or pieces, but an *Urverhältnis,* "incomparable to any sort of relation obtaining within the sphere of the sensible" (*LP* 175).

If the object as understood by transcendental logic is thus paradigmatic (*urbildlich*), not representational (*nachbildlich*), meaning, this concept of meaning is nevertheless inscrutable to nonphilosophical ways of thinking. It—and not some metaphysical concept like substance or subject—is the primary "philosophical epithet" for what is (*LP* 123), but it is a specifically transcendental notion, intelligible neither in the terms of straightforward experience nor in those of empirical science. For in these latter the concern is exclusively with what Lask calls the object *material* (*LP* 122); one simply "lives" in the realm of meaning without "knowing" it as such (*LP* 191 f.). But "if we as logicians characterize the existing object as meaning," we have turned our attention to categorial form as such in reflection upon what implicitly makes our first-order cognitive grasp possible (*LP* 123). In transcendental logic we "know" the object as meaning because we grasp the category *as* form—not as itself an existent, but as a moment of validity.

Heidegger explicitly adopts Lask's concept of categorial form. He notes that "the concept of form plays an equally decisive role in Aristotelian and transcendental philosophy," though it is not always "clearly and above all unambiguously conceived" (GA 1:223). In Aristotelian philosophy form has "metaphysical significance as a forming principle of psychical, physical, and metaphysical reality"; it is a metaphysical entity. But if form is an entity, and if it is supposed to be that which constitutes an entity *as* an entity, there is an infinite regress (GA 1:221). Kant, in contrast, "raised the concept of form to its definitive position of power within the region of the logical" but did not decisively break free of psychologism (GA 1:223).[13] For Lask, however, categorial form simply has the character of holding, and since to hold is always to hold *of* something (*Hingelten*), form is intrinsically bound up with particular material. It is thus unthinkable that form could either exist apart (Aristotle) or be imposed on the material by thinking (Kant). Moreover, if there is a plurality of forms (a "table" of categories), the principle of differentiation must lie in the material itself. From this, Lask's principle of the "material determination of form," it follows that the discovery of categories will be, as Heidegger demanded, an empirical phenomenological affair (*LP* 63).

The principle of material determination means that the object cannot, in Hegelian fashion, be sublated into the absolute concept, even at the infinite remove of Natorp's Hegelianizing neo-Kantianism. But if form is not an existing element of the object either, as the branches or DNA of a tree are its elements, how is its "holding" to be conceived? Lask answers that "form is nothing other than a particular objective *Bewandtnis* pertaining to . . . the material" (*LP* 69), a certain ordering inherent in the material itself.[14] It is a "moment of clarity," that by which the way things stand with the material is "lit up" (*LP* 75). Object material cannot be reduced to logical form (Panlogism), but is instead logos-immanent, "held" within form as within its own involvements ("hegemony [*Panarchie*] of the logos") (*LP* 133). For Heidegger, too, form is neither an entity nor an existing element of entities, but a "moment of clarity"; the category "brings nothing new" to the object material, it only brings "more clarity." It is nothing but a "certain *Bewandtnis* with the object," the arrangement, relevance, or involvement of the material itself (GA 1:224, 235). As "a moment of order in the given" the category makes the latter "graspable, cognizable, intelligible"; in other words, it holds (GA 1:224). For Heidegger as for Lask, then, form is not a metaphysical principle but a principle of intelligibility; yet it belongs to the material itself and does not arise first through the constitutive activity of thinking.

This view of logical form, and thus of the object as paradigmatic meaning, undergirds Lask's concept of truth. Cognitions, judgments, can strictly speaking only be called "in accord with truth" or "contrary to truth," since they arise from an "artificial" destructuring of the object in the subjective process of empirical knowledge. That against which their contrariness or accordance is measured is truth in the genuine sense: the object itself as *übergegensätzlich* meaning, beyond the opposition of truth and falsity (*LvU* 413 ff.). As a unity of *valid* form and material, the object can rightfully be called "true": "Particular objects are particular theoretical meaning unities, particular truths." For example, "spatiotemporal objects *are* truths," though they are not "cognitions, judgments, propositions" but "unities of meaning in the paradigmatic sphere" (*LP* 41). Lask's transcendental object concept thus satisfies the condition laid out above for a logical account of correspondence, since it shows how the object can in principle serve as the measure of truth in the judgment. For if "the object itself is nothing other than meaning," it follows that the "distance between meaning and the object" (the skeptical distance between judgment-meaning and the thing itself that gave rise to the antinomy in the problem of truth) "amounts to a distance between meaning and meaning" (*LP* 43; *LvU* 394).

Formally, Lask's theory of meaning solves the antinomy of truth by providing a transcendental logical counterpart to the neo-Scholastic concept of ontological truth, which Heidegger deemed insufficient because it could not establish an intrinsic connection between the metaphysically conceived object (truth) and logic (knowledge). The question, however, as Heidegger discovers when he employs Lask's position as the framework for his interpretation of Scotus's logic, is whether Lask's formal solution goes far enough toward a genuinely *critical* account of how the "distance between [judgment] meaning and [object] meaning" can be negotiated in concrete knowing.

Heidegger formulates Scotus's doctrine of ontological truth—the convertibility of *ens* and *verum*—in a logical idiom: "Every object is a true object" (GA 1:265). Though sharing a motive with neo-Scholasticism's appeal to ontological truth, Heidegger's reconstruction replaces the latter's metaphysical "encumbrances" with logical principles derived from the theory of validity. To say that every object is a true object is not to make a metaphysical claim (a metaphysical judgment always pertains to supersensible object *material;* it is not a judgment about the object *qua* object). Rather, it is to register the categorial nature of the category itself, to identify the *Bewandtnis* reflected in the category of validity as such, namely, "the possibility of a relation to knowledge" (GA 1:267). But such a *Bewandtnis* is not intelligible apart from reference to the knowing subject. If the object, the unity of category and material, is true as a unity of meaning "beyond the opposition" of truth and falsity, and if thus "in mere givenness consciousness may be oriented toward 'the true,' " Heidegger nevertheless emphasizes that this object "contains only virtually" those moments that are brought out explicitly and conjoined into a unity of meaning in judgment: "The true constitutes itself in cognition" (GA 1:268, 285, 271). Through the "position taking acts of the subject," the categorially formed "true" object—"the significative content of the object material that has come to givenness, together with its particular form of reality"—is "taken up into the judgment" (GA 1:270).

Here Heidegger's account closely follows Lask's theory of how the already logos-immanent paradigmatic meaning "becomes immanent" to the *subject* (*LvU* 414).[15] And with that, it seems, the elements for a logical account of correspondence are in place. The theory of categories is grounded in the object by way of the third "form of reality," valid meaning. The idea of material determination of form clarifies the object of knowledge in the various sciences without reductionism, and it establishes the "hegemony of logical meaning" without metaphysical dogmatism or Kantian skepticism. But *does* this transcendental recasting of ontological truth suffice? How is the "taking up" of the object into knowledge—the very *Bewandtnis* of validity upon which the transcendental sense of the object as "true" depends—to be understood? As we saw in chapter 3, the "transcendence" that contrasts with such "becoming immanent" renders a noetic inquiry into the relation of object and judgment impossible for Lask and hence was rejected by Husserl. Here Heidegger too finds it necessary to go beyond Lask in the direction of phenomenology, for reasons suggested in the second bit of unfinished business in the *Schluss.*

4. Logic and Subjectivity

The first horizon of the category problem is to delimit the region of reality of the object domain of meaning. This cannot be approached without the second, namely, its "insertion into the subject and judgment problem" (GA 1:401). A logic of truth demands that a lacuna in Scotus (and thus in contemporary neo-Scholasticism), as well as in Lask (and thus in contemporary neo-Kantianism), be filled. So long as a theory of categories remains, like Lask's, focused wholly on "genuine transcendence" (the object "untouched by all subjectivity"), it has not yet shown how knowledge, as *knowing*, is possible. The antinomy still arises, since "it is simply not possible to compare judgment-meaning with the real object" (GA 1:273). Lask's isomorphism between the elements of object-meaning and judgment-meaning is only a necessary condition for knowledge (*LvU* 394). A sufficient condition would involve showing how that isomorphism can be *given*.

In contrast to Lask, Heidegger addresses this problem phenomenologically. Knowing is not comparison but *Erfüllung*. That is, the object *as given*—"the significative content of the given, the intuited state of affairs *simpliciter*"—is "the measure of judgment-meaning; from it the latter derives its objective validity" (GA 1:273). But this implies that the givenness of Lask's sphere of logos-immanence (the site or "clearing" of the object as paradigmatic meaning) must itself be situated logically, that is, clarified philosophically as to its possibility. The logical clarity of the object is unintelligible without reference to the subject; hence ontological truth must be grounded in a "correctly understood concept of immanence" (GA 1:273), one toward which Scotus already points. The convertibility of *ens* and *verum* implies Lask's thesis of "the convertibility of the '*ens logicum*' with the objects" (GA 1:279). But for Heidegger/Scotus the *ens logicum* (the object from the transcendental logical viewpoint) is an *ens in anima*. This cannot be an existing, psychically real entity, an act or representation, but only "what today one expresses as 'noematic meaning' " (GA 1:277).

The allusion to Husserl is crucial to Heidegger's understanding of the *Bewandtnis* that characterizes knowledge and its object. The noema, the significative content of the given, is nothing but the thing itself grasped in the *secunda intentio* of reflection, where consciousness is not oriented (as in the *prima intentio*) toward the "real object in its immediate reality" but "toward its own content" (GA 1:279), toward the intelligibility *of* the real object, thus also its categorial structure. For Heidegger, though not for Lask, the logical distinction between the object of knowledge and knowledge of the object falls *within* an immanence governed by the (phenomenological) distinction between reflective and unreflective consciousness. The "cardinal distinction among modes of reality is that between consciousness and reality; more precisely, between nonvalid modes of reality which can in turn always only be given in and through a context of meaning having the character of validity" (GA 1:279). If it is true that "only because I live in the realm of validity do I know anything concerning what exists" (GA 1:280), it is also true that only because I can reflect on such "living" can I know anything concerning the realm of validity.

With his phenomenological concept of immanence, Heidegger can place Lask's theory of categorial validity "within the subject and judgment problem." If categories—"elements and resources for interpreting the meaning of the experienceable" (GA 1:400)[16]—are not copied from the real but are ordering principles "with respect to" the material, then what needs explaining is, roughly, their *Erfüllungsbedürftigkeit* (Lask) or semantic quality, their *Hin-gelten* or holding "of" the material. Where Lask takes validity to be an irreducible transcendental category, Heidegger argues that it must be grounded in *intentionality:* "Intentionality is the 'defining category' of the logical realm," that is, the "moment that determines and characterizes order in the realm of logic" (GA 1:283, 281). Without taking this "subjective side" of logic into account, then, an "objective logical" theory of categories "necessarily remains incomplete" (GA 1:404).

The category is the "most general determination of objects," but to speak of an object already implicates the subject (GA 1:403). First, in the "mere givenness" of life consciousness is "oriented toward the 'true' " (GA 1:285); and second, one becomes "conscious of it as true, valid meaning only through judgment" (GA 1:285). The theory of categories thus confronts the traditional problems of givenness and "predication" (GA 1:403). How is the object as valid meaning (the "true") given, such that the subject can "become conscious of meaning" through its "accomplishments" as a "position-taking" judging subject (GA 1:285)? To ask how this predicative activity and its immanent logical construct—judgment-meaning—can hold of transcendent objects ("nonvalid modes of reality") takes one from the theory of categories to the theory of signification, and so must remain untreated here. But in the *Schluss* Heidegger sums up as follows: Only "by beginning with the judgment" can the "problem of the 'immanent' and 'transeunt' (lying 'outside of thinking') validity of the categories . . . be solved," since "without taking 'subjective logic' into account it makes no sense even to speak of immanent and transcendent validity" (GA 1:404).

Heidegger had already touched on issues of subjective logic, though without developing them, when he introduced the term "projection" (*Projektion*) in discussing how an object domain is constituted by the category. For example, only by "projecting them into a homogeneous medium," or "*Lebenselement,*" governed by the category can I count otherwise radically particular object materials as "two *trees*" (GA 1:255). And Husserl helps him unravel the hints of subjective logic in Scotus when the latter appeals to a subjective or "act" analysis in distinguishing between modes of givenness (*essendi, intelligendi, significandi*) (GA 1:321).[17] But in Scotus, too, there is a lacuna: He lacks a "precise concept of the subject" (GA 1:401). Together with the predominately "objective-noematic orientation" of Scholastic psychology (GA 1:205), this means that Scotus never fully coordinates a logic of the object (theory of categories) with the subjective logical problems of givenness and the constitution of objectivity in judgment.[18]

If medieval logic fails finally to coordinate subjective and objective logic, Heidegger is quick to note this same failing in contemporary logical theories. He contrasts two rival modern positions—Külpe's critical realism and neo-Kantian transcendental idealism—to suggest that neither successfully clarifies the connection between knowledge and the object.

The critical realist position distinguishes between empirical (psychical) and rational (categorial) aspects of knowledge and holds that the latter allows us to move from merely "positing" a transcendent object (on the basis of subjective givenness) to predicating something of it truly.[19] This avoids psychological idealism since categories are not principles of association working upon the givens of perception. But Heidegger notes that on Külpe's view the "real-world objects to be determined by knowledge" are not as such "present in perception, not simply given in consciousness, but only first of all to be grasped through the process of knowing, in particular through scientific research," and that this is just the principal claim of Marburg formal idealism: The object of knowledge is not the given, but the valid judgment achieved by an infinitely pursued science, an Idea in the Kantian sense. Failing to recognize the significance of the problem of judgment (built into its own scientistic object concept) for the "grounding of objectivity" (GA 1:403), critical realism is not critical enough.[20]

But Marburg idealism also falls short, though in the opposite direction. First, it sidesteps the problem of givenness by treating space and time as categories. With this logicizing of Kant's transcendental aesthetic, formal idealism fails, on Heidegger's view, to "incorporate the principle of the material determination of form organically into its position" (GA 1:404). If categories receive their sense from the material, they cannot be understood apart from phenomenological recourse to the givenness of different types of material. And second, out of fear of psychologism it relegates the noetic or act sphere to the status of a categorial *construction* in "rational psychology." But if the material is given first of all not to a "theoretical" subject but to consciousness engaged in the pretheoretical, pragmatic life of the world, then such a formal reconstruction of "objectively valid" thinking will bypass the very dimension in which the origin of categories can be sought, namely, the intelligibility or clarity that belongs to "life."

It was Lask who came closest to overcoming the inadequacies of current realism and idealism. He "unquestionably achieved something significant" with his theory of materially determined categorial form (GA 1:405). But the problem of *how* the material determines form—the *site* of the *Urverhältnis*—ultimately opens onto a "new sphere," and Lask was unable to "take sufficient account of the difference between sensible and nonsensible material" (GA 1:405). That is, if the category is itself the "material" for *transcendental logical* knowing, Lask's elision of the question of how the category can be given (as sensibly existent material is given in perception) will not do. Lask's "aletheiological realism" of meaning ultimately remains uncritical, since he deems all such questions psychologistic. Heidegger points toward a solution to this problem by grounding validity in intentionality; and his preoccupation with Husserl's "categorial intuition" shows how seriously he took it in his later work.[21] Here, however, he simply remarks that without first getting clear about the "judging subject" one will "never succeed in bringing out the full sense of what one designates as 'validity' " (GA 1:405).

Regarding the second horizon of the category problem, then, Heidegger suggests the need to bring the motives of critical realism and transcendental idealism "into a higher unity" (GA 1:404). Külpe's realism properly preserves the transcendence of the object of knowledge, but its naturalism does not do justice to the peculiarity of meaning. Marburg idealism properly insists on the logical primacy of valid meaning but does not recognize, as Lask did, that "the most elemental problems of logic only show themselves to those logical investigators who take 'prescientific' knowledge into account" (*LP* 185), where the origin of materially determined form is to be sought. But if Lask grasped the material determination of form, his treatment of the relation between judgment and category remains stuck in a quasi-dogmatic sphere of "genuine transcendence," concerned with "structural problems" in abstraction from how structure is achieved, uncovered, or given in immanence. The issue of material determination does not lead him to the "unavoidable principled investigation into the value and limits" of the form/matter dichotomy itself, and thus his "extremely fruitful" concept of meaning as the object "beyond the opposition" of truth and falsity drives him to "metaphysical problems of which he perhaps never became fully conscious" (GA 1:405, 406).[22] But then, what sort of "higher unity" does Heidegger propose? This is the third horizon of the category problem.

5. The Question of Metaphysics

The previous two problem areas belonged to logic as such, implying a coordination between its objective and subjective aspects. The third issue, however, requires a move beyond logic and thus raises the question of the relation between logical inquiry as a whole and what Heidegger here calls "metaphysics." On the basis of the foregoing, we are now in a position to say something about the problematic character of this move.

If the first problem (categorially delimiting the logical realm of meaning) cannot be solved without appeal to the second (the subject and judgment problem), Heidegger goes partway toward this goal by appeal to Husserl's notion of immanence. Husserl's *Ideen I* has provided "decisive insight into the riches of 'consciousness' and has destroyed the oft-expressed opinion concerning the emptiness of consciousness in general," but finally this is not enough: "One is not at all able to see logic and its problems in their true light unless the context from which they are interpreted becomes a translogical one" (GA 1:405). In particular, the concept of immanence that contextualizes the subjective (phenomeno-) logical problems cannot be understood on the model of any traditional or current idealism or realism. Evidently, the categories that would clarify this immanence are not to be gained by reflecting on the *Bewandtnis* of knowing, on the logical "epistemological subject." It is necessary to go beyond logic, beyond the "theoretical attitude," which "is only *one* among a wealth of formative directions of living spirit." The third horizon of the category problem thus appears as "the task of an ultimate metaphysical-teleological interpretation of consciousness" in terms of the notion of "living spirit" (GA 1:406). Since this is "essentially historical spirit" (GA 1:407), it is necessary that "history and its culture-philosophical, teleological interpretation" become an "element that determines significance within the category problem" (GA 1:408); that is to say, history belongs to the meaning-determining *material* in a theory of categorial form.

These notions raise a number of issues crucial to a full account of Heidegger's early logical work. For instance, though the call for metaphysics reflects his proximity to the neo-Scholastics, Heidegger's own terms are far from the Aristotelian realism of a Geyser or a Sentroul; they derive from Hegel, or rather, from Dilthey's post-Hegelian *Lebensphilosophie.* But here we shall simply indicate the way Heidegger's call for metaphysics pertains to the logic of truth. It is the "truth problem," says Heidegger, that demands a "metaphysical-teleological interpretation of consciousness" in which philosophy leaves the logical "study of structures" and "breaks through to true reality and real truth" (GA 1:406). If the space of meaning (truth) is neither psychical nor metaphysical, Heidegger nevertheless demands that what might be called its "ontological" status be specified in some way. The structural form/material unity may suffice within logic, but "logical meaning must be made into a problem with respect to its ontic significance as well" if one is to ground logic's ability to "guarantee us true reality and objectivity" (GA 1:406).

These elliptical remarks amount to the claim that transcendental logic fails to answer the question, What is meaning?[23] "Metaphysics" is supposed to provide access to "ontic significance," but it is clear that Heidegger's usage in the *Schluss* does not correspond to the sense of metaphysics (a science of supersensible entities) found in the main text. What is ontic significance? When Heidegger suggests that this would be a "transcendental-ontic interpretation of the object concept," it is possible to hear in the term "ontic significance" what he will later develop as ontology, namely, a (transcendental) investigation of the meaning of the being of entities, the successor discipline to the transcendental logical investigation of paradigmatic meaning as the ground of truth.

That a "metaphysics of meaning" arising from transcendental logic calls finally for something other than metaphysics is evident in the problem of trying to coordinate metaphysics and logic in the systematic terms of the main text. Given the absolute hegemony of logic as the theory of theory, its principles hold for metaphysics as a theory of supersensible entities as well. And given that object, form, and material are all logical principles, an ontic interpretation of the object could only be a grasp of the "ontic" significance of the *Urverhältnis* of form and material. For example, what does it mean to say that material "determines" form, or that form "clarifies" material? But if metaphysics is the science of supersensible entities, what can it tell us about that relation that logic cannot, since it already presupposes it? Whence come its "translogical" principles? Heidegger does not say, but two remarks point up the difficulty.[24] First, Heidegger insists that metaphysics and mysticism "belong together" in medieval philosophy—that "philosophy as a rationalistic construction cut off from life is powerless, mysticism as irrationalistic experience is purposeless"; thus, rationalism and irrationalism must be seen in some sort of higher unity (GA 1:410). And second, in connection with the problem of material determination he promises to show the philosophical relevance of Eckehart's mysticism for "the problem of truth" (GA 1:402).[25] It thus appears that the form-determining material does not call for metaphysics as a "science" of supersensible entities. Instead, a breakthrough to the "true reality and real truth" of logical meaning, its "ontic significance," seems to require an incorporation of mysticism. Yet it is also to have the character of a "*transcendental* ontic interpretation"—meaning, I take it, that it remains focused on the critical, phenomenologically understood, "unique relation of being conscious" (GA 1:277). Here the tension in Heidegger's work that I discussed in the introduction to this book is manifest: on the one hand, the mystical desire to "eff the ineffable"; on the other, the critical desire to do so *philosophically*.

Hence, the metaphysical horizon of the category problem calls for a transcendental ontic interpretation of the *subject* as well. The "true reality" of the subject, in whose immanence the problem of truth is structured and answered logically, is historical. The category cannot be deduced from a timeless consciousness in general, since it is a *Bewandtnis* of the material itself. Thus, the discovery of categories—the emergence of the "resources for interpreting the meaning of the experienceable"—is a historical issue that must be brought to bear on an "ontic" interpretation of the nature of categories. If it is not first of all in science but in the pretheoretical intelligibility, the "living in validity," of everyday life that the *Bewandtnisse* of the material originally show themselves, it is artificial to limit the theory of categories to the principles of intelligibility of *science*. Intelligibility, categoriality, is not found only in theoretical life; consequently logic must recognize that the origins of meaning lie in all the meaning-full formative directions of living spirit. Only by grasping the "fundamental metaphysical structure" of this historical living spirit "and its relation to the metaphysical 'origin' " can one understand how the "uniqueness and individuality of *acts* is amalgamated into a living unity with the universality and subsistence in itself of *meaning*" (GA 1:410).[26]

Here then is the ultimate horizon of a metaphysics of meaning, a "metaphysics of the truth problem." The difference between meaning (the logical object) and acts in the psychological sense is presupposed, while Husserl's theory of intentionality shows that this is not incompatible with a nonpsychological, logical investigation of acts. But at the metaphysical or "ontic" level there is still need to understand the being of the relation between individuality and universality, act and meaning, by investigating the fundamental metaphysical structure of historical living spirit. Making logic philosophical again demands a "transcendental ontic" interpretation of the phenomenological sphere of immanence, of consciousness. Epistemological immanence must be referred to the translogical context of historical living spirit as the original space (though not, apparently, the origin) of meaning. Heidegger does not say how one is to do this, nor what the logical status of such interpretation would be.

It would be possible to show that this demand very soon led Heidegger to one of his central innovations, his move from the transcendental *logical* identification of meaning and "object" to the transcendental *ontological* concept of meaning as "world." But this would require consideration of his early Freiburg lectures, as would a complete account of how and why he came to drop the 1916 idea of the "deeper, essentially worldview character of philosophy" (GA 1:410) underlying his mystically tinged metaphysics. These topics we shall reserve for later chapters, recalling here only that the demand for a theory of categories—for philosophical science—continues to exert a hold on the text that investigates the *existentialia* of Dasein. In its own way, and in spite of radical advances, *Sein und Zeit* continues to heed the challenge laid out in the logical truth problem—that it clarify how knowledge is possible in all the different modes of scientific inquiry, *including* its own. This represents neither a metaphysical, nor a mystical, resolution to the problem of knowledge but something much more interesting: a transcendental ontological reinterpretation of it.

PART 2

PHENOMENOLOGY AND THE VERY IDEA OF PHILOSOPHY

6

Heidegger's Phenomenological Decade

For years, readers of *Being and Time* had little external evidence to help them resolve ambiguities in that complex text. Heidegger's publishing silence between his *Habilitation* in 1916 and the appearance of the existential analytic in 1927 meant that the question of his "intentions" could be approached only via the philosopher's own autobiographical utterances, notoriously shifting and self-serving as these often were, combined with recollections of former students whose views on the motivations of *Being and Time,* for all their value, often reflected their authors' own philosophical concerns as much as Heidegger's. All that has changed. With the publication (in a controversial *Gesamtausgabe* "aus letzter Hand") of the lecture courses Heidegger delivered during what Theodore Kisiel rightly calls his "phenomenological decade,"[1] we are now inundated with an enormous, often confusing, mass of Heideggeriana documenting his peregrinations on the way to *Being and Time* and beyond. Today we are coming to see how the "astonishing torso" heralded in Herbert Spiegelberg's well-known mot is tattooed with the name of every philosophical paramour who inflamed Heidegger during those silent years.

At this early stage of assimilating the new material there is need of a reliable and reasonably comprehensive overview of the terrain, a map that details both the way stations visited by the young Heidegger and the major ways linking them. Just this is provided by Theodore Kisiel's subtle, scholarly, and authoritative "book about a book" (*GH* 312), *The Genesis of Heidegger's Being and Time,* whose publication is a major event in Heidegger studies. Incorporating ten years of work in the archives, and informed by Kisiel's extraordinary sensitivity as a translator attuned to every nuance of Heidegger's shifting language, the book delivers a carefully wrought "story" of "Heidegger's development from 1915 to

1927" (*GH* 2). Given the slovenly editorial policies of the *Gesamtausgabe,* scholars concerned with any facet of Heidegger's thought will be grateful to have this report from a researcher who has done more than anyone else over the years to expose the philosophical consequences of bad philology. Kisiel's book offers both a context and a corrective that can facilitate responsible use of the early material.

This does not mean that a philosophical grasp of *Being and Time* necessarily becomes any easier. Indeed, one important result of the genetic treatment is that Heidegger's book ceases to stand in systematic isolation and enters instead into a flux of texts, drafts, notes, and lectures produced by Heidegger in response to issues determined, as often as not, by the contingencies of teaching, university alignments, speaking engagements, publication demands, and other happenstance. Little wonder, then, that the "genealogical approach" tends to operate "against the grain of many an old interpretation" (*GH* 5). It is a leitmotif of *The Genesis of Heidegger's Being and Time,* for example, that the "concept of *Existenz,*" whereby *Being and Time* became "a book inaugurating *Existenzphilosophie,*" was "a remote by-product" of Heidegger's real topic "and, over the years, an increasingly obfuscatory one" (*GH* 419). Archival checking reveals that the existentialist language peppering the published version of the WS 1921–22 course is a later addition, "not to be found at all in student notes of the same course" (*GH* 232). Heidegger does discuss *Existenz* in a 1920 "private communication," the "Critical Comments" on Jaspers's *Psychology of Worldviews,* but this finds no immediate echo in his subsequent courses. The term is officially first used in 1922, but with a narrow meaning akin to the later "authenticity" (*GH* 249), and its occurrence in SS 1923 is far rarer than the published text would indicate. Right up to the final draft of *Being and Time,* then, Heidegger was "wary" (*GH* 275) of the modish language of Kierkegaardian existentialism (though not unsympathetic to the ideas) and preferred to express his position either in life-philosophical or ontological-categorial terms.

If *Existenz* does not name the topic of *Being and Time,* then what does? It is tempting to follow Heidegger's self-interpretation and answer "being," but this should be resisted. Kisiel's story introduces us to the many names Heidegger gave his "topic" throughout the phenomenological decade—"primal something," "facticity," "life," "meaning," "being," "time," among others—and the core of Heidegger's thought is not to be identified with any one of them. But Kisiel's real achievement lies in his extremely nuanced presentation of a more complicated kind of coherence in Heidegger's thinking; for he shows that Heidegger's "topic is a double play of matter and method, What and How, drawn to a point where they are one and the same" (*GH* 21). The constant proves to be

Heidegger's concern with *method;* he is above all the philosopher who questions radically about what philosophy itself is, about its distinctive practice and the nature of its authority. Perhaps the most important lesson to be learned from Kisiel's reconstruction is that the various intellectual and spiritual currents nourishing Heidegger's early *Denkweg*—interest in the history of concepts and the historicality of life, in Protestant theology and religious consciousness, in Aristotelian ethics, physics, and "psychology," and so on—are all filtered through Heidegger's commitment to a "categorial," *wissenschaftlich,* philosophical project.[2] The implications of this fact, as I shall argue in this chapter, are not always fully appreciated by commentators on early Heidegger—Kisiel included.

The question of the possibility of philosophy defines Heidegger's sense of himself as a *phenomenologist,* and this touches on a central thesis of Kisiel's story, namely, that the genesis of *Being and Time* contains the seeds of its demise (*GH* 10). Why? Because the topic that emerges at the threshold of Heidegger's mature thought involves the "almost contradictory" demand that phenomenological philosophy—as scientific yet pretheoretical—grasp and express the ineffable (*GH* 17, 457). Response to this demand reaches its apotheosis in *Being and Time* where, in a way "perhaps more theoretical ('scientific') than Heidegger would eventually wish," Heidegger articulates the ontic grounding of ontology such that "theoretical transparency is to become one with its concrete evidence" (*GH* 430). Kisiel's judgment on this is that "ontic founding . . . is at once ontology's foundering" (*GH* 428). It is certainly true that Heidegger eventually came to abandon the project of fundamental ontology, and the issue of its "ontic founding" may have played a role in his decision.[3] One of the benefits of restoring the fluidity of its context to *Being and Time,* however, is that it becomes possible to retrieve impulses entering into it that may serve to modify such a judgment and to glimpse fruitful paths not taken. The present chapter shall follow one part of Kisiel's story that suggests such a path: the one leading toward a hermeneutic transcendental phenomenology. To begin with, a glance at the book's overall structure will be helpful.

Kisiel's narrative highlights Heidegger's persistent effort to gain access to the pretheoretical origins of meaning while overcoming the theoretical paradigm in philosophy by recourse to a vital, kinetic, historical, ec-static conception of the "I am." It is grounded in "the BCD methodology" (*GH* 459)—biography, chronology, doxography—and in this schema chronology dominates. Kisiel labors tirelessly to set the record straight. One appendix gives us the first accurate list of what Heidegger taught and when, noting discrepancies between the announced titles and what was actually delivered; a second lays out the publication history of

Being and Time, the text that finally appeared in Husserl's *Jahrbuch;* while a third provides a "Genealogical Glossary of Heidegger's Basic Terms" that should forestall many an error arising from use of the unreliable *Gesamtausgabe.* The main text, further, devotes particular attention to contextualizing the "very firsts"—the very first use of "situation" (SS 1919), "facticity" (SS 1920), "Dasein" (SS 1923); the first appearance of the "ontic/ontological" distinction (SS 1924), the nuclear structure of the *Daseinsanalytik* (Aristotle-*Einleitung* of 1922), the identification of ousia with presence (in a lecture of 1923–24), and the like.

Biography, in contrast, is narrowly conceived. Important biographical moments are noted—the conversion, the relation with Jaspers, the alienation from Husserl, the rocky road to Marburg, the wavering in publication strategies—and are linked to shifts in Heidegger's ideas and terminology. In general, though, the account remains focused on the homo academicus, on Heidegger's encounter with books and ideas rather than with people and situations. We learn, for example, that in 1919 Heidegger was (as he writes to Elizabeth Blochmann) "constantly learning in my association with Husserl" (*GH* 76) and that in 1924 Heidegger penned what turned out to be one of the "very first passages written for the famous book of 1927," namely, "the sentence acknowledging Husserl's 'incisive personal guidance' (SZ 38n)" (*GH* 322). But we learn little about the nature of this association or about the details of this guidance.[4] This is because in invoking biography to mediate between chronology and doxography Kisiel does not seek some psychological or political explanation, but the phenomenological "motivation" present *in* the factic "problem situation" (*GH* 4). Biography thus has a "metaphilosophical" significance (*GH* 5), in line with Heidegger's claim that to philosophize is not to repeat "timeless" problems but to question radically out of the *jeweilig* hermeneutic situation, to work "concretely and factically out of [one's] 'I am.' "[5] Still, if the very sense and rigor of one's philosophy must therefore be judged, at least in part, with reference to one's situation, the inclusion of biography at the metaphilosophical level of phenomenological motivations poses the tricky question of what form *systematic* evaluation of Heidegger's thought might take.[6]

Hence, finally, the narrative rests on doxography. Kisiel's book is largely a careful exegesis of the lecture courses, relevant *Vorträge,* and manuscripts of the period, by means of which we gain a detailed sense of what Heidegger said and when. This doxography is organized so as to show the threefold origin of *Being and Time*—as a *topic,* as a *project,* and as a *text.* In establishing origins, Kisiel looks for originality, for Heidegger's "philosophical departure from the tradition" (*GH* 15). By that criterion, the breakthrough—simultaneously phenomenological and theological—to the *topic* dates from the *Kriegsnotsemester* (*KNS*) of 1919. Phenomenologically, Heidegger's logical investigations in the *Habilitation* thesis of 1916 prefigure his breakthrough to the dual topic of the proper "object" of philosophy and the proper "access" to it. Theologically, the topic emerges from his reading of medieval mysticism and devotional literature (Eckehart, Bernard of Clairvaux, Teresa of Avila) in the years 1917–19, during the struggle to break with his Catholic worldview and achieve a more experiential approach to religion glimpsed in Schleiermacher's work, a struggle culminating in his conversion to protestant "free Christianity." This bears fruit in the religion courses of 1919–21 where—in dialogue with Luther, Paul, and Augustine—Heidegger achieves crucial insights into the "kairological" character of lived time and the historical, "concernful" character of "factic life" that enable his appropriative "destruction" of Dilthey. Part 1 of the *Genesis* relates this story in detail.

Part 2 of the *Genesis,* then, shows how the topic first became a project during Heidegger's intensive reading of Aristotle beginning in 1921 and developed in a series of courses and writing projects through 1924. At this time Heidegger first outlined his plans for a systematic phenomenology of life/Dasein, together with a destruction of the history of ontology to counteract life's complacent, *ruinant* tendency toward inauthentic employment of the traditional philosophical concepts available to it for such a phenomenology.

Finally, part 3 of the *Genesis* relates how the text of *Being and Time* originated in the "overlapping publishing projects" (*GH* 311) of a book on Aristotle (only the *Einleitung* was written) and "The Concept of Time" (first a lecture and then a never-published journal article on the Dilthey-Yorck correspondence). Kisiel treats this latter as the first of three "drafts" of *Being and Time,* each reflecting Heidegger's *jeweilig* preoccupation. In this "Dilthey" draft the preoccupation is with history and the ground of historiography; in the second, "ontoeroteric," draft (WS 1925), the focus is on the being "in question" in Dasein's being; while in the final (published) "Kantian," or "kairological," draft, time becomes central.

If *Being and Time* thus has a threefold origin, it is the first of these—the "breakthrough to the topic"—that proves indispensable for a *philosophical* understanding of Heidegger's development. For the genuine phenomenological motivations behind the other two origins will be understood differently, depending upon how the topic is described. In turning to Kisiel's characterization of this topic—his conception of the relation between the object of philosophy and our access to it—it will be important to attend closely to matters that we have seen to be at stake in Heidegger's earliest writings. In particular, I have argued that the "topic" of the early Heidegger's philosophy is the "ontological difference" between meaning and entities. What becomes of this in Kisiel's story? How, for instance, does Kisiel configure Heidegger's insight that the space of meaning—the transcendental field of inquiry presupposed by both physics and metaphysics—cannot be approached wholly structurally (logically) but requires *phenomenological* grounding in terms of its distinctive constitution and modes of givenness?

As Kisiel tells it, by 1915 Heidegger had already sought to probe behind the neo-Kantian topic of theoretical "validity" for the "pretheoretical" sources of meaning. Drawing upon Rickert (the "heterothesis"), Husserl (intentionality), and Lask (material determination of form), Heidegger found in Scotus's logic a sense for the pretheoretical involvement of consciousness and facticity (*GH* 25–38). In contrast to my claim that Heidegger's topic is already fully in play in the early work, Kisiel suggests that it is only in *KNS* 1919, as he pursues the Husserlian question of how philosophy can be a self-grounding "primal science," that Heidegger stumbles on what Kisiel refers to simply as "the KNS experience," the very topic of *Being and Time.* Behind the empty formal-logical category of the "something in general"—which differs from content-laden species concepts because it is not attained through a sequential "generalization" but all at once, through "formalization"—Heidegger discovers its phenomenological motivation in a preworldly, pretheoretical *experience* of the "primal something" expressed in the *es gibt.* The breakthrough may thus be formulated as a move through impersonals[7]—from the neo-Kantian *es gilt,* the "it holds" of logic and propositional truth, to the underlying *es gibt,* the pretheoretical It that is not a "given" but to which I am, in Lask's phrase, "given over" (*Hingabe*) such that, finally, as "the basic moment of life as such," *es weltet* as the flowing, streaming immediacy of the *Er-lebnis* (*GH* 40–56). Kisiel thus construes Heidegger's topic in a way that I would call metaphysical or mystical—focusing not on the *difference* between being/meaning and entities, but on a pretheoretical primal *something.*

This same experience informs the theological breakthrough, where "religious experience" becomes "a phenomenological paradigm" (*GH* 80). Behind the encrustation of Scholastic tradition, Heidegger finds, with the mystics, that "the stream of consciousness is already religious," that the motivations of genuine religion are to be sought in the immediacy of life (*GH* 113). And in the religion courses following his conversion (1919–21), inspired by Kierkegaard and Luther, Heidegger begins his critique of received historiography on Augustine and Paul, deconstructing the worldly-Greek-theoretical concepts that conceal the primal experience of primitive Christianity, which "lives temporality as such" (*GH* 189). Crucially, however, though the topic is *lived* in the paradigmatic religious life, Heidegger does not dissolve philosophy into a religious worldview. Even before he first proclaims the "fundamental atheism of philosophy" in 1922, the ontic ground of his thinking exhibits a "deep philosophical need to make questioning a virtue" (*GH* 113, 218). Hence the importance of the second aspect of his topic, the question of *access*.

This is because the very first question raised by the *KNS* experience is whether the impersonal immediacy of this pretheoretical origin is "mute or meaningful" (*GH* 42). If it is the latter, how can the philosopher bring it to language? Are there "categories" with which to speak of the It that precedes all objectification, hence eluding all the categories of the positive sciences and traditional object-oriented logic? Can there be, in Lask's terms, a "logic of philosophy"? This task Heidegger assigns to *phenomenology*, which in 1919 emerges beyond all neo-Kantianism and worldview as the sole candidate for the primordial science, the sole conceivable method of scientific access to the primal something, the sole hope for a rigorous thinking *about* the pretheoretical. What, then, is phenomenology?

Though Kisiel deals with this question extensively, his strategy of focusing on novelties and departures has the paradoxical consequence that we come away from his account of Heidegger's phenomenological decade having learned little about Heidegger's *positive* debt to the founder of phenomenology, Edmund Husserl. In this Kisiel echoes Heidegger's usual way of presenting his relation to Husserl: generally acknowledging "breakthrough" achievements (intentionality, the a priori, categorial intuition), while insinuating that, in their Husserlian form, they are philosophically useless. Thus, we learn how impulses from Lask, Natorp, Dilthey, Aristotle, Kant, and others led to modifications of Husserl's program, but the details of Heidegger's understanding of that program itself are not extensively explored. Though defensible in a book devoted to identifying what is *echt* Heidegger, such reticence may cost us something in our understanding of his development. For example, if in 1921 Heidegger was able to come to "a transformed understanding of Aristotle," able to break free of his old Scholastic view of Aristotle as the author of a "heavily scientific, naturalistic, and theoretical metaphysics of being"[8] and (as Kisiel notes) to reintroduce the theme of truth after a silence of five years (*GH* 226), is it not plausible that this was facilitated by his "practice of phenomenological seeing, teaching-learning in proximity to Husserl"?[9] If so, is it sufficient to read Heidegger's "confrontation with the ontological tradition" solely for what it reveals about how Heidegger used Aristotle to *get beyond* Husserl? And if, in WS 1925–26, "it was as if scales fell from [Heidegger's] eyes" in his grasp of Kant, it is because, as he says, he read the first *Critique of Pure Reason* "against the background of Husserl's phenomenology" (*GH* 409). One would like to know more about how that background functioned.

By emphasizing originality, then, Kisiel gives us a Heidegger for all seasons except the phenomenological. There is the Lask-Heidegger who develops a logic of philosophy by way of the reflexive-general categories; there is the Dilthey-Heidegger who adopts the term "life" and seeks an ontology of historicality; there is the Saint Paul–Heidegger whose "actualization-historical" situation leads paradigmatically to the kairological core of *Being and Time;* there is the Aristotle-Heidegger whose triad—poeisis, phronesis, techne—breaks through the theoretism of the ontological tradition; and finally there is the Kant-Heidegger whose "horizontal schema" of temporality is the central innovation of *Being and Time* as published. But there is no Husserl-Heidegger; or rather, Husserl is ubiquitous but as a backdrop or foil.

Does this matter? It does, if we wish to be clear about how Heidegger understood the methodological problems facing philosophy, how he approached the question of "scientific" access to "the KNS experience," and further, if we are perhaps to seize upon undeveloped possibilities within the patchwork of early Heidegger's thinking. To support this point, let us look at what Kisiel presents as the pivotal moment, in 1919, of Heidegger's appropriation of phenomenology.

How can phenomenology get at the topic of philosophy, the immediacy of flowing factic life, the birth of meaning in the pretheoretical ground of everyday and scientific understanding? What does it mean to "get at" such a topic? In the terms of Heidegger's earlier work the question amounts to this: If philosophy seeks a *categorial* elucidation of what gives itself in primal experience, it is seeking to make explicit the *Bewandtnis,* or mode of involvement, in which that primal "material" already stands *in* such experience. At the same time, it must show how such "making explicit" is itself possible—all the more so since, as it concerns what lies at the deepest, original, "pretheoretical" level, philosophy cannot simply proceed on the basis of presupposed "theoretical" canons of self-justification. For this reason Husserl rejected neo-Kantian theorizing, which constructs the preobjective by means of an objective categorial logic. For him, the only conceivable access to the topic that could claim to be transcendentally self-justifying would be one that sought to *clarify* its contours through a *reflective intuitive description* of the place where it shows itself—for Husserl, the intentional stream of *Erlebnisse.* But while Heidegger follows Husserl's argument against neo-Kantian constructivism, Kisiel claims that he also adopts as his own Paul Natorp's two "simple but ingenious objections against Husserl's phenomenology," thereby signaling its hermeneutic transformation (*GH* 47).

Natorp argued, first, that the phenomenological claim to *intuitive* access to the immediacy of the *Erlebnisse* is belied by the very nature of its *reflective* approach; reflection necessarily dissects and objectifies the reflected-upon, transforming its character by "stilling the stream" of mental life. Philosophical grounding can thus be achieved only through *reconstruction,* not by the phenomenological "principle of all principles" that insists upon intuitively evident apprehension. Second, Natorp rejects the phenomenological claim to capture pretheoretical experience through "immediate description," since all language generalizes and objectifies such experience. There is no language of the things themselves. Thus, philosophical discourse will not seek to conform itself descriptively to the given but will attempt to articulate a transcendental logic for reconstructing the given.

If Heidegger made these objections his own we should expect him to abandon the phenomenological notions of justification through intuitive evidence, the priority of reflection over rational reconstruction, and the commitment to a language arising from submission to the It of "the *KNS* experience." But things are not so simple. Instead he proposes a "form of access which hermeneutics calls understanding . . . a certain familiarity which life already has of itself and which phenomenology needs only to repeat," a "streaming return of experiencing life upon already experienced life" which is "the immanent historicity of life" (*GH* 48). Further, in WS 1921–22 Heidegger will seek "in life and on life itself" (GA 61:88) for a language of "less intrusive pre-cepts or preconcepts which at once reach back into life's motivation and forward into its tendency" (*GH* 48)—"formal-indicating" (*formal-anzeigende*) concepts that neither objectify nor describe, but interpret.

In place of intuition, reflection, and description, then, we have understanding, repetition, and formal indication. Kisiel brilliantly traces the methodological function of these notions right up through *Being and Time.* In particular, he brings considerable light to the hitherto obscure role of formal indication, "the very fulcrum of *Being and Time*" (*GH* 529) and the source of Heidegger's ontological transformation of both hermeneutics and phenomenology. For Kisiel, the "logic of philosophy" consists not of objectifying categories but of formal indicating concepts. Terms such as care, guilt, death, and Dasein itself (to name just a few from the 1927 text) arise from life's own self-interpretation but are "formalized," emptied of their everyday reference (their "what")—a process that goes hand in hand with historical *Destruktion*—while retaining reference to their attitudinal motivation (their "how") in life such that they can "indicate" the immediate life situations out of which they arise and toward which the philosopher, thinking by means of them, comes to be directed

(*GH* 165–70). They thereby open up recollective access to the origins of meaning as lived. "Life" itself is such a formal indication. Formalized, it no longer draws upon the "theoretical" connotations explicit in the life sciences and still at work in *Lebensphilosophie,* but indicates the phenomenological field that precedes these derivative senses. The philosopher follows this indication to recover his own prephilosophical receptive submission (*Hingabe*) to primordial immediacy.

Kisiel argues that formal indication allowed Heidegger to dislodge Husserl's idea of phenomenology as rigorous science by treating categories as means toward "an intensification of life" (*GH* 59). The new reading of Aristotle—where Heidegger supposedly finds a "phronetic" sense of philosophy more appropriate to the variable "situation of factic life" (*GH* 270) to replace the Cartesian legacy infecting Husserl's understanding of phenomenology—presses Heidegger toward the realization, attained fully only in the (presumed) collapse of the project of fundamental ontology, that "philosophy is more a form of life on the edge of expression rather than a science" (*GH* 59). The displacement of Husserl is said to be complete in WS 1925 when Heidegger offers his "first systematic treatment" of *Verstehen* as a formal indication. Emptied of psychologistic dross and formalized free of its ties to method in the human sciences, understanding "follows life in familiar accompaniment without reflective intrusion." It is an "understanding access that life has to itself" and thus "presents the possibility of nonobjectifying foreconceptions which, in a precursory indication, at once retrieve and forerun life's course without intrusion. Replacing objectifying intuition with nonobjectifying understanding thus resolves both [of Natorp's] objections against phenomenology" (*GH* 376).

Perhaps; but will it be said that *Verstehen,* so described, also preserves what Heidegger sought from phenomenology in the first place—not merely one "interpretation" of life, but *philosophical method?* To agree with Kisiel regarding the centrality of formal indication for the early Heidegger is not necessarily to embrace the suggestion that phenomenology is phronesis or else a "form of life on the edge of expression." This is one direction in which Heidegger's thoughts on phenomenology tend, but it is not the only one. Granted, Heidegger deconstructs the Cartesian interpretation of the key phenomenological notions (intuition and reflection) upon which it bases its claims to be "scientific." Exclusive emphasis on the sense in which formal indication might be said to *replace* the Husserlian notions of intuition and reflection, however, obscures the fact that Heidegger's (and Kisiel's) account of it becomes philosophically compelling only by tacit—and not always tacit—appeal to versions of those very notions. And though he tends to highlight how they depart from Husserl's ipsissima verba, Kisiel notes many passages from the early courses in which Heidegger seeks to preserve the force of Husserlian principles even as he rethinks them—where he speaks of "hermeneutic intuition" for example, and "reflexivity" (*GH* 56), or in the frequent invocations of "evidence," whose continuing relevance is well expressed in a passage Kisiel cites: "The phenomenological criterion is nothing but the understanding evidence and evident understanding of experiences" (*GH* 61).[10]

The importance of maintaining even indirect methodological contact with Husserlian notions such as intuition and reflection can be instanced in Heidegger's answer to the objections of another neo-Kantian, Heinrich Rickert. In his 1920 polemic against *Lebensphilosophie,* Rickert had argued that a *philosophy* of life must be a categorial-theoretical reconstruction of life; the attempt to follow the contours of life's immediacy is but a useless "repetition" of that immediacy. The project of *Lebensphilosophie* fails to distinguish between *living* life and thinking *about* it.[11] It is tempting to raise this very objection to any reconstruction of Heidegger's hermeneutic phenomenology that would place exclusive emphasis on its phronetic over its categorial moments. It is one thing to say that a better account of life is found in Aristotle's *Ethics* than in post-Cartesian subjectivistic theories; it is quite another to say that philosophy itself is essentially *phronesis.* That is simply the obverse error of the theoretism it is supposed to replace. It is not an error Heidegger makes, however. Instead, he seeks to defuse Rickert's objection by claiming *both* that philosophy is repetition of life *and* that it is not re-living but *categorial research* in which life's re-collectability (*Wieder-holbarkeit*) "simultaneously brings its evidence to fruition" (GA 61:88).

Can this notion of research as repetition—the difference between living life and thinking about it—do without the phenomenological concepts of reflection and intuition? There is an implicit reflectivity (or "recursivity" if one wants a neutral word) in Kisiel's customary way of glossing the "historical" aspect of Heidegger's concept of life as "the experience of experience, the movement of turning back upon itself by which life becomes familiar with itself and so understands" (*GH* 379). But *this* sort of "turning back upon itself"—historicality—will not suffice to distinguish living from (philosophical) thinking. Philosophy must be a special sort of turning back if it is not to reduce to mere repetition in Rickert's sense. The point can also be made more technically, using the terms adopted by the early Heidegger to clarify the phenomenon of intentionality: Even if the *Gehaltsinn* of life and philosophy is in some sense the "same," their *Bezugsinn* and *Vollzugsinn* must differ.

Roughly, the *Bezugsinn* (relating sense) is the manner in which life "goes about" (*umgeht*) what concerns it. That concern is its *Gehaltsinn* (content sense). Thus, the course of life will involve many different relating senses—loving, perceiving, questioning, willing, and so on—but we may follow the early Heidegger and formalize them all under the notion of care (*Sorgen*) while simultaneously formalizing the corresponding content senses under the notion of significance (*Bedeutsamkeit*) (GA 61:89–90). Thus, the recursivity Kisiel describes belongs to care in general, but the crucial issue is to specify the relating sense meant when philosophy is described as "repetition" (research). In 1921 Heidegger argues that the relating sense of philosophy is "cognitive comportment" toward its specific content sense, which is "beings as being" (GA 61:58). What does "cognitive" mean here? Kisiel hears a *contrast* between this description of the *Bezugsinn* and a later addition to the text where Heidegger calls it "illuminating comportment" (*GH* 235, 238), but there is no contrast if (as I think) Heidegger all along follows Husserl's view that philosophical cognition, phenomenology, is not objective theory but "clarification," a kind of comportment that works by methodologically exploiting the "turning back upon itself" implicit in life's own course. Repetition *is* "reflection."[12]

Similarly, the phenomenological criterion of intuitive evidence reappears as soon as one tries to distinguish the *Vollzugsinn* (actualization sense) of life from that of philosophy. The actualization sense is, again roughly, the manner in which the *Bezugsinn* is enacted, thus governing the modality in which the content is presented. This corresponds to Husserl's distinction between intending something "emptily" and in an intuitively "fulfilled" manner, a distinction Heidegger redescribes as the difference between authentic and inauthentic "having" (*Habe*) of the content sense. Heidegger claims that the actualization sense of life in its living immediacy is for the most part inauthentic, *ruinant* (later "fallen"), such that it does not "have" itself genuinely. The actualization sense of philosophy, in contrast, is a "countermovement," a "struggle . . . against [life's] own factic *Ruinanz*" in which life comes to its "genuinely developable self-givenness" (GA 61:153). Beginning with "inauthentic having" (*GH* 235), then, philosophy's formal-indicating concepts "lead the way" (*methodos*) into the "authentic evidence situation" (GA 61:35) where genuine having of life itself is possible. Explicating the difference in the *Vollzugsinn* of life and philosophy requires appeal to a way of evident *having*, or access, which—like Husserl's functional notion of intuition but unlike Natorp's caricature of it—is sensitive to what Heidegger calls an object's "genuine manner of *coming to be had*" (GA 61:18).[13] Formal-indicating concepts thus do not replace the intuitive givenness of phenomena but are precisely the means for achieving it. One sees, then, how Heidegger's notion of research might answer Rickert. The method of formal indication does "repeat" the self-interpretation of life, but it *differs* from a mere going-along-with lived life because it is an explicitly cognitive-illuminative self-recollection (reflection) and is oriented toward evident (intuitive) self-having.[14]

Kisiel is certainly aware of these issues, and Heidegger's struggle to articulate the special character of philosophy in the phenomenological decade is a central theme of his book. It seems to me, however, that he constructs that theme upon too sharp an opposition between understanding and intuition—as in the previously cited contrast between "objectifying intuition and nonobjectifying understanding" (*GH* 376; cf. 400)—and that this obscures Heidegger's more positive appropriation of Husserl.[15] If Kisiel does not think that Husserl's concepts of intuition and reflection are exhausted by what Natorp makes of them, the *Genesis* provides little evidence of it, for he swerves from a direct account of the two places where Heidegger discusses Husserl in detail, WS 1923–24 and WS 1925.[16] An exercise in phenomenological destruction, WS 1923–24 starts by considering Husserl's phenomenology and moves back to the source of his "theoretical" distortions, Descartes. Because Husserl and Descartes are said to be "essentially" the same regarding their inadequate attention toward "the question of the being of consciousness" (GA 17:254), Kisiel's equation of the two as he ("for reasons of space") omits discussion of this "destruction of Descartes (i.e., Husserl)" is not without some justification (*GH* 280). But it obscures the point that in this lecture Heidegger *also* inserts a chapter on the "fundamental *differences* between Descartes and Husserl" in which a more positive account of Husserlian notions—including evidence, consciousness, and the reduction—can be found. Let us close, then, by listening to what Heidegger says about *Reflexion*.

According to Husserl's "fundamental comprehension of it," writes Heidegger, reflection is not the basis for a "formal-ontological thesis" (Descartes), nor is it concerned with "psychic occurrences" (Natorp's view!). It thematizes "the manners of comportment toward the world of objects." Thus, it is a "fundamental error" to interpret Husserl's phenomenology as "an act-phenomenology or transcendental psychology" unless one understands "act" as Husserl does, namely, as characterizing the "entirely new domain" of "modes of self-relating-towards" together with their "towards-which" (intentionality). "As long as I lack this ground I am in no position, in the direct observation of the entity, in any way to see anything like a character of being, or to pursue anything like ontology." Phenomenological reflection thus leads beyond "the form of mere reflection" and enables "ontological research in the manner of scientific investigation" (GA 17:261–62). Here, I take it, the theme of the reflective difference between an entity (including a "psychic occurrence") and the "character of its being" (that is, meaning) announces itself. To focus on those places where Heidegger emphasizes the positive contribution of Husserl's phenomenology is to suggest that this—no less than the ineffable "primal something" which supposedly underlies this difference—has a claim to being considered the genuine "topic" of Heidegger's phenomenological decade.

Given the scope and ambition of the *Genesis,* such reminders are mere quibbles. Kisiel's magisterial (and perhaps unique) grasp of the whole of Heidegger's early thinking is not to be undermined by the remark that there are things that might have been emphasized differently. Still, just because his story is one of a probing, experimental thinking that finds itself on several "ways" at once, it may be useful to recall that if, at a particular point on that itinerary, Heidegger holds a certain project to be a dead end—if, for example, it comes increasingly to seem that "the very nature of Dasein puts into question . . . any attempt to 'have' it . . . conceptually" (*GH* 406)—this may not be treated as some sort of necessary outcome of "the" genesis of Heidegger's thought. In hinting at a sequel tracing the "demise" of *Being and Time,* Kisiel suggests that there is a deep unity to it. Can it be, he asks, "that the hermeneutic breakthrough of 1919 already contains in ovo everything essential that came to light in the later Heidegger's thought" (*GH* 458)? But because he has shown how Heidegger's development includes impulses never fully exploited, we who reach the "impasse" of 1927—where Heidegger "is subtly downplaying, disguising, or otherwise distorting some of the deepest roots of his thought" (*GH* 422)—now have *two* directions to turn. We may follow the later Heidegger forward into what many consider an unphilosophical "mythology of being," or we may look back and, thinking with Heidegger against Heidegger, reappropriate the potential of some of those fecund impulses from the phenomenological decade's research into the space of meaning.

7

Question, Reflection, and Philosophical Method in Heidegger's Early Freiburg Lectures

Being and Time can be read as a treatise on transcendental method investigating the conditions of possibility for philosophical knowledge. As such, it finds its model in the transcendental-logical tradition, specifically in Kant's *Critique of Pure Reason,* which "is a treatise on the method, not a system of the science itself."[1] "Method" here does not denote a procedure that would apply indifferently to any subject matter but rather the way in which a particular sort of subject matter becomes scientifically accessible in the first place. In this sense, Heidegger's considerations of method in *Being and Time* are not limited to the sections explicitly so identified, but consist in the entire spiraling movement from everyday being-in-the-world to the authentic temporalizing of anticipatory resoluteness. The question of how philosophical inquiry is possible governs the general structure of the book, Heidegger's choice of phenomena to investigate, and the limits within which he pursues the investigation. Dasein's structure is articulated only so far as is necessary for understanding how philosophical knowledge of being is possible, that is, only so far as Dasein (like Kant's a priori synthesis) is to be seen as the transcendental condition for ontological knowledge.[2] Anthropological interpretations of *Being and Time*—for instance, those that bemoan its one-sidedly gloomy picture of "man"—fail to appreciate these limits.

When Heidegger turns to the "entity which each of us is himself" as the starting point for working out the question of being, he insists that the term "Dasein" is "a pure expression of being," not just an idiosyncratic name for "man" (GA 2:10, 17/27, 33). The same is true of those concepts, *existentialia,* that articulate Dasein's structure. The being of human beings does not yield itself to empirical, experimental, or cultural comparativist methods; "ontological foundations" are not hypotheses "subsequently disclosed on the basis of empirical material" (GA 2:67/75). Heidegger sets out to clarify the conditions of possibility for ontological knowledge, and because human beings are entities distinguished by the basic condition for such knowledge (an "understanding of being"), the term "Dasein" is "filled in" exclusively by those determinations necessarily attributable to an entity possessing such an understanding. The structures Heidegger attributes to Dasein may be phenomenologically inadequate in certain ways, and the particular possibilities he seizes upon may be open to criticism, but what is genuinely contestable cannot even become visible if one reads the work anthropologically. Weaknesses in the analysis are such only in light of fundamental ontology's methodological project of accounting for that entity capable of philosophizing—capable of grasping meaning as meaning so as to illuminate the conditions that make any empirical encounter of entities possible.

The claim that *Being and Time* seeks a transcendental clarification of that entity capable of grasping meaning as meaning may seem contentious. Is it not the express aim of that work to clarify an entity's understanding of *being?* It is, but the methodological character of the work calls first for an ontological understanding of understanding, and since meaning—"that wherein the intelligibility [*Verständlichkeit*] of something maintains itself" (GA 2:201/193)—is the horizon for any understanding, it is this aspect of Dasein that must be rendered perspicuous. It is here that fundamental ontology represents a radicalization of Husserl's transcendental phenomenology. Husserl's reflection on transcendental subjectivity sought to lay bare the absolute horizon in which objects are constituted as "unities of meaning."[3] Heidegger, however, denies that transcendental consciousness is an adequate phenomenological ground for an account of meaning since the meaning thanks to which objects are "there" is not itself an object and thus cannot be constituted. Hermeneutic phenomenology remains a transcendental philosophy, but one that attends to this ontological difference between meaning and entities.

I do not intend to explicate and defend these claims fully here. The present chapter aims only to suggest the grounds for such an interpretation of *Being and Time* through the prism of those lecture courses Heidegger held in Freiburg following the First World War. More precisely, I shall not deal with all of Heidegger's Freiburg lectures but with three in particular whose topics exhibit an inner systematic connection:

"Die Idee der Philosophie und das Weltanschauungsproblem," delivered during the *KGN* of 1919; "Phänomenologie und transzendentale Wertphilosophie," delivered during the summer semester of 1919; and "Phänomenologische Interpretationen zu Aristoteles: Einführung in die phänomenologische Forschung," delivered during the winter semester of 1921–22. As we have seen, Heidegger's earlier work had centered on problems of transcendental logic and the theory of categories, guided largely by Husserl's methodological standpoint of phenomenological immanence. Heidegger's postwar lectures begin to question the assumptions of his earlier work, though without abandoning the essential tenets of a phenomenological approach. On the contrary, the lectures set out precisely to show that phenomenology is the method demanded by philosophy as an inquiry concerned with meaning. In them the issues of meaning, being, and phenomenological method emerge together. While touching upon nearly every theme that will later surface in *Being and Time,* these lectures show, more explicitly than the later text does, how "existential" issues gain their systematic sense from the context of Heidegger's argument that phenomenological method alone provides access to the thematic field of philosophical inquiry—the space of meaning.

Though various aspects of Heidegger's appropriation of phenomenology could be illustrated by tracing the issue of philosophical method as developed in these lectures, I will concentrate on the idea of phenomenology as a *reflective* method. It is somewhat surprising that the topic of reflection has received relatively little discussion even among those who have explored other features of Heidegger's early appropriation of phenomenology in some detail.[4] The reason for this seems to be the existence of something like a "received view," most recently and fully articulated by Kisiel.[5] On this reading, the move to a hermeneutic method, via Dilthey, displaces the Cartesian model of reflection as objectifying self-inspection, a model (it is claimed) that characterizes Husserl's view of reflection as an *intentional* structure. With Heidegger's recognition that intentionality is not primary—so this interpretation goes—reflection becomes both unavailing and unnecessary.[6] Against this, I want to show in this chapter that a closer look at the lectures reveals a more complicated picture in which reflection is not abandoned but reinscribed (without being denoted) into an account of philosophy as a distinctive sort of *questioning* comportment. In this way the lectures lead to the threshold of *Being and Time* and the methodological centrality—the ontico-ontological priority—of Dasein as the entity "whose being includes the possibility of questioning" (GA 2:10/27).

1. What Is Philosophy?

Our previous consideration of Heidegger's earliest work has suggested important ways in which the question of being derives from the phenomenological thematization of meaning (*Sinn*). An emblem of this connection reappears in the lecture course on *Wertphilosophie* from SS 1919. Criticizing Rickert's theory that the "valid" meaning (or content) of a judgment is not a kind of being (*Sein*) but a kind of value (*Sollen*), Heidegger remarks dismissively that "validity" is used to describe the "atemporal subsistence" or "being-true" of meaning "when one wants to avoid the expression 'being.' "[7] But even if Rickert is right that valid meaning cannot be counted as a being, as something existing, this does not mean that it is a "value." For since "what it is to be a being [*Seiende*] is indicated by being [*Sein*]," and since Rickert nowhere clarifies the latter, it would first be necessary to investigate the meaning of being itself, moving out from the question of what meaning "is" (GA 56/57:198–99).

This is not simply one issue among others. It is the pivot upon which an understanding of philosophy's own essence turns: "We must renounce the attempt to locate meaning in the sphere of beings [*Seiendes*]. Then in which sphere is it to be located? With this we stand before an ultimate problem of principle that shall decide the basic character of logic (theoretical philosophy) and philosophy in general" (GA 56/57:199). Here the problem of philosophical method becomes pressing. To identify the categorial sphere in which meaning is located, philosophy must secure genuine access to the theme—valid meaning. As the lecture from the previous *KGN* shows, Heidegger understands the mode of access, or method of categorial research, to be phenomenology. That lecture is structured around two ideas: (1) that there is a necessary distinction between positive-scientific and philosophical method, and (2) that this difference stems from the essentially *circular* character of philosophical questioning. After explicating the circle (sec. 1), I will argue that Heidegger's way of dealing with it is essentially a reinterpretation of phenomenological reflection (sec. 2 below), and that such reflection remains salient in Heidegger's move toward a "hermeneutic of facticity" (sec. 3 below).

The lecture begins where Husserl's 1911 article, "Philosophy as Rigorous Science," had broken off, namely, with the claim that weltanschauung "presents a phenomenon altogether foreign to philosophy" since philosophy's innermost claim is to scientific status; it is to be nothing less than "primordial science" (*Urwissenschaft*) (GA 56/57:17).[8] What does it mean to call philosophy scientific? No satisfactory answer can be derived from nonphilosophical sciences; what primordial science is can be determined scientifically only in the manner appropriate to primordial science itself. The circle here, "the Münchhausen problem of the spirit" (GA 56/57:16), distinguishes philosophical from positive-scientific inquiry, since the latter can and must appeal to a ground lying outside itself (GA 56/57:95). Heidegger argues further that

> the circularity of presupposing itself, of grounding itself, contained in the idea of a primordial science . . . is not some forced, cleverly devised difficulty, but already the stamp of an essential characteristic of philosophy and of the essential sort of method it has—which must put us in a position to *sublate* [*aufheben*] this seemingly insuperable circularity in such a way that we gain immediate insight into it as necessary, a matter of essential law. (GA 56/57:16)

Philosophical method will thus necessarily operate within this circle; it cannot be called upon to deny it.

The major philosophical movements of the day, however, sought precisely to deny or avoid such circularity, and one element of Heidegger's solution to the Münchhausen problem becomes apparent as he proceeds to criticize these movements. To provide a noncircular philosophical grounding of fundamental axioms, for example, Windelband and Rickert's "critical-teleological method" proposed to follow a "substantive, material clue," a certain "pregiven material" from which an axiom is said to arise as the telos of a process of normative idealization (GA 56/57:37). Heidegger will also appeal to this pregiven material as a fissure in formal circularity, but he rejects the critical-teleological method since, on that view, the pregiven material takes the form of "an empirical psychical nexus" of experiences (*Erlebnisse*) that already fall within the object domain of scientific psychology and history. A primordial science, however, cannot derive its material from these or any other positive sciences. Only as phenomenology, as pure "description" of what presents itself as it presents itself (GA 56/57:61), can philosophy incorporate the *Erlebnisse* prior to their scientific elaboration. But is phenomenological description any less burdened by presuppositions than are empirical sciences? What, indeed, can be said to be "there" phenomenologically? As Heidegger puts it, "Gibt es das 'es gibt?' " (GA 61:62)[9] He states further: "We stand at the methodological fork in the road, an abyss that is decisive for the life or death of philosophy in general. Either we fall into the nothingness of absolute positivism [*Sachlichkeit*], or else we leap successfully into *another world,* or more precisely, into the world itself for the first time" (GA 56/57:63). Phenomenological description must deliver a world other than the fact world constituted by positive-scientific presuppositions, and in such a way that the scientific character of philosophy becomes perspicuous. In the course of his negotiation of this demand, as I shall now argue, Heidegger works out an amalgamation of phenomenological reflection and interpretation that he denotes "hermeneutic intuition."

Unprejudiced phenomenological description of what there is discovers tables, chairs, and books, not colors, shapes, and tones. Though this initial description of "the environmental" (*das Umweltliche*) shows no reliance upon a specifically reflective stance, Heidegger does not limit himself to such picture-book phenomenology. He goes on to identify an eidetic feature of the environmental—its "moment of significance" (GA 56/57:72)—that can be noted as such only if, while attending to what presents itself, I simultaneously attend to the way it presents itself. As Husserl would say, significance pertains to the mode of givenness of environmental things and becomes perspicuous as such only in reflection upon the experiencing of the experienced. Heidegger does not emphasize this reflection contained in his own description, however, for his interest is in the distinctive way significant things are "there": "Living in an environing world [*Umwelt*], it is everywhere and always significant for me, all is worldly, it worlds [*es weltet*]" (GA 56/57:73). Heidegger's neologism "*es weltet*" is meant to preserve the phenomenological primacy of significance in the face of the scientific—psychological and historical—approach to the *Erlebnisse* in which an interest in what is "really there" predominates, such that "the character of world is extinguished" (GA 56/57:73).[10] This "theoretical" interest is what he warned against as the abyss or nothingness of "absolute *Sachlichkeit.*" In contrast, if phenomenological method is to fulfill its mission of providing access to the genuinely pregiven material, "this privilege of the theoretical must be broken—*not,* however, by proclaiming the primacy of the practical . . . but because the theoretical itself and as such refers back to something pretheoretical" (GA 56/57:59). Thus, the first methodological task is to clarify "the essence and meaning genesis of the theoretical" without falling victim to an unphilosophical pragmatism (GA 56/57:88).

This means that phenomenology cannot approach the environing world as something *given,* for "a given environing world is already conceived theoretically," its lived texture is extinguished, reconceived as something that "stands *before* me." The idea of givenness already involves "a quiet, barely apparent, yet certainly genuine theoretical reflection," an objectifying categorial elaboration of the environing world, a product of the theoretical attitude (GA 56/57:88, 89). From here it is but a short step to the full-blown "de-worlding" (*Ent-weltlichung*) of the environing world that reduces it to a real thing. Primordial science can be concerned neither with the apodictic description of the given, nor with the "altogether valuable" investigations into the "different levels of theoretical founding" pursued by philosophers from Lotze to Natorp and Husserl. Its task is to negotiate this "passage over the boundary from environing world experiencing to the primary objectification" contained already in the idea of givenness (GA 56/57:91).

But even if phenomenological method proposes to concentrate on pretheoretical world experience (significance), does it not presuppose the real (theoretically determined) world just the same? Will that not undermine its claim to be primordial science (GA 56/57:93)? Against this objection Heidegger offers a version of Husserl's claim that phenomenology is presuppositionless, arguing that the notion of presupposition (*Voraus-setzung*), like the notion of givenness, makes sense only in the context of the theoretical attitude. A presupposition is something supposed in advance, posited in advance. While positing requires an attitude that explicitly objectifies, description of environing world experience reveals no such attitude; instead, "according to its essence," it is not a function of "positing" or "supposing" at all (GA 56/57:94). Thus phenomenology, which is nothing but a recovery of this experience, can strictly speaking be said neither to presuppose anything nor to operate without presuppositions. Here Heidegger finds a way to acknowledge the circle in the idea of philosophy while sublating it by undermining the reasons one has for thinking it a difficulty. If philosophical beginnings are presuppositions, something posited as known, a primordial science that proposes to ground the *possibility* of knowledge cannot even begin without begging the question. If the beginning need not be construed as a presupposition, however—if it is such only for the theoretical attitude—then "the circularity is a theoretical and *theoretically created* difficulty" (GA 56/57:95). Philosophy need not remove, but only move within, the circle of its material beginnings.

But with the suspension of one difficulty, another emerges. Heidegger's argument holds only if philosophy is something other than theory. Will it then still be a primordial science? What makes up its scientific character? Heidegger's answer follows Husserl in seeing philosophical science as reflective clarification rather than theoretical explanation. In the *Logical Investigations* Husserl argued that

> theory of knowledge, properly described, is no theory. It is not a science in the pointed sense of an explanatorily unified theoretical whole. . . . The theory of knowledge has nothing to explain in this theoretical sense, it neither constructs theories nor falls under any. Its aim is not to *explain*

> knowledge in the psychological or psycho-physical sense as a *factual* occurrence in objective nature, but to *shed light* on the *Idea* of knowledge in its constitutive elements and laws. (Hua XIX/1:26–27/264–65)

For Husserl, such a clarificatory science is made possible by the "principle of all principles," which Heidegger at a crucial point quotes, approvingly, as "everything originarily . . . offered to us in 'intuition' is to be accepted simply as what it is presented as being" (GA 56/57:109).[11] The key, for Heidegger, lies in the fact that this principle, which no theory could possibly shake, is "not of a theoretical nature" but is rather "the primordial intention of a truthful life in general, the primordial orientation of experiencing and living as such" (GA 56/57:110). Phenomenological method stakes its claim on the philosophical dimension concealed in the very living of a truthful life, and the methodological significance of all Heidegger's subsequent "existentialism" can be glimpsed here:

> The "*rigor*" of the scientificity awakened through phenomenology gains its originary meaning from this basic orientation [of life toward genuine seeing] and cannot be compared with the "rigor" of derivative, nonprimordial sciences. Thus it becomes clear why the problem of method has a more central place in phenomenology than in any other science. (For this reason the whole lecture has actually moved entirely within the scope of the method problem.) (GA 56/57:110)

Phenomenology is thus not brought to experience from the outside but is the very "method" of experience, tracing, in Husserl's terms, the orientation toward fulfillment adumbrated in every intention. The question of the sort of science to be carried out on its basis is inseparable from the question of how life is to be clarified from within.

The idea that phenomenology is in essence *hermeneutic* expresses the distinctively nontheoretical character of philosophical science. Since on this account *mere* life is also essentially interpretive, however, it is necessary to explain how philosophical method differs from nonphilosophical interpretation. Husserl marks this distinction by the term "reflection": "Phenomenological method operates exclusively in acts of reflection" (Hua III:177/174). Rather than follow Husserl explicitly in this regard, however, Heidegger concludes the lecture course by recalling Natorp's objection to phenomenological reflection: that it cannot genuinely grasp the *Erlebnisse* as *lived* since it would seem to be a theoretical, objectifying act that would necessarily "still the stream" of what it reflects upon (GA 56/57:100–1). Because Heidegger clearly takes this objection seriously, it might be thought that he follows Natorp in rejecting the methodological significance of phenomenological reflection.[12] However, the text is not clear on this point. In the final fifteen pages Heidegger proposes to "develop the issue further on the terrain of phenomenology," yet without explicit reference to Natorp's position, whose criticism is said to be too bound up with the "basic position of the Marburg school" to make discussion of it feasible in the present context (GA 56/57:102). Thus, the extent of Heidegger's agreement with the criticism does not become clear here (or in any other lecture course, so far as I can see). The text concludes rather obscurely with a characterization of phenomenology as "hermeneutic intuition," a kind of seeing that is not an objectification of the *Erlebnisse* but rather "the possessing, self-accompanying experience of experience" (GA 56/57:117). Methodological seeing is something that accompanies experience in such a way that it remains experience while recurring simultaneously to the experiencing of this experience. No doubt this is other than the objectifying *secunda intentio* of theoretical reflection criticized by Natorp. Nevertheless, in the following section I argue that the demand that hermeneutic intuition be "self-accompanying" expresses a reappropriation, rather than a rejection, of the genuinely phenomenological concept of reflection.

2. Phenomenology as Formal Indication

Heidegger's lecture course of WS 1921–22 explores the conditions necessary for actualizing the idea of primordial science outlined in 1919. Methodological access to the pretheoretical, and so a philosophical beginning that is other than a presupposition, comes to be understood in terms of the phenomenological concept of *Evidenz.* Existential themes emerge as this radicalized phenomenology pursues an "unavoidable methodological reflection [*Besinnung*]" whose aim is to "achieve access to the original *evidence situation*" of philosophy (GA 61:157, 35).[13] Like Husserl, who had called upon the philosopher to "decide" between scientific and weltanschauung philosophy,[14] Heidegger argues that carrying out philosophy as primordial science demands a "primordial decision [*Urentscheidung*] about the accomplishments [*Vollzüge*] of philosophizing" (GA 61:35). Thus, the existential theme of decision is introduced exclusively as a methodological condition for making phenomenological evidence accessible within the philosophical project.[15]

The 1919 lecture course argued that the pretheoretical world with which philosophy is to begin should not be taken as something given. If this is now to be thought in terms of evidence, then evidence cannot have the structure of a datum, but, in the words of *Being and Time,* of something that needs to be brought "closer" to us (GA 2:37/50). The lecture of 1921–22 calls this the "original evidence situation," and because of its unusual structure the method that is to provide philosophical access to it cannot be one that moves linearly, from one point to another, but circularly, *clarifying* the place one already occupies. Thus, as a "continual movement of rigorous gaining-access" (GA 61:157) to the evidence situation, philosophical method is interpretive in the sense of moving within a part/whole structure.

It is also reflective, however, for the evidence situation is *my own;* it is "not a positing but a historistic-historical Dasein-in-advance" (*Voraus-dasein*), or facticity (GA 61:158–59). The evidence situation can require "decision" precisely because I am implicated in it—I myself am always "in question," as Heidegger says at the end of the lecture. The initial consequence Heidegger draws from this, however, is that a methodological beginning requires that the evidence situation as "factic life," a "cultural-historical situation," be "appropriated understandingly" by philosophy. Crucially, this does not mean that philosophy turns to "the most modern lyric poetry" or advocates "the latest sociological theory." Rather, it seeks to grasp the very concept of situation in a "factically radical" sense, to clarify "the meaning of *its* being" *as* the Dasein-in-advance "in which and through return to which philosophizing is accomplished" (GA 61:161). Philosophy is concerned with "being situated" just so far as that makes up a condition of possibility for philosophizing.

If this methodological sense of Heidegger's turn to facticity is overlooked, his distinction between weltanschauung and primordial science collapses. If facticity, as the Dasein-in-advance of philosophy, is taken to be the empirical historical-cultural determination of the "subject," a factic point of departure can yield only historically and culturally relative world-views. Hence, while Heidegger's appeal to facticity does challenge certain aspects of Husserl's concept of a transcendental ego, the lecture provides no ground for seeing this as a rejection of the transcendental aspirations of phenomenology. It remains an attempt to identify those transcendental or categorial aspects of the (situated) "subject" that make philosophical inquiry possible. For this reason there is a doubling in the thematic of philosophical method: To provide access to the philosophical "object" is simultaneously to clarify the one to whom such access is granted, the philosopher.

This doubling was not fully present in Heidegger's earliest publications. Philosophy was seen as a theory of meaning, a theory of those logical forms or categories that, together with alogical material, constituted the "truth" or "objectivity" of an object. However, as we saw in chapter 5, the origin of such categories was not so much investigated as posited in the promissory "historical-teleological interpretation of consciousness."[16] In 1921–22 Heidegger continues to see philosophy as research into the categories that determine the meaning of entities, but categories are no longer abstract logical forms; they emerge as something like paths in the process of understanding, interpretive accomplishments (*Vollzüge*), so that the primary philosophical task becomes categorial clarification of factic life as the basis for any investigation of categories.[17] Failing to grasp this, the transcendental-logical tradition has "suppressed a radical problematic of logic": If philosophy is essentially "categorial research," then its first task is to clarify its own possibility categorially. Here is it not enough merely to recognize that the subject is always situated; rather, one must uncover the categories that define being in a situation in such a way that the possibility of philosophical knowledge becomes intelligible. The whole point of a *phenomenological* interpretation of factic life is to uncover the situation categories that make philosophical inquiry itself possible (GA 61:21, 26, 27).

Against the objection that any appeal to a "factual situation" would preclude the philosophical claim to "absolute validity" and so imply skepticism or relativism, Heidegger remarks that such formal arguments simply miss "the meaning of the accomplishments of philosophical knowledge . . . and the meaning of its relation to the object" (GA 61:164). The question of validity in philosophical inquiry is not the question "of whether [its] presuppositions are provable as universally valid, whether one can compel the agreement of most or of all," but rather "whether the intended bindingness of the interpretation has become a *living* one, that is, whether the accomplishment of philosophical knowledge in its point of departure, initial conceptualization, and method is so rigorous that it can bring to fruition [*zeitigen*] in itself the vitalization [*Verlebendigung*] of the genuinely binding claim that the object makes upon it" (GA 61:166). In spite of the unfamiliar language, there is little here with which Husserl could not agree. To say that the question of philosophical validity is not a question of whether its presuppositions can be "proved" to be universally valid, or whether one can "compel" the agreement of others, does *not* mean—as the personalist interpretation of Heidegger suggests—that Heidegger is rejecting the very idea of "universal validity" or "agreement" in philosophy. Rather, it expresses a peculiarity of philosophical inquiry upon which Husserl, too, insists. Ultimately, there can be no external court of appeal for determining the truth ("bindingness") of a position in philosophy; there is only the demand that one think for oneself in such a way that the philosophical matter shows itself in the inquiry as evident *already* in factical Dasein-in-advance. As in *Being and Time,* the point is "to enter the circle in the right way" (GA 2:203/195).

Heidegger thus turns to factic life to facilitate a "vital working-out and appropriation of the *basic phenomenological orientation,*" which means "to unlock in oneself, through openness to the object-meaning that springs from the carrying out [*Vollzug*] of philosophical questioning itself and the objectivity intended in it, the character of commensurateness to the object and the object-connectedness that belongs to philosophical investigation" (GA 61:166). Once more, the problem of philosophical science: The "objectivity" of philosophical knowledge is attestable only in raising philosophical questions in such a way that what is asked about, the "object" of philosophy, shows itself *in* the process of accomplishing such questioning and so serves to measure the bindingness of the interpretation. As in 1919, phenomenological method is seen to be a radicalization of a tendency inherent in truthful life itself, in which access to the philosophical "object" is accomplished. But this leads to a further layer of complication.

If the aim is to discover the categories that make philosophy possible, Heidegger argues, the specific character of philosophical inquiry must be brought into view. This—the task of "defining" philosophy—already involves us in a self-referential, and specifically reflective, movement. To define philosophy one must attend not only to *what* it is but to what Heidegger calls its "genuine mode of coming to be possessed" (*Gehabtwerdens*) since philosophy, like all "objects," involves "a particular mode of access, of holding oneself to it or of *losing* it" (GA 61:18). Thus, a definition must not merely "determine the object in its what and how being," but must do so in a way "appropriate to the situation and fore-conception" in which the object is possessed and addressed, one that arises from the "fundamental experience" (*Grunderfahrung*) of it (GA 61:19). A definition of philosophy—a categorial determination of it in the "what and how" of its being—will thus involve reference to a situational mode of genuinely possessing the object, a "fundamental experience" in which philosophizing is itself "there." Now as we saw in the 1919 lecture, philosophizing has an intimate relation to pretheoretical experience; it is in a certain way continuous with life's immediate self-interpretation. The definition of philosophy must therefore make reference to that pretheoretical situation. But philosophy is not pretheoretical comportment or experience tout court; it is "categorial research." So the definition of philosophy must also indicate how the pretheoretical situation is itself "categorially" structured so as to be "the origin of phenomenological research into the categories" (GA 61:19). To the peculiar structure of such definitional discourse, Heidegger gives the name "formal indication" (*formale Anzeige*).[18]

On Heidegger's view, a definition is categorial—*prinzipielle;* a principle is not a given basis for deductions but is *formal-anzeigend.* A definition must "indicate" the way of access appropriate to its object by pointing back to an evidence situation in which that object is originally possessed, to an "accomplishment of understanding" (*Verstehensvollzug*) that becomes explicit in the articulated definition such that "the factically decisive . . . fundamental experience can be taken up concretely into the business of the inquiry" (GA 61:20). Thus, the definition indicates explicitly a gaining-access that is implicitly accomplished in a particular fundamental experience. That the content of the definition "indicates" means that I do not take this content as a static theme. Definition is, rather, dynamic in two directions. It has the methodologically *negative* function of warding off common assumptions about what philosophy must be; it "inhibits" the tendency toward "blind, dogmatic fixation" upon verbal formulas by forcing me to reflect upon my own "accomplishment" of what is experienced (GA 61:32, 142). In this, says Heidegger, it captures the "positive sense of Husserl's 're-duction' " (GA 61:39). Definition also has the *positive* function of providing a directional sense for an act of understanding. Definition indicates a "way"; it adumbrates a method (GA 61:52).[19]

Yet a definition *is* not this way itself, since its indication is only "formal." It indicates a "point of departure" such that to understand it is to be set on a path that "*leads into concreteness.*" Formality here is not the emptiness of logical formality, but rather like Husserl's "empty" intentions that contain directions for their own fulfillment. As Heidegger says, "the understanding that grasps [the content] must follow out the directional sense [*Sinnrichtung*] indicated." The object is "there inauthentically" in a formal-indicating definition, but the "meaning structure of the emptily present content is what at the same time provides direction to the accomplishment," to the task of bringing to fruition (*Zeitigung*) "the original fulfilling of what is indicated" (GA 61:31, 32, 33). The formal definition becomes deformalized when the one who understands it returns explicitly to an implicit accomplishment of evidence, possession in factic life, such that the accomplishment gets "repeated" in a methodologically perspicuous or self-conscious way. In Heidegger's earlier terms, the formal-indicating definition brings to explicitness the *Bewandtnis,* the specific sort of experiential involvement, in which the "object-material" of philosophy itself, meaning, stands in pretheoretical life, the kind of clarity or intelligibility meaning itself possesses in its "logically naked" (in Lask's words)—prereflective—state. Formal indicating categories are thus not forms of objects but indicators of tasks that, in the optimal case, yield the fullness of evidence in the phenomenological sense, the "authentic" possession of the object.

Definition does not provide a starting point in the sense of something unquestioned (the basis for inferences), then, but is the originally *questionable,* that which gives direction to a path of *inquiry.* As Heidegger claims, "The authentic foundation of philosophy is the radically existential grasping and bringing to fruition of questionability" (GA 61:35). Heidegger's reference to Husserl's reduction suggests that definition demands a decision to question the familiar, a kind of "skepticism" as Heidegger calls it. If authentic thinking means accomplishing access to the evidence situation adumbrated in the definition, then the definition situates one before the "primordial decision" to philosophize by accomplishing the indicated questioning. To say that philosophy is a mode of questioning does not go very far toward characterizing it, however. Not all questioning is philosophical, and presumably philosophy does not consist solely in asking questions. Once more, then, Heidegger draws upon the contrast between worldview and science to develop the definition of philosophy. Agreeing with Husserl that the phrase "scientific philosophy" is a "pleonasm" (GA 61:46), Heidegger is nevertheless more circumspect than Husserl about what it means to call philosophy scientific. The claim that philosophy is scientific is itself formal-indicating; it thus indicates the direction of a question or task, namely, to access the evidence that embodies what philosophical cognition is, along with its scientific character (GA 61:45).

In a framework best understood as Heidegger's initial stab at the reinterpretation of intentionality that will come to fruition in the lecture course of SS 1925, Heidegger explores what is indicated in the idea of scientific philosophy by way of a phenomenological analysis of science as a particular mode of cognitive comportment, that is, in light of "the full meaning in which it is what it is. Full meaning = phenomenon" (GA 61:53). Not merely a system of true propositions governed by laws, science is a kind of comportment; it thus involves a noetic component ("betaking *oneself*") and a noematic component ("betaking oneself *toward X*"). This structure is analyzed into four aspects: (1) *Bezugssinn,* the way one is oriented toward the object (Husserl's noetic act character or quality—e.g., judging, wishing, willing, imagining); (2) *Gehaltssinn,* the way the object is "taken" in such orientation (Husserl's noematic act content); (3) *Vollzugssinn,* the character of the act as accomplished (which suggests the noetic aspect of Husserl's distinction between authentic and inauthentic thinking—e.g., the distinction between merely "thinking" an act of categorial combination such as conjunction and actually accomplishing the synthesis indicated therein); and finally (4) *Zeitigungssinn,* the noematic correlate of *Vollzugssinn* as the manner in which the object either does or does not bring evidential fullness to the *Gehaltssinn,* fulfilling the intentional implications of the act and bringing it to maturity or fruition.[20] With these distinctions in place, Heidegger has a frame in which to analyze philosophizing as scientific comportment.

Because philosophizing seeks to determine objects as such, to say "what and how the object is," its *Bezugssinn* involves a concern for truth. Philosophy is thus "cognitive comportment," as opposed to wishing, willing, desiring, imagining, and so on. Yet the *Gehaltssinn,* or "object," of such comportment is unlike that of any other science. Each science confronts its object as "belonging within a more or less precisely delimited context of beings," an "object domain," whose boundaries are established by the *Gehaltssinn* of the particular scientific practice, that is, by the noematic aspect of the object which is materially relevant to a particular science (GA 61:55).[21] What domain pertains to philosophy, then, and through what *Gehaltssinn* is it determined? In fact, philosophical comportment is not oriented toward a circumscribed domain of beings; its *Gehaltssinn* does not carve out a specific domain of entities. As "principled cognitive comportment toward beings," philosophy seeks "what is fundamental for such beings as such." The *Gehaltssinn* of philosophizing is "that upon which beings ultimately depend"—"being"—so that philosophy is "cognitive comportment toward beings as being." Heidegger notes, however, that it is still unclear "what the 'as' implies, the sense in which it is to be understood" (GA 61:58). For how is being to be understood in relation to those beings for which it is "fundamental," though it is not any particular noematic aspect of beings and thus does not categorially define any positive scientific object domain? How, in short, is one to think the ontological difference?

Here the essentially reflective character of philosophy's cognitive comportment must be recognized, for Heidegger is quite explicit that to thematize being is neither to posit a metaphysically supreme or ineffable entity, nor to identify a universal or "highest" region (a kind of "real predicate" of entities), but rather to proceed transcendentally, phenomenologically, "with reference to the way in which such 'being' is comprehensible: the *meaning* of being" (GA 61:58). To say that philosophy is concerned with the meaning of being is to say that its very *Gehaltssinn* (the "towards which" of its comportment) includes reference to being's being "comprehended," thus to Dasein and to the specific sort of *Vollzugssinn* in Dasein's philosophizing comportment whereby the comprehension of beings as being is accomplished. Thus, the full definition of philosophy implicates a moment of reflection, since the being who philosophizes must concern itself with its own being as being:

"Philosophy is principled cognitive comportment toward beings as being (meaning of being) in such a way, indeed, that in the comportment and for it the being (meaning of being) of the having of the comportment is always decisively also at issue" (GA 61:60). If Heidegger now designates philosophy as "ontological phenomenology,"[22] the order of terms is significant: Philosophy is ontology, but ontology must be understood as an adjectival modification of phenomenology. Phenomenology is the "authentic *Vollzugssinn*" of philosophy (GA 61:60).

This means that Heidegger cannot dismiss the reflective character of phenomenological method but instead must recast reflection in a phenomenologically more adequate form, namely, in terms of the structure of formal indication. Even if the idea of reflection as a higher-order objectification of *Erlebnisse* is abandoned as a result of Natorp's criticisms, its methodologically essential feature is retained, since in order to accomplish philosophical questioning on the basis of authentic evidence I must at the same time attend explicitly to my own "act" of questioning. The circularity of philosophy as *philosophizing* is an index of this self-reflexive (and not merely recursive or self-referential) character, since as oriented toward being "with reference to the way in which such 'being' is comprehensible" (as *meaning*), my own being as comprehender must always at the same time be an issue. As self-reflexive, philosophy is unavoidably tangled up with the question of its own authenticity.[23] Its very definition formally indicates the phenomenological task as one of accomplishing "the *Seinssinn* of the having of the comportment" itself (GA 61:61). That is, to achieve its *Zeitigungssinn,* or authentic fulfillment through evidential clarification of the meaning of being, philosophy must attend to the being of that entity in which philosophizing, as self-reflexive questioning, is accomplished. In 1921–22, as in *Being and Time,* Heidegger turns to investigate the categories of factic life, of "Dasein, 'to be' [*Sein*] in and through life" (GA 61:85).

3. Phenomenological Reflection and the Categories of Life

The very possibility of attending in a philosophically distinctive way to the "life" in which philosophy is embedded is threatened from two sides, however, and Heidegger prefaces his account of the categories of factic life by responding to both. On the one hand, there is the danger that phenomenology will collapse into *Lebensphilosophie.* Though he defends the impulses motivating the projects of Dilthey and Bergson, Heidegger nevertheless accuses them of failing to clarify life itself categorially, thus leaving it a "fashionable word" for "philosophers and literati who prefer to enthuse rather than think" (GA 61:80). On the other hand, Rickert had argued that such categorial clarification could only be transcendental-*logical* construction; a phenomenology based on intuiting lived experience could only be a nonscientific "repetition of life." Heidegger agrees that "*Wieder-holung*" does describe phenomenology as the categorial investigation of life, but he cautions that "everything depends on what that means" (GA 61:80).

To make his point, Heidegger must employ the structure of phenomenological reflection, though again it is not named as such. The key lies in Heidegger's idea that a category, as formal indication, is "something that according to its meaning *interprets* a phenomenon in a particular way or direction of meaning, principally, that brings the phenomenon, as *interpretandum*, to understanding" (GA 61:86). The term "life" itself is such a category: *Leben* ("to live") indicates (1) "reach" (*Erstreckung*), a "unity of succession and maturation" (*Zeitigung*) that is characterized (2) by "possibilities" on the basis of (3) "reality" in the sense of "its specific opacity as power, destiny" (GA 61:84). The context wherein these aspects of life show themselves is "world." Life and world "are not two independently existing objects," and they can only be clarified together. Recalling his previous analysis, Heidegger designates living as a certain *Bezugssinn* whose *Gehaltssinn* is world (GA 61:86). As basic categories, intrinsically first for philosophy as primordial science, life and world must indicate directions of meaning (*Sinnrichtungen*) that enable an actualized philosophical understanding of the phenomenon of understanding itself, an "interpretive accomplishment of that interpretation that accomplishes itself in, through, and out of factic life" (GA 61:87). In a by now familiar circle, the categories that philosophy is to bring to light as conditions of the intelligibility (meaning of being) found in factic life must already belong to it insofar as philosophy, too, is an accomplishment of life. Thus, against Rickert, Heidegger argues that categories are "nothing invented, no 'framework' or independent society of logical schemata; they are rather in an originary fashion *in life itself of life;* of life, to 'cultivate' it. They have their own mode of access which, however, is not such as would be foreign to life itself, imposed upon it arbitrarily from without, but is just the eminent way in which *life comes to itself*" (GA 61:88). Philosophy is not a theory about life but life's own homecoming.

Categorial research thus cannot (as the neo-Kantians thought) be an autonomous construction grounded in an act of theoretical will. Rather, "categories come to be understood only so far as factic life is itself *compelled* to interpretation" (GA 61:87). Here, as in *Being and Time,* such compulsion arises from breakdown in the ordinary course of factic life.[24] Categories of life become visible when the taken-for-granted intelligibility in which life moves (Heidegger calls it *Diesigkeit*) collapses and I can "decide" to come to terms with myself explicitly, "categorially." Such categorial interpretation is, according to Heidegger, a specific kind of *repetition* of that movement of understanding locatable in life itself: "In its genuine and ever more rigorous repeatability the evidence [grounding such interpretation] comes to fruition [*zeitigt*]" (GA 61:88). At this point, however, Rickert's objection becomes pertinent: How can such self-interpretation be anything but a nonscientific "repetition" of the interpretation already carried out in life itself? If philosophizing neither adds a new content to life, nor imposes on it a new categorial form, what is the difference between philosophical and nonphilosophical understanding?

Heidegger's tacit reworking of the phenomenological concept of reflection in his notion of "repetition" is crucial for answering Rickert. Initially, he employs the opposition between what is "implicit" (in prephilosophical life) and what, through philosophical repetition, becomes "explicit" (GA 61:89)—an opposition essential to Husserl's theory of philosophical evidence as reflective clarification. For Husserl, philosophical evidence is gained by reflectively making explicit the achievement of meaning constitution taken for granted in the natural attitude. Now Heidegger does not accept the idea that philosophical understanding is accomplished by a *Reflexion* upon an absolute transcendental ego. Nevertheless, the reflective movement of Heidegger's philosophical method becomes apparent when one combines his claim that the "transition from implicitness to explicitness is 'categorial' in the eminent sense (category interpretation!)" (GA 61:93),[25] with the earlier claim that categorial analysis concerns the *meaning* of being. What gets made explicit, then, is not some hidden aspect of an entity, but meaning, which can be thematized only together with reference to the *Vollzug* of comprehending or understanding. Repetition, "making explicit" in this sense, is thus the method whereby the "difference" between meaning and entities can be grasped. The difference between life oriented toward entities *through* meaning and philosophy oriented toward meaning (being) *as* meaning must be seen as the difference between naive and reflective life. Otherwise one does not have a phenomenological philosophy of evidence, but an a priori construction, a "dialectical joke" (GA 61:129), or a "*schwärmerisch*" immediate repetition of life.

If Heidegger does indeed retain the phenomenological concept of reflection, its trace must be evident in his sketch of those categories of factic life that, for him, are more primordial than Husserlian intentionality.

For Heidegger, the "full meaning of intentionality lies in an original dimension" that the "theoretical attitude" (hence the theoretical reflection criticized by Natorp and practiced, according to Heidegger, by Husserl) "denatures" (GA 61:98).[26] To this end Heidegger fleshes out the formal indications contained in the categories of *Leben* and *Welt* by a pair of correlative notions—care and significance—that do not have an intentional structure: "Significance as a categorial character is not the *object* of care, but always some worldly entity is" (GA 61:90, 93). Life, care, is not care for significance but for some significant *thing;* yet an experience, or "having," of significance as significance *is* possible in phenomenological self-experience, that is, in the methodological transition from implicitness to explicitness. If, therefore, ordinary experience is first of all a living toward the world made possible by significance, philosophical clarification as explicit repetition or self-experience must initially clarify "what it 'is' and means to live factically 'in' significance" (GA 61:93).

Since what is to be clarified is living "in" significance—and not the intentional objects made accessible thereby—phenomenological self-experience cannot take the form of a reflective objectifying act directed upon first-order objectifying acts. Heidegger thus carefully distinguishes it from "self-reflection in the usual sense of the word reflection," which would stage a self explicitly into the nexus of care and significance (GA 61:95). Yet if Heidegger rejects reflection "in the usual sense of the word," he can also be seen to recast the methodological role of reflection in an *un*usual, phenomenologically more perspicuous sense, through his account of how specifically philosophical self-experience is accomplished in life itself. Philosophy, phenomenological interpretation of factic life, is possible only because life is characterized by care for self (*Selbst-Sorge*). In sketching the basic categories of life that clarify this possibility, Heidegger uncovers a reflexivity altogether different than Cartesian theoretical self-consciousness. I shall conclude, then, by discussing the methodological significance of one such category, *Ruinanz,* whose counterpart in *Being and Time* is "fallenness."[27]

Heidegger seeks to understand philosophy as a possibility of factic life. Factic life is accomplished as care, which includes "care for self" (GA 61:135). Heidegger's argument that self-relatedness is not equivalent to the Cartesian or Husserlian reflective thematization of one's experiences turns on the previously mentioned character of factic life as reach. Reach is a form of motility (*Bewegtheit*), a movement which is interpreted "kairologically," grounded in primordial time as maturation (*Zeitigung*). Such temporal motility is no neutral flow, however; it has a distinctly lived character: "This . . . motility of factic life (which is as such constituted by its world) we indicate with the term 'plunge' [*Sturz*]; a movement that cultivates itself and yet not itself, but the emptiness in which it moves; its emptiness is its possibility of movement. Thus we have the basic meaning of the motility of factic life, which we fix terminologically as *Ruinanz* (*ruina,* plunge)" (GA 61:131). Life's "cultivating" itself as movement is not *self*-directedness but *ruinant* directedness toward the *world* on the basis of an enabling, though concealed, emptiness. It might seem, then, that philosophy, as life's explicit self re-collection, would be impossible since, seen categorially, the movement of life is *ruinant.* But this would follow only if the categories of life had the fixed quality of logical forms. Instead, the reach of life is also its "possibility"—in other words, the categories are as such *modalized.*[28] Hence, "life is 'still' something other, which other to be sure is, occurs [*vorkommt*], in *Ruinanz* but in the mode of being suppressed" (GA 61:132).

To understand what Heidegger means one needs to recall that categories are principles that interpret (clarify, illuminate) the factic life from which they arise. Factic life has been interpreted as motility, but if motility is *ruinant,* then illumination itself becomes ambiguous. On the one hand, care is "concerned" thematically with beings themselves, not with the meaning of their being. Factic illumination initially attends to entities, while that which enables such attention, significance, remains implicit. On the other hand, factic life is itself a being—hence care, as *Selbst-Sorge,* already involves a potential for self-illumination. In carrying out such interpretation, however, life generally remains caught up in its *ruinant* movement toward worldly entities, thereby concealing its own specific categorial character as temporal motility. It is for just this reason that "formal indicating" is "possible and factically necessary" as the "methodological point of departure for existential categorial interpretation" (GA 61:134), for as we saw above, its methodologically negative function resists the world-oriented plunge of *Ruinanz.* If formal-indicating categories are to be deformalized, interpretively accomplished authentically on the basis of phenomenological evidence, factic life itself must attest (make evident) a concrete alternative to this "natural tendency of interpretation."

Heidegger thus tries to show that *Ruinanz* contains both the basis of its self-forgetful plunge into the world and the possibility of a *countermovement* (self-recollection) as methodological condition of philosophy. That basis lies in the fact that "in the accomplishing of care, life occurs [*vorkommt*], encounters, if generally in a world-oriented way; nevertheless in this way, in this worldliness, it shines through in its ownmost [*Eigentlichen*]" (GA 61:137).[29] The philosophical coming-to-oneself made possible in this shining through of one's ownmost is not a form of consciousness of self as object, yet it is a form of finding, recalling, or recovering oneself explicitly that shares much with the methodological role of reflection in phenomenology. Though Heidegger does not carry his analysis of such self-recovery very far in the lecture course, one already begins to see how analyses of anxiety, guilt, and conscience in *Being and Time* belong to the project of reconceiving the reflective character of phenomenological method.

First, Heidegger introduces what *Being and Time* will call "disposition" (*Befindlichkeit*). Though the lecture leaves this dimension of care "terminologically undefined" (GA 61:138), it is clear what is meant. "Being-me" is "announced" in factic life by way of a certain affective quality which Heidegger terms "distress" (*Quälen*). This announcement "is not to be taken as a cognitive preindication or referring back, but is a way (in the being-me of the distressing) of wanting to lay claim to factic life on the basis of itself" (GA 61:138). As in *Being and Time,* where the fundamental mood of anxiety reveals the possibility of Dasein's transparent return to itself as well as its tendency to turn away from itself toward the world, distress here announces the ambiguously accomplished illumination of being-me in factic life. *Ruinanz* thus proves to be a *possibility,* a *Richtungssinn* in which self-interpretation is often "tempted" to cultivate itself. But as possibility it also points to an alternative, a countermovement initiated by a primordial decision of "wanting to lay claim to factic life on the basis of itself."

Heidegger's account of the "temptation" behind the directional sense of *ruinant* interpretation is specifically tailored to the "explication of the *Vollzugssinn* of philosophy" (GA 61:142, 143). The impulse for the plunge of factic life cannot be blamed on something external: "There is for this motility no passing it off onto something that would be of another object- or being-character than it itself." Rather, "the toward which of the plunge is . . . 'the nothing of factic life itself' " (GA 61:144, 145). The nothing, as *Nichtung,* is the particular "emptiness" of factic life, distinct from all formal, theoretical, and dialectical conceptions: "The nothing of factic life is its own *Nichtvorkommen* in the *ruinant* Dasein of its self, which *Nichtvorkommen* belongs to [life] and is for it as temporalized, vital, and world-oriented (facticity)" (GA 61:148). This *Nichtvorkommen* of its self underlies the possibility of a concern for worldly entities and the interpretation of being in terms of the givenness of objects.[30] The immediacy of worldly entities is a function of this "plunging oneself into the matters" (GA 61:149), but just for that reason immediate givenness cannot be taken as a philosophical beginning, nor can direct self-inspection be an adequate philosophical method. Unless the *Ruinanz* of its interpretation is explicitly recognized, the self that gets inspected will be conceived in terms originating in the objectifying attitude of *ruinant* concern with the world. To conceive philosophical reflection as a *secunda intentio* does not adequately take *Ruinanz* into account; it cannot represent the self's "authentic" having of itself (GA 61:131).

What would such authentic having be, then? Is there a way that "the possibility of access" to the occurring (*vorkommen*) of factic life in its own facticity "can be won from the indicated movements of factic life" itself, and is it possible that "life as authentic" has its own kind of "immediacy" (GA 61:150)? Heidegger's conclusion to the lecture anticipates the point of departure of *Being and Time* and returns to the themes with which he began. For the authentic immediacy of factic life is not to be found in the objectifying attitude but in the attitude of *questioning*. Authentic philosophizing begins in a "readiness for questionability," the "readiness for seizing upon concrete, factically encountered, not invented, possibilities of access to its object" (GA 61:150–51).

In turning to the attitude of questioning, "the philosophical interpretation of facticity gets serious" since it thereby "maintains, in living experience, the actualization of the access to factic life" (GA 61:152). Only the attitude of questioning authentically maintains the ambiguity of illumination. Because factic life is characterized by a tendency toward illumination (self-interpretation), philosophy as explicit clarification is possible; but because this tendency is initially *ruinant,* philosophy must be accomplished by a countermovement whose *Vollzugssinn* (phenomenology) is precisely to put this initial tendency—which is self-forgetful, unreflective—into question (GA 61:153). Such questioning cannot be "an absolute eternal decision" but is the ongoing demand for a "counter-*ruinant* motility"—not a "methodological dictum" but "the continual struggle of philosophy against its own factic *Ruinanz,* a struggle carried out simultaneously with the actualization of philosophy" (GA 61:152, 153). Arising as a possibility when I am compelled to self-interpretation, the primordial decision for authentic philosophy accomplishes an illumination ("in the eminent mode of questionability") in which "factic life comes . . . to its own genuine cultivat*able* self-givenness" (GA 61:153).

Thus on the one hand phenomenological interpretation, as counter-*ruinant* movement or hermeneutic reflection based on a "readiness for the questionable" (GA 61:132), clarifies the ground of theoretical comportment (and its species of reflection) by revealing its origin in the *ruinant* tendency toward illumination. On the other hand, it also lays claim to a philosophical or nontheoretical illumination (access to an "original evidence situation") whose own bindingness can become an issue only "if such factically immediate life becomes questionable within itself" (GA 61:152). The self-givenness achieved in questionability is not immediate in the sense of providing an apodictic ground for knowledge, but is cultivat*able,* progressively *clarifiable,* though always at risk of going astray. Without going into it, Heidegger here touches upon the deep methodological problem of philosophical validity, and it is here that the account of truth in *Being and Time* (for which there is no analogue in the lecture course) will become crucial. Heidegger's lectures bring us to the threshold of *Being and Time* by distinguishing between positive science and philosophical inquiry, necessitating a search for the methodological conditions for the possibility of philosophy, for an authentic access to meaning as meaning. The lectures accomplish this by rethinking the nature of phenomenological reflection in terms of "questioning"—not just any interrogation, but a specifically counter-*ruinant* movement concerned with an authentic possession of its own capacity to think. What this suggests, finally, is that the transformation of Husserl's methodological point of departure achieved in the hermeneutic phenomenology of *Being and Time* is not primarily a "pragmatic" substitution of the practical for the theoretical, but a reinterpretation of reflection as the specifically philosophical species of self-*question.* In the next chapter it should become clearer how *Being and Time*'s "existentialism" is in fact a consequence of thinking the "scientific" character of phenomenological philosophy, begun in the early lectures, through to the end.

8

Philosophy as a Vocation: Heidegger and University Reform in the Early Interwar Years

Avoiding both hagiography and idle moralizing, some recent biographically oriented studies of Heidegger provide a reliable context for approaching his thought.[1] The connection between context and sense, however, remains elusive. That there is some intimate connection between the philosophy and the man is a thesis that Heidegger himself appears to authorize when, in *Being and Time,* he suggests that ontology is nontrivially grounded in the ontic or "existentiell" affairs of the individual philosopher.[2] This thesis does not merely acknowledge the situation of the philosopher in order to bracket it (as Husserl might); it advances the view that one's factic situation remains somehow productively sedimented in the very *sense* of ontological knowledge. But this only makes the task of understanding the connection more difficult. It is easy to establish that Heidegger spoke the language of his time and can be located, more or less, on a grid drawn by ideal-typical historical or sociological analyses. Still, if the question is how particular philosophical positions taken by Heidegger reflect an "ontic ground" in the life, the more philosophically interesting the ideas, the less they will be intelligible in terms of ideal types. In such cases, it is the individual whom we want to understand, and so there is no substitute for a kind of microanalysis whose terminus ad quem is the atypical in the typical.

Thus, global frameworks like the one developed in Fritz Ringer's influential book, *The Decline of the German Mandarins,* where Heidegger appears as just another "conservative revolutionary" professor, may be sufficient for many purposes. If we wish to understand any more intimate connection there may be between Heidegger's philosophy and his "political engagement," however, it is, as Hans Sluga has shown, the nuances of difference that matter.[3] This chapter will not make a direct assault on this question, which has by now generated an enormous literature.[4] Instead, under the aegis of Heidegger's claim that he got caught up in politics "by way of the university,"[5] it will intentionally *complicate* our picture of Heidegger's relation to his historical circumstances during the interwar years by examining the university as a theme in Heidegger's thought, beginning at a critical juncture in German history and in Heidegger's own development, the year 1919. "The university" is, in fact, the first name that Heidegger gives to the ontic ground of ontology; it designates a condition of philosophy's possibility. At the same time, it provides an important topical frame of reference for assessing the development of Heidegger's thinking between the summer of 1919—when he opened his first postwar lecture course with the question of "Science and University Reform" followed by a course on "The Essence of the University and of Academic Study"—and the spring of 1933, when he spoke on the "Self-Assertion of the German University." Focus on the *early* interwar years (1919–23) suggests reasons for thinking that this development is in important respects discontinuous. In spite of all that links the young privatdocent to the rector of 1933, the former grasps the university solely as the site for renewing the vocation of philosophy and specifically rejects the latter's call, however qualified, to reform the university in the service of the state. While this shift in Heidegger's conception of the relation between politics and philosophy postdates *Being and Time* and coincides with the displacement of a Husserlian by a Nietzschean idiom in Heidegger's thought, the present chapter will concern itself almost exclusively with the central elements of the earlier, less well known, part of the story. These elements show forth what is most distinctive about Heidegger's early philosophy. In order to place the young Heidegger's remarks on the university in a focus that will let us see this distinctiveness, it will be useful first to say something about the interest in university reform in general among German intellectuals of the period

1. University Reform and the Question of Modernization

As Fritz Ringer has argued, the surprising and disastrous outcome of World War I forced into the open doubts and anxieties about the German university that had their source in the "modernization" of society and the organization of science taking place since the 1870s.[6] The cultural elite (or "mandarins") within the university were all more or less antimodern in the sense of seeking to defend their privileged position against socialist calls for democratization and against the ever-growing subordination of scientific research to the exigencies of industry, but among them Ringer distinguishes two camps. In one camp were the "accommodationists"—those who sought to reconcile the "technical necessity" of democracy with maintenance of "mandarin cultural values and the whole tradition of the cultural state."[7] In the other camp were the "orthodox," who—playing endless variations on the theme of modern cultural decline and degeneracy—looked back to a supposed golden age of the university and preoccupied themselves with (re)establishing the "unity of knowledge" on the basis of an authentically German worldview.[8] If one asks where Heidegger fits on this grid, it will appear that his thinking between 1919 and 1929 involves aspects of both. In particular, if the orthodox position is most appropriately labeled "antimodern," and if virtually no one within the German university system welcomed modernization with open arms, then Heidegger's early position can perhaps be called "anti-antimodern."[9] The present chapter will clarify this by establishing a certain isomorphism between Heidegger's views on the relation between philosophy and the university in 1919 and those of the "traitor"[10] to the mandarin class, Max Weber, whose controversial "Wissenschaft als Beruf" was delivered in the same year. First, however, Weber's descriptions shall provide us with a sense for the ideal that all parties to the debate saw as deeply threatened.

Reflecting on the situation of the university and its central ideal, the life of *Wissenschaft,* Weber remarks that "inwardly as well as externally, the old university constitution has become fictitious." Once the affair of an "intellectual aristocracy," research has become the preserve of a legion of "mediocrities" through expanding specialization, bureaucratization, and democratization, while teaching has become a popularity contest thanks to the "chance," rather than merit, that governs appointment to a chair. The ideal of a life devoted to *Wissenschaft* has proved to be other than expected. Once pursued as the avenue to "true being," today's youth look upon "the intellectual constructions of science [as] an unreal realm of artificial abstractions"—and they are partially correct in doing so, for no one anymore believes that the "findings" of science can "teach us anything about the *meaning* of the world." It is the "inescapable condition of our historical situation" that the pursuit of (natural or historical) "learning" has become one "career" among others and not an affair of "dispensing sacred values and revelations" or contemplating the "meaning of the universe."[11] A product of the German university in its idealistic heyday, Weber does not look upon this state of affairs as altogether desirable, but he resigns himself to the situation and asks what is left of the "value" of science. His resignation signals the collapse of that specific integration of science and life values envisioned in the idea of the Humboldt University.

At the beginning of the nineteenth century, during what might be called the first *Modernismusstreit,* the German university system was reformed on the basis of the "neo-humanist" ideas of Fichte and other German idealists.[12] Searching in the Napoleonic period for an indigenous alternative to the French model (in which research was consolidated in nonteaching academies, while the universities, dominated by the state-connected faculties of theology, medicine, and law, were little more than higher gymnasia devoted to transmitting the static knowledge thought to be characteristic of these fields), Wilhelm von Humboldt at Berlin proposed an organization of the university with the philosophical faculty (i.e., the humanistic and scientific disciplines) at the center. Arguing that *Wissenschaft* is essentially open-ended research, von Humboldt maintained that the "internal" vocation of the university lies in "linking objective science with subjective cultivation [*Bildung*]" while its external organization involves "the transition from dependent schooling to autonomous study." Emphasis is thus placed on the *unity* of science as research grounded in the cultivation of the person. The university is not to be a technical or special school, nor should the state demand that it pursue only "what immediately and directly concerns it"; rather, the state should assume that if the university fulfills its own autonomous goal, the goals of the state will also be achieved, and indeed "from a much higher point of view."[13] Grounded in the ideal of individual *Bildung,* academic freedom would, in the long run, advance the spiritual aims of the state.

Already by the 1850s the specialization of the sciences, later noted by Weber, was undermining this neohumanistic idealism. By then, the idea of a systematic unity of the sciences—even one grounded in the cultivation of the personality and not, as with Hegel, in the absolute idea—seemed irreconcilable with the antisystematic practices of the technical disciplines.[14] The failure of the revolution of 1848, too, fostered collaboration between the state and a university that ideologically asserted its autonomy vis-à-vis the directives of state utility while being bound to such directives (and the corresponding censorship) through financial necessity. McClelland writes that "by the end of the nineteenth century, the German academic world invoked the principles of Humboldt and Fichte like a litany, but the practice of the governments and even the evolution of the ideology of *Wissenschaft* had combined to make the utilitarian needs of the state, rather than the intellectual needs of the society, paramount."[15] By the last two decades of the nineteenth century, then, both the ideal of *Bildung* (as the existing ground of the unity of knowledge) and the idea of academic freedom had been compromised. If in 1800 the appeal to *Bildung* had been progressive, in the changed circumstances of 1900 it could just as well be reactionary, an attempt to preserve prerogatives on the part of those whose station had been elevated—both materially and in terms of prestige—by the state/university coalition.[16] One sign of this rearguard action within philosophical faculties at the turn of the century is the obsession with the debate over "science and worldview."

The neo-Kantian movement, with its "methodological" conception of philosophy and its goal of a "scientific worldview" constructed from a transcendental theory of categories, represents the last attempt to redeem the notion of the unity of knowledge on the basis of the older neohumanistic idealism. Starting with the plurality of cultural and historical values, for example, Heinrich Rickert held that one could, by reflecting upon their conditions of possibility, arrive at the "suprahistorical in the historical" and so establish an idealistic worldview.[17] But the outcome of the war, and the collapse of the economic base of the university system, made all such forms of idealism ring hollow. It is significant that Heidegger, the student of Rickert, comes of age in the academy just as Max Weber, schooled in the tenets of Southwest German neo-Kantian *Wertphilosophie,* attacks the pretense of Rickert's claim to move from a reflection on values to a rational grounding of them. If Heidegger does not altogether take the same line as Weber, this is due in part to the "ontic" circumstances of the path he traversed to the decisive year 1919.

2. Heidegger's Biographical Situation

A product of a Catholic family of modest means and of Catholic secondary education, Heidegger entered the university (which only financial support from the Church enabled him to attend) only to find himself at odds with the dominant *Bildungsidee* and its conception of *Wissenschaft.*[18] At Freiburg, the neo-Scholastic movement that was Heidegger's milieu represented a distinct form of antimodernism best illustrated, perhaps, by the Münster philosopher Joseph Geyser. Author of epistemological treatises that adopted the framework of neo-Kantian problematics, Geyser's aim was to undermine the modernist identification of epistemology with "first philosophy" and thereby advance the antimodern thesis of the priority of ("realistic") metaphysics.[19] Heidegger began as an antimodern in this sense. His earliest publications (1911), in the Catholic journal *Der Akademiker,* praise the Church's stand against the "influences of modernism"—against the "decadence of individualism" and "the trendy wave of subjective worldviews" that are "adapted to life instead of the reverse." For Heidegger, the authority of objective, logical thinking must be tempered by the fund of "ethical power" that "only the genuine, irrevocable Catholic worldview can provide."[20]

Already by 1912, however, these sentiments are in conflict with what Ott calls a "research program of astounding modernity"—focusing on studies in "mathematical logic" and the "space and time problem oriented toward mathematical physics"—that Heidegger was developing for himself.[21] When he subsequently found it necessary to abandon his ambitions for a Church career, the conflict became more than an intellectual issue: Even after migrating from the theological to the philosophical faculty, his philosophical pursuits would have to have a Thomistic orientation if he were to keep his financial support. Under such circumstances, Heidegger's adoption of the "positivist" Husserl's phenomenological way of posing problems in logic reveals more about the core of his thought than either the neo-Kantian terminology or the neo-Scholastic topics of his early work. Already in 1914, in a letter to his friend, the theologian Engelbert Krebs, Heidegger could mock Pope Pius X's demand that Catholic scholars take an (anti) "modernism oath": The cure for "anyone who took a notion to have an independent thought" is "to remove his brain and fill his head with Italian salad."[22] If such sentiments do not manifest themselves overtly in Heidegger's scientific writing at the time, the reason is obvious enough. Supported by a grant tied to work carried on in "the *spirit* of Thomistic philosophy," Heidegger's *Habilitation* thesis will still conclude with an appeal to the "genuine worldview essence of philosophy" and a demand that philosophy not neglect its genuine "optics, metaphysics" (GA 1:410, 406). But its internal tensions (some of which we noted in chap. 5) already hint at what Ott calls the "break with his ancestral faith."[23]

In 1916 Heidegger became a privatdocent in a university system that, prior to the war, was quite comfortable for full professors but excruciatingly difficult for docents (especially ones perceived, as Husserl put it, to have "confessional ties").[24] Thus, when the chair of Christian philosophy at Freiburg went to Geyser instead of Heidegger, the latter turned to Husserl, newly appointed to Rickert's chair, for intellectual support. The difficult years of war and revolution yielded "epistemological insights" that finally made "the *system* of Catholicism problematic and unacceptable."[25] When Heidegger officially broke with the Church he gave his reasons partly in the language of von Humboldt's vision of the university: He possesses the inner *Beruf* of a philosopher, and his justification before God will come by using his powers to "fulfill that calling through research and teaching for the sake of the eternal *Bestimmung* of the inner man"—not the life of a "mere scientific grind" (*wissenschaftliche Handwerker*), but of a genuine philosopher, whose demand for "inner *truthfulness* to oneself" requires "sacrifices."[26]

With that, the young Heidegger finds himself in the situation to which the old Weber gave expression in the same year of 1919, the situation of questioning what it means to devote oneself, without the "comfort" of an "irrevocable worldview," to the calling of science. And just as Weber appeals to "intellectual integrity" and to being "faithful" to oneself as the virtues of a life of science, so Heidegger appeals to the "inner truthfulness" of the scholar.[27] But while Weber is truly modern in his resignation—specifically, in his view that philosophy has nothing scientific to say about meaning—Heidegger draws a different conclusion from the demand for disenchanted scientific truthfulness. In 1919 Heidegger begins his philosophical itinerary by mounting a protest against two sorts of worldview philosophy—the antimodern "metaphysical" worldview of Catholicism and the equally antimodern "mandarin" worldview of neo-Kantianism—and it is in this sense that his position is anti-antimodern. But Heidegger is not modern either, since the conception of *Wissenschaft* in whose name he carries out his critique, unlike Weber's, is *phenomenological.* Heidegger thus rejects Weber's resignation and holds out hope that philosophy, as phenomenology, can recover "scientific" access to meaning. As Heidegger argues in a lecture course delivered in the summer semester of 1919, the "ultimate problem of principle decisive for the fundamental character of logic (of theoretical philosophy) and of philosophy in general" is the question of meaning itself. "If we cannot allow that meaning [*Sinn*] can be located in the sphere of entities [*Seienden*]," then "to which [sphere] does it belong?" (GA 56/57:199) Heidegger's biography helps us to understand the circumstances thanks to which this question is posed, but it is the university, as the name for the hermeneutic situation *in* which it is posed, that provides the point of departure for answering it.

3. Philosophy beyond Science and Worldview

If the Heidegger of 1933 proposes a new vision of the university for the sake of the state—for "that spiritual mission that impresses onto the fate of the German Volk the stamp of their history"[28]—it is just this sort of engagement that he *rejects* in the *KNS* of 1919 when he opens his lecture with remarks on "Science and University Reform." The "much-discussed university reform"—with its protest gatherings, programs, orders, and organizations—involves "thoughtless [*geisteswidrige*] means in the service of ephemeral ends" (GA 56/57:4). For accommodationist mandarins on the one side, these ends included reconciling the old university with the new democratic demands; for the orthodox on the other, the goal was to paste up the shreds of the *Bildungsidee* by appeal to a synthetic vision or worldview.[29] Heidegger, an outsider to both camps, speaks of "genuine spiritual renewal," thus echoing the orthodox call to resist the merely technical organization of the university, but he rejects the orthodox prescription for "cultural programs" and mocks the "usual attempts to grace the sciences with a 'worldview' by means of the phrase-mongering of a degenerate philosophy." Today, he writes, "we are not yet mature enough for *genuine* reform in the realm of the university," and the task of becoming mature enough "is the affair of an *entire generation*." Speaking the language of Dilthey and Husserl,[30] Heidegger calls for a "rebirth of genuine *scientific* consciousness," a renewal of that "habitus of personal existence," the specific "consciousness nexus" and "typical motivational nexus," characteristic of science as "vital genuine research." His name for the scientific habitus echoes Weber: "the *inner truthfulness* of value-filled, self-constructing life" (GA 56/57:4–5).

In the following semester, when he lectures on "The Essence of the University and of Academic Study," Heidegger reiterates his claim that truthfulness is the exclusive motivation of genuine research. The "nexus of scientific life" is distinguished from all other "life experiences" of the "situational ego" because it requires one to "tear oneself free of the natural attitude," and so from the immediate claims of all other commitments—whether political or personal (i.e., one's worldview). The genesis of such freedom involves an "education to truthfulness" that germinates in the exploratory questioning and noticing of everyday life (*Kenntnisnahme* as "submission to the world") and grows into a "need for absolute truthfulness." This need takes hold when truthfulness becomes "a new *duty*." At this second level (*Erkenntnisnahme*) I am "purely given over to the matters," I am "wholly free from every life context and yet wholly bound to the truth." Scientific consciousness is radically individual: "To other subjects I have only the duty of absolute truthfulness."[31] Here Heidegger, like Weber, takes up the "*Berufsfrage*": Can I "maintain the habitus of absolute truthfulness?" To do so will involve constant "recourse to origins," an "eternal youth" that will keep me at odds with the direct living of life; it will also involve the threat of "fragmentation" in other spheres of life (art, religion, politics); and finally, under critical questioning "what is handed down will lose its character as [authoritative] tradition" (GA 56/57:211–14).

What compensates me for these "labilities"? What is the "value" of a life devoted to science? Weber answered that "philosophy," if it remains true to its sole "internal" value of "intellectual integrity," can at most help the individual to "give an account of the meaning of his own conduct."[32] This description fits Heidegger's 1919 conception as well. Like Weber, Heidegger rejects the idea that the philosopher is a "prophet of values." And like Weber—as becomes clear in his treatment of the worldview question—Heidegger determines the idea of philosophy and its role in the university wholly in terms of the goal of *self*-clarification on the basis of the moral desideratum of self-responsibility. The way to this end leads not through Weberian objectivism, however, but through Husserlian phenomenology. What Heidegger proposes, then, is not reform of the university but reform of *philosophy* through a radicalization of phenomenology as the "primordial science" of factic life.

In his programmatic essay of 1911, "Philosophy as Rigorous Science," Husserl had anticipated the central thesis of Weber's 1919 paper: "For modern consciousness the ideas of culture, or Weltanschauung, and science . . . have been sharply separated, and from now on they remain separated for all eternity" (Hua XXV:51/135).[33] Though "the spiritual need of our time has become unbearable," this very need "has its source in science" and "only science can definitively overcome the need that has its source in science" (Hua XXV:56–57/140–41). Heidegger seeks to work this thesis into his own idea of philosophy, thus suggesting how Weberian self-clarification, as *phenomenology*, can at the same time provide rigorous access to meaning.[34]

On the one hand, Heidegger agrees with Husserl that "worldview represents a phenomenon alien to philosophy" (GA 56/57:17). He thus rejects those positions (such as Geyser's neo-Scholasticism) that hold that philosophy, as "metaphysics," is *essentially* a worldview; and he also rejects those positions (such as Rickert's neo-Kantianism) that hold that critical philosophy can, in the "depths of the personality," *lead* to a worldview (GA 56/57:8–9). Further, he nominally agrees with Husserl that the "idea" of philosophy is the idea of a "primordial science" (GA 56/57:12). But for Heidegger this is precisely the title of a *problem*. Working on this problem over the next several years, Heidegger challenges both the Weberian identification of science with positive or empirical science and the Husserlian alternative, a philosophy of absolute validity.[35]

Already in his lecture course of 1919–20, for example, Heidegger asks whether the choice between scientific philosophy and worldview is justified. What is needed is a "deeper grasp of the idea of scientific philosophy (primordial science)" (GA 58:235). In the following semester he wonders whether Husserl's own conception of a rigorous science of philosophy is really "necessarily and fully motivated from the idea of the basic phenomenological orientation" itself, since it is developed merely from the *contrast* between science and worldview (GA 59:10). Better to deconstruct that contrast by attaining a "more originary" position than that at which the contrast arises (GA 59:12).

Is this to revert to a position that ignores the force of what Husserl and Weber held to be the "eternal" separation of science from worldview? Referring specifically to Weber, Heidegger does remark that "it is particularly difficult to separate scientific objectivity and personal evaluation in philosophy," since philosophy's " '*facts*' and their grasp are of a radically different sort" (GA 58:191). But this just means that "every genuine philosophy is, in its deepest driving force, a struggle over *method*" (GA 58:135). The phenomenologist's response to Weber lies in developing the method appropriate *to* the aim, shared by both, of "clarifying the meaning of one's own condition." On the one hand, unlike the method of "objectifying" science (which, according to Heidegger, guides both Husserl's and Weber's thinking about science), phenomenological method does not aim at amassing "cognitive propositions" step-by-step into a "treasury of knowledge." Heidegger claims that "*this* concept of science is absolutely heterogeneous to the idea of philosophy" (GA 58:236). On the other hand, even if the " 'rigor' of [philosophical] method has nothing to do with the rationalistic exactness of natural science," it is anything but "mystical or mysticism"; it involves "no arbitrary eccentricities or tepid presentiments" (GA 58:137). In 1921–22 Heidegger still joins with Weber and Husserl against "vulgar Lebensphilosophie." The popular idea that philosophy is not rigorous, but can only be "experienced," an idea that reduces philosophy to the utterly private, is mere "enthusiasm" (*Schwärmerei*) passing for "profundity" (GA 61:36).[36]

The key to unpacking these seemingly conflicting tendencies is to see that while Heidegger abandons Husserl's *concept* of scientific philosophy, he retains the fundamental phenomenological criterion of *evidence*, "intuitive demonstration" (GA 58:240). The "rigor" (*Strenge*) of philosophy, its scientific integrity and the aim of its method, lies in its "striving [*Anstrengung*] toward a pure submission to the situationn"; thus access to the matter of philosophy, meaning, involves an evidential experience in which the inquirer is peculiarly implicated (GA 58:137). The grasp of meaning occurs in an act of understanding, and since understanding has "necessary conditions that do not lie in axioms or propositions but in the subject's lived experiencing of vital, concrete situations," the problem of an "introduction" to phenomenological "method," of *access* to the phenomenological field, is irreducibly individual (GA 58:238). Hence, the *norm* of "phenomenological understanding" does not lie in "truth in the sense of correctness" but in "Ursprünglichkeit" (GA 58:244). How does Heidegger understand such "originariness"?[37]

Our analysis of the lecture course of 1921–22 in the preceding chapter made it plain that this term reflects Heidegger's attempt to radicalize the phenomenological idea of evidence. Where Weber denies the possibility of a rigorous thematization of the meaning of existence, Heidegger seeks to renew philosophy by phenomenological research into the "categories of factic life," categories that are conditions of possibility *for* meaning as such (GA 61:85 ff.). In circular fashion, the grasp of such categories itself presupposes a "concrete" *understanding of philosophy* as the "way" in which such a grasp is executed. But since what it means to philosophize cannot be learned by drawing upon models from other sciences, such research entails a kind of self-responsibility at its outset (GA 61:27 ff.). To philosophize is to "bring questionability to fruition in a radical and concrete way" (GA 61:35). This is to open one's eyes, so to speak, to "accomplish [*vollziehen*] access to the originary *evidence situation*." Heidegger's emphasis is on the accomplishment, *Vollzug:* The evidence situation is "the experience in which the object [here, the "what-and-how being of philosophy" itself] genuinely gives itself as that which it is and in the way it is"; it is the point of "originary access" to one's thematic, on which basis alone it is possible to philosophize with intellectual integrity. But "as" such a situation of access "it is the situation of *primordial decision* for the accomplishments of philosophizing (*Existenz*)" (GA 61:35).[38] Hence, the starting point for categorial investigation must take critical stock of the situation in which such an understanding arises[39]—and that means the university.

This much should suffice here to indicate that Heidegger's 1921–22 appeal to originariness is not an idle invocation of "nonrational" sources of wisdom in the face of a supposedly empty or soulless "reason," but rather belong in the context of his 1919 reflections on individual truthfulness and the "nexus of scientific consciousness." He does not abandon these themes for some mystical or dogmatic appeal to being. This is further reflected in the fact that when Heidegger again takes up the question of the university, it is solely for the sake of elaborating this originary "situation of access" to philosophy. One last time, then, let us see how Heidegger positions himself with respect to the debate over university reform.

4. University Reform?

In the name of a certain "historicity" and against the prevailing obsession with the effects of "historical consciousness," Heidegger identifies the university as the "situation" in which rigorous access to the categories of factic life is accomplished, the ontic ground of ontology. The task of coming to philosophize is possible "here and now" only if the "factic life nexus called the university" is taken up phenomenologically (GA 61:190, 64). But this is easily misunderstood. It is not as though the situation "were simply there" (GA 61:187). On the contrary, the current "circumstances" (*Lage*) of the university—with its fruitless disputes between a sentimental *Lebensphilosophie* and the pseudorationality of "the" sciences, its ceaseless opinion mongering, trends, sociologies, theories of culture, and the rest (GA 61:187 f.)—must first of all be *transformed into* a "situation," that is, into the individual's "factical ground" whereupon "one's own *resolve to philosophical cognition*" grows (GA 61:169). It is "tempting" to approach the issue in terms of "objective history" and the "historical consciousness" that assesses "the" university in light of what it has been (GA 61:65). This was Weber's way of establishing what he called "the inescapable condition of our historical situation,"[40] but Heidegger rejects it. To understand the prospects for philosophical research in this way leads to false alternatives—modernism versus antimodernism, "fact" versus "personal evaluation"—hence to resignation. To transform mere circumstances into a situation in which philosophy can take root, one must overcome the prevalent "blindness for the current *geistige Situation*" where one speaks of the effects of "historical consciousness" and, contrasting this with absolute truth, bemoans the corrosive effects of relativism or seeks a philosophy modeled on established sciences (GA 61:38 f.). Many other passages in this 1921–22 lecture course (e.g., GA 61:74 f., 161) express Heidegger's disdain for the superficiality of the then-current obsession with "historical consciousness." This kind of historical consciousness has "fallen as far away as possible" from the frame of mind in which philosophy could be grasped as the genuine *Urwissenschaft* (GA 61:64).

Consequently, Heidegger distinguishes his philosophical interest in the university from the political goals of either camp of reformers: "So long as it remains true to itself," he writes in 1920, "philosophy is not called to save or redeem the age, the world, or to relieve the misery of the masses or to make men happy or to form and advance *Kultur*" (GA 59:170). In 1921–22 he dismisses orthodox mandarins such as Rickert who appeal to scientific *Bildung* to restore the "unity of knowledge" in the personality of the researcher. However much Heidegger emphasizes existential appropriation of the evidence situation (an ontic/ontological connection of life and science), the point is not to attain "some philosophical '*Bildung*' or possession" (GA 61:41). If there is a crisis in the university, if there has been a "rupture in the tradition," this is "not to be healed by providing practitioners of the sciences with a so-called philosophical *Bildung* drawn from the circle of contemporary philosophies"; for indeed "the damage lies deeper." Philosophy is "itself responsible for the rupture," and, to the "extent that it still 'exists,' " it is "no longer capable of transmitting its own heritage" because it either merely "rummages around in its own history" or else "allows itself to be claimed by literati who propagate it in the form of a pseudoreligiosity" (GA 61:46).

There is, then, no good old philosophical culture to preserve, but instead the task of "radically overcoming what belongs to yesterday" (*das Gestrige*)—for without one's own originary access to genuine philosophizing, the source of any authority the tradition might have remains hidden, its claims mere claims (GA 61:65, 75–76).[41] The point of emphasizing the university as the "situation of access to the *decision* to philosophize," Heidegger explains, is to forestall the temptation to speak in general about philosophy, to avoid all half-baked "prophesizing wisdom schools" and their self-designated "cultural missions." To the extent, however, that "the situation named with the term 'university' is allowed to become radically relevant and free" it may foster "the most unconditionally radical possibility of accomplishing philosophy" (GA 61:66–67). Freeing up the situation does not occur in proposals for university reform but through phenomenological *Destruktion* of the commonplaces governing our everyday understanding of the "circumstances." Thus overcoming yesterday's world (*das Gestrige*) remains exclusively a *philosophical* desideratum and a far cry from calls for university reform in the manner of 1933. Heidegger's appeal to the university as situation lies "in principle outside all discussions of the ends and means, necessity or superfluousness, of so-called *university reform.*" Scoffing at the fact that "today one even writes about the *Führerproblem!*" Heidegger insists that his reflection on the university serves a methodological aim and must be pursued without the least hint of "prophethood and leader allure" (GA 61:69–70). It is addressed to those who would conceive philosophy as a vocation.[42]

Thus, rather than address the issues that most concerned the reformers—"whether the university should be further oriented toward [social and technical] needs, or remodeled to take into account the continually sinking level of an intellectual preparation [on the part of students] that is even now only halfway sufficient"—Heidegger offers a series of either/or's that call for decision: Either we carry out our research on the basis of these untested needs and vague opinions, or we attain our "Dasein" in and through the concrete grasp of a radical Idea—quite apart from whether this Idea, culturally speaking, signals "decline [*Untergehen*] or progress," since our work "is not concerned with cultural profit and loss." And if it does signal decline, then either this will bring us to "wrestle genuinely with our own facticity"—that is, to "exist" as "radical existentielle distressed concern" (*Bekümmerung*)—or else we "lose ourselves in the trappings of mythical and theosophical metaphysics and mysticism, in that dreamy state of busying oneself with piety one calls religiosity" (GA 61:70). Heidegger abjures any "premature for and against." If he refuses to abandon the idea of rigorous philosophical inquiry into the grounds of meaning (and so is not modern in the sense which led Weber to resignation), he does so without the then-current nostalgia (and is to that extent anti-antimodern). In the early interwar years, Heidegger keeps his distance from university reform so as to renew "science" by cultivating the genuine "passion" of a "resolve to understand," one all the more certain the more it can "wait and keep silent" (GA 61:71).[43]

As is well known, Heidegger broke this silence decisively and, to some, surprisingly, in 1933. The philosopher who in 1921–22 saw the university solely as the site of a radical reform of philosophy now calls upon philosophy, and the university "reformed" around it, to participate in the renewal of the German state. The philosopher who in 1921–22 mocked the overheated concern with the "leader question" now insists upon the *Führerprinzip* and corresponding restrictions on "so-called academic freedom." The philosopher who in 1921–22 spoke of "decision" as access to originary *evidence,* and whose remarks to students finding their way to philosophy turned on *individual* truthfulness, responsibility, and personal evaluation, now subordinates research to "the Führer" and truthfulness to Will, the individual to the Geist of the German Volk. Does the same philosophical vision speak in both cases? In light of the ambiguity in Heidegger's writings—noted in our introduction—between the mystical philosopher who wants to "eff the ineffable" and the critical-transcendental philosopher who recognizes the absurdity of that ambition, it will never be easy to establish conclusively that a "change," turn, or similar fundamental reorientation of thought has taken place between one phase or path and another. Nevertheless, more localized questions might be capable of being answered with some confidence, and by following the theme of the university one seems to confront the trace of a shift in Heidegger's thinking that is not without significance for judging the relationship between the philosophy of *Sein und Zeit,* at any rate, and Heidegger's political engagement.

The evidence suggests that right up through 1927, for all his distance from (and indeed personal disdain for) Husserl, Heidegger continued to respect the constraints of the project of philosophy conceived in terms of phenomenology as primordial science—as categorial investigation grounded in the truthfulness and responsibility of the inquirer's methodological "struggle" for originary access to evidence. In this he lies closer to the modernism of Max Weber than either to *Lebensphilosophie* or to neo-Kantian scientific worldview. But after 1928 two things change in Heidegger's discussion of philosophy: (1) In connection with his interest in Scheler's work, there arises a *positive* employment of the term "metaphysics" to characterize his own project, and (2) there is an increasing tendency to describe philosophy in *Nietzschean* terms.[44] As Pöggeler notes, the break with Husserl was only part of a more general "break from every merely academic philosophy" that found public expression "at Davos in the discussion with Cassirer" (1929).[45] What this signals may be expressed as a fundamental shift from a scientific or academic to a *political* sense of the "ontic ground" of ontology. Mediated by Nietzsche, this "outsider" conception of philosophy reverses the priorities of Heidegger's earlier work, forging a link between philosophy and directly political ends.[46] To some (e.g., Habermas) this may alert us to the presence of crucial shortcomings in the otherwise defensible project of the earlier work; to others (e.g., the French poststructuralists) it may represent the crisis that leads Heidegger beyond the outdated "humanism" of that work into his genuinely postmetaphysical maturity. Perhaps Heidegger himself was closer to the mark, however, when (as the story goes) he lamented: "Nietzsche hat mich kaputt gemacht."

9

Husserl, Heidegger, and Transcendental Philosophy: Another Look at the *Encyclopædia Britannica* Article

Sometime in 1927 Husserl began work on an article he had been asked to contribute to the *Encyclopædia Britannica*. Eventually, in the fourteenth edition of 1929, "Phenomenology" was published over the initials "E. Hu." This version was Christopher V. Salmon's very free—and much abridged—translation of Husserl's much longer text. Husserl's own final draft of the article is of interest in itself as a rich, concise introduction to phenomenology, but for several decades now scholars have been drawn to "the *Encyclopædia Britannica* article" not so much as a text, but as an episode in the history of phenomenology.[1] For Husserl's initial work on the article seems roughly to have coincided with the publication of Heidegger's *Being and Time* in February 1927. Husserl, who had long considered Heidegger to be his most promising student and true heir of phenomenology, but who had recently been experiencing misgivings about the "unorthodox" direction of Heidegger's work, appears to have taken the occasion of the article as an opportunity to measure the distance between himself and Heidegger and, if necessary, to attempt a reconciliation. Thus, he invited Heidegger to collaborate, and their mutual engagement yielded four drafts: Husserl's original; a second draft with an introduction and numerous marginal comments written by Heidegger; a transitional third draft; and the final version that contained little trace of Heidegger's participation. The final version testifies to the collapse of the collaboration. Though Husserl did subsequently name Heidegger as his successor at Freiburg, he never again considered

Heidegger his "student" and came, finally, to speak of him (together with Scheler) as "my antipodes."

Scholarly attention has focused on the documents of this failed collaboration (especially the original version and Heidegger's revisions of it) as evidence for the gulf that existed between Husserlian and Heideggerian conceptions of phenomenology, concluding from them that Heidegger altogether rejected Husserl's transcendental phenomenology—with its characteristic doctrines of the transcendental-phenomenological reduction and transcendental constitution—in favor of a phenomenological ontology that broke free of Husserl's egological idealism. But without denying the evident differences between Husserl and Heidegger, the texts at hand can be seen to support a very different conclusion, namely, that Heidegger's *Being and Time* "represents" (as Lévinas has claimed) "the fruition and flowering of Husserlian phenomenology" and that, Husserl's disappointment notwithstanding, the real issues concern not so much Heidegger's rejection, as his reinterpretation, of central Husserlian notions.[2] This chapter and the one following shall be devoted to the clarification and defense of that thesis: first, by focusing on the conception of transcendental philosophy Husserl introduces in his article, together with the conception that emerges from Heidegger's criticisms of it (chap. 9); and second, by indicating the extent to which Heidegger's ontology must be read, in spite of its focus on being and existence, as an essay in transcendental phenomenology (chap. 10).

At the outset it will be useful to recall the distinction introduced by J. N. Mohanty between "*prinzipientheoretisch*" and "*evidenztheoretisch*" varieties of transcendental philosophy, a distinction crucial for understanding the sense in which Husserl's phenomenology is "transcendental."[3] The former proceed by way of a kind of *argument* that seeks to justify, on the basis of some principle or principles, particular truth claims or categorial frameworks (*quaestio juris*). The latter, of which Husserl's philosophy is an example, proceed by way of a kind of *reflection* that seeks to clarify, on the basis of an original field of evidence, the meaning structures that make any truth, indeed any intelligibility, possible at all.

This distinction has not always been heeded by those who have undertaken an analysis of the relation between Husserlian and Heideggerian phenomenology. Thus, for example, commentators have interpreted the second, Heidegger-revised, draft of the *Encyclopædia Britannica* article as showing Heidegger's implicit rejection of Husserl's doctrine of constitution and so his rejection of Husserl's transcendental philosophy.[4] But if, like Husserl's conception of phenomenology, Heidegger's conception is *evidenztheoretisch,* then the issue can be seen to be not so much a rejection of the doctrine of constitution as a deepening of it. In other words, the fault line that runs between Husserl and Heidegger should not be seen as "phenomenology: transcendental philosophy or ontology?" (as though Heidegger rejected Husserl's transcendental turn in favor of realism) but rather as "transcendental phenomenology: epistemology or ontology?" It would not be over the interpretation of phenomenology per se that the two disagree, but over the interpretation of "transcendental," that is, over what reflection on the phenomenological field of evidence accomplishes. Support for this can be gleaned from another look at the drafts of the *Encyclopædia Britannica* article itself. What follows does not, however, present a full account of this episode. Its aim is simply to suggest the way in which the specific character of Heideggerian transcendental ontology can be seen to emerge from the common basis of the Husserlian/Heideggerian phenomenology of evidence.[5]

1. The First Draft: Psychology and Transcendental Philosophy

In the first draft Husserl begins with the natural attitude of everyday experience and describes how all "natural experiencing" of things admits of a "phenomenological turn" transforming it into a "process of phenomenological experience" (Hua IX:237). Husserl argues that such phenomenological experience provides the basis for a pure phenomenological psychology by way of a reduction to the "experiencing of the experienced" as such. The initial phenomenological turn from the attitude of natural world experience is thus a *reflective* one. Instead of living straightforwardly in our world experience as *Weltkinder,* we exercise a "universal phenomenological reflection" (Hua IX:239) whereby what is implicit in such experience, its intentional structure, can be made explicit. But if phenomenology is to be distinguished from psychology (the positive science of inner experience), Husserl must distinguish between a psychological phenomenological reflection and transcendental phenomenological reflection. Hence, he introduces the notion of the "phenomenological reduction" as a move beyond psychology (Hua IX:243). This move needs to be examined in more detail.

Reflection on experience in the natural attitude suggests the possibility of a pure science of "subjective experiencing" that would thematize the intentional structure of psychic life. Just as the science of physics abstracts from all those predicates of its objects that are seen to be bound up with the *experiencing* of such objects, so Husserl thinks a pure psychology is possible that abstracts from those predicates of its object, experience as such, that go beyond what belongs to that experiencing itself. But this is just to practice the epoche:

> To grasp the purely psychical in a *cogito* of the type perception requires . . . that the psychologist put out of play every position taking with respect to the true being of the perceived (of the *cogitatum*), that he practice in this respect an epoche and accordingly make no natural judgment of perception, to whose meaning indeed a continual assertion of objective being or nonbeing belongs. (Hua IX:243)

Such an epoche, or "phenomenological reduction" (Hua IX:245), leaves us with a field of phenomena, a field of pure psychic experience that remains what it is in its descriptive features whatever the ontological status of the *cogitata* inscribed within it may prove to be.

What is really involved in such an epoche? In carrying it out, the psychologist "puts out of play every position taking with respect to the true being of the perceived"; she "make[s] no natural judgment of perception." Such descriptions at first only make explicit that we are dealing here with a *reflective* procedure, one in which the theoretical interest does not extend to questions having to do with the elements of the object as a natural object. They express the truism that investigation of my experiencing of an object is not a sufficient evidential basis for ascribing ontic predicates to the ("physical") thing. The reduction in this sense merely confirms what belongs to the essence of reflection.

To the extent that this is what the phenomenological reduction (or epoche) means, then Heidegger, too, accepts the reduction. Though Heidegger does not explicitly invoke the epoche in *Being and Time,* this is only one example of several cases in that work where phenomenological procedures are in play without being acknowledged as such.[6] Properly understood, Heidegger's ontological phenomenology does not "take a stand" regarding the factual presence of any particular object; as ontologist, Heidegger "makes no natural judgments of perception," nor does he compromise the phenomenological field by presupposing positive or physicalistic premises going beyond what shows itself in phenomenological experience. To be sure, he speaks of phenomenology as a way of access to the being of things, but what he means by "being" is no more drawn from the natural attitude as a nonphenomenological presupposition than is Husserl's "transcendental" concept of being. On the contrary, Heidegger takes his point of departure from a feature that Husserl himself frequently emphasizes, namely, that in the reduction to pure experience nothing is lost from the descriptive content of what is experienced in the natural attitude. To use Husserl's example, a reflectively considered perception is still perception-of-this-house; it includes the sense of perceptual "believing in" the house as "actually existing" (*wirklich Daseiendes*). Under the epoche the house is taken in its full descriptive content "as meaning content (perceptual meaning) of the perceptual belief" (Hua IX:243). The being-character of the perceptual object is itself a descriptive feature of the experiencing of the object for Husserl. And, I would argue, for Heidegger also.[7] To describe a "natural view of the world" is not to occupy such a view; to speak of *Vorhandensein* is not to predicate real being of any particular entity.

But the reduction to the pure psychical is still distinct from a transcendental phenomenology. Phenomenological psychology sets itself the task of explicating the evidential levels of constitution of intentional objects by exploring "the several forms of synthesis . . . through which in general consciousness with consciousness comes to be a unity of consciousness" (Hua IX:244). When Husserl goes on to charge the phenomenological psychologist with the task of seeking "the necessary structural system without which a synthesis of manifold perceptions as perception of one and the same thing would be unthinkable," Heidegger notes "transcendental questions!" (Hua IX:245). But for Husserl such phenomenology is not yet transcendental. What more is required?

Husserl admits that transcendental phenomenology and phenomenological psychology deal with "the 'same' phenomena and essential insights"; it is possible to move from one to the other through a mere *Einstellungsänderung* (Hua IX:247). The demand for such a "change of attitude" does not arise from the project of establishing a pure psychology, however, but from the idea of carrying out a "reform of philosophy to a rigorous science" (Hua IX:247), which for Husserl was always equivalent to establishing philosophy on a firm *epistemological* foundation. So the *Einstellungsänderung* is introduced as necessary for the "project of a theory of knowledge, a transcendental philosophy" (Hua IX:248). Toward the solution of this problem a phenomenological psychology can contribute nothing, since it finds itself caught in the "absurdity of the epistemological circle" (Hua IX:249)—which Husserl in the second draft called the "transcendental circle"—namely, the attempt to ground the possibility of knowledge on a basis that itself presupposes the (unexamined) validity of certain forms of knowledge. But what sort of mere change of attitude can prevent such circularity? In what sense are the phenomena of phenomenological psychology both mundane and transcendental?

Husserl introduces the *Einstellungsänderung* by recalling the discovery of Descartes that "subjective conscious life in pure immanence is the place of all meaning giving and positing of being, all verification of being"

(Hua IX:248). Inquiry into this "pure immanence" must provide the foundation, the *meaning*, of all problems arising with regard to empirical and metaphysical modes of knowing. Phenomenological psychology has not yet revealed this realm since it is still "positive science, it has the world as pregiven ground" (Hua IX:248). The reduction to the purely psychological still carries the sense of a reduction to a "worldly" stream of conscious experiences, to an entity within the world. The subjectivity of phenomenological psychology is thus not yet in a position to address the transcendental-epistemological question of the foundation of all worldly knowledge, including its own. Husserl thus introduces the concept of a "fully universal phenomenological reduction (the transcendental)" (Hua IX:249) that will overcome the remaining "naïveté" of phenomenological psychology. Whereas the phenomenological reduction brackets the facticity of the *cogitata* so as to focus on them as purely given intentional "meaning contents," the transcendental reduction carries this bracketing one step further by applying it to the "worldly" character of the subject itself, to its stream of intentional experiences. In this way the sense of these experiences is altered: From being particular properties of a human subject they become the pure intentional field upon which even this sense of "human subject" is constituted in its meaning and posited being.

Here the last vestige of "posited" being, the posited reality of *human* psychological subjectivity, is overcome in favor of an inquiry into the transcendental "positing" life of a "pure" subject.[8] Thus, Husserl can write that as I reflect within the reduction I grasp a subjectivity which cannot "be taken as I, this man" (Hua IX:249). But when Heidegger attaches to this the rejoinder "Yet certainly as humanity (understood as the essence of man)," we stand before the very issue over which the collaboration will collapse. How is it to be understood? Heidegger does not object here to Husserl's move toward a transcendental phenomenology, to "transcendental subjectivity" as such. Instead, he indicates the locus of a disagreement over how this field of transcendental subjectivity (or "transcendental life," as Husserl calls it) is to be interpreted. What for Husserl, guided by epistemological considerations, must be seen as prior to the naturally posited sense "human subject" is, from Heidegger's ontological perspective, a possibility of the human subject—not qua human (in the anthropological sense) but qua subject (in the transcendental sense).

Before proceeding further with an account of this divergence, it is important to recall that Husserl's recourse to the pure subject is not based on an argument, but on a reflection carried out in methodologically controlled fashion. Transcendental subjectivity is not a *principle*, but a field of *evidence*, a space of meaning that is to be grasped as that "thematic field of an absolute phenomenological science which is called transcendental because it includes within itself all transcendental or reason-theoretical problematics" (Hua IX:250). The difference between Husserl's concept of transcendental phenomenology and the *prinzipientheoretisch* versions of Kantian and neo-Kantian transcendental logic stems ultimately from their different conceptions of what these "reason-theoretical problems" are.[9] Concerned with the so-called *quaestio juris,* the question of how (empirical and a priori) truths are to be *justified,* the neo-Kantians had recourse to formal principles of argument (and a formal subject) to construct a transcendental foundation for specific truth claims. Central to Husserl's advance beyond such a conception of transcendental philosophy is his claim that meaning is more primordial than truth—that truth is itself a particular type or structure of meaning. Thus, the genuine transcendental project would not be to justify truth claims but to *clarify* the "intentional sense" of such claims, as well as that of all other unities of meaning, or "objectivities." Such a philosophy will of course make truth claims, and it will also seek to justify them. However, it will not be constructed as a special form of metajustification (transcendental argument) that employs principles of justification unknown in other cognitive disciplines. Phenomenological clarification of what it means to justify a truth claim uncovers the relation between assertion and evidence; hence this conception of evidence must be carried over to the reflexive problem of how the cognitive claims of transcendental philosophy are themselves to be justified.[10] Thus, Husserl's conception of a nonformal transcendental field allows him to speak of "transcendental facts," and in *Being and Time* Heidegger approvingly called Husserl's philosophy a "philosophical empiricism" (GA 2:67/490).

Husserl's transcendental philosophy is an investigation of the field of reflection as a field of meaning-constitution purified of all uncritical positing of being—"and in nothing else," continues Husserl, "consists its transcendental idealism" (Hua IX:250). "Idealism" here refers to the fact that the space of meaning, the intelligibility that is presupposed in all positive inquiry, can be clarified only by recourse to the intentional structure of conscious experience. Because it is upon this basis alone that any "meaning of being" can be elucidated, transcendental idealism contains within itself a "universal ontology," including the "a priori ontology" of the form of any "world" whatsoever (Hua IX:251). Transcendental idealism is thus not a metaphysical idealism; it is a rejection of "every metaphysics that moves in empty formal constructions [*Substruktionen*]" (Hua IX:253). Heidegger also rejects metaphysics in this sense as something "carried out in the natural attitude and always tailored to it in particular historical situations of life, with its merely factical possibilities of knowledge" (Hua IX:253). Against the tendency such metaphysics has to lose itself in aporetic dichotomies—including "ontologism and transcendentalism"—for which desperate formal (dialectical or logical) solutions are sought, Husserl demands phenomenological work that progresses "from the intuitive givens to the abstract heights" (Hua IX:253). In this way it can be shown that "transcendental idealism contains natural realism entirely within itself" (Hua IX:254), that the meaning of natural realism is itself constituted in evident intentional ways.

This sketch of Husserl's notion of transcendental phenomenology as presented in the first draft suggests that Heidegger is, in important respects, committed to the idea of phenomenological idealism. For Heidegger, too, metaphysical dichotomies are to be admitted, if at all, only after phenomenological reconstruction of their sense; and he finds no incompatibility between a *kind* of phenomenological idealism and *that* realism which alone can be at issue in the natural attitude. For Heidegger, too, the "transcendental" is a field of evidence embedded within mundanity rather than a formal construction of principles deduced to explain (or justify) mundanity.[11] Accessible solely through a reflective inquiry, through recourse to *Verhaltungen* of Dasein, transcendental questions are concerned not with beings per se, but with their meaning. There is thus a good sense in which Heidegger can be said to adopt the program of inquiry into transcendental constitution.[12] If there are nevertheless essential differences between the two they must be discovered further back, in terms of the issues and problems that are brought to this field by each and so influence the philosophical significance it is taken to have. These issues are already quite apparent in the second draft of the article.

2. The Second Draft: Ontology and Transcendental Philosophy

Where Husserl's first draft had introduced transcendental phenomenology indirectly, by way of contrast with pure psychology, Heidegger's introduction to the second draft begins with the question of philosophy's claim to be "fundamental science."[13] The "totality of beings," writes Heidegger, is parceled out to the various positive sciences as "object domains" for their research. What then is left for philosophy? Not the determination of entities in their particular factual constitution, but the determination of entities as entities, "to understand them with respect to their being" (Hua IX:256).

Next Heidegger notes that whereas the positive sciences pursue their task by immersing themselves in the object as theme, philosophical inquiry has at every stage of its history sought "illumination of being" by way of a reflective turn "from entities to consciousness." Is this an accident? To see in it an essential necessity is the epoch-making contribution of phenomenology, which Heidegger defines as "the fundamental clarification of the necessity of the recourse to consciousness, the radical and explicit determination of the way and the laws of the stages in this recourse, the principled delimitation and systematic exploration of the field of pure subjectivity that discloses itself through this recourse" (Hua IX:256). In keeping with his conviction that the article should emphasize the transcendental nature of phenomenology from the outset, Heidegger writes that "pure subjectivity" can be called "transcendental" since in it "the being of all that is experienceable for the subject in varying ways, the 'transcendent' in the widest sense, is constituted" (Hua IX:257).

To this point, in spite of the unfamiliar language of "being" in which it is expressed, nothing in Heidegger's introduction would necessarily conflict with Husserl's idea of phenomenology. The various object domains of the positive sciences (including psychology) all contain "transcendent" objects in Husserl's sense and are "ontologically" grounded in the fundamental categories, regional ontologies, expressing the "essential being" of such objects. These in turn are referred to transcendental subjectivity as the source of their ultimate clarification, a referral that takes place through reflection on the constitution of the intentional space of meaning. The issues separating Husserl and Heidegger do not become visible until the interpretation of this intentional field, transcendental subjectivity, is explicitly addressed.

In section 2 of the article, we find Husserl's revised presentation of the progress from pure psychology to transcendental phenomenology. Again Husserl's point is that the epistemological investigations of modern philosophy "continually presupposed the existential validity [*Seinsgeltung*] of the experienced world" and so, falling into "transcendental psychologism," did not recognize that the transcendental problem was to clarify this world's *Seinsgeltung* itself. Regarding the evidence of the world and worldly entities, the transcendental question is not whether it is valid (*ob es gilt*)—this is the task of empirical inquiry, which tests hypotheses and secures true propositions through positive criticism—but rather "what meaning [*Sinn*] and scope [*Tragweite*] such validity can have" (Hua IX:265).

For Husserl it is "universally dominant naturalism" that impedes recognition of transcendental subjectivity as a "field of transcendental experience" (Hua IX:267, 269). Overcoming naturalism is made possible only by the "method of the transcendental-phenomenological reduction" (Hua IX:270) that "raises up the totality of the positive to the philosophical level," bracketing the lingering naïveté in psychological reflection, which posits the realm of subjective experience as a natural entity, a bit of the world. With the reduction, however, a "cloud of unintelligibility" spreads over the world as the "taken-for-granted reality and pregiven field of all our theoretical and practical activities" (Hua IX:271). The world, whose reality before the reduction was never so much as questioned, is now seen to be "constituted in whatever meaning it may have, and whatever existential validity is attributed to it, 'in ourselves,'" in the "immanence of our own perceiving, representing, thinking, valuing, etc., life" (Hua IX:271).

The problem identified here—that of the "meaning genesis of the world"—is, as Heidegger notes, "the task of transcendental philosophy and must be identified as such at this point" (Hua IX:271). In a letter to Husserl, Heidegger emphasizes that what needs to be discussed is the precise sort of unintelligibility that spreads over the taken-for-granted world under the reduction: "In which respect is such being [*Seiendes*] unintelligible? . . . [W]hat sort of higher claim to intelligibility is possible and necessary" (Hua IX:602)? Husserl envisions a transcendental clarification of the sense in which the world and all worldly objects are constituted as "*an sich seiend*" (Hua IX:271) in order to gain insight into the genuine sense of all epistemological problems concerning "knowledge of what transcends consciousness." With his eyes on the *same* field of transcendental experience, Heidegger envisions a clarification of the being of entities disclosed through phenomenological reflection on their constitution, a clarification of that which enables these entities "in truth" *to be* as they are encountered in the natural attitude.

Even at this stage there is no necessary conflict between the Husserlian and Heideggerian projects. The being of which Heidegger speaks is in no sense equivalent to the "posited being" bracketed by the reduction, the admission of which leads to the absurdities of "transcendental psychologism" attested in the traditional problem of proving the existence of the external world (Hua IX:265). Genuine difficulties do emerge, though, as Husserl continues his explication of the sense of the transcendental reduction. If "the transcendental problem concerns the existential sense [*Seinssinn*] of a world in general," then the "decisive point" that distinguishes the transcendental from the psychological-phenomenological reduction is the "*universal* inhibition" of "natural experience as the pregiven ground of possible judgments" (Hua IX:273). The world as something "on hand for me" in the natural attitude is bracketed in order to reveal "pure subjectivity as source of meaning and validity." Pure subjectivity is no longer "my ego as soul"—an idea which "already in its own meaning presupposes an existing or possible world"—but rather "my ego" as transcendentally reduced "self-contained field of experience with all its intentional correlates" (Hua IX:273–75). With regard to the sense of this transcendentally reduced ego, Heidegger poses the decisive question: Is it not the case that "a world in general belongs to the essence of the pure ego" (Hua IX:274)?

Before evaluating this question, one must note an ambiguity in Husserl's concept of world. On the one hand, Husserl tends to use the term "world" to mean "the totality of objects."[14] World in this sense would be that subset of things posited as "being" by the theorizing and pretheoretical subject in the natural attitude that can *truly* be posited, that is, that truly are. World itself is thus synechdochically posited, as it were, in every "taking-for-true," every positing of an object; and when the reduction is said to bracket the world, what is meant is the putting out of play of this sort of positing, which locates everything within this set understood simply as existing "in itself." The posited being of the world is bracketed in order to focus on the positing (including the modes of givenness) in which it is posited. On this view it could seem that the transcendental ego must, as reduced, be worldless to the extent that world is equivalent to naively posited being.

However, Husserl also sometimes speaks of the world as a nonobjective "horizon" of all positing, as the "transcendental phenomenon 'world.' "[15] Not only does this have a structure very different from any posited entity; it cannot at all be thought of as "the same" as the world in the previous sense. It is far from clear that the transcendental ego could be worldless in this sense. For if nothing is lost under the reduction, reduction to pure subjectivity as intentional field must *also* include the world horizon as pure phenomenon.[16] Indeed, it would seem that Husserl's claim to avoid the formal "epistemological subject" would demand that transcendental subjectivity have an a priori content, a world, as the horizon of constituting activity. Heidegger indicates this to Husserl by reminding him of "our Totnauberg conversation [1926] on 'being-in-the-world' . . . and its essential difference from presence at hand 'within' such a world" (Hua IX:274). Thus, when Heidegger writes in his letter to Husserl that "we agree that being [*das Seiende*] in the sense of what you call 'world' cannot be clarified in its transcendental constitution by recourse to being [*Seiendes*] of precisely the same sort" (Hua IX:601), one must be careful to note just what such agreement means. For "world" in Husserl's sense here means all being that, in the natural attitude, is taken simply as existing "in itself." This is of course precisely not what Heidegger means by "world." Agreement consists in the fact that for both Husserl and Heidegger the being of what Heidegger calls the present-at-hand, its constitution, must be clarified by recourse to the transcendental dimension that, as reflectively disclosed, is precisely not present-at-hand within the natural attitude. But on Heidegger's view such a transcendental dimension would in fact be worldly—precisely as the "transcendental phenomenon" of world that therefore "belongs to the essence of the pure ego."

In continuing his letter, Heidegger voices a related point of divergence. Even if the constituting dimension is not an entity present-at-hand, "this does not imply that that which makes up the place of the transcendental is not being [*Seiendes*] at all—rather it precisely raises the problem: what is the mode of being of that being [*Seinsart des Seienden*] in which 'world' constitutes itself? That is the central problem of *Being and Time*" (Hua IX:601). The issue here concerns the meaning of the limits to phenomenology set by the transcendental reduction. When Husserl argues that the transition from the psychological to the transcendental standpoint is effected "in one stroke" by a "universal theoretical will" that "spans the totality of current and habitual life" (Hua IX:274), Heidegger asks "And this will itself?" Heidegger's elliptical question indicates the problem of the motivation for performing the transcendental reduction. How is a will to the disclosure of the transcendental possible, given that for Husserl there can be no motivation within the natural attitude for moving to the pure transcendental level (for engaging in reflective *philosophy*) since, ex hypothesi, it is altogether concealed from "man," the subject of the natural attitude?[17] Heidegger, however, for whom "man" is never "merely present-at-hand," never merely an item in the world of the natural attitude, tries to offer an account of such motivation by interpreting the transcendental as a "'marvelous' existential possibility ['*wundersame*' *Existenzmöglichkeit*]" (Hua IX:275) of "the subject," man, already in the natural attitude. The ground and possibility of the will to transcendental reflection lies in the ontological constitution of the subject itself: Dasein is that being in whose "very being that being is an issue for it." Dasein is "ontically distinctive in that it is ontological" (GA 2:16/32). The psychological subject is not merely a transcendent entity; properly seen in its ontological constitution, it "is transcendental." Only so is it possible to *account* for the fact (one Husserl continually emphasizes) that psychological reflection can be seen as transcendental experience through a simple, though decisive, "interpretive turn [*Umdeutung*]."

Yet for Husserl this *Umdeutung* meant that the question of ontology (regional or otherwise) had been left behind. If "being" is equivalent to worldly (posited) being, then recourse to the transcendental level of positing is a departure from all questions of ontology. For Husserl, the fact that the transcendental subject is "identical in content" with the psychological but "freed from its '*seelischen*' [worldly real] sense" (Hua IX:275) means that the question of the "existence" (i.e., worldly existence) of such a subject can no longer have *any* meaning. But though Heidegger too distinguishes between "man" and Dasein (as the being or transcendental constitution of man), he insists, against Husserl, that transcendental subjectivity must be seen as an existential possibility of man: "Is not this act [the transcendental reduction] a possibility of man, but precisely because man is never simply on hand; a comportment, i.e., a mode of being, that it secures for itself and so never simply belongs to the positivity of what is on hand" (Hua IX:275)?

What Heidegger argues against here is not the reduction per se, but the implicit ontology in which Husserl locates the entity "man"—specifically, his restriction to the conception of man as an entity present-at-hand which is thematized in psychology, psychophysiology, the social sciences, and so on. Husserl's regional ontological assumptions about man cloud his view of what reduction to the transcendental means. This issue comes to the fore at the end of the second draft where Husserl identifies the *Umdeutung* from phenomenological psychology to transcendental phenomenology as the key to the "riddle of the Copernican turn" of Kant. Here Heidegger notes that following Husserl's own presentation the *Umdeutung* is simply a "supplemental development of the transcendental problematic which you found incomplete in pure psychology so that . . . now everything positive becomes transcendentally problematic" (Hua IX:277). If so, then the naive sense of the psychical with which psychology begins must itself be put into question. It will not be enough to identify it, as Husserl did, by analogy with the physicist's reduction to the purely physical. Inquiry into transcendental constitution cannot avoid the quest for proper ontological categories of the psychical since, as Heidegger writes, "the focus on that which belongs purely to the soul has never grown out of consideration of the ontology of the full human being, that is, not from a genuine perspective on psychology—rather, it has emerged since Descartes primarily from epistemological considerations" (Hua IX:602). In other words, "that which belongs purely to the soul" has been misinterpreted to exclude the proper *transcendental* determinations of "world" (of the "soul" as being-in-the-world). This is not, as Husserl thought, anthropology. The specifically naturalistic sense that Husserl gives to "human being" plays *no role* in Heidegger's transcendental phenomenological descriptions.

It would appear, then, that the essential difference between Husserlian and Heideggerian interpretations of the meaning of transcendental phenomenological reflection does not concern the legitimacy of the reduction, which both accept insofar as it places into question the ontological presuppositions of the natural attitude. Rather, the issue turns on whether the phenomenological clarification of being, proposed by

Husserl, must be extended to the being of the transcendental subject itself. For Husserl, who identifies being with "being posited," the question of the being of the transcendental subject—that is, the being of the field of positing/constituting acts, the being of the space of meaning—can have no sense. But Heidegger argues quite plausibly: "That which constitutes is not nothing, and thus it is something and in being [*seiend*]—though to be sure not in the sense of the positive. The question about the mode of being of that which constitutes is not to be avoided. The problem of being is thus directed toward the constituting and the constituted alike" (Hua IX:602). Indeed, even on Husserl's own terms there is something artificial about his restriction of the question of being. For if, as Husserl argues in *Ideen I,* the "formal" sense of *Etwas überhaupt* is the basis of all ontology—if "to be" (formally) means to be the "subject of possible true predications" (Hua III:15/10)—then a transcendental phenomenology must leave open the possibility of an ontology of transcendental subjectivity, since there can be no denying that Husserl thinks true propositions concerning such a subject are possible.

If it is pointed out that Husserl does indeed envision an ontology of the transcendental subject and in fact attributes to it an "absolute being" (Hua III:115/110), one should recall that such "ontological" characteristics of the transcendental subject arise not from an inquiry into the meaning of being per se (ontology), but from *epistemological* considerations that everywhere presuppose that the meaning of being is simply given (as "posited" being). Thus, Husserl most often speaks of ontology as a branch of formal logic (which includes formal apophantics and formal ontology), that is, as an objective discipline concerned with what it is to be an object in general and with specific "regional" differentiations among objects.[18] Such a discipline, though in need of transcendental (epistemological) grounding, is not yet transcendental. Husserl will even state that "in itself . . . ontology is not phenomenology" (Hua V:129/117). When, however, he speaks of "another 'formal ontology,' which relates to everything that exists in any sense: to what exists as transcendental subjectivity and to everything that becomes constituted in transcendental subjectivity" (Hua XVII:277/271), and when he helps himself (as in *Ideen I*) to the language of "absolute being" in characterizing such a subject, he encounters systematic problems.[19] For on his conception of reflection, if the subject is to be brought into view ontologically it must be "objectified," turned into something posited for the reflective gaze. But the transcendental subject was glimpsed initially through the reduction of everything positive, as the positing or constituting origin of objective meaning. The result is that Husserl can characterize the absolute being of the transcendental subject only *negatively* and, in particular, with regard to its *epistemological* privileges. As Heidegger puts it in a criticism of Husserl on just this point: "Husserl's primary question is simply not concerned with the character of the being of consciousness. Rather, he is guided by the following concern: How can consciousness become the possible object of an absolute science?" For this reason, Husserl's "ontological" determinations of transcendental subjectivity "are not derived by considering the intentional in its very being, but to the extent that it is placed under scrutiny as apprehended, given, constituting, and ideating taken as an essence" (GA 20:147, 146/107, 106). Though Heidegger's criticisms do not do full justice to the subtlety of Husserl's view of consciousness here, it does seem fair to say that Husserl largely derives the ontological characteristics of what he calls "absolute being" from epistemological considerations. He thereby closes off the possibility of a genuine phenomenological ontology based on unprejudiced recourse to the "things themselves."[20]

So with regard to the phenomenological investigation of the domain of transcendental subjectivity, Heidegger can ask, "What is the character of the positing in which the absolute ego is posited? To what extent is there no positivity (positedness) found here" (Hua IX:602)? The mode of being of the absolute ego must itself become a transcendental problem. Only so can it be phenomenologically clarified how the pure ego both is and is not "the same" as the factic ego (Hua IX:602). The ground upon which entities are encounterable explicitly in their meaning structure must itself be inquired into as to its *Seinssinn*. At the same time, such an inquiry preserves a genuine sense and direction for Husserlian constitutional investigations within the projected (fundamental) ontology of *Being and Time.* Of course, Heidegger's criticisms of Husserl's views on the relation between phenomenology and ontology involve problems of their own. Yet the form they take in the *Encyclopædia Britannica* episode shows that whatever else Heidegger had in mind, the "parting of the ways" between the two phenomenologists makes better sense as an immanent criticism of Husserl's transcendental program rather than as its wholesale rejection. It thus becomes possible to project a significant rapprochement between Husserl and Heidegger, one that leaves neither totally unrevised.

10

Ontology and Transcendental Phenomenology between Husserl and Heidegger

In 1983 Timothy Stapleton advanced the claim that Husserl's transcendental phenomenology was largely motivated by an ontological problematic and not, as was argued in the previous chapter, an epistemological one.[1] Critical examination of this claim provides a convenient framework for clarifying the new sense of ontology demanded by phenomenological philosophy so far as it is genuine "first philosophy," in which (as Husserl claimed in *The Crisis of European Sciences and Transcendental Phenomenology*) "the total sense of philosophy, accepted as 'obvious' throughout all its historical forms, [is] basically and essentially transformed" (Hua VI:16/18). As I have argued throughout this book, such a new sense of philosophy arises with the recognition that the space of meaning cannot be approached with the resources of traditional metaphysical (ancient) or epistemological (modern) philosophical paradigms. The *systematic* relation between the phenomenologies of Husserl and Heidegger turns on what is required to move beyond this impasse, namely, the apparently paradoxical notion of an ontological transcendental philosophy. In this chapter, then, I shall continue my argument that Heidegger is better seen as developing and advancing Husserl's transcendental philosophy rather than as rejecting it altogether.

The issue of the relation between transcendental and ontological phenomenology is often framed in something like the following terms: Heidegger admired the "realistic" Husserl of the *Logical Investigations,* whose categorial intuition opens up a new avenue to being and to the question of the unity of being. But he (along with other erstwhile followers of Husserl) rejected the master's "transcendental turn" in *Ideen I,* especially the "transcendental reduction," which discloses the constitutive activity of absolute consciousness with its noematic correlates. The reduction opens up the transcendental dimension, but it appears opposed to any ontology. The existence of things is bracketed in order to thematize their modes of givenness (as noemata), and the worldly existence of consciousness is bracketed to thematize its pure and self-contained act life, the syntheses in which noemata are constituted as unities of meaning. In Husserl's view, ontology is a worldly, or pretranscendental, discipline, a branch of logic that can be pursued, without the reduction, as an eidetic science of formal and regional object types.[2] It remains "transcendentally naive" unless relativized to the evidential syntheses of transcendental constitutive consciousness grasped in a specifically *reflective* direction of inquiry. The transcendental turn therefore uncovers the ground of ontology, but it is not itself an ontological form of inquiry.[3] Thus, in order to develop an ontological phenomenology Heidegger had to reject the reduction, thereby rejecting transcendental philosophy. There could be no ontological transcendental philosophy.

Stapleton, however, offers a different account. He argues that it is a mistake to see the transcendental reduction as motivated by epistemological considerations: Husserl is concerned with apodicticity, with indubitable evidence, but that issue is distinct from his search for "ultimate foundations," for evidence that is "first in itself" (*HH* 42). The claim that transcendental consciousness is characterized by such evidence arises in a search for a kind of being that would escape the epoche, the foundation for an "ultimate science of being" (*HH* 17). The transcendental reduction is "merely a variation and logical extension of the eidetic reduction" (*HH* 57) in which "eidetic rationality" completes itself by drawing the ultimate consequence of the theory of wholes and parts from the *Logical Investigations,* namely, that transcendental consciousness alone can be the ultimate "*concretum,*" that which is truly self-sufficient in the order of being. On this basis Husserl's transcendental phenomenology does *not* result in "a surrender of the ontological problematic" (*HH* 4). Heidegger's hermeneutic phenomenology, oriented toward the ontological difference, can be directly compared with Husserl's transcendental phenomenology, oriented toward consciousness, because they are both engaged in the same enterprise: "The reversion to consciousness . . . in Husserl's phenomenology, the bracketing of Being, is undertaken in order ultimately to clarify the meaning of the Being of entities" (*HH* 89).

Stapleton's thesis thus brings Husserl and Heidegger together at the level of an ontological problematic, but he continues to see a dichotomy between transcendental and hermeneutic phenomenology. It is this that I would like to begin to question here, since I hold that Heidegger's phenomenology is transcendental. Thus, in the first part of this chapter I shall raise some critical questions concerning Stapleton's understanding of the distinction between epistemological and ontological valences in Husserl's concept of transcendental phenomenology; then, in the second part of this chapter I shall investigate what it is, exactly, that Heidegger is supposed to reject in Husserl's transcendental phenomenology. My aim is to suggest the horizon for an *ontology of meaning* that opens up within Husserl's transcendental phenomenology, though it is one that Husserl himself never fully incorporates.

Stapleton admits that "the explication of the movement to transcendental consciousness" he offers "does not necessarily correspond with Husserl's explicit intentions" (*HH* 76). His distinction between ontological and epistemological motives is supposed to reflect an "inner rationale" which "could" serve as the implicit telos of Husserl's thinking, though Husserl's texts often run the two problems together. I argue, however, that the two problems are more intricately entwined than this. Stapleton makes his case more plausible by construing epistemology too narrowly as a concern for apodictic evidence, thus obscuring the way epistemological issues inform the question of being as Husserl raises it. Even if the transcendental reduction is motivated by the search for an ultimate stratum or meaning of being, the very question is formulated in terms of a certain epistemological conception of the conditions of possibility for philosophical knowledge. To the extent that it is distinct from traditional metaphysics, Husserl's transcendental question of being derives its sense from critical (epistemological) restrictions upon the nature of rational discourse. In *The Idea of Phenomenology*, for example, Husserl claims that the ultimate "science of being . . . grows out of a 'critique' of natural cognition in the individual sciences." And when he notes that "the critique of cognition . . . is the condition of the possibility of a metaphysics" (Hua II:23, 3/18, 1), this is not without importance for understanding the nature of his transcendental turn.

The point I am making can also be illuminated by noting an overlap, and a significant divergence, between Stapleton's thesis and Heidegger's 1925 interpretation of Husserl. Like Stapleton, Heidegger reads the "Considerations Fundamental to Phenomenology" of *Ideen I* as an exercise in ontology. The "suspension" of the being of natural reality discloses the region of pure consciousness; subsequently,

> on the basis of this pure region it now first becomes possible to define the suspended being, reality. The question of being is thus raised, it is even answered. We have to do solely with the genuine scientific way of answering it, which attempts to define the sense of the reality of something real insofar as it manifests itself in consciousness. (GA 20:155/112)

Here "the reduction itself has no other task than to fix and demonstrate this fundamental distinction of being" (GA 20:158/114), the "cardinal distinction" between consciousness and reality. Heidegger nowhere claims that the transcendental reduction is motivated by the search for apodicticity. In particular, when he lists the characteristics which distinguish the priority of consciousness for Husserl, there is no mention of its status as apodictically known (GA 20:142–46/103–7). Heidegger, then, appears to agree with Stapleton that the quest for apodicticity is not the motive for the transcendental reduction. But he does not, apparently, agree that Husserl's motive is exclusively ontological either. Instead, "Husserl's primary question is simply not concerned with the character of the being of consciousness. Rather, he is guided by the following concern: how can consciousness become the possible object of an absolute science. The primary concern which guides him is the idea of an absolute science" (GA 20:147/107). That is, "the formation of the region of pure consciousness is undertaken for the purposes of theoretical reason" (GA 20:153/111). Hence, the ontological characteristics Husserl attributes to consciousness are not drawn from the "things themselves" but from a consideration of consciousness as an object for theoretical reflection. This suggests that the ontological motive for the transcendental reduction is more intimately entwined with a kind of epistemological motive than Stapleton allows and that a certain revision of his characterization of Husserl's transcendental turn is called for. To flesh out this suggestion one must delve a bit more deeply into the "Considerations Fundamental to Phenomenology" found in Husserl's *Ideen I.*

1. Epistemology and Transcendental Phenomenology

To evaluate the claim that epistemological motives are secondary in Husserl's path to the transcendental reduction it is necessary to get clear about what the project of epistemology is understood to be. Stapleton tends to treat it as equivalent to one aspect of the traditional and Husserlian conception of epistemology, namely, the search for apodictic evidence, for certainty. Epistemology can also mean the project of justifying particular kinds of knowledge claims—as in Kant's *quaestio juris,* and, more broadly, in attempts to refute skepticism. Stapleton correctly notes that Husserl is not engaged in this sort of project; instead, his is "that of comprehending or understanding, not securing objectivity" (*HH* 115). But this is just what Husserl took the primary task of epistemology to be. In the *Logical Investigations,* for example, he claims that the task of a "theory of knowledge" is not to construct an explanatory theory, but rather "to shed light on the Idea of knowledge in its constitutive elements and laws" (Hua XIX/1:27/265). Epistemology in this sense enters deeply into the motivation for the transcendental reduction, for the question of being is posed as a question of the object and of "objectivity"—that is, of "valid" (*geltend*) being. If for Husserl "transcendental" derives its sense from "transcendent," the latter derives its sense from the epistemological idea of validity.

Stapleton seeks to answer the question of what motivates the reduction by analyzing Husserl's opening moves in *Ideen I.* What could lead an individual *in* the natural attitude to abandon the very sorts of beliefs and evidences which *define* the natural attitude, and to do so "radically," reflecting the "chasm" between the natural and the philosophical attitudes (*HH* 9)? Some would locate such a motivation in the search for absolute certainty; however, Stapleton suggests that "the deepest motives underlying this philosophical turn are ontological in nature" (*HH* 17). This means that "if the philosophical (transcendental) level is to be attained, the existence problematic must itself be introduced" (*HH* 23). The transcendental turn is thus motivated by the search for an "existence stratum" that escapes the epoche, one that is "not a product of the affirmation of the Being of the world" characteristic of the natural attitude (*HH* 18).

Husserl describes the natural attitude in order to distinguish a specifically philosophical attitude from it. Stapleton argues that this description turns on an ontological issue, "a certain thesis concerning the Being of the world" (*HH* 16). Thus the "alteration" of the "general thesis" that Husserl proposes appears to be motivated by the search for a stratum of being untouched by the worldly commitments of the natural attitude. But if we recall part 1 on "Essence and Eidetic Cognition," which precedes the "Considerations Fundamental to Phenomenology," we find that the ontological problem is by no means independent. It is itself motivated by the same need for a "critique of cognition" Husserl alluded to in *The Idea of Phenomenology.* Indeed, the section closes with the claim that dogmatic scientific research stands opposed to "scientific research peculiar to the *epistemological,* to the *specifically philosophical* attitude"(Hua III:56/47). Here, as elsewhere, Husserl identifies the philosophical attitude as one "reflectively turned back upon itself" in a concern for "the possibility of the validity of all modes of cognition" (Hua III:56/48). To recognize that Husserl equates an epistemological reflection with the "philosophical attitude" does not undermine Stapleton's claim that an ontological motive is at work in Husserl's path to the reduction, but it does undermine his claim that the two inquiries are distinct.

This becomes clear also in the reason why Husserl inaugurates the move toward transcendental philosophy by means of "psychological" reflections (*HH* 18–20). After Husserl describes the general thesis of the natural attitude, he proposes to "alter it radically." First, he identifies one aspect of Cartesian "universal doubt" that enters into the epoche, namely, a "certain annulment of positing," parenthesizing, or "refraining from judgment"(Hua III:54–55/58–59). Husserl recognizes the need to "limit" the epoche, but since it is "in our perfect freedom" to suspend judgment about any positing whatsoever, *any* restriction will in a certain sense be arbitrary. Analyzing this moment in the text, Stapleton writes as though the problem *already* concerned a region of being which would escape the attempt to suspend judgment about worldly being: "If the source of all existence, with respect to its meaning, lies in the thesis of the natural attitude which affirms the being out there of the world, and ultimately of all transcendent entities, then all Being, all existence, falls within the scope of such an epoché. . . . How could the epoché be limited so as to leave a residuum of some sort?" (*HH* 18–19). In fact, however, the problem of a "residuum" has not yet arisen. Any region, however absolute, could be subjected to a suspension of judgment. The restriction Husserl actually places on the epoche is precisely the restriction to suspending the general thesis: "The restriction can be designated in a word: We put out of action the general positing which belongs to the natural attitude" (Hua III:67/61).

It is only now that the question of a "residuum" arises. Why then does Husserl choose just *this* restriction at the outset? In part, certainly, because he is searching for a "new region of being never before delimited in its own peculiarity." But Husserl also acknowledges that the "exclusion of the world" leaves *other* regions of being untouched—for instance, the world of "the number series or arithmetic" (Hua III:70/63). Thus, the motive for "not taking this path" and instead engaging in an "eidetic analysis" of "any consciousness whatsoever" cannot be simply that consciousness is a region of being that escapes the epoche of the natural attitude, since there are other such regions. Instead, it turns on the aim of illuminating "the field of a science of consciousness" (Hua III:72/66), since this has some special philosophical significance. What sort of significance? Husserl writes:

> Concerning our terminology we may add the following. Important motives, grounded in the epistemological problematic, justify our designating "pure" consciousness . . . as transcendental consciousness and the operation by which it is reached the transcendental epoché. . . . From an epistemological point of view we shall refer to transcendental reductions. (Hua III:73/66)

The term "transcendental" emerges from an epistemological problematic (to identify the specifically philosophical attitude of critical reflection), and Husserl's designation (in edition D) of "the phenomenological world" as "the transcendental sphere of being" attests that the ontological characterization of this sphere is inseparable from its epistemological/transcendental function.

The same move is found in the *Encyclopædia Britannica* article. There the transcendental reduction follows upon the reflection on phenomenological psychology *not* because of an ontological problematic, but as necessary for "the project of a theory of knowledge, a transcendental philosophy" (Hua IX:248). Phenomenological psychology, as "natural knowledge," is caught in the "absurdity of the epistemological circle" (which in the second draft Husserl calls the "transcendental circle") and so cannot provide presuppositionless grounds for clarifying the possibility of cognition. For Stapleton, "the most fundamental difference in Husserl's thought, that between the transcendental and the nontranscendental, is grounded in the distinction between the sense of existence in the two" (*HH* 24). But differences in modes of being alone do not exhaust the distinction designated in Husserl's use of the term "transcendental."

So far I have been arguing that the ontological sense of the transcendental reduction is deeply entwined with an epistemological problematic. In particular, the term "transcendental" itself inscribes Husserl's basic orientation toward the "critique of cognition" as first philosophy. Stapleton does not wholly neglect this fact, but for him the "epistemological characteristics" that distinguish "pure consciousness" in its philosophical relevance "rest upon an ontological basis" (*HH* 24). It is first by pursuing the ontological problem that epistemological questions arising in the relative domain of transcendent cognition and the absolute domain of transcendental philosophical cognition get answered. If, as I argue, the epistemological problem plays a more determinative role in Husserl's account of the region of pure consciousness than Stapleton acknowledges, it should be possible to provide some evidence to support this from Husserl's ontological remarks in the text.

A crucial moment in the investigation is reached when Husserl identifies as the "cardinal" distinction "among modes of being," that between "consciousness and reality" (Hua III:96/90). Husserl arrives at this ontological distinction by noting a difference in the way these two kinds of being are present to consciousness: "It belongs to the regional essence, Mental Process [*Erlebnis*], . . . that it can be perceived in an immanental perception . . . [and] it belongs to the essence of a spatial physical thing that it cannot be so perceived" (Hua III:95/89). Though Husserl goes on to speak of the "further fact" that this contrast "includes an essentially fundamental difference between the corresponding kinds of givenness" (Hua III:96/90), it is really this difference in modes of givenness that led to the ontological determination in the first place. Modes of being are defined in terms of different modes of givenness.

Stapleton recognizes that it is tempting to see this reflection as "basically epistemological," since "to talk about 'modes of givenness' is to talk about the 'for us'; what is at issue is a characteristic of human knowledge and not of things themselves" (*HH* 23). But since Husserl anticipates this objection and devotes the following section to criticizing one version of it (the Kantian theory that what is given is "mere representation"), Stapleton concludes that "reflection on the modes of givenness of different types of objects discloses something about the objects themselves" and is thus genuinely ontological. However, if one asks what "being" signifies in this context, the most reasonable answer would be that it connotes the epistemological notion, "being an object." The importance of this appears in Stapleton's reproduction of the following argument by Husserl: "If God is to know nature as nature, then he knows it perspectivally, and hence imperfectly. This imperfection is a negativity built into the very Being of nature, and as long as nature is to be nature, this characteristic of its existence must be preserved" (*HH* 23). This is altogether correct as a representation of Husserl's thinking, but if used as an argument for the claim that the epistemological characteristics rest upon an ontological basis, it is circular, since the ontological basis is itself determined in terms of the way things show themselves to perception. The cited argument determines the "imperfection" inherent in nature through the "perspectival" way in which it must appear. In what sense is this an imperfection in the very being of nature? If it is true that the assumption of "an infinite intellect for whom natural objects are not given perspectivally is an absurdity, for it subverts the very meaning of the Being of the objectivity in question" (*HH* 23), one should still not overlook the fact that being and its meaning are here understood in terms of how things show themselves as objectivities, as presences to consciousness. An epistemological or critical decision precedes such an ontology.

It is extremely difficult to decide whether the epistemological status of things is a result of their ontological status (determined independently of all epistemological considerations) or whether ontological status is determined by a certain kind of commitment rightly called epistemological. Both moves are found united in Husserl's text. Thus, Husserl can claim that "the spatial thing" (he does not say "object") is "nothing other than an intentional unity which of essential necessity can be given only as the unity of such modes of appearance" (Hua III:98/92). The same ambiguity is found in the fluctuation of the title heading of section 44 (which Husserl admitted "cannot be used"). As published it reads, "Merely Phenomenal Being of Something Transcendent, Absolute Being of Something Immanent"; in edition A Husserl amends it to read, "Merely Phenomenal Givenness of Something Transcendent as the Absolute Givenness of Something Immanent" (Hua III:100/94). What authorizes the equation between the way things are (or can be) given and the way things "are" *simpliciter?* Husserl writes: "If the meaning [*Sinn*] of the physical thing is determined by the data of physical thing-perception (and what else could determine it?), then that sense demands such an imperfection and necessarily refers us to continuously unitary concatenations of possible perceptions" (Hua III:101/95). Ontology—the being of things—is here referred to a meaning that is determined (and can be determined) only by the data of perception, by modes of givenness. Absolute being is defined by its nonadumbrated modes of appearing, and "absolute" signifies the lack of an "open presumption of non-being" (Hua III:103/96)—an epistemological criterion. The very meaning of being, whether absolute or relative, is determined by the status of the evidence in which different sorts of objectivities present themselves. The being of things is derived from the epistemological modalities of being an object.

I believe that Husserl does provide a new, specifically phenomenological, way of dealing with the old "for us/in itself" problem and that he points the way toward a new sort of ontology in which the true ontological question concerns the meaning of being. But the whole problem of the meaning of being in Husserl emerges from an essentially epistemological orientation—an orientation toward the problem of objectivity and validity (*Geltung*). The question of being arises initially in terms of the epistemological question of clarifying the cognition of transcendent objects, a problem treated by phenomenological analysis of the way they are given. Transcendent being, the "genuine concept of the transcendence of something physical which is the measure of the rationality of any statements about transcendence, can itself be derived only from the proper essential contents of perception" (Hua III:111/106). Ontology is preceded by a definite conception of rationality and by a definite way of understanding being, namely, in terms of objective validity. This ontology is not based on logic (as both traditional metaphysics and Husserl's own understanding of ontology are), but on a prior transcendental/epistemological reflection on valid meaning.

It is easy to gloss over the importance of this notion of validity in the economy of Husserl's thought about being. For example, Stapleton quotes a passage from *Cartesian Meditations* in which Husserl claims that "the being of the pure ego" is "antecedent to the natural being of the world" since "natural being is a realm whose *Seinsgeltung* is secondary;

it continually presupposes the realm of transcendental being" (Hua I:61/21). Stapleton concludes from this that "the sense of the transcendental in Husserl has simply to do with the way in which we think the relationship between ego and world" (*HH* 50)—which is true as far as it goes but which fails to note that the passage above links the priority of the ego specifically to the secondary *Seinsgeltung* of nature. It is the objective *validity* of nature that is relative to consciousness. That Husserl identifies such validity with being (or, more accurately, with the "meaning" of being) is true; that an epistemological motive informs such a determination of transcendental priority is no less true. Thus, Husserl acknowledges that "the hypothetical assumption of something real outside this world is, of course, 'logically' possible" since it involves no "formal contradiction." Yet it is inadmissible since "if we ask about the essential conditions on which its validity would depend, about the mode of demonstration demanded by its sense," we find that it would have to be connected to the possible experience of "any *actual* ego" (Hua III:113/108). This argument shows that if such reality is to have a "valid sense" as "transcendent," then it must be part of the ongoing possible concatenations of experience. This may be a legitimate argument, but it is an epistemological one.

The implications of this for traditional ontological questions about realism and idealism are not always easy to determine. What is the force of Husserl's suggestion (made *prior* to invoking the reduction, and so in terms which are supposed to be intelligible from the natural attitude) that "the whole spatiotemporal world . . . is according to its sense a merely intentional being, thus one that has the merely secondary sense of a being for a consciousness. . . . Beyond that it is nothing" (Hua III:117/112)? This sounds like a strongly ontological assertion, yet in copy A Husserl inserts the clarification "or, more precisely, its being anything beyond that is a countersensical thought." Are these statements really equivalent? Again, Husserl writes that "nature is only as being constituted in regular concatenations of consciousness," but he adds, "that will be misunderstood" (Hua III:121/116). What is the meaning of the "is" here? I submit that the question is unanswerable apart from a grasp of how the issue of validity, of "objectively valid meaning," guides Husserl's ontological thinking from the outset.[4]

For Husserl, the connection between ontology and validity ultimately rests on what Stapleton calls the "pre-beginning" of philosophy in the "will to science," an "ethical imperative" that involves the "decision" to search for "absolutely rational grounds" (*HH* 35 f.). This decision is nothing other than the radicalization of what, for Husserl, characterizes human existence in general: "All life is position-taking," and in the "phenomenological analyses of consciousness this idea is articulated in terms of the identification of experience with evidence" (*HH* 36). Thus, Stapleton can express qualified agreement with Ricoeur's claim that phenomenology is preceded by "a commitment to truth" and a "definition of truth by evidence" (*HH* 39). Yet on Stapleton's account this talk of rationality, truth, and evidence does not appear to influence the character of Husserl's transcendental turn, the "logic of the transcendental reduction."

For example, one might hold that the "principle of all principles," an epistemological desideratum by which Husserl defines rationality, would be sufficient to motivate the transcendental turn.[5] But for Stapleton the "germ of transcendental phenomenology" lies in the movement from evidences that are first "for us" to evidences that are "first in themselves" (*HH* 42, 41)—the latter representing genuine ontological knowledge. The key here lies in Husserl's claim that, contrary to appearances, "worldly" evidence is not "first in itself." In Stapleton's view this move is not motivated by a demand for apodicticity but by an attempt to apply the logico-ontological theory of parts and wholes from the *Logical Investigations* to the question of absolute grounding. The transcendental ego represents what is first in itself, not because it is more certain than what is transcendent, but because it is "continually presupposed" by the world and all worldly evidence. Stapleton's analysis of the theory of parts and wholes, designed to show what is meant by such a presupposition, is wholly convincing so far as the logic of Husserl's argument goes. But it will appear that exclusive focus on this aspect of the argument further effaces the epistemological orientation of Husserl's transcendental phenomenology without providing a self-sufficient alternative.

The transcendental turn is motivated by the insight that the ego is "antecedent" to the world in the sense that the world "depends" upon the ego (*HH* 50). But what, exactly, depends upon the ego? Husserl says that it is the *Seinsgeltung* of the world and of all transcendent entities. Stapleton tends to read this as *Sein simpliciter,* arguing that Husserl's notion of "founding" is not epistemological, but derives instead from the logico-ontological whole/part relation:

> We can see . . . that in a certain sense the relationship of foundation is one that functions only within the domain of moments or abstract parts (abstracta). For the definition of foundation points to the presence of an essential relationship between elements or objects such that the condition for the possibility of the objects' *existence* lies in their necessary correlation with other objects. (*HH* 59; emphasis added)

The key to Husserl's transcendental philosophy would thus lie in recognizing that just such a relationship obtains between the transcendental ego and the world: Husserl argues that at some point our analysis of transcendent entities *must* yield an ultimate *concretum,* an object not further founded on anything else. Within the natural attitude it appears that the world, the horizon of all transcendent entities, is such a *concretum.* But "what Husserl's transcendental phenomenology attempts . . . is the replacement of the world as absolute *concretum,* with transcendental subjectivity" (*HH* 71). If successful, this move yields the ontological thesis that the condition of any transcendent object's *existence* lies in its correlation with the transcendental ego. It follows, further, that to ask what "unites" these two domains of being is absurd since "those wholes whose parts are moments, essentially dependent, require no external bond" (*HH* 60).

This is a neat argument that seems to be quite close to what Husserl wants to say, but is it possible to give it an exclusively ontological reading? What does it mean to say that the existence of transcendent objects "depends" upon transcendental consciousness? In Husserl's terms it means that such objects are constituted in consciousness. Like everyone else, Stapleton recognizes that this cannot mean that "consciousness so conceived creates beings in an ontic sense" (*HH* 29). Constitution is a "transcendental phenomenon"; it is "completely unintelligible" from a worldly perspective since worldly concepts "presuppose . . . an ontological concept of *relata*" (*HH* 11). But is that not precisely what is yielded by an exclusively ontological interpretation of the transcendental reduction based on the logic of parts and wholes, one that sees the transcendental turn wholly as an ontological thesis about the relation between the ego and the world? It would be fair to say that for Husserl the existence of *objects* depends on consciousness, since to be an object is to be constituted as valid meaning on the basis of evidence. But is it so clear that we can also say that the existence of *things* depends on consciousness? Here one has in view an altogether different sort of dependence, a causal one perhaps.[6] I have no objection to calling the phenomenological sort of constitutional dependence an "ontological" one—only it seems necessary also to acknowledge that this sense of ontology is tied to the epistemological motivation to say only what can be redeemed in terms of evidence generated through reflection on the noetic-noematic correlation. Conceived in its self-given purity and its self-chosen ascesis from all naturalistic theories, this is transcendental subjectivity.

To put the question another way: What is to keep us from supposing that transcendental consciousness is not in turn dependent on something other than itself and other than the world—on something inscrutable? Indeed, while insisting on the absolute being of transcendental consciousness, Husserl could at the same time speak of God, who would be "an 'absolute' in the sense totally different from that in which consciousness is an absolute" (Hua III:140/134). "For us," transcendental consciousness is absolute, an ultimate *concretum,* but only because it provides (if Husserl is right) the conditions for the possibility of *meaningfully* positing anything upon which it would be said to be dependent. This is why it is not dependent on the world, according to Husserl. But if this is an ontological thesis (as I think Husserl thinks it is), it is a new, specifically transcendental-phenomenological ontology, motivated by a specific conception of the "ideal of rationality" and by the (epistemological) limits this ideal imposes on what we can rationally say of things.

Thus, Stapleton rightly argues that "any question which cannot, in principle, be meaningfully answered from the perspective of transcendental phenomenology must be either a meaningless question, or must point to a limitation to transcendental subjectivity" (*HH* 77). This is his springboard to the interpretation of Heidegger, for whom, supposedly, "the sphere of origins escapes transcendental reflection" (*HH* 116). But here the opposite problem arises. For if the ontological dimension of Husserl's transcendental phenomenology is too frequently overlooked, the inner connection between Heidegger's ontological question and Husserl's transcendental thought is no less frequently denied. For example, in spite of the new way in which he construes the relation between Husserl and Heidegger, Stapleton still locates their differences in Heidegger's "rejection" of the "transcendental turn" (*HH* 94), arguing that for Heidegger "the presuppositions of the transcendental reduction cancel its [ontological] significance" (*HH* 93). In what follows, then, I want to problematize this common understanding of the relation between Heidegger's fundamental ontology and Husserl's transcendental phenomenology. I shall not pursue this goal by continuing the critical commentary on Stapleton, however. Instead I shall turn to the texts that document Heidegger's interpretation of Husserl and that, it seems to me, suggest that it is not simply from the "realistic" phenomenology of the *Logical Investigations* that Heidegger appropriates important elements of his project, but also from the "idealistic" phenomenology of *Ideen I,* thus making his rejection of transcendental phenomenology far more qualified than it is often taken to be.

2. Transcendental Phenomenology and Ontology

In *Being and Time* Heidegger claims that "only as phenomenology is ontology possible" and that phenomenological method yields "transcendental knowledge . . . *veritas transcendentalis*" (GA 2:48, 51/60, 62). What does "transcendental" mean here?

The two traditional sources for the term are (1) Kant's definition ("I entitle transcendental all knowledge which is occupied not so much with objects as with the mode of our knowledge of objects in so far as this mode of knowledge is to be possible a priori"),[7] and (2) the quasi-Aristotelian, Scholastic notion whereby transcendental knowledge is knowledge of those "transcendental" predicates "convertible" with being itself—e.g., *unum, verum, bonum.* Since Heidegger identifies being as "the *transcendens* pure and simple" (GA 2:51/62), and since he uses the Latin phrase "*veritas transcendentalis,*" one might imagine that he intends to ignore the Kantian definition in favor of an exclusively metaphysical/ontological conception of transcendental philosophy. Thus, he might be understood as obliquely dispensing with Husserl's critical reflective method concerned, as was Kant's, with "validity" and "modes of our knowledge."[8] Nonetheless, we have frequently noted Heidegger's standing concern, as Karl Lehmann put it, "finally to bring the long-postponed dialogue between ancient metaphysics and modern transcendental philosophy on track."[9] In Heidegger's early work, certainly, focused on the space of meaning and on a phenomenological "immanence" that is neither metaphysical nor epistemological in the traditional sense, the meaning of "transcendental" is always itself at issue. But even if the case could be made that a critical conception of transcendental philosophy was evident in Heidegger's early work, one might still argue that in his mature thought, when Heidegger explicitly adopts the term "ontology," he altogether abandons any connection with Husserl's transcendental problematic. Can a case be made for a continuing connection on the basis of that later work itself?

Evidence that Heidegger's conception of ontology still involves something of the critical sense of transcendental reflection can be found in his lecture course from the summer of 1927, where he discusses the difference between ancient and modern "categorial investigation" (GA 24:154–57/110–11). His earlier idea of a transcendental-logical theory of categories is now seen as an ontological project, but Heidegger has not relapsed into a precritical understanding of categories, which he calls "naive." As Heidegger notes, "Ancient ontology performs in a virtually naive way its interpretation of beings and its elaboration of [the categories]." Nevertheless, ancient ontology, "if it is ontology at all must already always, because necessarily, be reflective—reflective in the genuine sense that it seeks to conceive beings with respect to their being by having regard to the Dasein (psuche, nous, logos)." Ancient thought simply did not achieve methodological self-consciousness; instead "reflection remained in the rut of pre-philosophical knowledge." To achieve such self-consciousness it is necessary to carry out what Heidegger calls the "transcendental-ontological differentiation," a methodological "reduction" whereby the "ontological difference" between beings and being—the difference between entities grasped naively and the meaning structures that enable such a grasp—is disclosed (GA 24:453 f./319 f.).

Thus, it is clear that Heidegger does not simply *reject* the transcendental turn in phenomenology in order to clear a space for ontology. Transcendental reflection and ontology are not incompatible.[10] But then, what is to be made of the claim that Heidegger rejected Husserl's transcendental reduction, a claim that surely cannot be entirely without foundation? Where exactly does he part company with Husserl? The lecture course from winter semester 1925 provides part of the answer.

The long "Preliminary Part," where Husserl's ideas are examined in detail, has two main purposes: (1) to motivate Heidegger's immanent development (not wholesale rejection) of the central discoveries of Husserl's phenomenology, and (2) to defend the revolutionary philosophical impulse of Husserlian phenomenology from current misunderstandings (such as Rickert's). In pursuit of these aims, Heidegger explicates the concept of intentionality and, in that connection, both the reduction and the noema. The discussion suggests that his rejection of these is more qualified than it is usually taken to be.

Against Rickert's misinterpretation of intentionality, Heidegger explains and defends the view that the phenomenological "perceived as such" (or intentional object) is not "the perceived *entity* in itself but the *perceived* entity insofar as it is perceived." This is the "entity in the how of its being perceived" (GA 20:60/45), its modes of givenness. Heidegger recognizes that this is "a completely new structure" to which "I cannot now attribute all those determinations which I have thus far attributed to the [perceived entity]" (GA 20:53/40). He recognizes this new structure to be the noema. Now since Heidegger is here commenting on Husserl, one cannot simply assume that he is also echoing his own views. Nevertheless, it is clear that Heidegger does not conceive of the noema as a kind of "representation" that would cut intentionality off from the world. On the assumption that Heidegger held such a view, Frederick Olafson, for example, argued that while *Being and Time* preserves the idea of an active noesis from Husserl's theory of intentionality, it dispenses with the noema as a kind of abstract entity mediating between Dasein and worldly beings.[11] But Heidegger does not see Husserl's noema as an abstract entity and thus has no need to reject it on such grounds. He does express the reservation that since the pair "noesis/noema" is derived from "the sphere of theoretical knowing," the "exposition of the practical sphere" would be "drawn from the theoretical"—but the terminology is "not particularly dangerous" for an explication of intentionality (GA 20:61/45). And though I cannot argue this here, his account of Husserl's theory of truth suggests that the noema might well remain indispensable for a clarification of theoretical intentionality even within Heidegger's own framework.

But if Heidegger is able to see that reflecting on the intentional object as such does not multiply existents—does not give rise to new entities—this is only because he has implicitly employed the reduction (as a bracketing of existence and as a disclosure of the field of intentional correlation). His account of intentionality appears to acknowledge implicitly the legitimacy of at least that aspect of the reduction whereby it sets aside the question of existence as it is raised on the ground of the natural attitude. This can also be discerned in Heidegger's discussion of constitution, which he interprets to mean not "producing in the sense of making and fabricating" but "letting the entity be seen in its objectivity" (GA 20:97/71). Heidegger's understanding of "objectivity" here is developed precisely in opposition to that sense of "reality" bracketed in the reduction. By setting aside the natural attitude's concept of reality, "we can come to see that the objectivity of an entity is really not exhausted by this narrow definition of reality, that objectivity in its broadest sense is much richer than the reality of a thing, and what is more, that the reality of a thing is comprehensible in its structure only on the basis of the full objectivity of the simply experienced entity" (GA 20:89/66). Such objectivity is encounterable only through a reflection on the "constitutive syntheses" or categorial acts whereby the entity "becomes expressly visible precisely in what it is" (GA 20:86/63). The "in" here indicates that new, specifically phenomenological, concept of being toward which Heidegger is working, the "a priori" as a "feature of the being of entities and not a feature of entities themselves" (GA 20:102/75). This being becomes visible as such only through a reflection that first sets aside or reduces the naturalistic thesis about being inherent in everyday life—the same reflection that, in Heidegger's earlier work, uncovers the "difference" between entities and their transcendental condition, meaning.

The textual support for this large claim is admittedly ambiguous. Somewhat clearer are the remarks Heidegger makes in connection with his rejection of Husserl's thesis that consciousness is absolute being. Heidegger examines four features by which Husserl characterizes the being of consciousness as "absolute." In each case he argues that these are not "original" determinations of the being of consciousness but are instead "relative," derived from the epistemological problematic (examined in sec.1 above) that articulates those aspects of how consciousness is given such that it can become the "region of an absolute science" (GA 20:147/107). Heidegger defines the "sense and methodological task of the phenomenological reduction" in relation to this project (GA

20:150/109). Now it is already quite interesting that instead of simply rejecting the reduction here—as though it were a sheer impossibility, an imaginary move to a domain having no claim to philosophical validity—Heidegger remarks that the "consideration" of consciousness as an absolute region by means of the reduction "is in fact possible" (GA 20:149/108).[12] One might even argue that the Husserlian reduction uncovers an indispensable ground for epistemological investigation and that Heidegger's own approach to epistemological issues (e.g., the theory of propositional truth in *Being and Time*) avails itself of just such a move through tacit incorporation of significant aspects of Husserl's analyses.

A perhaps even more surprising implication resides in the remark already cited concerning the question of the being of the real, the "objectivity structure" grasped as the correlate of reflective intentionalities. Heidegger claims that by means of Husserl's reduction to the "pure region" of consciousness "the question of being is thus raised, it is even answered. We have to do solely with the genuinely scientific way of answering it, which attempts to define the sense of the reality of something real insofar as it manifests itself in consciousness" (GA 20:155/112). Though difficult to interpret with confidence, this statement suggests that Heidegger has no quarrel with Husserl's transcendental approach to the question of the being of entities, no objection to approaching being by way of that space of meaning in which entities are as they are for (reduced) consciousness. This has its analogue in *Being and Time,* where Heidegger will refuse to separate the being of entities from the *Seinsverständnis* that, as an existentiale of Dasein, provides the only "scientific" way of developing an ontology. It thus seems that even here Heidegger is not willing to depart from one of the features most distinctive of Husserl's transcendental phenomenology.[13]

Still, this leads to the crucial point. For Heidegger explicitly states that "in its methodological sense as a disregarding . . . the reduction is in principle inappropriate for determining the being of consciousness positively" (GA 20:150/109). What is lost in Husserl's reduction to the sphere of intentionality is any way of giving a positive ontological characterization of the "being of the intentional," that is, of that entity who *is* intentional. If with Husserl the approach to a positive characterization of being lies in showing how its sense is constituted in specific modes of givenness, a problem arises concerning how to specify the being of the one who constitutes. Husserl held the question to be meaningless, but Heidegger insisted that phenomenology could not shrink from giving an account of the ground that made the constitution of objectivity possible. As he says in his notes to the *Encyclopædia Britannica* article, "[T]hat which constitutes is not nothing, and thus it is something and in being . . . the question of the mode of being of that which constitutes is not to be avoided" (Hua IX:602). At this point, then, transcendental philosophy must renounce the epistemological orientation and become genuinely ontological, thus collapsing Husserl's distinction between transcendental phenomenology and the "worldly" discipline of ontology.

In 1925, then, Heidegger does not argue that the reduction makes ontology impossible. His concern is rather that the strategy of bracketing naive acceptance of being in order to make it an intentional theme seems not to be "sufficient for the question of the being of the intentional." He claims that whereas the reduction succeeds in thematizing the "what" or the "structure" of intentional acts, it does not at the same time "thematize their way to be, their being an act as such" (GA 20:151/109). This somewhat obscure objection seems to mean that in the case of intentional acts (and in their case alone) the very being of the acts gets lost in the move from "fact" to "essence." This can be the case only if the being who is intentional is "an entity whose what is to be and nothing but to be" (GA 20:152/110)—only if such a being is Dasein, that entity, as *Being and Time* put it, whose "essence . . . lies in its 'to be' " (GA 2:56/67).

But if this identifies the point where Heidegger rejects the reduction, one should note that the objection pertains not to the transcendental, but to the eidetic, reduction. The transcendental reduction traces constituted meaning to constituting accomplishments. In this regard Heidegger clearly questions the adequacy of Husserl's *interpretation* of that to which meaning gets reduced (since he claims that Husserl does not give consciousness a "positive" ontological characterization), but he does not necessarily reject what this reduction is supposed to accomplish. Indeed, Heidegger himself comes to trace meaning to the enabling structures of Dasein's thrown project, or disclosedness.[14] And it is here that transcendental philosophy would recognize its ontological character in a new, specifically phenomenological, sense as oriented toward meaning. The claim would be that if transcendental constitution of meaning has ontological conditions, the primary task of philosophy—as "fundamental" ontology—is to specify those conditions while *at the same time* specifying the transcendental conditions for the possibility of ontological knowledge itself. Fundamental ontology would thus recall Aristotelian ontological first philosophy without abandoning the modern critical demand for reflective, transcendental clarification of the methodological possibility of its own inquiry.

Such an interpretation implies that significant aspects of the reduction are not only not rejected in Heidegger's ontology, but are actually presupposed in its formulation. How is one then to account for Heidegger's undeniable demand that we dispense with the reduction in turning to *Existenz?* By way of conclusion (thus very briefly), I will approach this question by asking what it is, in fact, that Heidegger "dispenses with" in his methodological turn to *Existenz* in *Being and Time.*

First, one might claim that it is not the eidetic reduction but the epoche that Heidegger rejects, insofar as the epoche is the negative move that brackets a concern with being prior to the phenomenological and transcendental reductions. But Tugendhat correctly argues that "Heidegger no longer needed the *epoché* in order to investigate the dimension of modes of givenness because . . . he stands within it from the outset." Heidegger's approach is not, "as Husserl thought, a relapse from the transcendental phenomenological problematic, but rather its own radicalization."[15] The epoche is the suspension of naive validity claims—not so as to deny or to ignore them but so as to make them the theme of investigation by recognizing their dependence on (to use Heidegger's idiom) the way things show themselves in the space of meaning opened up by Dasein's ec-static being in the world. This is only to say that Heidegger's phenomenology is no more "naturalistic" or "realistic" in the naive sense than is Husserl's. It is concerned with the meaning of entities, a transcendental theme that is clarifiable only through phenomenological reflection.

Second, in *Basic Problems of Phenomenology* Heidegger can still appropriate the term "reduction" in a way that suggests a continuing recognition of its significance for making what Husserl called the "transcendental field" accessible to philosophy. The reduction is said to lead "phenomenological vision back from the *apprehension* of a being, whatever might be the character of that apprehension, to the *understanding* of the being of this being (projecting upon the way it is unconcealed)" (GA 24:29/21). There is certainly a difference between the idea of tracing the apprehension of a being back to syntheses of absolute consciousness and tracing it back to "the understanding of the being of this being" with reference to "the way it is unconcealed." But the difference has little to do either with the concept of being (which is thematic only as meaning) or with the transcendental character of the inquiry itself.[16]

But is it not precisely "existence" in the sense of *existentia* (as opposed to essentia) that Husserl once and for all disregards in his version of transcendental philosophy, leaving it as a problem for metaphysics (one for which phenomenology has perhaps nothing to offer)? And does Heidegger not wish to restore precisely this in his talk of *Existenz?* Leaving aside the problem of whether this is a correct interpretation of Husserl's position, one must acknowledge that Heidegger is not Sartre and that his notion of *Existenz* is not the traditional *existentia.* As Dasein's "way to be," *Existenz* is by no means the sheer "being on hand" thought in the term *existentia*. And if *existentia* is indeed what Husserl's reduction brackets, an inquiry that "restores" it to consideration would, in the first instance, be an empirical science concerned with particular existing entities in their existing particularity. But Heidegger's fundamental ontology is not an empirical inquiry. Nor is it meant to be a philosophical anthropology, an exploration of the regional type "man" (which on Husserl's view would still be carried out against the existential positing of the background of the "world" in the sense of the natural attitude, since the meaning of man's "existence" is inseparable from such world positing).

Perhaps this leads to the central point. Isn't there in fact a sense in which Heidegger's concern *is* with a particular existing entity in its existing particularity—namely, Dasein as being-in-the-world—if not as an empirical instance in the usual sense, then at least as a "worldly" entity in a sense that conflicts with Husserl's bracketing of the world? For Heidegger insists that Dasein is "factic," *jeweilig*, and characterized by *Jemeinigkeit*. Are these not worldly notions that transgress the strictures of the reduction and thereby rule out any transcendental sense for Heidegger's inquiry, stamping it as a kind of pragmatism or historical relativism? Perhaps, but then something like these notions can also be found in Husserl's idea of the transcendental ego, which, though not "I, this man," is nevertheless concrete (not a formal principle) and "identical" to the corresponding field studied by phenomenological psychology.[17] The deeper point, however, is that for Heidegger these are categorial features of Dasein's being; they pertain necessarily and universally to Dasein, in spite of Heidegger's apparent rejection of the eidetic reduction in 1925. Heidegger argues that these aspects of Dasein must be taken into account in any analysis of the way an "understanding of being," the space of meaning, is opened up through Dasein's being. But however such an analysis might proceed (e.g., in the direction of a historicist conception of world disclosure, or in a pragmatic approach to understanding), it cannot possibly be interpreted so as to render an investigation into the "a priori" impossible. Appeal to facticity cannot rule out knowledge of genuine transcendental conditions since, in Heidegger's view, these aspects are themselves just such conditions.[18]

But if Heidegger's turn to *Existenz* can dispense neither with the epoche (as a bracketing of the naive positing—or understanding—of being in order to investigate its meaning) nor with the eidetic reduction (as the move that enables a grasp of universal and necessary features of entities, including those whose essence is "to be"), what is left of Heidegger's claim that ontological phenomenology must abandon the reduction? It still appears that what Heidegger rejects is not so much the reduction itself as an *interpretation* (Husserl's) of what the reduction accomplishes. Heidegger does not accept the idea that the reduction discloses an absolute ground of constituting consciousness. Though he admits that the reduction to constituting consciousness is always possible, the notion of "absolute" does not thereby gain any genuine ontological sense. But this idea arises not so much from the reduction itself as from Husserl's almost exclusive concern with epistemological problems and questions of theoretical intentionality during the years of Heidegger's close association with him. A phenomenology oriented toward the question of being might well accept Husserl's claim that under the reduction I am no longer "I, this man" in the empirical sense, without claiming that I am thereby disclosed as "absolute" consciousness. If the reduction reveals that I am ontologically situated, this would call for rethinking both the method and the character of the knowledge claims of transcendental philosophy. And I believe that just this is at stake in the "hermeneutic" phenomenology of *Being and Time.* The whole cluster of issues loses any distinctly philosophical sense, however, if one fails to recognize that for Heidegger not only can there be an ontological transcendental philosophy—there must be.

11

Heidegger's Phenomenology and the Question of Being

As a motto for the edition of his collected writings, Heidegger proposed the phrase "Ways, not works," thus expressing his conviction that philosophical thinking does not aim at fixed results and systems but rather, in ever-renewed impulses of questioning, seeks to open up previously unsuspected paths into what, hidden within the familiar, calls for thinking. Thus, while Heidegger himself claimed that his topic from first to last was the "question of being," it is impossible to grasp what this means without also identifying the moment in his career when some specific version of the question is posed. The matter of thinking, and the way to it (method), are in Heidegger's writings inseparable. But if a certain periodization thus becomes necessary for understanding Heidegger, any such identification of stages or phases is controversial, since it presumes substantive decisions concerning what his philosophy is about. Following Heidegger's own not unambiguous lead, it is customary to distinguish between works done before and after the "turn" (*Kehre*)—that is, between works written primarily before 1930, focused on the human being's "understanding of being," and those written after the 1930 turn to being itself—but this is by no means fine-grained enough to capture even the most important interrelations among the ways traversed during a career that spanned seven decades, from the dissertation of 1914 to the last addresses of the 1970s. Since no alternative periodization commands consensus among scholars, however, the present chapter will resolve the issue by tracing the concept of meaning (*Sinn*) in Heidegger's thought—both because thematization of meaning distinguishes phenomenological philosophy from traditional epistemology and metaphysics and because it frames Heidegger's first formulation of the question of being as the question of the "meaning of being" (*Sinn von Sein*).

From this perspective, Heidegger's thought appears to develop in four stages. Drawn to the question of the "meaning of 'meaning' " through his earliest reflections on logic (1912–17), Heidegger spent the next decade (1917–27) refining and reworking Husserl's phenomenology, Dilthey's hermeneutics, and Aristotle's metaphysics into the question of the meaning of being, to which his first major work, *Being and Time,* was devoted. That volume solidified Heidegger's reputation as Germany's leading philosopher and became, against his own intentions, a sourcebook for subsequent existentialism. Though up to 1930 Heidegger continued to cultivate the phenomenological ontology established in *Being and Time,* already in 1929 a shift in orientation is noticeable. From 1930 to 1945, as Heidegger explored the relation between his thought and traditional metaphysics, the phenomenological question of the meaning of being came increasingly to be posed as a question of the "truth" of being—a transformation prefigured in Heidegger's own novel interpretation of truth as "disclosedness" or "clearing." After 1945 Heidegger pursued the task of "overcoming" metaphysical thinking—the hitherto exclusive form taken by the history of being (*Seinsgeschichte*)—until finally even the inquiry into the truth of being is displaced by an attempt to think about the primordial event (*Ereignis*) that grants or gives both being and truth. With considerable effort in previous chapters having been devoted to probing the phenomenological dimension of Heidegger's early work, it would perhaps be useful to step back for a moment to see how Heidegger's thought as a whole appears from this perspective. It should be emphasized, however, that this chapter makes no pretense of being a comprehensive interpretation of Heidegger's career. Rather, it tries to clarify something of what is at stake in each of the four stages mentioned if primary weight is given to the first two, in which Heidegger most clearly belongs to that phenomenological tradition committed to carrying on the Kantian impulse of autonomous philosophizing. At no stage does Heidegger truly abandon that impulse, but his later thought contains strong elements of postphenomenological or postmodern suspicion regarding both the matter and the method of philosophical inquiry.

1. From Meaning to Being: Ontological Phenomenology

Fundamental to Heidegger's thought is his claim that the metaphysical tradition fails to do justice to the "ontological difference," to the difference between entities (or beings) and the being of entities. Aristotle, for instance, registers this difference in his observation that the term "being" is equivocal, that it does not exhibit the unity of a highest genus of entities; yet he subsequently confounds the difference in his thesis that substance (ousia) is the primary meaning of being. Aristotle does not explain why ousia plays this paradigmatic role in defining being, but by 1923 Heidegger has his breakthrough answer: It is because the Greeks think being within the unreflected horizon of time. Ousia—what is present—appears primary because being is already understood in terms of presence, a modality of time. The modern period alters nothing in this regard since its own primary being—the self-certain knowing subject—is conceived as that which is permanently present to itself. *Being and Time,* then, will seek to recover the difference between being and beings by reflecting upon the hidden presupposition of both ancient and modern philosophy, namely, the structuring of all understanding (including the understanding of being) by time. The philosophy that uncovers time as the horizon of understanding will be "critical" in that it simultaneously uncovers the conditions of its own possibility as a mode of understanding. Here the importance of phenomenology for the early Heidegger becomes apparent, for phenomenology provided a way to raise the ancient metaphysical question of being without ignoring the claims of modern critical or transcendental philosophy.

In his *Logical Investigations* (1900), Husserl had rejected the idea that logical laws and concepts express psychological realities; instead, they designate ideal or necessary structural connections between meanings, given through (linguistically expressible) acts of thinking but not reducible to them. In his 1914 dissertation, written under the direction of the neo-Scholastic philosopher Arthur Schneider, Heidegger applied Husserl's critical insights to five psychologistic theories of judgment, showing how each fell into self-contradiction by failing to acknowledge the proper object of logic, valid meaning (*geltender Sinn*). Heidegger concludes by asking "What is the meaning of meaning?" (GA 2:171). Neither psychically subjective nor physically objective, meaning is irreducible and underivable; yet it can be "pointed out" phenomenologically. Traditional categories seem unable to capture it, but since logical validity pertains precisely to this domain of meaning, the very existence of logic seems to call the adequacy of traditional ontological dichotomies—such as realism and idealism—into question.

Heidegger's *Habilitation* thesis of 1915, written under the direction of the neo-Kantian Heinrich Rickert, deepens the inquiry into the meaning of meaning. In the context of examining "Duns Scotus's" (really Thomas of Erfurt's) theory of signification (a logical grammar or truth-functional theory of language), Heidegger employs the concept of intentionality to distinguish the realm of meaning from the metaphysically real and the epistemologically ideal. Drawing upon Husserl's description of consciousness as a field of evidence (the intentional correlation, consciousness-of-something), Heidegger identifies the origin of logical categories in the projective and constitutive character of the knowing subject, the *Bewandtnis* obtaining between subject and object. Neither the empirical psyche nor a formal epistemological construct, the being of this phenomenological subject now becomes Heidegger's lifelong theme. Already in the conclusion to his thesis, Heidegger insists that reflection on the intentionality of the knowing subject is not enough; the phenomenon of valid meaning will remain philosophically unclear until one goes beyond transcendental logic and, by means of philosophy's genuine "optics," metaphysics, recognizes the full being of what Heidegger, borrowing from Dilthey and *Lebensphilosophie,* calls the "living historical spirit." The future trajectory of Heidegger's move from meaning to being is adumbrated here. Collapsing the distinction between historical and systematic inquiry, the logical (categorial) theory of meaning must be grounded in the concrete life of the historical subject, or spirit, while avoiding both uncritical metaphysics and nonphilosophical empiricism.

Between 1916 and 1923 Heidegger explores this requirement in a series of reflections that culminate in a "hermeneutics of facticity." These years see two significant developments of the earlier work: First, Husserl's phenomenology is revised in the direction of hermeneutic theory, and second, the connection between meaning and being that Husserl had established at the level of logic is now made at the level of everyday practical life.

In the Emergency War Semester of 1919, Heidegger poses the question to which *Being and Time* provides the answer: How is philosophy, as the primordial science (*Urwissenschaft*), possible? In 1911 Husserl had argued that only as phenomenology could philosophy become rigorous science. Heidegger now pushes the question of a scientific philosophy to the point where the whole idea of scientificity—of philosophical knowledge and method—must be transformed. This is because the "theoretical" sciences with their "object-constituting" categories prove incapable of illuminating philosophy's genuine theme, the origin of meaning, which must be sought instead in the "pretheoretical" movement of "factic life." Reflecting on the problem of authentic religious life in Saint Paul, Augustine, and Luther, Heidegger came to hold that philosophy seeks what "is" prior to its diffraction into the objects that form the correlates of intentional consciousness. Because it seeks the "there is" (*es gibt*) before the "there is something," philosophy cannot take place as an objectifying reflection on experience but must instead engage in the indirect interpretive strategy that Heidegger refers to as "formal indication." Following Dilthey, Heidegger attempts to understand life's primordial movement by tracing the formal (initially empty) directions indicated in the very terms life uses to interpret itself (concern, significance, *Ruinanz*, torment, etc.) back to their evidential sources in pretheoretical experience. These "categories of factic life" thus serve as formal indications of that primal something (*Uretwas*) that sustains all scientific and prescientific grasp of objects.

The hermeneutics of facticity remains phenomenological in its conviction that this primal something is *meaningful*. In the early Freiburg lectures, Heidegger generally does not distinguish rigorously between being and meaning: To ask after being is to ask after the "being-meaning of a being" (*Seinsinn eines Seienden*). To grasp the being of an entity is to grasp the "full meaning in which it is what it is. Full meaning = phenomenon" (GA 61:53). Here Heidegger introduces the idea of an "ontological phenomenology" (GA 61:60) that will define his project through 1929. Having rejected traditional metaphysics, Heidegger will approach being exclusively through phenomenology—with reference to how being is evidentially given—thus by deepening the transcendental turn toward "the way such 'being' is understandable: the *meaning* of being" (GA 61:58). Heidegger holds that the full phenomenon of meaning/being does not have an intentional structure; it is rather, as Heidegger's intensive preoccupation with Aristotle in his Marburg years will reveal, an "opening" or temporal-horizonal framework that "situates" constituting subject and constituted object in Husserl's sense.

The attempt to grasp the phenomenon of meaning more originally than is possible in the theory of intentional consciousness led to crucial modifications in the understanding of philosophy's starting point. As early as 1921 Heidegger introduced the key that would allow *Being and Time* to break with the Cartesian conception of human being without abandoning the transcendental point of departure altogether. Instead of starting with a being who doubts, knows, and thus *posits* the world, Heidegger identifies the philosophically more primary sense in which the beginning philosopher is a *questioner*. To ask about the meaning of being is thus first to ask about the being of the one who raises the question, and that means, about the conditions for the possibility of raising questions at all. The systematic heart of *Being and Time* lies in the idea of a "preontological" understanding of being (*Seinsverständnis*) as the first such condition that any entity capable of raising the question of being must fulfill. For this reason Heidegger introduces "Dasein" as a *terminus technicus* to indicate that being for whom "in its very being that being is an issue for it," namely, a being for whom questioning is possible (GA 2:16/32).

Heidegger's project of "fundamental ontology," then, can be understood as one in which the philosopher tries to get clear about his or her own being insofar as that being makes it possible to raise the question of being in a fully "ontological" way, that is, to bring the preontological understanding of being into explicit philosophical comprehension. The "Analytic of Dasein" (a title that echoes Kant's "Analytic of Concepts" and announces itself as the successor to transcendental logic) is an attempt to articulate those categories (which Heidegger calls "existentials") that make possible not objects but meaning. On that basis, then, and mindful of the ontological difference between being and beings, one is in a position to raise the question of the meaning of being in an explicit, phenomenologically grounded, way.

Being and Time is thus conceived as a propaedeutic. That this propaedeutic can already be ontological knowledge, prior to answering the ontological question, is due to its phenomenological character as Heidegger understands it. For him, phenomenology is neither a school nor a method defined by arcane techniques but is the very way we come to understand ourselves in the course of our lives. This does not mean, however, that our ordinary ways of seeing things are to be taken at face value, or that the handed-down conceptions of being are simply to be cobbled together into a new theory. Rather, Heidegger (like Husserl) sees the task of phenomenology as one of bringing to light, making explicit, that which for the most part does not show itself—not because it is an inaccessible thing-in-itself, but because it is concealed by misinterpretation and by the very commonplaces of the tradition it supports. The process of phenomenology is thus "hermeneutic"; it interrogates our everyday understandings so as to reveal their experiential sources, interprets them so as to expose what they conceal, brings them into the fluidity of living thought.

Hence, in a historico-hermeneutic move that has little parallel in the more positivistic phenomenology of Husserl, the phenomenological method in *Being and Time* requires reflection on the history of philosophy, not in order to find precursors, but to deconstruct the categories that, in the present, conspire to veil the phenomena to which an inquiry into the meaning of being must attend. This "destruction of the history of ontology"—which was scheduled to appear as part 2 of *Being and Time*—thus has a positive aim, namely, to recover a sense for what was really at stake in traditional ontological inquiry and to reinvest its vocabulary (truth, being, logos, reason) with something of the evidential "force" it had in its original existential setting. Though this part of *Being and Time* was never published, some of the project was carried out piecemeal in the published pages, and, beginning with *Kant and the Problem of Metaphysics* (1929), Heidegger fulfilled its spirit in a series of critical reflections on figures in the history of metaphysics. The attempt to recover a concealed, but more authentic, impulse behind the official history of philosophy became increasingly important in Heidegger's thinking during the 1930s.

Being and Time offers a phenomenological reinterpretation of the being of human being (Dasein) such that both the ancient metaphysical concept of rational animal and the modern epistemological concept of a "subject" of representations are displaced. Against the view that holds reason to be the distinguishing mark of human being, Heidegger argues that human rationality is itself dependent on what he calls "care" (*Sorge*), a certain sort of self-relatedness irreducible to the metaphysical tradition's idea of self-consciousness. Care is reflected in the fact that my own being is an issue for me—that it matters to me. This cannot be explained in terms of my rational faculties alone, yet without such "care" those rational faculties would not find motive for their exercise. Both animality and rationality as traditionally understood can be clarified, as elements of Dasein, only by being derived phenomenologically from the structure of care.

The idea of structure here points to a crucial aspect of Heidegger's approach to Dasein; for care is not a property (even an essential property) of a substance—of human being—but rather a complex, articulated whole that makes possible those properties we can be said to have. Thus, *Being and Time* conceives care—the being (*Sein*) of human being—as a dynamic structure of "ways to be" (*Zu-sein*). Against the modern concept of subjectivity—which only repeats, on the level of reflection, the ancient tendency to think of being as what is present as an object—Heidegger argues that Dasein's mode of being is not that of a thing (whether object or subject), but existence (*Existenz*). Existence here is not the opposite of essence—the "that" as opposed to "what"—but signifies rather that Dasein "has its own being *to be*." In having it, it "has to be" it, has no choice but to take up its existing in one way or another precisely not as something given, whose meaning is determined once and for all, but as a "to be," as something that is always at issue (GA 2:56/67).

To say that Dasein "exists" is to say that it is primordially a "being possible." This does not mean that there is an ideal set of (logical or physical) possibilities that are consistent with Dasein as an actual being. Rather, it means that I always understand myself in terms of normative alternatives of success or failure. Socially, for example, I can be a citizen or a brother simply by fulfilling some institutional criteria; existentially, however, I can be these things only by continually succeeding (or failing) to live up to what being a brother or a citizen means. Existential possibility characterizes the very way existence is "mine," what it means to be oneself. As a function of *Existenz,* selfhood cannot be the simple identity or perdurance of a subject but is instead poised between the modalized alternatives (possibilities) of finding and holding oneself (which Heidegger calls "*Eigentlichkeit*") or of fleeing and losing oneself (which he calls "*Uneigentlichkeit*"). Such "authenticity" and "inauthenticity" are definitive of selfhood as such, and though they obviously involve a normative component, the evaluation they express is strictly speaking neither moral (which phrases evaluations in terms of the good or the right) nor aesthetic (which phrases evaluations in terms of the beautiful). To be authentic is to maintain oneself in a certain transparency with regard to the nature of one's own being—an understanding that selfhood has the character of a charge or responsibility and not a fixed ground—while to be inauthentic is to conceal this ungrounded quality of one's existence. Such existential concealment has complicated relations to moral, political, and other sorts of evaluation, but Heidegger says little about these in *Being and Time.*

The concept of authenticity has methodological significance and is intimately connected to those analyses of anxiety, death, conscience, and guilt that so impressed Heidegger's initial readers. Because Heidegger begins by describing Dasein in its everyday way of being—in which it is to a certain extent lost to itself, absorbed in the practical negotiation of its everyday affairs—it becomes necessary to show how it is possible for Dasein to come to an explicit understanding of its own being. To do this Heidegger explores those moments in which Dasein's everyday self-understanding is most radically challenged, its complacency most disturbed. In anxiety (*Angst*) this dislocation is accomplished in such a way that authentic self-understanding can be made explicit as an existential possibility (though it need not be). Only if it is, however, can the philosopher carry out the task of fundamental ontology, achieve the "transparency" necessary for making explicit the ontological structure of that being who is capable of raising the question of the meaning of being. Authenticity, a clear view of one's own being, is a condition of philosophy's possibility.

Authentic self-understanding grasps the finitude and situatedness of my being. To be situated is to see that the familiar and stable world that provides the unquestioned normative context of my everyday life is essentially contingent ("factic"), a historical, sociocultural milieu; while to be finite is to see that my own identity finally lies in the resoluteness (*Entschlossenheit*) with which I take responsibility for the choices I make in the clear-sighted acknowledgment of my "being toward death." With this the ultimate "horizon," the ultimate clarificatory framework for understanding the care structure of *Existenz,* comes into view. For what holds these possibilities together, makes them intelligible as a whole, is temporality (*Zeitlichkeit*). Dasein is radically temporal—not merely in time, as are all things, but rather "temporalizing," already in a world but always ahead of itself, pressing into possibilities. In temporalizing, Dasein clears a historically particular space in which things can show up, "present" themselves, as meaningful. At the limit of Heidegger's ontological phenomenology of the human being, then, is a kind of transcendental historicism: Historicality belongs to Dasein—hence to the very constitution of meaning—and selfhood itself has a narrative structure. Heidegger does not think that this sort of historicism implies thoroughgoing historical relativism, for if transcendental historicism recognizes relativity of meaning at the ontic level of particular historical and cultural traditions, as a phenomenological philosophy it also uncovers ontological structures that condition or account for such ontic relativization. The ultimate cogency of this distinction has been disputed, and Heidegger later seems to distance himself somewhat from it, tending toward a more radically historicized conception of philosophy.

Brief mention should be made of some principal features of Heidegger's description of Dasein in which his departure from traditional philosophical ideas becomes most evident. This departure is already clear when, in opposition to the Cartesian tradition and Husserlian phenomenology's presumed appeal to a "worldless" transcendental consciousness, Heidegger describes Dasein as being-in-the-world. *Being and Time* analyzes three mutually implicating aspects of this structure: worldhood, being-with, and being-in.

In one of his most celebrated contributions, Heidegger asks us to consider the being (worldhood) of the world. His analyses show that world cannot be understood as the collection of existing entities; it is not something pieced together out of independently existing things, but rather that in which and in terms of which these things show themselves as existing in one way or another. Thus (in his famous example) world is adumbrated in the workshop, which is itself no mere collection of tools but an organized context, or "referential totality," that remains a taken-for-granted background until such time as a tool in use (a hammer, say) breaks down. When the hammer becomes unserviceable, its references to other items in the workplace, oriented toward the work to be done (but now in danger of not getting done), become perspicuous to varying degrees. Even then I do not attain a "theoretical" grasp of the workplace as a well-defined object; its very mode of being—holistic and horizonal—precludes that.

While the workplace is a local context of meaning linked to specific practices of building, world is the ultimate context or horizon in which the practice or project of existing as such takes on significance. Thus world is prior to subject and object; these can emerge only as items *in* the world. Nor can the world be a system of representations grounded in a subject; representations arise only against the background of the world. As the workshop example makes plain, the worldhood of the world is not equivalent to the epistemological notion of an implicit theory (set of propositions) or categorial framework; it is rather linked to the skills and practices in which human beings are engaged in everyday life. Thus, the world belongs to a "form of life" in Wittgenstein's sense—a culturally and historically specific, normative, and finite horizon of intelligibility, the logically ungrounded space of meaning in which beings, entities, take on significance, show themselves as the things they are.

What Heidegger calls "being-with" (*Mitsein*) follows from the nature of the world of being-in-the-world. The world is shared "with" others. Against the solipsism and mentalism of the modern tradition, Heidegger insists that the "who" of Dasein, the self, is hopelessly misunderstood if one begins with an isolated subject whose mental life would be radically private. Heidegger argues that since all understanding takes place within the horizon of shared norms, practices, rules, and conventions that belong to the world, so too does any self-understanding. Thus, my identity is formed in terms of the roles I take up within a specific community, roles that, as social possibilities, are anonymous and typical. Practically, I understand myself not in terms of how I differ from others but in terms of how I do not differ from them: I do what one ordinarily does in specific circumstances. This is not an accident that somehow befalls a self that would otherwise have a presocial identity; rather, to speak of a self at all is to speak of a socialized self, which Heidegger calls "the they" or "one" (*das Man*). Because features of Dasein's being—including selfhood as being-with-others—are existential possibilities, however, a Kierkegaardian reversal of the traditional solipsistic problem emerges: The question is not how an individual subject transcends its solipsistic condition toward genuine encounter with the other; rather it is how an initially undifferentiated anonymous "they-self" can become individuated. At this point, Heidegger's phenomenology of the self connects with the previous remarks on authenticity: Individuation begins with the collapse, in anxiety, of the they-self and the intelligibility of its taken-for-granted way of doing things.

With Dasein described as being-in-the-world, some have found it strange that Heidegger does not offer a phenomenology of embodiment in *Being and Time*. The primary reason for this is that Heidegger is trying to conceptualize the being of human being prior to the traditional distinction between mind and body. Thus, just as Dasein is not consciousness but cannot for that reason be said to be "unconscious," so too, though Dasein does not "have" a body it cannot be said to be "disembodied." Heidegger holds that what it means to talk either of consciousness or of the body as aspects of human being cannot be properly determined without first explicating the essential categorial features of that being who questions (Dasein). What is ordinarily referred to with the term "body" is, of course, everywhere present in Heidegger's analyses (as in the famous example of wielding a hammer), but to explain Dasein by appeal to some category of embodiment is to put the cart before the horse. Nevertheless, in *The Metaphysical Foundations of Logic* (1928) Heidegger does propose to take up the question of embodiment. Under the heading of "metontology," philosophy is called upon to reflect on the natural and cosmological situatedness of human being. Because of the turn in his thinking, Heidegger never carried out the project of metontology.[1]

Finally, being-in-the-world can be conceived according to the character of its "in," the Da (here/there) of Dasein. Taking aim at the tradition that sees this phenomenon primarily in terms of consciousness viewed on the model of a subject knowing an object, Heidegger shows how consciousness, intentionality, itself derives from a more complex structure whose aspects he terms "disposition" (*Befindlichkeit*), "understanding" (*Verstehen*), and "discourse" (*Rede*). These aspects—which must ultimately be understood as modes of Dasein's temporality—together yield that space of meaning thanks to which both subjects and objects can be encountered.

"Disposition" signifies the ontological structure of moods. Moods reflect the way I find myself already in a world, my thrownness (*Geworfenheit*); they disclose the particular way the world as a whole matters to me. Moods are not subjective colorations laid over an objectively given world; they are essential constituents of meaning, and without them nothing in the world could make a claim on me. Disposition always goes together with a certain "understanding"—which signifies the previously discussed aspect of Dasein's "projection" of possibilities. Such projecting is not a thematic deliberating over alternatives, but that know-how whereby I negotiate my everyday affairs, an ability to be (*Seinkönnen*). Together, disposition and understanding figure a meaningful context that can be "articulated," that is, "interpreted" in the sense that within it particular things can be encountered meaningfully as something. This kind of meaning (the "hermeneutic as") is inherent in practice and does not depend on any explicit judgment on things (the "apophantic as"), but because "discourse" also belongs to Dasein's being-in, the practically articulated and interpreted world can be spoken about.

Disposition, understanding, and discourse together make up Dasein's disclosedness (*Erschlossenheit*). On the basis of his understanding of the Greek term for truth, *aletheia,* Heidegger finds disclosedness to be the phenomenologically primary meaning of truth. Propositional truth, correctness of statements, is seen as a function of Dasein's practical "uncovering" of entities, a mode of pointing out and determining entities through linguistic behavior. But since entities can show themselves as they are (or be taken as they are not) only within the previously "disclosed" horizon of meaning opened up with the structure of Dasein's being-in, propositional truth depends upon "truth" understood as this meaningful disclosure. Truth is thus an existential category of Dasein and so must exhibit the structure of existential possibility: Insofar as a specific space of meaning (world) is opened up through Dasein's practices, Dasein is "in the truth"; yet because these practices close off other possibilities and so other aspects of things, other ways to be, Dasein is also "in untruth." The ultimate "truth of existence," then, is achieved in "resoluteness," when authentic Dasein attains insight into its inescapable responsibility for the finite and historical meaning things take on thanks to its choices in the world.

2. From the Meaning of Being to the Truth of Being

After the publication of *Being and Time* (1927) and Heidegger's return to Freiburg as Husserl's successor (1929), the terms "phenomenology" and "ontology" appear less frequently in his work. German philosophy during this period was characterized by renewed interest in the problem of metaphysics—closely associated with the desire for a philosophical worldview to address a perceived crisis of values—and Heidegger's lectures and publications of the 1930s reflect this trend. In part this follows directly from *Being and Time*'s call for a destruction of the history of ontology. But the path is new in its attempt (as Heidegger later put it) to use the "language of metaphysics" to make the turn from Dasein's understanding of (the meaning of) being to being itself, thereby completing the break with modern subjectivism. From this effort there would emerge, at about mid-decade, the project of overcoming (*Überwindung*), and finally recovering from (*Verwindung*), metaphysics.

The previously mentioned idea of metontology—something like a *metaphysica specialis* in Kant's sense, a metaphysics of nature, of animal being, and the like—was one consequence of Heidegger's new interest. Another was the idea of a "basic mood" or attunement (*Grundstimmung*). Introduced in the 1929–30 lecture course "Fundamental Concepts of Metaphysics," it would play a significant role in Heidegger's thinking during the first half of the decade. This concept reveals a subtle shift of emphasis when compared with Heidegger's previous analysis of disposition. Where disposition, in particular as anxiety, had been seen primarily in its methodological significance as a condition for radical individuation, basic mood is taken primarily as a mode of being with one another, a historical and social phenomenon. Thus Heidegger can characterize the *Grundstimmung* of the German people of 1929–30 as boredom (*Langeweile*), his subsequent analysis of which provides the methodological basis for a situated grasp of the relation between philosophical thinking and its "time."

The most enduring legacy of Heidegger's efforts to transcend modern subjectivism by means of metaphysics, however, was the transformation of disclosedness—the meaningful space that *Being and Time* had analyzed in terms of Dasein's resolute projection of possibilities—into the "truth of being," the structure of clearing (concealing/revealing) that conditions metaphysical thinking without being recognized by it. Though not yet named, an important feature of this idea is prefigured in Heidegger's Plato lectures of 1931–32. According to Heidegger, Plato was the first to conceive being as Idea (eidos) and truth as *homoieosis,* conformity between the mind and being-as-Idea. The being of beings is thus reduced to a being, and truth (including metaphysical truth) is conceived as correct representation of such being. Thereafter, metaphysics becomes focused upon entities and not upon the truth of being itself, that openness or clearing (*aletheia*) in whose light all entities, including the Ideas, show themselves. Similarly, the lecture "On the Essence of Truth" (1930) identifies truth with the unconcealedness of the "totality of entities" (the theme of metaphysics), an unconcealedness that, in revealing entities, conceals its own unconcealing. Publishing the lecture only in 1943, Heidegger heavily revised it to suggest that what was implicitly at stake was already the "truth of being."

With the gradual emergence of the idea of the truth of being came a need to rethink the role played by human beings in what is increasingly seen as a *happening* of truth. Along one axis, then, the trajectory of Heidegger's thinking between 1929 and the year 1945, when the Allies refused him the right to teach for his activities during the Nazi period, can be understood as a continual reflection upon, and revision of, the idea of authenticity as resoluteness. More specifically, Heidegger sought to grasp resoluteness as a response (*entsprechen*) to a claim (*Anspruch*) of being. This problem surfaces in his lectures on Kant's practical philosophy, Hegel's phenomenology, and Aristotle's metaphysics (all delivered between 1930 and 1932) and comes to pointed expression in Heidegger's rectoral address when, in 1933, he became the first Nazi rector of the University of Freiburg. There Heidegger combines language currently in use by Nazi ideologues with terminology deriving from *Being and Time* and early Greek philosophy (notably Heraclitus) to give political content to the idea of the "truth" of a people, a destiny deriving from being itself that calls for decisive action and "leadership" ungrounded in (unconstrained by) "ideas and concepts." By 1945, however, the voluntaristic strain in this conception of the relation of human being to being has given way to images of shepherding and to the idea of "letting be" as "releasement" (*Gelassenheit*).

Heidegger's tenure as rector was short and, for him, extremely disillusioning. The effects of this, and the relation between his politics and his philosophy, are topics of much debate. Regarding the question of the truth of being, however, there are clear differences between writings from the years just after the rectorate—such as the first lectures on Hölderlin (1934–35), *Introduction to Metaphysics* (1935), and "The Origin of the Work of Art" (1936)—and those belonging to the later 1930s and 1940s (especially the 1936 *Beiträge zur Philosophie* [*Vom Ereignis*], the 1936–40 lectures on Nietzsche, the new lectures on Hölderlin of 1941–42, and the 1942–44 lectures on Parmenides and Heraclitus). In the earlier set Heidegger still invokes will and decision and calls upon resolute Dasein to take responsibility for instituting (*Stiftung*) the space of truth or meaning. In the later set, however, and especially in the protracted struggle with Nietzsche, the very idea of will, of self-assertion and action, comes in for criticism.

In the earlier Hölderlin lectures, for example, Heidegger modifies his previous analysis of truth as disclosedness by introducing the notion of a primal leap (*Ur-sprung*), a historically originary decision or founding act that provides a people with its "destiny" or truth, those measures whereby it distinguishes what is for it great or small, noble or base, meaningful or meaningless. Thus truth—the normative horizon within which a people arrives at its judgments—is made to turn on the creative (*dichterisch*) originating act of those whom Hölderlin calls "demigods" and among whom Heidegger counts not only poets and thinkers, but political leaders as well. Given the historical circumstances, Hölderlin's poetry comes to be read as a call to the Germans to inaugurate "another" truth or normative order in essential tension with the first one established in the West by the Greeks.

In the mid-1930s Heidegger is thus preoccupied with the relation of Greece to Germany, that is, with the putative demand that resolute German thinkers and leaders take responsibility for the destiny of the West. As the 1935 lecture course, *Introduction to Metaphysics,* argues, the Greek beginning—in which the essence of truth as unconcealedness is forgotten in favor of correctness and in which being is forgotten in favor of beings—has now shown itself as nihilism. To that heritage—the "rational" and ordered world that has led to Germany's fate, clamped between the pincers of soulless America and totally mobilized Russia—the thinker must stand decisively opposed, in the name of what remains concealed in it. Here Heidegger's interpretation of the first chorus of Sophocles' *Antigone* takes on political resonance when, in conclusion, Heidegger claims that "the works that are being peddled about nowadays as the philosophy of National Socialism" have "nothing whatever to do with the inner truth and greatness of this movement." When the lecture was published in 1953, Heidegger glossed "this movement" as "the encounter between global technology and modern man," thereby introducing themes that come to prominence only in a later phase of his thinking (GA 40:208/199).[2]

That later phase, with its critique of the voluntaristic idea that will—resolute, rationally ungrounded decision—creatively contributes to opening up the truth of being, is prefigured in his massive *Beiträge* (1936–38). Here Heidegger rethinks the major themes from *Being and Time* and after, though now the point is not to grasp being from the perspective of Dasein's understanding of being but to situate Dasein within what he now calls the "truth of being" (*Wahrheit des Seyns*). This turn (*Kehre*) is reflected in the strategy of the Nietzsche lectures delivered between 1936 and 1940 (which, along with the Parmenides and Heraclitus lectures of 1942–44, Heidegger claimed to involve an implicit critique of Nazi ideology "for those who had ears to hear"—a claim that has proved controversial). In these lectures Heidegger tries to show that Nietzsche, the great antimetaphysician, was in fact the "last metaphysician of the West." Both Nietzsche and Heidegger present nihilism—the late modern sense that things as a whole lack meaning and value—as the outcome of metaphysical thinking. But whereas Nietzsche believes that nihilism arises because metaphysics ties meaning and value to a static "being" beyond the world of becoming and offers his doctrine of the will to power as a postmetaphysical answer to nihilism, Heidegger glosses the latter as mere "will to will," itself the last chapter of metaphysics and hence a form of nihilism. The basis for this is his view that metaphysics is an inquiry that conceals the truth of being, a concealing accomplished in Nietzsche's term "will to power" as the ultimate subjectivistic substitutional name for being. The issue that dominates Heidegger's last phase, then, is how to open a path to a genuine overcoming of metaphysics and so "another beginning" for thinking, one that would emphasize a listening, waiting attitude of questioning and reflection (*Besinnung*) in contrast to the Nietzschean will to will. Against nihilism, what Heidegger will come to call "thinking" (in decisive opposition to "philosophy") must seek—tentatively, questioningly—what Hölderlin called "a measure on earth."

3. Beyond Being

In the final phase of his thinking Heidegger follows out the logic of his project of deconstructing and overcoming metaphysics—seen now as the history of being (*Seinsgeschichte*)—to the point where its guiding terms, "being" and "truth," are themselves deemed unsuitable for naming the topic that provokes a new way, another beginning, for thought, namely, *Ereignis*. This term is meant to suggest that "event" whereby "there is" the ontological difference between being and beings. Prior to both being and time, *Ereignis* grants or gives both (*es gibt Sein, es gibt Zeit*). Heidegger's postmetaphysical thinking nevertheless still draws upon the "essential help of phenomenological seeing,"[3] which, in counterpoint to the technological ordering of all reality that is the heritage of metaphysics, he cultivates explicitly in a series of essays devoted to recovering the poetic possibilities in mundane things.

Though its roots lie earlier, this last phase begins publicly with the 1947 "Letter on Humanism," which marks Heidegger's return to publication after the silence of the war years. Here Heidegger is at pains to distinguish his project from then-current existentialism. Refusing to assimilate his earlier work to a humanism that places man or "human existence" at the center of philosophy—as had Sartre's interpretation of *Being and Time*—Heidegger insists that the task is to think being itself and to determine the human only on the basis of such essential thinking. In Heidegger's view *Being and Time* already indicated the need to make this turn, but his subsequent thought failed, he now believes, because it remained too dependent on the "language of metaphysics." In his emphasis on will and decision, for example, the disclosure of a normative meaningful space, or world, remained tied to the very metaphysical subjectivism Heidegger criticized in Nietzsche. As a result, the theme of language itself, first explored in the lectures on Hölderlin, emerges as central in Heidegger's essays from the 1950s. To overcome metaphysics, to think the truth of being in a non- (or post-) metaphysical way, a new relation to language is required. In the "Letter on Humanism," language is identified as the "house of being," and the image of human being as language user is displaced by the image of human being as one who "dwells" in the house, one who is the "shepherd" of being. In subsequent essays Heidegger emphasizes the proximity of postphilosophical "thinking" (as the response of the thinker to the call or claim of language) and the primordial "saying" of poetry.

By the end of this phase, as can be seen in the 1962 essay on "Time and Being" and the 1964 essay "The End of Philosophy and the Task of Thinking," Heidegger finally comes to reject all efforts at overcoming metaphysics. If the task of thinking is to think (the meaning of) being itself, this can only be done in light of that event (*Ereignis*) whereby "there is" being. Metaphysics, in contrast, always thinks being in light of beings, that is, as the being *of* beings. The very interest in overcoming this tendency (including Heidegger's own earlier preoccupation with the ontological difference) is now seen to keep thought in thrall to beings. Hence, in a line that anticipates some of the themes of Derridean deconstruction, Heidegger argues that one should "cease all overcoming and leave metaphysics to itself."[4] Heidegger is thus led to abandon the metaphysical language he had sought to reappropriate for his "other" thinking. With pointed reference to the method of phenomenological seeing, which nourishes itself upon the clearing (*Lichtung*) that grants and enables such seeing, Heidegger argues that while metaphysics has always thought about what shows up in the clearing—namely, beings—it "knows nothing of this clearing itself." More precisely, clearing must here be thought verbally as opening, and the philosophical term "truth" (*aletheia*) does no more than name it while remaining blind to its character. Hence, the clearing cannot be called the "truth" of being, and the "question of the *aletheia,* of the unconcealedness as such, is not the question of truth." Reflecting on the matter of thought, then, leads Heidegger to replace the metaphysical terms of his earlier project—"being" and "time"—by the postmetaphysical "clearing" (*Lichtung*) and "presence" (*Anwesenheit*).[5]

The character of such thinking can be gauged more concretely in the essays of the 1950s converging around the themes of technology and language. Heidegger sees the essence of modern technology as the "completion" of metaphysics, that is, as an event of truth in the history of being, an enframing (*Gestell*), or that horizon of meaningfulness in which all things show themselves finally as standing reserve (*Bestand*) for manipulation. Following Hölderlin, Heidegger calls this the "gravest danger" to humanity—not because it yields the means for destroying the planet (though this is dangerous enough, and true enough), but because it signals the concealment of the very meaningfulness of the question concerning its own limits—in the positivistic denial, for example, that the question of being has any meaning at all. Against this, Heidegger understands Hölderlin's claim (that where the "gravest danger" is, there also the "saving power grows") to mean that the counterpoint to the hegemony of technological thinking is to be sought in poetic language—not as aesthetic refinement but as poiesis, which like its cousin techne is an event of truth. Technological thinking leads to the contradictory conception whereby "man" is both lord of the earth (resolutely manipulating all things according to his own measure) and a kind of virtual reality or function of the system at various levels. In his 1962 interview with the magazine *Der Spiegel,* Heidegger claims that "only a god can save us" from this situation, but in the 1950s he sought a healing measure in the word of the poets. Why? Above all it is because in the poetic word a hidden aspect of our relation to language becomes audible.

In essays from the 1950s, as part of his "antihumanistic" attempt to decenter modern subjectivism, Heidegger rejects the view that language is a "tool" that is "used" by man. Again following hints in Hölderlin, he proposes that it is not man but language that should be thought originally to speak. Human speech is therefore at bottom an *ent-sprechen,* a co-responding to the Saying that has always already spoken. One may think here, in a less exalted vein, of Gadamer's idea of tradition. As Heidegger suggests in a series of reflections on the poets George, Trakl, Rilke, and Hölderlin, it is the poet whose response is the most adequate (*angemessen*), most attentive, to the call of language. Far from being a willful creation of something new and subjectively expressive, poetry arises as a deep response to what speaks in the silent Saying of language—a response which Heidegger calls "measure-taking" (*Maß-nahme*), that which registers the measure of what it means for us to be. The thinker's task is to follow up thoughtfully, in a meditative dwelling on meaning (*Besinnung*), the taking of our measure in the poem. To what end? Here, finally, the aim of another related series of essays from the 1950s becomes clear, those in which Heidegger tries to rethink the meaning of the earth.

Essays like "The Thing" (1950), "Building, Dwelling, Thinking" (1951), and "Language" (1951) reveal a phenomenological sensibility informed by a vocabulary derived from Heidegger's encounter with the poets, especially Hölderlin. With their talk of the fourfold (earth, heavens, mortals, divinities) that takes place as a roundelay or mirror play, many have seen in these essays little more than an attempt at mythmaking and a nostalgic yearning for the world of the Black Forest peasant at the moment when that world has decisively disappeared. Yet if one reads them in the spirit of phenomenological seeing and description, which Heidegger never abandoned in practice even if he abandoned it as a designation for his project, one may discern a keen attention to the way that the most ordinary things can continue to address us even in their very unobtrusiveness. Heidegger hopes to reawaken a sense for what *things* are (or mean) that is concealed, deeply but not perhaps irrevocably, in the technological contexts of contemporary life. Reversing the order of *Being and Time*—where the "thing" is seen as a derivative mode of the tool and the tool is relativized to Dasein's projects in the world as a totality of involvements (*Bewandtnisganzes*)—the essay on "The Thing" reflects on how it is precisely the thing's own "thinging" that "gathers" and organizes a world (the roundelay of the fourfold). A simple jug thus does not disappear into its use but is seen as a particular way of bringing together earth, heavens, mortals, and divinities. Reflection on a bridge in the essay on "Building, Dwelling, Thinking" moves in the same direction, toward phenomenological recovery of a kind of being (dwelling) attuned to measures other than those accorded value in the metaphysical matrix of meaning that is the essence of the technological world. Thinking, then, listens or hearkens to the traces of what remains hidden, for the most part, in the self-assertion of technological planning, a releasement (*Gelassenheit*) or "letting be" that does no more than "bring to word" what speaks in the primordial poem of the world. To that extent, then, even the later Heidegger does nothing more than seek a way "back to the things themselves" (Husserl's phenomenological slogan) and, in letting them speak, remains committed to the possibility of phenomenology.

12

Metaphysics, Metontology, and the End of *Being and Time*

1. Introduction

The term "end" in the title of this chapter should be understood in three senses:

1. Heidegger's unfinished book concludes in section 83 with a series of questions that are to prepare the way for the sequel, an interpretation of the meaning of being in terms of time. This preparation consists, strangely enough, in questioning the appropriateness of the method used in the previous four hundred or so pages. The analysis of Dasein's ontological structure is, Heidegger now reminds us, "only *one way* which we may take."[1] Indeed, "whether this is the *only* way or even the right one at all can be decided *only after one has gone along it.*" At the end of *Being and Time,* then, can we say whether the path has been the right one? Only if we know what was to be accomplished by its means—hence, a second sense of "end."

2. The end, or aim, of *Being and Time* is perhaps best understood through a comparison that Heidegger himself increasingly employed in the later 1920s, namely, with Kant's *Critique of Pure Reason,* which Kant described as "a treatise on the method, not a system of the science itself."[2] "Method" in this transcendental sense means demonstrating the conditions of possibility for synthetic a priori knowledge, preliminary to working out a system of such knowledge. Construing Kant's synthetic a priori knowledge as "ontological knowledge," Heidegger views transcendental critique as a reflection on the "ontological ground" of ontology. Similarly, the aim of *Being and Time* is to lay the groundwork for ontological knowledge (of the "meaning of being"), but in place of Kant's focus upon the cognitive comportment of *judging*, Heidegger turns first to the interrogative comportment of raising the *question* of being. Where Kant locates the ground of ontological knowledge in "a priori synthesis," Heidegger locates it in the understanding of being (*Seinsverständnis*) presupposed in all questioning. For this reason the focus of reflection falls on "Dasein," a *terminus technicus* indicating that being who, in a prephilosophical way, necessarily raises questions about its own being and thereby provides the inescapable starting point for philosophical inquiry, "the point where it *arises* and to which it *returns*" (GA 2:576, 51/487, 62). But if, given the aim of showing how ontological knowledge is possible, Dasein has a peculiar claim on our attention, by the end of *Being and Time* Heidegger detects a "fundamental problem that still remains 'veiled' " (GA 2:576/487). For if the possibility of ontological knowledge lies in Dasein's *prephilosophical* understanding of being, must not any such knowledge be limited to the particular, finite perspective occupied by the questioner? Heidegger has all along acknowledged—indeed emphasized—that philosophical inquiry is nothing but a "radicalization" of that everyday yet "essential" tendency that Dasein has to question the meaning of its being and that thus his own inquiry is ultimately "ontically rooted [*verwurzelt*]" (GA 2:20, 18/35, 34). But when Heidegger asks whether "ontology allows of being *ontologically* grounded [*begründen*], or rather requires in addition an *ontic* ground [*Fundamentes*]," he cannot be referring to the previously described priority of Dasein, for he immediately appends the further question, "and *which* entity must take on this function of grounding?" This question would make no sense if "ontic ground" merely referred to Dasein, the inquirer, as the inescapable starting point for philosophy (GA 2:576/487). It appears rather that when Heidegger asks for an "entity" in which to ground ontological knowledge, he stands poised to make a move that has since become familiar in philosophy, namely, to relativize such knowledge to some aspect of the context in which it arises. To ascribe a grounding function to the entity, "nature," for example, might yield something like that naturalism that seeks to explain ontological knowledge in terms of causal relations between environment and brain states. Similarly, to embrace the entity, "history," as such a ground might yield a kind of historicism in which the content of one's thought, one's ontological knowledge, is explained with reference to the conceptual resources of one's historical milieu.[3] Other candidates for the grounding entity could be proposed—society, language, even God—but the fact that in entertaining the possibility of an ontic ground of ontology Heidegger must ask "which" entity or context is to serve this function signals a methodological crisis that threatens *Being and Time*'s aim of making the transition from Dasein's understanding of being to the meaning of being. Hence, a final sense of "end."

3. The end of *Being and Time* also means the collapse of its project, the demise of fundamental ontology. What happened? Why was the announced sequel to *Being and Time* never published? This question, deeply entwined with the problem of the so-called turn (*Kehre*) in Heidegger's thinking, has occasioned much commentary. Our angle on it shall be established by the observation that at first the idea of a turn was immanent to the project of *Being and Time* itself; only later did it take on, in Heidegger's self-interpretation, the status of a turn away from that project, a rejection of its grasp on the problem. Though examining the immanent turn suggests an interpretation of the turn in the broader sense, that is not my main quarry. Instead, I shall show how the immanent turn at the end of *Being and Time* gets entangled with the very different issue of an "ontic ground" of ontology. To ask why Heidegger imagines that there should be an ontic ground of ontology is to expose a latent inconsistency in his magnum opus. Though I analyze this inconsistency in terms of an opposition between phenomenology and metaphysics (the terms in which Heidegger formulates the turn), the problem can be seen to have far wider provenance. For "phenomenology" here represents that aspect of Heidegger's project that adheres to the critical-transcendental formulation of philosophical questions, whereas "metaphysics"—the heading under which an ontic ground is sought—turns out to be a virtual cipher for any appeal to "contextualizing" discourses with pretensions to provide independent grounds for the transcendental problematic.

Though Heidegger did not immediately grasp the problem—indeed, he places great weight on his conviction that "ontology can only be founded ontically," a fact that "no one before me has explicitly seen or stated"—the collapse of his project results from the inconsistent belief that a turn is to be made from phenomenology to metaphysics.[4] Kept at bay in *Being and Time* (1927), this inconsistency comes glaringly to light in an appendix to Heidegger's last Marburg lecture course, *The Metaphysical Foundations of Logic* (1928). In order to complete his project, Heidegger here demands something called "metontology," a "turning around [*Kehre*], where ontology itself expressly runs back into the metaphysical ontic in which it implicitly always remains" (GA 26:201/158). To ask what metontology could be is to uncover the precise point where phenomenological and metaphysical (pretranscendental) motifs confront one another. This confrontation occupies Heidegger for a decade until, conceding in effect that appeal to an ontic ground involves what Kant calls "transcendental illusion," he formulates his idea for overcoming (*Überwindung, Verwindung*) metaphysics. Since Heidegger often seems to suggest that overcoming metaphysics leaves important aspects of the phenomenological project in place, it might be said that *Being and Time* did not altogether collapse and that Heidegger continued in the spirit of the claim that "only as phenomenology is ontology possible" (GA 2:48/60).

2. The Language of Metaphysics

Perhaps the best way of introducing the argument is to consider some famous passages in which Heidegger explains why *Being and Time* was never completed. In his 1947 "Letter on Humanism," he writes that the crucial section on "Time and Being," in which the immanent turn was to be made, was "held back because thinking failed in the adequate saying of this turning and did not succeed with the help of the language of metaphysics" (GA 9:328/231).[5] Crucially, the "and" here indicates that the thinking that failed did not already employ the language of metaphysics; rather, at a certain moment it turned to the language of metaphysics for help. The "and" thus distinguishes two distinct phases of Heidegger's thought: On the one hand, the thinking that failed employed the vocabulary of hermeneutic phenomenology, as in the published portion of *Being and Time;* on the other hand, the unhelpful language of metaphysics was the traditional Kantian-Leibnizian-Aristotelian language (specifically excluded from *Being and Time* in favor of its notorious neologisms) that Heidegger began to speak around 1928 and that he once more abandoned in the mid-1930s, when he called for overcoming metaphysics. Theodore Kisiel has labeled the years between 1916 and 1927 as Heidegger's "phenomenological decade"; I suggest that the years between 1927 and 1937 are Heidegger's "metaphysical decade."[6]

Though crucial to my argument, this reading of the conjunction as indicating two distinct phases of Heidegger's thought is not universally shared. Typically, the reference to metaphysics is understood to include the whole transcendental project of *Being and Time.* So Jean Grondin writes that "what the 'Letter on Humanism' teaches or confirms is that *Being and Time* fails to say this *Kehre,* remaining in a certain respect prisoner of the horizon of the intelligibility of metaphysics"[7]—an interpretation suggested by the later Heidegger's tendency to see the entire tradition, including his earlier thought, as part of the "history of metaphysics" that needs to be overcome. Yet precisely in our passage Heidegger seems interested in preserving a nuance of difference. More revealing is David Krell's remark that immediately following the publication of *Being and Time* Heidegger "still hopes to rejoin" the "tradition of metaphysics" in a "positive and fruitful way"—implying a certain distance between *Being and Time* and that tradition.[8] Having noted that in *Being and Time* the term "metaphysics" almost always occurs in scare quotes, Joanna Hodge captures the decisive point: After *Being and Time* Heidegger is "trying to retrieve a *disquotational* use of the term 'metaphysics.' "[9] To support my reading of the conjunction, then, a brief look at the "quotational" use in *Being and Time* is necessary.

As we have seen, the tension between metaphysics and phenomenology in Heidegger's thought goes back to his student years, when metaphysics was associated above all with neo-Scholasticism and its defense of Aristotelian realism against neo-Kantian epistemological idealism. In the debate over whether logic and theory of knowledge presupposed a metaphysics of the object, a theory of "ontological truth," Heidegger took the critical side.[10] Though Heidegger did not think that critical philosophy presupposed a metaphysics, he did believe that it *led* to one: Transcendental theory of knowledge is to be completed by "an ultimate metaphysical-teleological interpretation of consciousness" (GA 1:406).[11] Rather than developing such a metaphysics, however, between 1917 and 1927 Heidegger worked at the transformation of phenomenology into a "hermeneutics of facticity," an ontology intended as an immanent development of the critical-transcendental impulse. Even Heidegger's renewed interest in Aristotle during this period should not be seen as an attempt to revive metaphysics but to recover a more phenomenological kind of questioning concealed by the Scholastic tradition. Thus, while the project of *Being and Time* may be interpreted as a "repetition" or retrieval of Aristotle's "first philosophy,"[12] that retrieval casts itself as a transcendental inquiry opposed to then-current conceptions of metaphysics. Following Husserl, Heidegger saw phenomenological method as a liberation from traditional metaphysical pseudoproblems: mind-body dualism, doubts about the external world, realism/idealism debates, and so on. In *Being and Time* the term "ontology" does not "indicate some definite philosophical discipline standing in interconnection with others"; nor does it "have to measure up to the tasks of some discipline that has been presented beforehand" (GA 2:37/49). Further, method demands that ontological language be scrutinized for metaphysical prejudices through a deconstruction (*Destruktion*) of the history of ontology. As in Husserl's transcendental phenomenology, such traditional preconceptions are to be put out of play.

There are two main reasons, then, why *Being and Time* surrounds the term "metaphysics" with scare quotes. First, it serves notice that Heidegger's project is not to be confused with the popular postwar turn from critical neo-Kantianism toward neo-Hegelianism, *Lebensphilosophie,* and the like; and second, it points toward a new sort of inquiry whose nature can be established only on the ground of Heidegger's transcendental-phenomenological project. An example of the first is found in the claim that the question of being has been forgotten "even though in our time we deem it progressive to give our approval to 'metaphysics' again" (GA 2:4/21), and the second in the claim that "what might be discussed under the topic of a 'metaphysic of death' lies outside the domain of an existential analytic of death" and presupposes "an understanding . . . of the ontology of the aggregate of entities as a whole" (GA 2:330/292). We shall see that the intelligibility of metontology hinges on whether the "language of metaphysics" can help articulate what an inquiry into this "aggregate of entities as a whole" might be.

If it is therefore plausible to suggest that the "and" in Heidegger's 1947 recollection indicates a distinction, important to his thought in 1927, between phenomenology and metaphysics, it becomes possible to argue that the collapse of *Being and Time* has less to do with phenomenology than with what proved to be a transitory positive evaluation of metaphysics. Yet the same recollection also seems to preclude the claim that Heidegger resolved the inconsistency in *Being and Time* by overcoming metaphysics in favor of phenomenology, for it suggests that the hermeneutic phenomenology of *Being and Time* failed. But what about it failed? Is there evidence for how we should understand the failure, especially given Heidegger's statement that "the thinking that hazards a few steps in *Being and Time* has even today not advanced beyond that publication," or that "the road it has taken remains even today a necessary one"?[13] A clue is found in Heidegger's explanation that "in the poverty of its first breakthrough" the sort of thinking at work in *Being and Time* failed because it did not yet "succeed in retaining the essential help of phenomenological seeing while dispensing with the inappropriate concern with 'science' and 'research' " (GA 9:357/258–59). The "concern with 'science' and 'research,' " it seems, and not with "phenomenological seeing," spoils the project of *Being and Time.*

It would be a lengthy task to unpack this statement fully, but for the contrast between phenomenology and metaphysics it is not necessary to do so. Decisive is the connection between phenomenological "seeing" and the idea of *grounding* philosophical practice and discourse in the matter (*die Sache*) that calls for and authorizes thinking. Heidegger's appeal to phenomenological seeing recalls Husserl's "principle of all principles" underlying the phenomenological theory of *Evidenz:* "Every originary presentative intuition is a legitimizing source of cognition" such that "everything originarily . . . offered to us in 'intuition' is to be accepted simply as what it is presented as being, but also only within the limits in which it is presented there" (Hua III:52/44). The force of this principle for Husserl is to insist that grounding or justification in philosophy ultimately lies in direct confrontation, however achieved, with the matters in question and not in dialectical or logical theory construction concerning these matters, however useful or even indispensable they may at times be. Though Heidegger criticizes Husserl's view of evidence in various ways—challenging the reliance on visual metaphors, bringing out its interpretive structure—it remains a significant element of his thinking to the end of his life.[14] In contrast, as I shall now argue, Heidegger's transitory positive evaluation of metaphysics after *Being and Time* results from an "inappropriate concern with 'science' and 'research,' " an *esprit de système* that originates in his renewed enthusiasm for Kant and brings to the surface a latent inconsistency in *Being and Time* between phenomenological and metaphysical senses of "ground." What leads Heidegger's project astray is its flirtation with a "disquotational" sense of metaphysics largely motivated by his desire to find a successor discipline—a "metaphysical ontic" or "metontology"—to the dogmatic metaphysics ruled out by Kant's transcendental dialectic. Perhaps this too was a consequence of his long-standing desire to effect a rapprochement between Kant and Aristotle—though a regrettable one.

3. Ontology and Metontology

It was noted above that between 1926 and 1929 Heidegger came increasingly to view his project in Kantian terms. In particular, in his *Kant and the Problem of Metaphysics* (1929, based on a lecture course from WS 1927–28), Heidegger tied Kant's transcendental project (and so also his own) to the distinction between *metaphysica generalis* and *metaphysica specialis*. The former indicates transcendental inquiry into the ground of ontological knowledge, while the latter is the system of such knowledge: rational psychology, cosmology, and theology. In contrast to the previously cited statement from *Being and Time,* according to which phenomenological ontology does not need to "measure up to the tasks of some discipline that has been presented beforehand," Heidegger's eagerness to see his project as a retrieval (*Wiederholung*) (GA 3:220/154) of Kant's now exerts pressure toward "system" on that very project. For instance, according to Kant's transcendental dialectic, *metaphysica specialis* proves to rest on a "transcendental illusion" (*Schein*) and cannot yield any genuine theoretical knowledge.[15] Because Heidegger views *Being and Time* as carrying out Kant's Copernican turn at the deeper level of "Dasein's finitude" (GA 3:232/163) and thus as roughly congruent with the task of *metaphysica generalis,* he must take a stand on the dialectic's negative judgment on the possibility of *metaphysica specialis.*

The conclusion of the Kant book hints at taking such a stand. Having identified *Being and Time* with a retrieval of the problematic of the transcendental analytic, Heidegger asks whether, "by extension," he should not also be able to retrieve "a positive problematic" in the apparently purely negative "characteristic of the Transcendental Dialectic." In a series of elliptical remarks he suggests that what Kant identified as "transcendental appearance [*Schein*]" or illusion needs to be rethought in light of *Being and Time*'s theory of truth, such that the "infinitude" presupposed in raising the question of Dasein's finitude can itself be brought into focus (GA 3:245–46/172). Thus, while sharing Kant's strictures against dogmatic metaphysics (he does not deny that transcendental appearance is an illusion, for example, calling it "transcendental untruth"), Heidegger nevertheless demands a reassessment of the dialectic, one that entertains the possibility of some sort of *metaphysica specialis,* some legitimate form of metaphysical inquiry. Heidegger's turn to the language of metaphysics for help in completing the project of *Being and Time* seems intended to occupy the terrain opened up by his reassessment of the transcendental dialectic. For having liberated this metaphysical problematic from "that architectonic into which Kant forced it," it becomes possible for Heidegger to imagine that reflection on "infinitude" might stand in a hermeneutical relationship to the analysis of Dasein's finitude from which it sprang, thus providing a "metaphysical" ground for ontology. And just here we encounter the puzzling idea of metontology.

When Heidegger introduces metontology a further connection with Kant's transcendental dialectic becomes explicit. He distinguishes broadly between *Being and Time*'s ontological inquiry (*metaphysica generalis*) and another sort of inquiry, a "new investigation" that "resides in the essence of ontology itself and is the result of its overturning [*Umschlag*], its μεταβολή," namely, "metontology," a "special problematic which has for its proper theme beings as a whole [*das Seiende im Ganzen*]" (GA 26:199/157). Kant's transcendental dialectic is concerned precisely with inquiry into beings as a whole—that is, with reason's claim to be able to grasp the "totality" of a series of conditions for every conditioned.[16] But where Kant judges metaphysics cognitively wanting in this pretense, Heidegger, thanks to his reassessment of the dialectic, seems to believe that an inquiry that "makes beings thematic in their totality in light of ontology" (GA 26:200/157)—hence an inquiry with the *scope* of *metaphysica specialis*—is possible after all. Significantly, metontology cannot simply be equated with the immanent turn called for in *Being and Time,* since that turn was intended not as an overturning (*Umschlag*) of ontology but as a move, *within* ontology, from Dasein's understanding of being to the meaning of being itself. Even though it is to be developed "in light of ontology" (that is, phenomenology), metontology must be a new *kind* of inquiry. As David Wood has argued, the idea of an inquiry into beings as a whole can arise only because "Heidegger thinks through again the idea of fundamental ontology."[17] Because this rethinking exploits an inconsistency in *Being and Time,* however, Heidegger's attempt to rescue metaphysics from Kant's transcendental dialectic fails—or so I shall argue.

One clue to how metontology is supposed to relate to ontology is found in Heidegger's 1928 characterization of the project of *Being and Time.* Because it aimed solely at elucidating Dasein's "understanding of being," the "analysis of the existence of Dasein" was neither an "anthropology nor an ethics." It focused instead upon Dasein "prior to every factual concretion," thus with a "peculiar neutrality" regarding a whole host of questions that, Heidegger now suggests, would fall within the scope of a "metaphysics of Dasein"—questions, for example, of sex and gender, embodiment, historical particularization, sociocultural dispersal, and entanglement in "what we call 'nature' in the broadest sense" (GA 26:171–74/136–38). This suggests that the metaphysics of Dasein would be a chapter within metontology as an inquiry into beings as a whole—a return to *homo humanus* that appears very much like the philosophical anthropology with which *Being and Time* is still too often confused.[18] However, this return is complicated by the fact that Heidegger, turning to the "language of metaphysics" for help, has significantly transformed the question he is asking.

During his Aristotelian-Husserlian phenomenological decade, Heidegger held the basic question of philosophy to be ontological: What is the *meaning* of being? Against this, Max Scheler objected that philosophy begins with the "absolute wonder" that "there is anything at all and not nothing," and this Leibnizian question—Why is there something rather than nothing?—comes to dominate Heidegger's metaphysical decade.[19] Yet it stands in a certain tension with the central argument of *Being and Time.*[20] For instance, if the question asks after a reason or ground "for" beings as a whole, in *Being and Time* this ground can only be understood transcendentally. Being, "that which determines entities as entities," is that "on the basis of which entities are already *understood*"; further, this "being of entities is not itself an entity" and so not a ground in the ontic sense, an *ens realissimum* or totality of entities of any kind (GA 2:8/25–26). The completion of *Being and Time* was to involve a turn from Dasein's understanding of being to the meaning of being; hence it was to remain within the scope of a ground of meaning. But Heidegger's new question appears suspiciously like the search for an ontic "explanation" for beings as a whole, one that threatens to annul his genuine insight into the difference between being (meaning) and beings. The question of why there is something rather than nothing thus forces a confrontation between a transcendental (ontological or phenomenological) and a metaphysical concept of grounding, and "metontology" names the confusion of the two.

The whole problem is that it is not at all clear what status an *inquiry* into beings as a whole could have within the framework of *Being and Time.* The care with which that text handles the question of bringing Dasein into view "as a whole"[21] might lead us to expect an equally gingerly approach to questions of metaphysical totalities. After all, Kant did not deny that we somehow *think* of ourselves as belonging within what is as a whole; indeed, he analyzed various experiences (e.g., the sublime) in which that sense overcomes us. He denied only that we could rationally inquire into the "whole of what is." So if Heidegger is to give a positive sense to the idea of metaphysical inquiry, he owes an account, consistent with *Being and Time,* of how metaphysical totalities can be comprehended sufficiently to be inquired into.[22] Some natural candidates for such an account present themselves; none, however, can stand up to scrutiny.

First, the idea of an inquiry into *das Seiende im Ganzen* as the ontic context for a metaphysics of Dasein clearly tracks Heidegger's new interest in something like philosophical *cosmology,* stimulated by Max Scheler's work. As Pöggeler argues, "[I]t was through impulses from Scheler's question concerning man's place in the cosmos that Heidegger was led to recontextualize his fundamental ontology in a metontology or metaphysical ontic."[23] But if Heidegger shared with Scheler the desire to "risk again the step into authentic metaphysics," he judged the latter's own attempt a failure—not "authentic" metaphysical inquiry but mere weltanschauung—precisely because it did not address the "central question of general ontology" (GA 26:165/132). Having confronted that question head-on in *Being and Time,* does Heidegger's metontology avoid Scheler's fate? Does he describe a plausible notion of cosmological inquiry?

A second candidate is suggested when one notes that the very language Heidegger uses to describe metontology—that it cultivates a "metaphysical ontic" by way of "existentiell questioning" (GA 26:200, 199/158, 157)—poses a puzzle from the perspective of *Being and Time,* since there these terms ("ontic," "existentiell") refer to a pretranscendental concern with entities from empirically particular points of view.[24] Might it be, then, that Heidegger's cosmology is prepared to make the naturalizing move that has become familiar in late-twentieth-century philosophy? His remoteness from all that becomes obvious, however, when he contrasts his proposal with the then-popular "inductive metaphysics" of Oswald Külpe, a position Heidegger had criticized already in 1912. Külpe held that the goal of philosophy, metaphysics, could be achieved by projecting the findings of the sciences of nature (physics and psychology) to the point where they intersected and formed a unified picture of the world. In 1912 Heidegger objected that the "hypothetical" basis of such naturalism contradicted the very idea of philosophy.[25] In 1928 he reiterates that even though metontology is like empirical science in having "beings for its subject matter," it "is not a summary ontic in the sense of a general science that empirically assembles the results of the individual sciences into a so-called 'world-picture,' so as to deduce from it a world-view and guide for life" (GA 26:199–200/157). Heidegger thus implies that metontology does not aim to naturalize what *Being and Time* calls *veritas transcendentalis,* transcendental truth.

Indeed, metontology is to "make beings thematic in their totality in light of ontology" (GA 26:200/157)—that is, in light of the transcendentally disclosed meaning of being. Should we see it then as supplying the complete "system of categories" hinted at in *Being and Time,* the regional "ontologies themselves which are prior to the ontical sciences and which provide their foundations" (GA 2:15/31)? This third candidate would be consistent with the transcendental standpoint of *Being and Time* and could, without much semantic strain, be labeled a "metaphysical ontic," since it would concern the a priori constitution of the object domains or ontic regions cultivated in anthropology, psychology, biology, history, and the like. Two considerations—one structural and one substantive—tell against identifying metontology with regional-ontological inquiry, however. First, considered structurally, Heidegger's conception of fundamental ontology already contains a place for regional ontologies, and that is not the place of metontology. Fundamental ontology consists of three phases (GA 26:196/154). The first is a "grounding that establishes the intrinsic possibility of the being question as the basic problem of metaphysics—the interpretation of Dasein as temporality" carried out in *Being and Time.* Second, there is "an explication of the basic problems contained in the question of being—the temporal exposition of the problem of being," a task sketched in what Heidegger called a "new elaboration of division 3 of part 1 of *Being and Time.*"[26] Here, in addition to the move from Dasein's temporality (*Zeitlichkeit*) to the temporality (*Temporalität*) of being, we find the elaboration of four "basic problems contained in the question of being."[27] One of these problems is "clarification of the existence mode of things and their regional constitution." Here is the place for regional ontologies of "history and artworks," of "nature" and its "diverse modes: space, number, life, human existence itself," and so on (GA 26:191 f./151), but it is not metontology, and not what Heidegger means by *metaphysical* inquiry. The latter is reached only with the third phase of fundamental ontology—"the development of the self-understanding of the problematic, its task and limits—the overturning [*Umschlag*]" (GA 26:196/154).

The second, substantive, reason why metontology cannot be identified with regional-ontological (categorial) inquiry within the framework of *Being and Time* follows from the last remark. For categorial inquiry into the "unity of the idea of being and its regional variants" (GA 26:191/151) still operates with the phenomenological concept of grounds of meaning. Metontology, on the other hand, is not to be grounded in Dasein's understanding (or the "idea" of being) but is to provide grounds *for* Dasein. The "language of metaphysics" thus invokes a second, as yet unclarified, sense of "ground," whereby the phenomenology of *Being and Time* is itself to be grounded in that "metaphysical ontic in which it implicitly always remains" (GA 26:201/158). The inconsistency in *Being and Time* emerges with this idea of a double grounding.

4. The Problem of Double Grounding

What exactly is meant by "double grounding," and why is it a problem? These questions are best answered by considering a passage where Heidegger explains why there is supposed to be an "intrinsic *necessity*" that ontology turn back to its ontic point of origin. Heidegger writes:

> The being "man" understands being; understanding of being effects a distinction between being and beings; being is there only when Dasein understands being. In other words, the possibility that being is there in the understanding presupposes the factical existence of Dasein, and this in turn presupposes the factical extantness of nature. (GA 26:199/156)

The first sentence in this passage merely restates the thesis of *Being and Time* that the transcendental ground of ontological knowledge lies in Dasein's understanding of being. Problems begin in the next sentence: How are we to read the first occurrence of "presupposes"? If it means no more than that there is no thinking without a thinker, it is trivial. By introducing it with "in other words," however, Heidegger signals that it too must be read in light of *Being and Time,* where the term "factical existence" does not refer to the "fact" of whether a being of such and such constitution is currently found among the furniture of the universe, but to the *constitution* of that being itself.[28] "Factical existence" is shorthand for the full ontological character of Dasein, the "facticity" and "existentiality" that together account phenomenologically for Dasein's understanding of being (GA 2:254/235). Read this way, the first occurrence of "presupposes" is nontrivial because it adumbrates the transcendental ground. It is the second occurrence of "presupposes" in this sentence, however, that signifies the supposed necessity of a passage from ontology to metontology, and here Heidegger seems to rely on the trivial sense when he claims that "the factical existence of Dasein . . . in turn presupposes the factical extantness [*faktische Vorhandensein*] of nature." Ontology thus finds a second ground in the "factical extantness of nature"—it is possible "only if a possible totality of beings is already there" (GA 26:199/157). Metontology is to inquire into *this* sort of dependency.

There is, then, an equivocation on the notion of "presupposition" in this passage. The claim that "the possibility that being is there in the understanding" presupposes "the factical existence of Dasein" refers to a transcendental-phenomenological sense of ground concerned with conditions of intelligibility, while the claim that "the factical existence of Dasein" presupposes "the factical extantness of nature" refers to an entirely different sense of ground—an ontic sense—whose relation to the first is by no means clear. By itself, the existence of this equivocation is not a problem; it becomes one only if the relations between the two senses of "ground" are not identified and respected. In *Being and Time* the equivocation is present but is contained by Heidegger's Husserlian procedure of bracketing all question of ontic grounds, and overt inconsistency is avoided. It breaks out only when Heidegger tries to remove the brackets with help from the language of metaphysics.

That the problem of double grounding lurks in *Being and Time* is not hard to show. When Heidegger claims that "readiness-to-hand is the way in which entities as they are 'in themselves' are defined ontologico-categorially" (phenomenologically), for example, he immediately notes that "only by reason of something extant [*auf dem Grunde von Vorhandenem*] 'is there' anything ready to hand." Hence, the extant is presupposed. Nevertheless, it does not follow that "readiness-to-hand is ontologically founded on extantness" (GA 2:96/101), and an ontological ground must therefore be other than whatever sort of ground belongs to the presupposition of the extant. Such examples could be multiplied, but they all yield the same distinction: Ontological grounding concerns the *priority of meaning*, that which enables understanding, and in that sense we are able to grasp the extant only "through" the ready-to-hand, or better, through the "world" as the meaning-horizon of entities within the world. "Only on the basis of the phenomenon of the world can the being-in-itself of entities within-the-world be grasped ontologically" (GA 2:102/106).[29] To claim that "only by reason of something extant 'is there' something ready-to-hand," however, is to invoke another sort of priority, one that does not concern relations of meaning but relations between those entities—of which "man" is one—that show up in the world via Dasein's understanding.[30] Hence, the question raised at the end of *Being and Time:* Can ontology be ontologically grounded, or does it also require an ontic ground?

What Heidegger says of Kant expresses the paradox of his own position: "Ontology is grounded in the ontic, and yet the transcendental problem is developed out of what is thus grounded, and the transcendental also first clarifies the function of the ontic" (GA 26:210/164). Has *Being and Time* clarified the function of the ontic such that it becomes possible to inquire into an ontic ground of ontology? Heidegger has all along insisted, against subjective or empirical idealism, that entities are not reducible to Dasein's understanding of being; they have a certain "independence."[31] In asking after an ontic ground of ontology, he seems to want to make this independence thematic in such a way that the phenomenological project can be clarified, grounded, in terms of it. But can ontology really be said to presuppose nature in any nontrivial sense? Heidegger certainly cannot intend to offer empirical-causal explanations for what was presented in the transcendental account, a story about how the natural entity, man, evolved and how its understanding of being can be explained in terms of natural laws—perhaps as an adaptation of neurological, psychological, or sociocultural factors. Such inquiries can be carried out, but to see them as grounds of ontological knowledge relativizes the latter in a way that Heidegger shows no interest in doing: "Being cannot be explained through entities" (GA 2:275/251). Yet a metaphysical appeal to entities, such as metontology is said to be, is no less objectionable. To see why, it will be useful to glance briefly at how Husserl negotiated the same impasse Heidegger reaches at the end of *Being and Time,* avoiding the inconsistency that undermines Heidegger's thinking.

As is well known, Husserl's breakthrough to phenomenology in the *Logical Investigations* came with the idea that no noncircular explanation of knowledge as a factual occurrence is possible, hence, that philosophical grounding of knowledge can only strive to clarify the *meaning* of cognition by reflection on cognitive intentional experiences (*Erlebnisse*). However, the *Logical Investigations* was still caught in a double bind. On the one hand, while the structure of the *Erlebnisse* could be adequately grasped in direct reflection, that appeared merely to be psychological immanence, shut off from the physical world. Phenomenology thus seemed to yield a kind of skepticism. On the other hand, to speak of the "psychological" presupposes reference to the supposedly unavailable real world after all, thus rendering the phenomenological delimitation of its sphere of evidence dogmatic.[32] Husserl's escape from this naturalistic double bind came through his theory of the phenomenological reduction.

The reduction interests us here solely in relation to the idea of phenomenological grounding, and the main point to note is that through it the field of phenomenological evidence explored in the *Logical Investigations* is freed of those presuppositions that identify it, prior to philosophical criticism, with a particular region of being, a particular slice of the world. This it does first by "bracketing" all scientific theories (including metaphysical theories) that seek to explain what is given to reflection, and together with these, all interpretations of the given that depend on what Husserl calls "transcendent" assumptions—for instance, the assumption of an ontological distinction between the mental and the physical. This move yields a specifically *transcendental* idealism, distinguished from empirical or psychological idealism in that the latter, but not the former, makes first-order claims about the nature of objects (e.g., that they are really "mental" constructs). What Henry Allison says of Kant's position holds equally of Husserl's, namely, that "transcendental idealism must be characterized primarily as a meta-philosophical or methodological 'standpoint,' rather than as a straightforwardly metaphysical doctrine about the nature or ontological status of the objects of human cognition." What distinguishes Kant's from Husserl's transcendental idealism is that the former considers objects in light of what Allison calls "epistemic conditions"—conditions "necessary for the representation of an object or an objective state of affairs"—while the latter casts a wider net, reflecting upon grounds of intelligibility or meaning per se, thus upon the entire sphere of intentionality—conscious life in its meaningful connections.[33] Because these grounds concern conditions that make entities intelligible, there is no sense in which they could in turn be relativized (reduced) to one or another region of entities.

Put otherwise, the relativity of meaning to transcendental subjectivity is not a case of causal dependence, an epistemological species relativism, or a metaphysical claim about a peculiar "absolute" entity. These are versions of *subjectivism* that transcendental idealism, as a metaphilosophical standpoint achieved through the reduction, leaves behind. Whether one denies the predicate "being" to this transcendental subject, as Husserl does, or exploits this standpoint as a way of raising the whole question of the meaning of being in a new way, as does Heidegger, the real danger lies in misconstruing these transcendental relations as ontic ones, thereby succumbing to what Husserl, in *Cartesian Meditations,* calls "transcendental realism." Transcendental realism is the "absurd position" into which one falls if one mistakes the sphere of transcendental subjectivity for a "tag end of the world," an entity supposedly defined by the worldly nexus which is its own phenomenologically disclosed correlate (Hua I:63/24). By bracketing the validity claims of worldly being, the reduction yields a kind of phenomenological evidence whose significance is prior to the mesh of the world. There is no sense, then, in which such evidence presupposes the factical extantness of nature.

Now Husserl, no less than Heidegger, saw that the transcendental ground is reached by reflecting upon the "natural attitude"—on what Husserl calls psychological subjectivity or what Heidegger calls average everydayness. Thus both recognized that their starting point was entangled in the world, yet both sought a distinct perspective on that entanglement (a phenomenological ground) from which the meaning of that entanglement could be clarified. It is true that Husserl appears more rationalistic in his belief that the natural attitude can be thoroughly clarified, while Heidegger doubts that the conditions of meaning can be made fully transparent.[34] However, these are interphenomenological disputes about the reach of phenomenological evidence (or grounding) itself, whereas the real danger—one that neither Husserl nor Heidegger can altogether resist—lies in the pull of traditional, nonphenomenological problems.[35] Ultimately, it is something like the phenomenological reduction from entities to meaning that enables Heidegger to thematize the ontological difference between being and beings, while the impasse he reaches at the end of *Being and Time* arises from a confusion about its implications for *Existenz,* Dasein's mode of being. For example, "world" in *Being and Time* is a structural feature of Dasein's being, that is, a transcendental condition of intelligibility and thus the meaning-ground of what shows up within the world. "Nature," in contrast, is "an entity within the world" (GA 2:280/254) and "can never make *worldhood* intelligible" (GA 2:88/94). To suggest that Dasein's understanding of being presupposes the factical extantness of nature thus implies a shift toward a transcendental realistic perspective that is not supplemental to, but *inconsistent* with, the phenomenological project. Empirical inquiries into "man's" entanglement in nature are certainly possible, but only on the ground of Dasein's understanding of being. Even the mere *possibility* of a metaphysical reading of this entanglement that could avoid the objection of transcendental realism, however, has yet to be shown.[36]

5. The End of *Being and Time* and the Overcoming of Metaphysics

If transcendental realism is the error of treating being-in-the-world as just another worldly entity, we have already encountered Heidegger's closest brush with it, namely, in his suggestion that the transcendental "neutrality" of the analysis of Dasein be supplemented by a "metaphysics of Dasein." There, the categorial features of Dasein that in *Being and Time* were defined exclusively with reference to the transcendental project of grounding ontological knowledge are to be reinterpreted in terms of the "factical extantness of nature."[37] Heidegger certainly felt that this metontology would provide a distinctively philosophical ground, for it was to be neither an empirical inquiry nor a development of transcendental philosophy's implicit regional ontologies. As in our earlier discussion of Kant's transcendental dialectic, Heidegger seems to have hoped that metontology would restore philosophical cosmology and provide a metaphysical ground for the phenomenological project of *Being and Time.* Yet it is hard to avoid the suspicion that cosmology of this sort is rather less inquiry than construction of what Heidegger himself describes as worldview—an "all-inclusive reflection on the world and the human Dasein," one that is "existentiell," that is, "determined by environment—people, race, class, developmental stage of culture"; not so much "a matter of theoretical knowledge" as "a coherent conviction which determines the current affairs of life more or less expressly and directly," an outlook that "always arises out of the particular factical existence of the human being" (GA 24:7–8/5–6). Now Heidegger's relation to the worldview question is complex,[38] but given his critique of Scheler we know that he envisioned something more for metontology; indeed, it must be something more, since "philosophy itself never gives a world-view, nor does it have the task of providing one" (GA 26:230/179). If we ask what the relevant distinction between philosophy and worldview is, the preceding discussion suggests that where philosophy inquires into grounds or reasons, worldviews presuppose such grounds and build upon them. Cosmology, then, seems to get us no further than worldview; but perhaps the genuine metaphysical ground is to be found only by moving through cosmology to retrieve rational *theology* from Kant's dialectic.

This would certainly provide an answer to Heidegger's question, at the end of *Being and Time,* concerning *what* entity was to function as the ontic ground of ontology. If the factical existence of Dasein presupposes the factical extantness of nature (beings as a whole), metontology might be seen as providing the metaphysical-ontic ground for ontology by referring this cosmological whole to its ground in God. Many things speak in favor of such a suggestion. For instance, Heidegger links metontology with *metaphysica specialis,* that is, with "metaphysics as final purpose," and this, in turn, is identified with that part of πρώτη φιλοσοφία Aristotle called θεολογία (GA 26:229/178). From this angle, Heidegger's metaphysics is essentially a retrieval of Aristotle's metaphysics. *Being and Time* focuses upon ontology, an inquiry into being qua being (τὸ ὂν ᾗ ὄν), while metontology takes up theology or the "problem of transcendence," an inquiry into "the highest kind of being" (τὸ τιμιώτατον γένος εἶναι), τὸ θεῖον.[39] A metaphysical ground would thus be a theological one, and the relation between phenomenology and metaphysics would be the relation between transcendental philosophy and theology.

Even if this suggestion is right, however, it is hard to see how it avoids the charge of transcendental realism. Appeal to God could no more consistently serve as an account of Dasein's understanding of being (ontology), independent of that very understanding, than could cosmological appeal to the contexts of nature or history. Heidegger's earlier point still holds: "Being cannot be explained through entities."[40] But in fact the suggestion does not really get us beyond cosmology at all, since Heidegger's reading of theology is essentially cosmological: τὸ θεῖον signifies "simply beings—the heavens: the encompassing and overpowering, that under and upon which we are thrown, that which dazzles us and takes us by surprise, the overwhelming" (GA 26:13/11).[41] Heidegger does link this "understanding of being qua superior power [*Übermächtig*]" with "holiness" (GA 26:211/165), and Pöggeler is surely right to say that Scheler's way of asking the "why" question has "stimulated Heidegger to reopen the question of the divine [*Göttlichen*] in terms of which human beings have understood themselves," thus taking up again the thread of his theological beginnings.[42] Nevertheless, Heidegger is not identifying the ontic ground of ontology with God. Almost as if he had the objection of transcendental realism in mind, he explicitly states that in discussing being as the overpowering the "dialectical illusion is especially great," and he also states that it is therefore "preferable to put up with the cheap accusation of atheism which, *if it is intended ontically,* is in fact completely correct" (GA 26:211/165; emphasis added). The "being that must take over the function of providing" an ontic ground, invoked at the end of *Being and Time,* cannot be God.

There is, then, apparently nothing left but to see the ontic ground as Dasein itself—not insofar as it understands being, but insofar as it finds itself already in the midst of a totality of beings "under and upon which we are *thrown.*"[43] Heidegger claims that the two sides of Aristotle's first philosophy—"knowledge of beings and knowledge of the overwhelming"—correspond "to the twofold in *Being and Time* of existence and thrownness" (GA 26:13/11). Having concentrated on a phenomenological clarification of Dasein's understanding of being—so the argument goes[44]—*Being and Time* concludes by acknowledging that the projection or interpretation of existence upon which such phenomenology draws is itself compromised by ontic presuppositions due to the inquirer's thrownness or facticity, her being always already particularly situated in the midst of beings as a whole. Since, as Heidegger reminds us, *Being and Time* employs a "factical ideal of Dasein," an "ontical way of taking existence which . . . need not be binding for everyone," the "ontological 'truth' of the existential analysis is developed on the ground of the primordial existentiell truth" (GA 2:411, 413, 419/358, 360, 364). It is plausible, then, to think that metontology turns back to investigate this primordial existentiell truth in some way, as the ontic ground of the ontological project.

The value of this suggestion does not lie in any precise insight it gives into what metontological or metaphysical inquiry could be; it adds—and *can* add—nothing to what we have already considered. Indeed, though this appears to be the interpretation of these matters favored by most commentators, I mention it only at this late stage because anyone adopting it must already have conceded that there can be no purely metaphysical grounds distinct from phenomenological ones, hence that there can be no metaphysical (metontological) inquiry into them. It is impossible that metontology could *investigate* thrownness—in the sense of demonstrating the natural, social, or historical limits of Dasein's understanding of being—since such investigation would already be grounded in that very understanding. Further, *Being and Time* has already analyzed the finitude of Dasein's understanding, and our access to it, by appeal to the existential categories of disposition (*Befindlichkeit*) and mood (*Stimmung*). If the "primary discovery of the world" is by way of "bare mood," we do not have the basis for an inquiry, but precisely the reverse: "The 'whence' and the 'whither' " of our being in the midst of what is "remain in darkness" (GA 2:183, 179/177, 173). What more can metontology hope to do but reaffirm this? And when Heidegger revisits these issues at the start of his metaphysical decade—in the 1929 "What Is Metaphysics?"—nothing has changed: The distinctive mood of *Angst* is said to reveal the nothing (*das Nichts*), that is, to bring us before the phenomenological fact that reasons—ontic answers to the question of why there is something rather than nothing—*give out.*[45] Yet the fact that metaphysics or metontology represents, on this reading, less an inquiry than the impossibility of one is, for those who adopt it, just the point: The ontic ground of ontology is understood precisely as something the recognition of which *undermines* the project of ontology, signaling the end, the collapse, of *Being and Time.*

Thus, Jean Grondin thinks that "Dasein proves to be too finite and too historically situated to enable it to derive . . . transcendental structures of its most fundamental being," while John Sallis holds that appeal to the "overwhelming" in the midst of which we find ourselves leads to "the sacrifice of the understanding."[46] More modestly, Robert Bernasconi concludes not that Dasein's finitude, its ontic situatedness, precludes it from grasping transcendental (ontological) structures, but that "Heidegger is not readily able to sustain the *purity* of the distinction between the ontic and the ontological."[47] This, however, does not imply that no such distinction is to be made, or that such "impurity" requires "sacrifice of the understanding." Similarly, David Wood recognizes that "it may be vital to shift from ontic discourse, discourse about beings and their relation to each other, to discourse about being," but we nevertheless cannot ignore "back-door entanglements between the ontic and the ontological"; indeed, "the transcendental . . . is nowhere else but *in* the empirical."[48] But if *that* is what the collapse of *Being and Time* amounts to, I would take it as good evidence for my earlier claim that what "failed" was not phenomenology ("phenomenological seeing"), but the "inappropriate concern with 'science' and 'research.' " For what must be abandoned in the face of ontic-ontological entanglement is the *esprit de système*—far more evident in Heidegger's appropriation of phenomenology than it is in Husserl's original[49]—that demands a successor discipline to traditional metaphysics. The hermeneutic phenomenology of *Being and Time* is already nothing but the continual attempt to negotiate this impurity, seeking the transcendental *in* the empirical. If philosophy can never constitute itself as absolute, infallible, secured, unrevisable—a fixed system of permanent possessions—the reflection on something like transcendental conditions of meaning is nevertheless inseparable from the project of philosophizing, a necessary "illusion" (GA 26:201/158), as Heidegger comes to call it.

Why "illusion"? Perhaps because although we acknowledge our finitude (the fallible, impure character of ontological inquiry), after we arrive phenomenologically at what we understand to be necessary, a priori (transcendental) truths, the claim that our insight has arisen from our limited abilities as thinkers "is no more exciting"—as J. L. Austin once put it[50]—"than adding 'D[eo] V[olente].' " At a deeper level, though, reference to a necessary illusion points to the confluence of ethical and epistemological motives in the notion of philosophical grounding. The phenomenological project, as a philosophical *practice,* proves to be an "art of existing" (GA 26:210/158), and it is no accident that this art—the ontic ideal informing the analysis of existence in *Being and Time*—exhibits what Bernasconi calls "an unstated bias toward what . . . might be called the 'virtues of the philosopher.' "[51] For that ontic ideal reflects an ethics of philosophy—those motives, collected by Husserl under the heading of the philosopher's "ultimate self-responsibility," that lead to the insistence on "phenomenological seeing" itself. Thus, even if phenomenology cannot provide a systematic foundational science, the phenomenological concept of ground has a distinct—*though ethical*—priority over the "adventure" of metaphysical cosmology, theology, and psychology.

It should be emphasized that Heidegger did not consistently understand metontology this way. At least during his metaphysical decade, he remained seduced by a kind of dialectical illusion. Faced with the phenomenological encounter with the nothing—with the fact that ontic grounds for the whole give out—he did not stay within the ethical space of phenomenological reasoning but believed instead that the finitude of thinking demanded anchor in ontic political and historical affairs, "decision" about the "meaning" of das *Seiende im Ganzen*. To this extent, Habermas is right that Heidegger transformed the transcendental philosophy of *Being and Time* into an inflated historicism and decisionism, something like a worldview.[52] The notorious "political engagement" would thus be a consequence not of the phenomenology of *Being and Time*, but of Heidegger's confusion between the ethical ground of thinking and the ontic involvements of the thinker. In this respect Heidegger's long struggle with the question of the existential dimension of philosophy—the beginnings of which we encountered in his reflections on university reform in chapter 8—would have ended in an unfortunate reversal. The earlier subordination of political involvement to the project of renewing philosophy gives way to the illusion that philosophy's direction must be determined by political commitments.

But one ought not to agree entirely with Habermas's further claim that, after his metaphysical decade, Heidegger retreated ever more into a mythical self-indemnification. It took Heidegger a decade to realize that there could be no *Umschlag* from ontology to metontology, that phenomenological grounds need no supplement from metaphysics, or politics either. Though Heidegger never got so far as to see that the ontic ground of ontology is exclusively ethical,[53] his later work no longer makes any appeal to metontology, or to a metaphysical ground. Rather, in the midst of many different motives (some of them perhaps suspect), one finds Heidegger engaged in a phenomenological project of getting back to the *ground of metaphysics* itself in order to confront the metaphysical way of thinking that "represents" beings as a whole.[54] Rather than follow the fruitless path toward worldview formation—a path that confuses being (meaning) with beings, phenomenological with ontic grounds—Heidegger tries to think the "truth of being," to "experience" (bring to phenomenological evidence) that which, in allowing access to beings, conceals itself. To overcome metaphysics in this way is not to reject philosophical reflection on nature but merely to deny that phenomenology (or *Denken*) can be contextually grounded as a being among beings.[55] If preserving the radical impulse of phenomenology thus requires rejecting the claims of metaphysics, the demise of *Being and Time,* its end, was only the end of the inconsistency still infecting its concept of philosophical reason giving. Paraphrasing Jacobi, then, Heidegger might well say that "I need the assumption of phenomenology to get into metaphysics, but with this assumption it is not possible for me to remain in it."

13

Gnostic Phenomenology: Eugen Fink and the Critique of Transcendental Reason

No friend of transcendental phenomenology can contemplate the face it reveals in that hybrid text, the *Sixth Cartesian Meditation,* without a profound sense of uneasiness.[1] Like Scrooge confronting the vision conjured by the Ghost of Christmas Yet to Come, one recognizes oneself in it but hopes that it is only a dream, that the future is not fixed, that there is still time to reform. Here the philosophy that emerged in the *Logical Investigations* promising to bring clarity to fundamental problems in philosophy—and did bring clarity in abundance—gets entangled in speculations so murky and outlandish that they often sound like a parody of Derrida.[2] Once presented as a liberation from the constraints of old systems of thought and well-worn philosophical language games, phenomenological appeal to the intuitive self-showing of "the things themselves" is here felt to be unacceptably constraining, a mere first stage infected with "Cartesian" naïveté. And here too the thought that found a path from the natural attitude to its transcendental ground, having admitted one fundamental paradox (namely, that man, subject within the world, is also constituting subject of the world), explodes into an endless shower of paradoxes, indeed, embraces paradox as its proper discursive modality. The culprit in all this, the maker of all this mischief, is of course the phenomenological reduction, and for someone who defends the reduction as an indispensable feature of transcendental phenomenological reflection, as I do, a glimpse into Fink's text must have a chilling effect.

And yet, one sees precisely the motives that produce such thoughts; it is out of the question to suppose that they are Fink's alone. The desire for something more than what transcendental reflection on experience seems able to provide has long been part of the heritage of phenomenology, and one need look no further than Husserl himself to find it. The "Nachwort zu meiner 'Ideen' " (1931) reveals well enough how Husserl chafed under the characterization of phenomenology as an "intellectualism" that skirts the "so-called problem of 'existence.' " He seemed to believe that "all questions" are contained within the field of phenomenology, including "all so-called metaphysical questions, insofar as they have possible sense in the first place" (Hua V:140–41),[3] and perhaps he was right. The problem is to say whether a metaphysical question, after its "possible sense" has been established in genuinely phenomenological terms, remains a metaphysical question. Or perhaps Husserl was wrong, perhaps metaphysics transcends phenomenology. This was Alfred Schutz's view of the matter, and his verdict on Husserl's efforts to move into metaphysics was harsh. Transcendental phenomenology "begins with the construction of the world of experience by consciousness and ends up with the creation of the world by the ego-become-god," an outcome for which Schutz holds Fink responsible: "What I have heard from him about so-called 'constructive phenomenology' (dealing with birth and death, life and aging, and other genuinely metaphysical questions) has not made me confident that the publication of the literary estate of Husserl will offer a solution to the metaphysical questions."[4] The publication of Ronald Bruzina's superb translation of the *Sixth Cartesian Meditation* provides an appropriate occasion for revisiting the provocation contained in Schutz's dismissal. For we can hardly read that text without taking a stand on the question of whether what is found there is on the way toward the formulation of metaphysical problems "insofar as they have possible sense in the first place," or whether it takes phenomenology to a place where it loses all sense and ceases to be phenomenology. And if the latter is the case, is this an idiosyncrasy of Fink's interpretation, as Schutz suggests, or is it inherent in the very nature of transcendental phenomenology?

Toward the end of his extraordinarily sensitive "Translator's Introduction," Bruzina raises the decisive question. Having laid out the textually apparent difference between Husserl and Fink on "the question of being," he asks: "Does the difference result from development within phenomenology, or must it be accountable to importation from outside it?" Does it "corrode and negate, or does it consolidate and reestablish? It is not," he continues, "a simple matter" (*SCM* lix). Nor shall a definitive answer be given here. Still, fully aware that what follows are mere headings for problems that need to be worked out in detail, I would like to propose something specific—namely, that the particular shape given to the "phenomenology of phenomenology" in the *Sixth Cartesian Meditation,* the particular conception of what belongs to (and is implied by) a "critique of transcendental reason," does indeed come, if not precisely from outside phenomenology, then at least from failure to recognize a trap lying within it, namely, the potential for "dialectical illusion [*Schein*]" in Kant's sense. And Fink is indeed responsible for this, if only because he actually tried to prepare the move from phenomenology to metaphysics that Husserl only pined after.[5] Thus, though Husserl insisted that Fink was neither a Heideggerian nor, more to the point, "ever an 'Hegelian,' " adding that it "would be completely wrong to think that new intellectual motifs that are alien to the consistent thrust of my earlier development have taken effect on me though him,"[6] it is obvious—and would have been obvious to Husserl—that Fink steers transcendental phenomenology toward Hegelianism, repeating in a precisely identifiable way the move from Kant to Hegel. Behind this is indeed something alien to the consistent thrust of Husserl's earlier development, namely, a "gnostic" reading of the transcendental reduction. I shall explain and defend this thesis with reference to four prominent topics in the *Sixth Cartesian Meditation:* the nature of the "phenomenological onlooker," the identification of being with "mundane being," the idea of "constructive phenomenology," and the issue of whether natural language is adequate to the expression of transcendental truth. Taken together, these suggest an answer to the question that Fred Kersten, following Maurice Natanson, asked when discussing this same text: "Can phenomenology of phenomenology complete or advance beyond the Copernican Revolution?"[7] Not only can it not do so, it is a mistake to want to.

Before addressing these issues, however, something should be said about the way they are so judiciously framed in Bruzina's "Translator's Introduction." Of its numerous virtues I shall mention only four. First is Bruzina's indispensable account of the tangled context in which the *Sixth Cartesian Meditation* was produced. Torn by the "betrayal" of Heidegger, stung by the judgment of Georg Misch, struggling to achieve a systematic presentation of his philosophy that would demonstrate its power in the changed philosophical climate, and all the while continuing to refine and develop his original insights, Husserl in the early 1930s was not in a position that could be described as ideal for the kind of careful concentration on particular phenomena that seemed to be a condition of his best work. Keeping this situation in mind, Bruzina, second, is able to discern Husserl's various endorsements of Fink's drafts and articles. Are we really to believe that there is "no statement" in Fink's *Kant-Studien* article that Husserl "could not explicitly acknowledge as [his] own conviction," as Husserl claimed?[8] Better than anyone before him, Bruzina helps us to see what such avowals meant in a context where both Husserl and Fink, for different reasons, needed allies and each other. Bruzina succeeds here precisely because, third, he concentrates on the evident *differences* between the two original thinkers in order to develop his own provocative thesis of a genuine "cophilosophizing." Could Husserl, he asks, perhaps have been as mistaken in his judgment of Fink's thought as he had been, a decade earlier, about Heidegger's (*SCM* xxx)? Though much more familiar with the former's work than he had been with the latter's, "the question remains," according to Bruzina, whether "Husserl really grasped the differences that might lie in Fink's treatment of phenomenology, in contrast to his own" (*SCM* xxxi). Eschewing imputations of ignorance and disingenuousness, Bruzina teaches us to see this collaboration in a new light: Husserl did not even have to agree with the content of Fink's proposals to accept them as his own, since the differences between them "were genuine problems for and within transcendental phenomenology, genuine problems that developed intrinsically within it rather than antagonistically confronting or undercutting it from the outside." That is, Fink's position cannot be seen as coming from outside phenomenology since Fink has become, so far as Husserl's philosophizing is concerned, Husserl's own alter ego (*SCM* xxxii). Under these conditions of genuine cophilosophizing, phenomenology itself "was not just Husserl's—it was Husserl's *and* Fink's" (*SCM* xxviii).

The claim that there can be a genuine cophilosophizing in which phenomenology produces itself, as it were, deserves more attention than we can give it here.[9] But it suggests a fourth virtue of the "Translator's Introduction," namely, its detailed analysis of the *motives* that led Fink to his position. In a moment I will question whether these are in fact quite as intrinsic to the phenomenological project as Bruzina claims they are—whether, for example, a nonintuitive, constructive phenomenology is really necessary "in order for phenomenology actually to fulfill its objectives" (*SCM* xlvii). For now, though, one may certainly say that the thesis of cophilosophizing considerably complicates the question of what "its" (transcendental phenomenology's) objectives are. Does the anti-Cartesianism that Bruzina and others discern in the Husserl-Fink collaboration belong to phenomenology, or is it already the sign of a misunderstanding? Does the idea of transcendental intersubjectivity, for example, already "challenge . . . the intuitive evidential immediacy basic to Husserl's phenomenology" and lead inexorably to "constructive" phenomenology—as Fink, and Bruzina too, seem to think (*SCM* xliv)? Or does it simply place us before a limit to phenomenology, however we are finally to assess the nature of such limits? What *is* essential to a philosophy that can call itself phenomenological? Part of my answer to that question will be evident from what follows. In resisting *gnostic* phenomenology, however, I merely join on the field of Husserl studies a contest that everywhere rages in philosophy today: Hegel or Kant? Metaphyiscs or critique? Dialectic . . . or dialectical *illusion?*

1. The Phenomenological Onlooker

In what sense does Fink's position amount to a "gnostic" reading of the phenomenological reduction? An answer may be suggested by taking up the first of our four issues, the question of the "phenomenological onlooker." This is the very problem over which, several years earlier, the attempt at a collaboration between Husserl and Heidegger on the *Encyclopædia Britannica* article came to grief.[10] This time, however, it is Fink who, by pushing to the limit the position Husserl had earlier insisted upon, exposes the unsettling paradoxes contained in it.

Beginning in the natural attitude, the philosopher reflects upon her experience of the world that is simply "there" for her. If the philosopher is a phenomenologist, she makes a further move, or series of moves (reductions), whereby the naive positing of worldly entities is bracketed. In such reflection I disregard the question of whether what presents itself as being truly *is,* and I concentrate solely on the way it gives itself as being. I thereby thematize the *intentional* relation that holds between consciousness and things: Though the positing of being has been suspended, the meaning of the thing *as* being remains. In suspending the positing of being, my own being as the worldly entity, "man," is likewise suspended. Yet that, too, insofar as it pertained to me before the reduction, remains as phenomenon, a meaning to be examined—and we must not be too quick to claim to know what is entailed in or given with such a phenomenon. Under the reduction, then, the very same intentional life I led prior to the reduction, and continue to lead, is considered apart from the natural attitude's "commitment" to the *Seinsgeltung* of what is given through the intentional syntheses that constitute things as unities of meaning for me. If I permit myself to speak of the reduction as revealing "the constituting life of transcendental subjectivity," I must always keep in mind that this is *absolutely nothing other* than the life I have always lived and continue to live and that I am *absolutely nothing other*—so far as anything the reduction could teach me is concerned—than what I was before. As a purely negative gesture so to speak, the sort of bracketing put into play here cannot reveal another type of being behind the being that is bracketed—let alone a "nonbeing" or "prebeing"—because all such ontic questions have been suspended. So where does that leave us?

In his collaboration with Heidegger on the *Encyclopædia Britannica* article, Husserl makes an argument that Fink seizes upon as the seed of his own full-blown "meontology." Insisting that ontology is oriented toward constituted objectivities while the "transcendental" question posed under the reduction concerns the constituting of such objectivities, Husserl argues that to raise the question of being with regard to transcendental subjectivity—the "being of the constituting"—makes no sense. This is not yet meontology, for to say that the question of being is out of place under the reduction is not yet to say that transcendental subjectivity is a *me-on,* a nonbeing, or Nothing. But it lends itself to development in that direction if, following Fink, the reduction is taken as the starting point for "metaphysical" questions. Heidegger, in contrast, insisted that "that which constitutes is not nothing, and thus it is something and in being—though to be sure not in the sense of the positive. The question about the mode of being of that which constitutes is not to be avoided. The problem of being is thus directed toward the constituting and the constituted alike" (Hua IX:602). For him, the meaning of "constituting" had to be sought as a "possibility of Dasein," that is, of the human being—the very being who carried out the reduction. Husserl saw this as a complete misunderstanding; but if that is so, how should one thematize the relation between the "constituting" in the reduced sense and "human" subjectivity? Here the wisdom of Heidegger's refusal of the meontic path proves itself.

For consider what Fink is led to by adhering to Husserl's original line. First, he insists, against Heidegger, that "the self-reflection of the phenomenological reduction is not a radicality that is within human reach; it does not lie at all within the horizon of human possibilities" (*SCM* 32). Appearances to the contrary notwithstanding, then, it is not "I this man" who engages in phenomenological reflection, but the "transcendental onlooker" who "produces himself" precisely by means of his "disconnection of all belief-positings" (*SCM* 20, 39). However—and here we find a central tenet of Fink's gnosticism—this self-production is not really an emergence from nothing; rather, the onlooker "is only *freed* of the *shrouding cover* of human being" by the epoche (*SCM* 40). In his remark on this passage, Husserl substitutes for "the *shrouding cover* of human being" the phrase "the barrier of anonymity in which transcendental life proceeds as that which constitutes the world and me the man in the familiar forms of pregivenness" (*SCM* 40). Here human being is not the dark lord's creation into which I have fallen, the shroud in which the spark of true life is imprisoned, but rather a constituted sense that is separated from transcendental life only by what Husserl calls "anonymity."

This is no mere nuance; nor did Fink see it as such. For where he is willing to maintain only that it is an "undisputed appearance-truth" (in his special sense) "that the subject of phenomenologizing is man" (*SCM* 120),[11] he acknowledges that Husserl himself "disputes the idea that man philosophizes only 'seemingly' [*scheinbar*], since the transcendental ego is indeed itself 'man.' " In other words, "Husserl does not carry the distinction between transcendental subject and man over into the dimension of individuation" (*SCM* 1). Gnosticism is, I take it, precisely the idea that there is an *individuating* distinction between the transcendental subject and man. Husserl, in contrast, in one of his longest marginal remarks, takes the antignostic line that "what must be avoided in the whole presentation is for things to look as if the mundanization of phenomenology . . . were an evil thing that only occasioned errors and misunderstandings." For since there is no individuating distinction between transcendental subject and man, the reduction achieves a breakthrough to "a new, higher *humanity*" (*SCM* 130). With this, Husserl's position is practically indistinguishable from Heidegger's.[12]

Nevertheless, Fink's gnostic reading easily arises from Husserl's own view that the question of being can only concern the constituted, never the constituting. If that is true, then human *being* can only be something constituted, and an individuating distinction between it and the one who engages in transcendental reflection, the phenomenological onlooker, becomes inevitable. But perhaps the phenomenologists have been too quick to identify being with constituted being. Do we actually know that the meaning of "human being" is *exhausted* by the anthropological framework in which Husserl and Fink place it? What if Heidegger were right that the "being of man" does not refer to some entity that is ever simply "on hand" in the world and that to think the meaning of the human is to think precisely the site of the constituting-constituted dyad?[13] When I as phenomenologist reflect upon the reduced life of transcendental subjectivity, I can bracket only that stratum of the sense, "human being," that refers to the constituted *anthropos*—but this does not exhaust the meaning of human being. Commenting on a slightly different matter, Burt Hopkins seems to press a similar point. Claiming that Fink treats the "human apperception" as a "wholeness structure" that "is something seemingly 'given' all at once"—hence something from which we can be freed, a shroud we can throw off—Hopkins rightly counters that "according to Husserl, what is freed by the reduction is '[a]cceptedness in being [*Seinsgeltung*]' . . . and not the apperception in question." That is, "in contrast to *Seinsgeltung*," which "can be bracketed and thus freed from acceptedness because it is first intuitively given in some sense as a whole, mundane apperceptions for Husserl must be, in effect, descriptively unfolded."[14] I would simply add that not all apperceptions of the human are mundane.

Much more would have to be said about these matters to make any real headway, but I will simply point out one further paradox that shows up in Fink's account. We may call this the "already there" problem. Because transcendental reflection is not supposed to be a possibility of the human being in any sense, Fink argues that the transcendental subjectivity it reveals "is neither given nor pregiven in the natural attitude, it is in no sense there" (*SCM* 38). Here too Husserl is more cautious, since in his marginal emendation he puts scare quotes around "there," as if he recognized the dilemma facing Fink. For if transcendental subjectivity is in no sense there, then what Fink acknowledges as the "phenomenological fore-knowledge that first makes it possible to pose the radical questions" becomes wholly enigmatic (*SCM* 36). The gnostic gospel of hiddenness itself requires that transcendental subjectivity is in some sense "already there" in the natural attitude, for Fink himself argues that "transcendental cognition can flash out" in specific "extreme situations" (*SCM* 34). Here as everywhere Fink has "exaggerated," as Husserl put it, the situation that obtains in carrying out the reduction (*SCM* 81).

2. The Mundanity of Being

We may locate the motive for this exaggeration by turning to our second topic, Fink's identification of being with mundane being. This too is an important tenet in Fink's gnostic reading of the reduction. Husserl, at least initially, had invoked the reduction to maintain neutrality with regard to ontological questions such that the meaning of being in any region whatsoever could be studied and explicated. Thus, as Heidegger pointed out in a critical vein, for Husserl the meaning of being "in general" meant no more than "being posited" as such (GA 20:148–57/108–14). Fink, on the contrary, strongly "regionalizes" the idea of being: It is "the natural attitude itself" that is "the situation of origin and home for the Idea of being and the concept of being" (*SCM* 74). Fink's point here is a complicated one (recalling, among other things, Heidegger's analysis of *Verfallenheit* and the resultant equation of being with *Vorhandensein*), but it has the consequence of introducing a meontic distinction into phenomenology. Since it lies "as it were 'analytically' in the concepts of knowing and theoretical experience" that "all natural cognition is cognition of what is existent [*Seiendes*], all experience is experience of what is *existent*"—in short, that "*being and knowing*" are "the two inseparable components of the cognitive relation"—it follows that what is known and experienced under the reduction cannot "be" in any sense at all (*SCM* 71).

Thus, where Heidegger saw the epoche of the natural attitude as an occasion for reawakening the question of the meaning of being in general, Fink sees in it an opening to meontology, a "thematic reduction of the Idea of being" that guards against the dangers of ontifying transcendental subjectivity (*SCM* 71). At this point the gnostic language and its paradoxes reappear: When we "interpret what comes to givenness for us through the phenomenological reduction," we initially remain "ensnared" in or "captivated" by the "mundane Idea of being" (*SCM* 72); we are "in bondage to the Idea of being," so "spellbound" by it that we tend to posit transcendental subjectivity as something existent (*SCM* 74). The reduction is the gnosis that reveals "pre-being" (*Vor-sein*), "the sort of thing which is 'in itself' not existent" (*SCM* 76). Nevertheless, this gnosis takes place as something like a double gesture, mental reservation, or hermetic doctrine. For even if by means of the reduction of the Idea of being we do not posit transcendental subjectivity as something existent, still "we must posit [it] *just as if* it were something existent," since otherwise (given the analytic relation between knowing and being) "we would lose the last possibility of making verifiable explications and assertions in regard to transcendental subjectivity" and would "fall into the danger of an incurable 'mysticism' " (*SCM* 74).[15]

But is it true that "there can in principle be no other object of cognition than what is existent" (*SCM* 71)? To this train of thought Husserl once more objects, claiming that "we are not spellbound by the old concept of being, but we are unclear, in danger of paradox, as long as we have not explicitly carried out reflection" (*SCM* 74). When I do so reflect, distinguishing between the existent and the constituted *meaning* of the existent, I have thereby shown that cognition and experience are *not* limited to what is existent. There is no need to treat this ontological difference as Fink does, gnostically arranging all being, all experiencing, and all knowing on one side of the ledger (the mundane), with a domain of "pre-being" or "non-being" (*Vor-sein* or *me-on*)—the " 'pre-existent' life processes of transcendental subjectivity"—on the other (*SCM* 76). This way of ontifying the findings of the reduction precipitates graver dangers than the alternative Fink tries so hard to avoid. For it guarantees that anything that is said about transcendental subjectivity will always be something less (or more) than the truth, will bear the mark of an incommunicable secret code, and will never mean what it seems to mean in all candor.

We shall return to this issue when we take up the question of whether natural language is adequate for expressing transcendental truth. For the moment, though, consider how the idea that being is essentially a mundane notion unnecessarily complicates Fink's doctrine of the transcendental onlooker. Fink identifies a "dualism in transcendental life," a radical "cleft" opened up by the distinction between transcendental subjectivity as world-constituting activity and the transcendental onlooker who reflects upon this constituting activity while remaining, supposedly, a "non-participant in world-constitution." The transcendental onlooker's "uncovering of constitutive becoming" is not itself "constituting" (*SCM* 20, 23). But why not? Are not all reflective acts, as acts, bound up in the stream of constituting subjectivity—and thus to the extent that the onlooker "looks" on, is this not also a reflective act in which objectivities of some sort are constituted? One would be tempted to deny this if one believed, as Fink does, that not only is the existent always the result of constitution, but also that "*constitution is always constitution of the existent*" (*SCM* 21). But the sole reason for this view seems to be that the idea of being is essentially mundane, and if one denies this, then there is no cleft in transcendental life or reflection, any more than there is in mundane life or reflection. Conversely, if we have no basis to posit a radical cleft within the transcendental sphere, then the gap between the natural and the phenomenological *reflector*—I, this man—narrows considerably.

Still, Fink's preference for emphasizing differences between mundane and transcendental experience would not matter much were it not that it seems to authorize a rejection (or at least restriction) of the phenomenological "principle of all principles." As Fink informs us in the "Preferatory Note" appended to the text when it was submitted as his *Habilitationsschrift,* phenomenology, with its commitment to the intuitive exhibition of its claims, has hitherto suffered from a "methodological naïveté" that "consists in uncritically transferring the mode of cognition that relates to something *existent* into the phenomenological cognition of the *forming* (constitution) of the existent" (*SCM* 2). I strongly suspect that Fink's evident willingness to abandon the principle of intuitive givenness is a function of the idea that being is always mundane, but I have not been able to find an actual statement to that effect. In the next section, however, I shall supply some indirect arguments for thinking that this is the case, as well as some direct arguments that show the dubiousness, phenomenologically speaking, of abandoning that principle.

3. Constructive Phenomenology

We thus arrive at our third topic, the idea of a "constructive" phenomenology. This poses a greater challenge to specific Husserlian principles than anything that has gone before, since constructive phenomenology "abandons the basis of transcendental 'givenness,' and no longer exhibits things *intuitively*" (*SCM* 5). What could possibly authorize such a move phenomenologically? According to Fink it is the job of the critique of transcendental reason, or the transcendental theory of method, to "put into question . . . the intuitional character of phenomenological cognition itself" and inquire "into the evidentness given there" (*SCM* 26). Here, as Hopkins notes, Fink seems to suggest "that phenomenology's intuitional character renders it incapable of calling into question the scope and limits of evidentness."[16] To get beyond its methodological naïveté phenomenology requires nonintuitive resources. But can a *phenomenological* critique of phenomenological method be carried out otherwise than by means of intuitive methods? We must examine what Fink has in mind a bit more closely.

Fink argues that a "movement out beyond the reductive givenness of transcendental life" is necessary because such givenness has an "external horizon" that, precisely as external, can be investigated only by a phenomenology that "no longer exhibits things intuitively" (*SCM* 7). Yet this notion of horizon cannot be understood in the usual phenomenological sense, which always belongs *within* the sphere of "reductive givenness" as the horizon *of* what presents itself thematically therein. An external horizon in this sense can involve intentional implications that point beyond what is currently intuitively given, and (as in the case of certain temporal or intersubjective references) even to what can be given only appresentationally. But in no case does it entail a move beyond reductive givenness as a whole. Fink seems to operate with a different sense of horizon, however. For on the one hand he construes reductive givenness as "the entire 'being' legitimated by the phenomenological reduction as transcendentally existent," that is, all that can be intentionally grasped through a *regressive* analysis and thus has "possible accessibility through the unfolding of the phenomenological reduction" (*SCM* 57). This whole regressively accessible life is then, on the other hand, said to entail "modes of referral" to "objects" that cannot in any sense be given. Because the referral is "to something that precisely by its transcendental mode of being is *in principle* deprived of 'givenness,' " theorizing directed to this sort of external horizon must be "constructive" (*SCM* 56).

The referrals Fink has in mind all seem to concern totalities. For instance, one constructive problem is raised by the fact that the "*entire* being that is accessible by the reduction" already "stands in a 'history,' inasmuch as world-constitution is always already underway"; and another is "motivated" by the "mundane time-*whole* of human subjectivity" constituted by the limits of birth and death (*SCM* 58, 61). Constructive phenomenology is thus authorized by referral to totalities, external horizons that seem to frame regressive phenomenology itself. Fink argues that "even if these questions were in the end to be proven transcendentally inadmissible, still the proof of their eventual inadmissibility must take place in a problem dimension that in principle lies 'outside' regressive phenomenology" (*SCM* 60). He does not give any very clear reason for this view, but the claim is structurally similar to Hegel's argument, against Kant, that to set limits one must already be beyond them. Can such an argument be accepted within the context of phenomenology of phenomenology, such that it authorizes placing limits on the principle of all principles? And if so, does it provide any principle of its own for moving beyond those limits by way of constructive phenomenology?

Let us consider the example of the "wholeness" of human lived time. According to Fink, the reduction reveals "the transcendentally existing stream of experience" that has been disconnected from "all worldly representations of the wholeness-structures of this stream" (*SCM* 61). Though the stream of experience has a monadic unity, temporal totality is not a datum of the reduced sphere. There is, however, a "special 'coincidence' " between the "temporality of bracketed human immanence and that of the transcendental stream of experience"; indeed, they are "the same" except that human temporality "is enclosed in transcending, enworlding apperceptions," while the transcendental stream "is freed from these mundane construals by the reduction." Hence, one is led to ask whether the latter *fully* coincides with the former. If the "time man in the world has begins at birth and ends in death," does that mean that "the transcendental time of world constitution" also has "a beginning that corresponds to worldly birth and a transcendental 'end' that corresponds to worldly death? Or are 'birth' and 'death' only elements of sense constituted in reductively given transcendental life such that, for example, transcendental subjectivity constitutes 'death' by withdrawing itself from worldly self-objectification?" (*SCM* 61–62). Fink's point seems to be that any answer to that question must go beyond reductive givenness, since already the phenomena of *human* birth and death are external horizons that cannot be thematized in regressive (intuitive) inquiry.

One might well wonder whether this is so. Fink's view depends on treating human being exclusively as "an entity merely on hand in the world" and birth and death exclusively as "natural" phenomena. But why should a phenomenology of birth and death be limited to confirming the approach to these phenomena characteristic of the "naturalistic" thinking of the natural attitude? That *some* account of these naturalistic evidences must be given does not mean—as Heidegger has shown in *Sein und Zeit*—that the question of the "wholeness" of "human temporality"

(Dasein) must be raised in terms of the totality of a "temporal stream of experiences" (GA 2:314–54/279–311). In that case there would be little force to the argument that a phenomenology of *death* demands that one abandon the principle of givenness. Nevertheless, our response to Fink's challenge need not be left hanging by what some might consider the precarious thread of Heidegger's status as a phenomenologist. A criticism of Fink's formulation of the problem can be crafted in the very Kantian terms he uses to formulate it.

Consider the question, "Does the transcendental stream have a beginning and an end, like human temporality, or does it not?" So formulated, it resembles Kant's first antinomy.[17] Within the sphere of reductive givenness (regressive phenomenology), there appear to be motives for either way of answering it. Following up referrals to an external horizon, constructive phenomenology should enable us to decide whether or not the coincidence between the reduced human temporal stream and the stream of transcendental life implies a beginning and an end to transcendental time. Constructive phenomenology will start with what is given in intuition, for only so can it move beyond it in a systematic and methodologically secure way. As Fink puts it, "only a fully mastered analytic understanding of the transcendental events of beginning and end *in* time lends methodological security and material insight to the constructive project of inquiry into a beginning and end of transcendental time" (*SCM* 63).[18] But what can we really expect from constructive phenomenology? In particular, are we entitled to expect a *methodologically secure* relation between the intuitively given and the merely constructable? Is it not far more likely that on the basis of what is intuitively given (say, the temporal stream of consciousness as monadic unity, or the world as horizonal whole) we will be able to construct *antithetical* positions between which there will be no way to choose, since the basis for such choice, the rational ground of all cognitive decisiveness—*Evidenz*—is in principle absent? To ask this question is, of course, to evoke the position Kant defended in his transcendental dialectic, and a glance at how Fink appropriates this Kantian text reveals the contrast between his gnostic interpretation of the reduction and what I would like to call a "critical" one.

Fink explicitly links constructive phenomenology with Kant's transcendental dialectic, but his conception of the relation between this and the "transcendental analytic and aesthetic" (regressive phenomenology) suppresses what Kant took to be the most important aspect of the relationship (*SCM* 60). In Kant's view, the attempt to move from principles of understanding, based in experience, to Ideas of reason, transcending experience, yields nothing but *illusion.* Transcendental "dialectic" for Kant contains no positive doctrine but provides only "a *critique of dialectical illusion*."[19] In contrast, Fink clearly imagines that constructive phenomenology can provide substantive insight. Fink recognizes that constructive phenomenology covers the same terrain as Kant's "cosmological antinomies" and "paralogisms of pure reason," but there is no hint of the Kantian insight that no rational answer to these questions can be constructed—that they must be critically dissolved lest one succumb to the illusion of an answer that seems to go beyond experience but in fact leads only to dogmatism or skepticism (*SCM* 64).[20] To bring out this contrast let us ask, in an admittedly sketchy way, what a Kantian or critical approach to Fink's question about the coincidence of the human and transcendental temporal streams might look like.

Recall that Kant described space and time as "infinite given magnitudes" because their unity was not that of a *compositum* (composed of separable elements) but a *totum* (whose elements are only "limitations" of the one space and time).[21] The antinomy arises when we come to consider the status of such an infinite given magnitude. If I simply construct an argument on the basis of how time is given, it appears that I can assert both that world must have a beginning in time and also that it cannot have such a beginning. By producing such arguments in his dialectic, Kant hopes to convince us that construction can get no further than this contradiction.[22] A critical solution is possible, however, if we recognize that both thesis and antithesis share a common, though false, presupposition that renders both false in turn. If we deny that presupposition—namely, that the world "exists in itself independently of the regressive series of my representations"—we can also assert that "it exists in itself neither as an infinite whole nor as a finite whole."[23] The critical solution is thus wholly diagnostic, showing why we must reject the temptation to move from intuitability to nonintuitability.

Though there are many disanalogies between Kant's position and Husserl's on these matters, there are also certain analogies that bear on the question Fink raises.[24] For instance, the monadic unity of the temporal stream suggests an analogy to Kant's notion of time as an infinite given magnitude. Thus, it seems phenomenologically justified to say that whatever may hold of what is constituted *in* the temporal stream, the temporal parts of the stream itself are given not as "pieces" from which it is composed but as "limits" of the one stream. It would follow, then, that a critical solution to the question of what can be constructively asserted about the reduced temporal stream, based on the intuited coincidence between it and human immanence, must hold that both the thesis that it has a beginning or end, and the antithesis that it has no beginning or end, are false. Common to both is the erroneous assumption that it "is" something in itself, that it is distinguished in "the dimension of individuation" from human subjectivity. In the reading I prefer, the reduction rules out such an ontic interpretation of the stream of transcendental temporality, much as Kant's Copernican hypothesis rules out treating the world as a totality "in itself." Thus, to say that the reduced stream does not show itself to be limited by birth and death (assuming of course that human immanence *does* show itself to be so limited)[25] could never authorize constructive phenomenology to assert that it is not limited by birth and death. That too would be false, since *as reduced* it is not something about which such a question can be raised. This is to say, in effect, that the very idea of an external horizon to what is revealed in the reduction makes no sense.

If my critical reading of the reduction and my Kantian response to Fink's problem is even remotely admissible, a clear contrast can be drawn with Fink's own hints at a treatment of the issue. For rather than dismissing both thesis and antithesis as false, Fink seems to suggest that both will be *true.* Interpreting liberally,[26] he seems to suggest that we may assert both that the temporal stream *as a consequence of secondary enworlding* can be said to "begin and end" (expressing what Fink calls an "appearance truth") and that in itself, speaking in terms of genuine "transcendental truth," it will also *not* have a beginning or an end. So considered, it looks as though Fink is treating the contradiction as an instance of what Kant calls a "dynamical" antinomy, which differs from the "mathematical" antinomy (exemplified by the cosmological Idea of composition discussed previously) in that both thesis and antithesis can be true.[27] However, this move is not available to constructive phenomenology since it depends on a distinction between phenomena and noumena—and finally on an invocation of a difference between theoretical and practical standpoints—that I think neither Husserl nor Fink would find congenial. Further, Fink is quite explicit about the fact that his dialectic culminates in a genuine phenomenological absolute. "The Absolute is the synthetic unity of anithetic moments," one that embraces constituted and constituting, being and prebeing, and other such "opposites" so radical that they really share no common term—hence an absolute that "cannot be grasped with the categories of formal logic." With this Fink shows that he is not convinced by Kant's argument that dialectic (or construction) is a logic of illusion (*SCM* 142–43). He drives phenomenology beyond Kant to Hegel and, alluding to Hegel's "speculative proposition," proposes a "theory of the phenomenological proposition" that embraces paradox and contradiction (*SCM* 70). Thus, "the givenness of the theme for phenomenologizing is in constructive phenomenology *non-givenness*" (*SCM* 65). But a phenomenology whose theme is given as nongivenness is a phenomenology that, if it tries to say anything more about the theme than precisely that it is nongiven, is on the verge of giving in to dialectical illusion—which is to say, it is on the verge of losing itself as phenomenology.

4. Phenomenological Truth and Natural Language

The notion that there is a special problem requiring a "theory of the phenomenological proposition" lies behind Fink's preoccupation with language in the *Sixth Cartesian Meditation* and leads to our fourth topic. The question is whether the language spoken in the natural attitude is adequate to the expression of transcendental truth. Is the very intelligibility of the transcendental compromised by linguistic expression; or conversely, is the ability of language to communicate compromised by the reduction? Fink's view on this matter depends in complicated ways on the idea that the reduction opens up a radical cleft between being and prebeing, and that "all concepts are concepts of being," that natural language "in principle speaks in regard to what is existent" (*SCM* 85). Thus, many of the criticisms raised earlier concerning this cleft and the identification of being with mundane being could be reiterated at this point. But I would like instead to develop the contrast between gnostic and critical readings of the reduction somewhat further by offering a relatively straightforward alternative to Fink's suggestion that predications made in phenomenological statements be understood as *analogies.*

As we saw, Fink holds that it is necessary to "ontify" the transcendental in order to speak of it at all (*SCM* 76), and he conceives the function of language in this process as a kind of analogizing. Since we must treat the transcendental *as if* it were the mundane, language cannot literally express what it knows; however, it can draw no ordinary analogy either, since it spans a radical cleft between things as disparate as being and prebeing. Yet if "the natural meanings of words and sentences cannot stand in a relationship of analogical predication to the intended transcendental sense-elements," there is nevertheless something like "an *analogy to the analogy* that is found within natural speech" (*SCM* 90–91).[28] Fink's gnosticism becomes clear when we consider the conception of the "life" of the phenomenologizing subject that lies behind his demand for a double analogy. The reduction "unhumanizes" the natural subject and places him "in the *monstrous solitude* of transcendental existence" where he attains the inexpressible gnosis concerning prebeing (*SCM* 110, 99). Now, there is no absolute "reason and no compulsion for predicative outward expression lying in phenomenologically theorizing experience as such"—which seems to mean that it can transpire without language, for if that is not what is meant then the next step becomes superfluous (*SCM* 99). For Fink goes on to say that the subsequent decision for communication requires a "non-proper or secondary enworlding" by means of which transcendental insights are brought back into the natural attitude in the form of "appearance-truths" (*SCM* 99, 110). It is the linguistic expression of such appearance truth that is, in relation to transcendental insight, analogical in Fink's sense.

What Fink means by "secondary enworlding" and by "appearance-truth" must be understood in contrast to "primary enworlding," which is the process whereby transcendental subjectivity anonymously (i.e., prior to recovering itself through phenomenological reflection) constitutes itself as "human" in terms of mundanizing apperceptions. With the breakthrough to phenomenology (a historical event), that anonymity is overcome, and transcendental subjectivity now knows itself *as* constituting, hence as distinct (in "the dimension of individuation") from human subjectivity. Though primary enworlding continues as it always has, the question arises as to how the newly self-conscious transcendental subject is to make itself known *as* such *in* the world. Here is where secondary enworlding comes into play, a process of self-manifestation by way of appearance truths involving the kind of ontification and analogization presently under consideration—a "humanization of reductive inhumanization" (*SCM* 110, 106–32). Thus, to take one example that will have to stand for many, Fink claims that thanks to secondary enworlding "we" (the transcendental onlookers practicing the reduction) "relate to transcendental world-constitution analogously to the way we relate to an existent," and when we speak of transcendental self-*experience* we express an appearance truth that uses the term "experience" analogically, since all experience is experience of the existent (*SCM* 73, 81).

Fink's recourse to the structure of analogy, then, turns on a view of language according to which linguistic sense is established in terms of paradigm cases and can be shifted more or less successfully to nonstandard or improper contexts. But Husserl's own earlier work suggests another, and to my mind superior, approach. For his treatment of terms like "intuition," "experience," "fulfillment," "sense," and so on, understands linguistic expression to be *functionally* generated—not dependent on a specific "proper" context of application but on phenomenologically attestable functional relations that range over any context.[29] This would mean that even if there were a cleft between being and prebeing, expression of the latter would not be irremediably compromised by the fact that natural language is initially and primarily used for expressing mundane truths. Indeed, Husserl himself seems puzzled by Fink's exaggerated claims concerning the merely analogical sense of terms like "experience" when used transcendentally. After all, he writes, "natural experience is . . . a transcendental mode, existent in the transcendental world as self-apperception of the natural attitude monad in the apperceptive universal-horizon, the natural world," and the "new, uncovered activity of the transcendentally redirected I" under the reduction "is precisely again an activity of the transcendental I of a new mode" (*SCM* 81). The relation between the two is thus far more intimate than what is implied in the notion of analogy. Analogy, especially when construed as an "analogy to the analogy," gnostically severs the I reflected upon from the reflecting I. But what is the alternative? If there is undeniably a difference between what is experienced in the natural attitude and what is experienced in reduced transcendental reflection, in terms of what trope may we understand the use of terms in moving from one to the other? If the relation between transcendental and empirical I, or transcendental and empirical experience, is not analogous to analogy, what is it?

According to the interpretation I have been developing, the reduction reveals transcendental life not as a "stranger" to the life of the natural attitude, a kind of prebeing lost in the world or shrouded by the sense "human being," but as that natural attitude life itself considered in light of its intentional meaning structure rather than in light of its ontic "commitments." It follows, then, that the only aspect of the language I use that will be "altered" by the reduction is that whereby it expresses a commitment to being. The "doxic positing" of assertions is thus quasi-neutralized, but in my view that is something that pertains equally to assertions about transcendental and empirical experience. I make no assertions about existence in either case, focusing solely on the different *Seinssinne* in each. What use of language is it, then, when I talk transcendentally of "experiencing" the "constitution" of meaning? It is true that in prereduced life the level of meaning is not attended to, that what is initially experienced are the things made possible as things for me by meaning-constituting activity. However, if the relation is as intimate as I have been suggesting, then to talk of transcendental experience is not merely an analogy. Instead, the transition from nonreduced to reduced language is governed by *metonymy*.

I shall not try to work out this suggestion in detail, but it amounts to the following. Metonymy is a trope where a term is used to substitute for something with which it is in some way associated—often by contiguity, as when I speak of the "crown" to refer to the king, but also in other more complicated ways as well, as when I claim that someone has a warm "heart." The point is that metonymy does not convey meaning by comparison—the issue is not one of discovering a bridge that spans the disparateness of two things, as it is with analogy. Rather, it trades on an intelligibility that must arise as it were from the juxtaposition itself, perhaps drawing upon a kind of familiarity established by tradition, but perhaps also by exploiting a relation between the reflective and the prereflective that we, following Fink, could associate with Platonic anamnesis (*SCM* 82). In this account, terms like "experience" or "life" make sense in a transcendental context because the natural attitude is already pervaded by the transcendental—not as something radically other, a gnostic spark hidden within it, but as something customarily overlooked, anonymous.[30]

It might be possible to go a step further here. One of the primary modes of metonymy is substitution of effect for cause—as when we use "weeping" to represent sadness. It seems to me that many phenomenological propositions employ metonymies of this sort. For instance, when we talk of the "life" of the transcendental subject we are not drawing an analogy between life and something else; indeed, we are not referring to the ontic notion of life "itself" at all, but to aspects of our *understanding* of it—hence to a meaning that is constituted transcendentally. In so doing we are returning the effect to the cause (or rather, we are returning the constituted to the constituting). And when we speak of transcendental subjectivity "constituting" or "producing" the world, we are not drawing an analogy between natural attitude production and a very different transcendental process. Rather—always presupposing the reduction, of course—we are characterizing transcendental life metonymically by designating it in terms of *a meaning* of which it is the source. Such language communicates because terms are functionally related to contexts. We "are not spellbound by the old idea of being" in the natural attitude but are concerned with beings by *way* of the transcendental life of meaning. Transcendental truths expressed in terms like "experience," "intuition," and "constitution" are not mere appearance truths, products of a nonproper enworlding, but genuine philosophical articulations of a complex that is already ours before the reduction, one that comes into focus through the reduction: the *contiguity,* so to speak, of beings and meaning. Metonymy is the phenomenological trope of the "always already" belonging together of the transcendental and the empirical. It expresses truths that, properly understood, stand in no absolute tension with the world and require no dialectical "synthetic unity of antithetical determinations." Thus, we can agree with Fink's claim that "the full-sided subject of phenomenologizing is transcendental subjectivity 'appearing' in the world"—if only we remove a tiny set of quotation marks (*SCM* 116). For there are no antithetical truths unified here, since the reduction entails no gnostic distinction between transcendental and empirical life. It is, as Heidegger knew and Husserl seemed close to acknowledging, nothing less—but also nothing more—than a possibility of that entity we call "human being."

Thus, my response to Kersten's (and Natanson's) question: Not only does the phenomenology of phenomenology not lead us beyond the Copernican revolution, it ought to teach us that the desire to go beyond it is a mistake. We should refuse Fink's dialectical absolute and steer clear of the transcendental illusion contained in moving beyond intuition to construction, even if that *seems* to condemn phenomenology to silence on questions of historical, cosmological, or psychological totalities.[31] The strength of phenomenology has all along been precisely its ability to illuminate what shows itself as it shows itself. History, the cosmos, the self—all of these show themselves in their way, and beyond that we cannot philosophize about them without falling into irresponsibility, contradiction, paradox, and error.

Notes

Introduction

1. The alternative, in my view, to articulating a phenomenological tradition in which Husserl and Heidegger are not perennially opposed to each other is the withering away of anything that might be understood as a distinctive contribution of "continental" philosophy to the philosophical tradition. In a recent book Robert D'Amico has claimed explicitly—though I believe prematurely—that this has already occurred. Claiming roughly that because the phenomenological movement from Husserl to Heidegger failed to establish itself as a genuine tradition—which requires "an open horizon of issues, problems, and possible clarifications" and cannot "consist of only the 'foundational' texts"—continental philosophy as a whole has in fact "ceased to be" a *philosophical* movement at all. Yet whatever might be said about the "end of philosophy" wing of continental philosophy, there has always been a *phenomenological* movement that fits D'Amico's description of a "philosophical tradition," and by reconceiving the relation of its founders, Husserl and Heidegger, in terms other than that of being "alternatives" (as D'Amico sees it), I hope to intervene in that tradition in order to strengthen it. See Robert D'Amico, *Contemporary Continental Philosophy,* 252–53.

2. I have in mind such works as Robert Brandom's *Making It Explicit,* Donald Davidson's *Inquiries into Truth and Interpretation,* John Haugeland's *Having Thought: Essays in the Metaphysics of Mind,* J. E. Malpas's *Donald Davidson and the Mirror of Meaning,* and John McDowell's *Mind and World,* among others. Though very different, all of these writers recognize something like the priority of meaning and pursue it in a quasi-Hegelian way that reminds one of the neo-Kantian movement rather more than of Kant (or Hegel) himself.

3. Nothing is easier than to find remarks on Husserl of the most dismissive sort, especially in Heidegger's letters. For instance, in a letter to Karl Jaspers on December 26, 1926, Heidegger writes that "if the treatise [i.e., *Sein und Zeit*] is written against anyone, then against Husserl"—whose work, Heidegger goes on to intimate, is "sham philosophy" (Walter Biemel, ed., *Martin Heidegger, Karl Jaspers: Briefwechsel, 1920–1963,* 71). Such statements are often used as license to ignore the manifest Husserlian content of Heidegger's text, explaining it away as the result of Heidegger's precarious academic situation.

4. John van Buren, *The Young Heidegger,* 44, 136, 25.

5. Ibid., 15, 55, 51.

6. Ibid., 38–39. Thus, van Buren, 39, cites with approval Thomas Sheehan's suggestion that "we might enhance the explanation of Heidegger's subject-matter by retiring the terms 'being' and the 'question of being' from the discussion." It is certainly true that these terms foster "remythologizing" tendencies both in Heidegger and in Heidegger scholars. For a recent forceful statement of the dangers, see Thomas Sheehan, "Nihilism: Heidegger/Jünger/Aristotle." However, a different view of Heidegger's "subject-matter" (the one I shall argue for in these chapters) suggests that there are more ways of avoiding such metaphysical mythologies than by abandoning philosophy altogether, even if Heidegger does not manage to hold to them.

7. Van Buren, *The Young Heidegger,* 242, 241, 202.

8. In this sense Heidegger's designation of philosophy as "skepticism" (see chap. 7 below) is not—as it perhaps is for Hume and Derrida—propaedeutic to overcoming the mania of philosophy altogether (an invitation to a personalistic or antiscientific stance) but rather is propaedeutic to a critical reorientation of philosophy itself, just as it was for Kant when he motivated his "critical solution" to the antinomy of reason by a "skeptical representation" of the issue that showed that either answer would be "mere nonsense." See Kant, *Critique of Pure Reason,* 436 (A485/B513).

9. Van Buren, *The Young Heidegger,* 232.

10. Ibid., 167, 325.

11. Ibid., 87, 219, 304.

12. Ibid., 203.

13. A similar confluence of existential and transcendental themes—though in a manner opposed to the Husserlian elements of the present proposal—has recently been given acute expression in John Haugeland's *Having Thought,* whose introduction is entitled "Toward a New Existentialism."

14. Van Buren, *The Young Heidegger,* 88.

15. Emil Lask, *Die Logik der Philosophie und die Kategorienlehre,* 43; henceforth abbreviated *LP.*

16. John McDowell, *Mind and World,* 85.

17. While there can be no question of pursuing this issue in detail here, helpful discussion of McDowell in relation to Lask, Fichte, Kant, and Heidegger can already be found in Sarah Lilly Heidt, "From Transcendence to the Open: Freedom and Finitude in the Thought of Martin Heidegger."

18. McDowell, *Mind and World,* xvi, xii, 7.

19. Ibid., 25, 26, 9; Lask, *LP* 43.

20. Lask, *LP* 109.

21. McDowell, *Mind and World,* 56–60, 170–73.

22. Ibid., 29.

23. Ibid., 78, 71. It would be valuable to develop this suggestion phenomenologically in terms of Husserl's distinction between the "naturalistic" and the "natural" attitudes. See *Ideas Pertaining to a Pure Phenomenology and to a Phenomenological Philosophy: Second Book* (Hua IV), and *The Crisis of European Sciences and Transcendental Phenomenology: An Introduction to Phenomenological Philosophy* (Hua VI).

24. McDowell, *Mind and World,* 64, 22.

25. More recently, McDowell has revised his opinion of Kant's philosophy and has rejected his earlier equation of transcendental philosophy with skepticism (see "Précis of *Mind and World,*" 365). So, too, he has moved in the direction of phenomenological questions by way of a Kant-inspired account of intentionality (see McDowell, "Having the World in View"). From a Husserlian perspective, however, McDowell's ingenious employment of the theory of synthesis in Kant's "Metaphysical Deduction" remains unphenomenological, the sort of a priori construction Husserl criticized in Paul Natorp. See chaps. 1 and 3 below.

26. McDowell, *Mind and World,* 124, 178.

27. Ibid., 155.

28. Ibid.

29. The fear that engaging in constitutional analyses in the space of meaning leads inexorably to idealism can be allayed by a look at John Haugeland's account of "letting be" in chap. 13 of *Having Thought,* 325 ff.—a text that also shows that the notion of phenomenological constitution is not tied specifically to Husserl's formulation of it and can be given a fruitful Heideggerian interpretation.

30. This sort of position has many recent defenders, among whom perhaps the most prominent is Klaus Hartmann. See, for instance, his essay "On Taking the Transcendental Turn."

Chapter 1

1. Hannah Arendt, "Martin Heidegger at Eighty," 294; Hans-Georg Gadamer, *Philosophical Hermeneutics,* 214, 230.

2. Gadamer, *Philosophical Hermeneutics,* 202.

3. Manfred Brelage, *Studien zur Transzendentalphilosophie,* 74.

4. Richard Rorty, *Philosophy and the Mirror of Nature,* 134 f., 393.

5. See Klaus Christian Köhnke, *The Rise of Neo-Kantianism: German Academic Philosophy between Idealism and Positivism.*

6. See Gerhard Lehmann, "Kant im Spätidealismus und die Anfänge der neukantischen Bewegung."

7. Köhnke, *Rise of Neo-Kantianism,* 280–81.

8. Ibid., 239.

9. Ibid.

10. Riehl was Rickert's predecessor at Freiburg in the chair that would eventually pass to Husserl, and then to Heidegger. On Riehl, see the article in Hans-Ludwig Ollig, *Der Neukantianismus.*

11. Heinrich Rickert, *Der Gegenstand der Erkenntnis: Einführung in die Transzendentalphilosophie,* 135 ff.

12. Heinrich Rickert, *Die Heidelberger Tradition und Kants Kritizismus,* 13–14.

13. Emil Lask, "Gibt es ein 'Primat der praktischen Vernunft' in der Logik?"

14. Lask, *LP* 41, 185.

15. Heinz Heimsoeth, "Die metaphysischen Motive in der Ausbildung des kritischen Idealismus."

16. Heinrich Rickert, *Die Philosophie des Lebens: Darstellung und Kritik der philosophischen Modeströmungen unserer Zeit,* 36, 50–51, 59.

17. Paul Natorp, *Philosophie, Ihr Problem und ihre Probleme: Einführung in den kritischen Idealismus,* 1, 3, 173, 184.

18. Ibid., 13.

19. Ibid., 38 ff.

20. Ibid., 14–15, 16.

21. Ibid., 44, 23 ff.

22. Ibid., 63.

23. Paul Natorp, *Logik in Leitsätzen zu akademischen Vorlesungen,* 7.

24. Natorp, *Philosophie, Ihr Problem,* 65.

25. Ibid., 50, 153–54, 50.

26. Paul Natorp, *Allgemeine Psychologie nach kritischer Methode, Erstes Buch: Objekt und Methode der Psychologie,* 32.

27. Ibid., 200–2.

28. Natorp, *Philosophie, Ihr Problem,* 153.

29. Karl Schuhmann, ed., *Edmund Husserl: Briefwechsel,* 5:110.

30. The Husserlian basis of Heidegger's approach to the university reform issue is the topic of chap. 8. In that context we shall have to consider further the sense in which Heidegger's conception of phenomenological "science" highlights an existential dimension only implicit in Husserl's conception, thereby complicating the issue of the relation between philosophy and worldview.

31. I shall return to the debate between Heidegger and Natorp in chaps. 6 and 8 below.

Chapter 2

1. Evidence of the high esteem in which Lask was held by the German philosophical community can be found in letters from Husserl to Natorp, February 1, 1922, *Edmund Husserl: Briefwechsel,* ed. Karl Schuhmann, 5:151; Husserl to Rickert, November 5, 1915, *Briefwechsel,* 5:176; Natorp to Husserl, June 3, 1917, *Briefwechsel,* 5:124; and Reinach to Husserl, August 21, 1915, *Edmund Husserl: Briefwechsel,* ed. Karl Schuhmann, 2:199. The phrase in the text is found in the letter from Reinach.

2. See, e.g., Hartmut Rosshoff, *Emil Lask als Lehrer von Georg Lukács;* Konrad Hobe, "Emil Lask: Eine Untersuchung seines Denkens"; Norbert Altwicker, *Geltung und Genesis bei Lask und Hegel;* Hanspeter Sommerhäuser, *Emil Lask in Auseinandersetzung mit Heinrich Rickert.*

3. The first full and systematic account of Lask's philosophy, focusing on the question of *Letztbegrundung* and the scientific character of philosophy, can be found in Stephan Nachtsheim, *Emil Lasks Grundlehre.* Nachtsheim's book also contains a useful bibliography of works on Lask.

4. See Heinrich Rickert, "Persönliches Gleichwort," x.

5. For a discussion of the intellectual situation in Germany between 1830 and 1881 and the sorting-out process which, by Lask's time, had established neo-Kantianism in its dominant forms (the Southwest German school and the Marburg school), see Köhnke, *Rise of Neo-Kantianism.*

6. Kant, *Critique of Pure Reason* 100 (A62/B87).

7. The terms "gnoseology" and "aletheiology" appear in Lask's second major treatise, published in 1912, *Die Lehre vom Urteil,* 423; henceforth abbreviated *LvU.*

8. Compare Hobe, "Emil Lask," 186: "The previous exposition . . . has shown that Lask rejects any justification of the categories (non-sensible forms) through transcendental subjectivity."

9. Lask's interpretation of Kant as it relates to the history of attempts to work out a doctrine of categories is found in his summary treatment (*LP* 243–63). On the rout of the psychologistic versions of neo-Kantianism by the later idealistic versions, see Köhnke, *Rise of Neo-Kantianism,* 240–80.

10. Lask thus both reinterprets and criticizes Aristotle's notion of *on hos alethes* (*LvU* 391, 403–4). Lask distinguishes between two dimensions of the "subjective." On the one hand, the cognitive activity of the *judging* subject yields an "artificial structural complication" (*LvU* 291) of the object. On the other hand, Lask hints at a *prejudicative* concept of the subject as "sheer submission to categorially embraced material" (*LP* 80). In neither case does the subject play a foundational role for the doctrine of categories, and in spite of his appeal to Husserl's notion of intentionality (e.g., *LP* 81), Lask's discussion of the "subject" generally has the appearance of an afterthought. For criticism of this view, see sec. 5 below; for a positive assessment see Schuhmann and Smith, "Two Idealisms: Lask and Husserl," 448–66.

11. For a discussion of such criticisms leveled at Lask by his contemporaries, see Wolf-Dieter Gudopp, *Der junge Heidegger: Realität und Wahrheit in der Vorgeschichte von "Sein und Zeit,"* 30–34. A more recent version of this charge will be examined in sec. 5 below.

12. As Gudopp (*Der junge Heidegger,* 34 et passim) correctly notes, the nuance at issue here was a main reason for the young Heidegger's enthusiasm for Lask. From his Marxist perspective, however, Gudopp holds both Lask's and Heidegger's attempts at a synthesis of Aristotle and Kant to be "products of the embarrassment into which bourgeois philosophy" had fallen in the period before the First World War (25). The kinship between Lask's meaning-realism and Heidegger's "ontological difference" is analyzed in chap. 4 below.

13. The locus classicus for Lotze's statement of the nature of validity (*Geltung*) is his interpretation of Plato's theory of Ideas in his 1838 *Logik—Drei Bücher: Vom Denken, vom Untersuchen, und vom Erkennen,* vol. 2, chap. 2.

14. A topic to be treated in sec. 4 below.

15. Schuhmann and Smith, "Two Idealisms: Lask and Husserl," 454, note that Lask's approach to categoriality through the "given" truth *in concreto* represents a challenge to orthodox neo-Kantian *Geltungslogik* and moves in the direction of phenomenology.

16. For a recent attempt to develop a transcendental logic with ontological, and not just epistemological (or "theory of science"), pretensions, see Hermann Krings, *Transzendentale Logik.* Important impulses from Lask are taken up in this work, especially regarding the nonmetaphysical (nonentitative) character of categories and the categorial foundation of the theory of judgment.

17. Lask's view on the possibility of metaphysics is further complicated by his distinction between *Erleben* and *Erkennen,* according to which it is possible that we "experience" metaphysical entities in some sense without having at our disposal the categories which would allow us to "know" them—to become "clear" about such experience (*LP* 130, 219). The implications of this position, though highly interesting, must be left aside here.

18. Lask's interest in the problem of the categories constitutive of historical objects is already evident in his dissertation, under Rickert's direction, on *Fichtes Idealismus und die Geschichte* (1902), which turns on the logical and historical-cultural significance of Fichte's notion of "individuality." Compare Köhnke, *Rise of Neo-Kantianism,* 124: "The Fichteanized Kant for whose creation and propagation Kuno Fischer above all must take credit was subsequently to become the distinguishing mark of the South-West German school of neo-Kantianism which derived from him."

19. On the meaning of "transcendence" for Lask, see *LvU* 414 f.; see also chap. 3 below.

20. Lask's attempt to steer clear of metaphysical realism and idealism provided the focus of Georges Gurvitch's appreciation of what he rather misleadingly called Lask's "metaphysical ontology." See Georges Gurvitch, *Les tendances actuelles de la philosophie allemande,* 153–86, esp. 178.

21. Krings, *Transzendentale Logik,* 142, notes that the "inappropriate" use of the term "*Gegenstand*" here reflects turn-of-the-century neo-Kantianism's "hostility to (or anxiety about) ontology."

22. The tension in Lask's theory of meaning as a transcendental *logic* is explored further in chap. 4.

23. Both Moltke S. Gram and Barry Stroud have discussed the problem of trying to move by way of transcendental arguments from epistemological questions of the conditions of our knowledge of something to conditions of *being,* the way things are. See Barry Stroud, "Transcendental Arguments," 241–56; Moltke S. Gram, "Transcendental Arguments," 15–26. The other side of the problem, of course, is that an account that makes no use of any verificationist moments, or "epistemological premises," threatens to abandon "transcendentality" altogether and relapse into an uncritical realism. Lask seeks to avoid both sides of the dilemma by means of the notion of validity.

24. Konrad Hobe, "Zwischen Rickert und Heidegger: Versuch über eine Perspektive des Denkens von Emil Lask," 371, argues quite plausibly that Lask distorts Aristotle's views in some important respects, but the adequacy of Lask's interpretation of Aristotle's form concept must be set aside in the present context.

25. As Krings, *Transzendentale Logik,* 279, writes: "Die kategoriale Synthesis besteht nicht darin, daß materiale Elemente *mit* dem Formelement, sondern

darin, daß materiale Elemente *durch* das Formelement verbunden werden. Kategorie und Kategorienmaterial sind nicht 'Glieder eines zwischen ihnen bestehenden Verhältnisses,' wie Lask diesen Sachverhalt zurückweist [*LP* 100], sondern die Kategorie ist das Verhältnis zwischen materialen Teilgehalten."

26. On the connection between Lask's use of the term *Bewandtnis* and Heidegger's use of the term in *Sein und Zeit,* see chap. 4. This view also informs Krings's understanding of categories. See Krings, *Transzendentale Logik,* 159 f., 201, 204, 259.

27. Lask's notion of clarity and of "living in the truth" implies, moreover, not only a prescientific comprehension of categories appropriate to "ontic" domains like nature, but a "prescientific philosophizing" (*LP* 185) and a logically naked familiarity with *Sinn.* This invites comparison with the Heidegger of *Sein und Zeit,* for whom Dasein is "in the truth" thanks to its preontological understanding of (the meaning of) being (*Seinsverständnis*), which in turn makes possible a reflective-transcendental-hermeneutic "fundamental ontology." Other commentators who have noted this connection—e.g., Theodore Kisiel, *The Genesis of Heidegger's "Being and Time,"* and van Buren, *The Young Heidegger*—have nevertheless failed, I think, to provide convincing explanation of how this prescientific philosophizing is supposed to make explicit philosophizing possible. As a consequence, the importance of critical-transcendental motifs in Heidegger's thought tends to be systematically downplayed, as are the positive aspects of his appropriation of Husserl's phenomenology. These matters shall concern us in part 2 below.

28. Nachtsheim, *Emil Lasks Grundlehre,* 231 ff., indicates where this view falls short as a grounding of philosophical knowledge.

29. In deference to "the usage of the age, schooled in positivism" (*LP* 6), Lask restricts his use of the term "being" to "sensible" being, but only with the reservation that another term be found for the "being" of supersensible beings, if there are any.

30. Nachtsheim, *Emil Lasks Grundlehre,* 231, also calls for a "meta-*categorial* level" upon which to complete the task of grounding, but on his view the turn to the subject will involve the search for principles of "thought" (gnoseology) and not of intuition.

31. Even had Lask known of the reduction, however, it is unlikely that he would have found it congenial. See Schuhmann and Smith, "Two Idealisms: Lask and Husserl," 465. The relation between Husserl and Lask is investigated in chap. 3 below.

32. Lask (*LvU* 415) refers to the role of the subject as "offering a place for [transcendent] meaning," that is, for the paradigmatic object. This is *all* he allows for the role of subjectivity with respect to this object as such. While he goes on to argue that this is not all the subject *does*—indeed, the whole text is a theory of how the judgment arises through the activity of the subject—the question of the legitimacy of a move from aletheiology to ontology concerns precisely the *prejudicative* role of the subject.

33. Michael Schweitz, "Emil Lasks Kategorienlehre vor dem Hintergrund der Kopernikanischen Wende Kants," 225, 227.

34. Ibid., 226. Lask (*LvU* 426) speaks in religious metaphors about the "original sin" of knowledge (judgment) that interposes itself between us and the "lost paradise" of the fully determinate paradigmatic object.

35. Hobe, "Zwischen Rickert und Heidegger," 360–76, 364.

36. Ibid., 368.

37. Ibid.

38. Martin Heidegger, *Sein und Zeit* (GA 2:220/263): "In its very structure Care is ahead of itself—Being already in the world—as Being alongside entities within-the-world; and in this structure the disclosedness of Dasein lies hidden. *With* and *through* it is uncoveredness; hence only with Dasein's disclosedness is the most primordial phenomenon of truth attained."

39. This becomes clear from the argument structure of the long *Vorbereitender Teil of the Prolegomena zur Geschichte des Zeitbegriffs* (GA 20:13–182/13–131).

40. This criticism, it seems to me, still holds of Krings's much more developed, yet still Laskian, notion of the "Wahrheit des ersten Vernehmens." See Krings, *Transzendentale Logik,* 86 ff.

Chapter 3

1. See Lask, *LP* (1911) and *LvU* (1912).

2. At the outset a word should be said about what Husserl knew of Lask. Husserl nowhere mentions Lask, a student of Heinrich Rickert, in his published writings. And though Lask sent both of his works on logic to Husserl, the underlinings in the copies preserved at the Husserl Archive in Louvain indicate that Husserl probably read only the first eighteen pages of *LP* and that he probably did not read *LvU* at all. In a letter to Rickert shortly after Lask's death in 1915, however, Husserl remarks that "eine der schönsten Hoffnungen der deutschen Philosophie ist mit ihm dahingegangen" (November 5, 1915, *Briefwechsel,* ed. Schuhmann, 5:176). And on the margin of a manuscript from 1923 dealing with the role of the "persönliche Einstellung" in Kant's doctrine of apperception (FII 7/162b), Husserl notes, "auch Lask muß endlich gelesen werden." It is perhaps at this time, when Husserl was finding affinities between his position and Fichte's, that he began to read Lask's *Fichtes Idealismus und die Geschichte* (1902), Husserl's copy of which is heavily underlined, though again only to p. 19. There are only three other references to Lask in all of Husserl's unpublished manuscripts, none of them substantial. In a letter from Lask to Husserl we learn that Husserl had sent Lask a copy of "Philosophy as Rigorous Science" and had also sent some criticisms of *LP* as (in Lask's words) being full of "Unexaktheit, Ungründlichkeit, Belastetheit mit Äquivokationen" (December 24, 1911, *Briefwechsel,* ed. Schuhmann, 5:34). The present chapter will indicate some of the points that might have served as the basis for Husserl's judgment here.

3. Kant, *Critique of Pure Reason,* 100.

4. Ibid., 96.

5. For Lask's view of Aristotle, see *LvU* 403–4 and *LP* 223–43.

6. Compare Edmund Husserl, *Erste Philosophie: Erster Teil* (Hua VII:63). On the interplay between Kantian and Cartesian motives in the development

of Husserl's transcendental phenomenology, see Iso Kern, *Husserl und Kant: Eine Untersuchung über Husserls Verhältnis zu Kant und zum Neukantianismus,* 109.

7. Kern, *Husserl und Kant,* 218–39.

8. Lask rejected the then-current *Abbildtheorie* but did not reject an account of propositional truth in terms of correspondence (*Übereinstimmung*). Compare *LvU* 353 ff.

9. Already by 1906 (Hua XXIV:45), Husserl had rejected the idea that judgment meaning was the act *in specie.*

10. Theodore de Boer, *The Development of Husserl's Thought,* 223.

11. For more on the relation between Lask and Husserl with regard to this problem, see Hobe, "Emil Lask," 186–201.

12. De Boer, *Development of Husserl's Thought,* 190.

13. To be sure, not under any impetus from Lask. Even if Husserl had studied Lask's position it is unlikely that he would have recognized anything useful in his notion of transcendence. This can be deduced from his response to Lask's mentor, Rickert's, notion of the "object of knowledge," Husserl's fundamental "misunderstanding" of which is noted by Kern, *Husserl und Kant,* 376–94.

14. Letter from Lask to Husserl, dated December 24, 1911, *Briefwechsel,* Schuhmann, ed., 5:34. Recall that the occasion for this letter was Lask's receipt of Husserl's "Philosophy as Rigorous Science," a work in which Husserl first indicated a fully universal (transcendental) program for phenomenology. Lask, we learn, cannot agree with Husserl that phenomenology contains "all of scientific philosophy." It may be a beginning, Lask admits, but it is still only a beginning. Presumably this means that the real problem is to move from the phenomenological standpoint of "transcendence in immanence" to the standpoint of genuine transcendence "untouched by all subjectivity"—that is, from phenomenology to ontology.

15. Kern, *Husserl und Kant,* 221.

16. For more on how Husserl's view of transcendental philosophy differs from other versions of it, and from other philosophical approaches to the problem of knowledge, see J. N. Mohanty, *The Possibility of Transcendental Philosophy.*

17. In this text Husserl uses the term "metaphysics" to refer to a study of the logical structure of the transcendent object ("ontology" in Lask's sense). He does not mean by it an investigation *other* than a logical one (a "metalogical" inquiry in Lask's sense). By the time of the *Ideas,* Husserl has dropped this use of the term "metaphysics."

18. For a sophisticated recent interpretation of these matters under the heading of "phenomenological semantics," see Olav K. Wiegand, *Interpretationen der Modallogik.*

19. On the various senses of "immanence" in Husserl, see Kern, *Husserl und Kant,* 212–13.

Chapter 4

1. W. V. O. Quine, "On What There Is," 1–19.

2. Kisiel's remark occurs in an earlier version of a paper that was subsequently published in *Man and World* as "Why Students of Heidegger Will Have

to Read Emil Lask," though without the cited words. This paper had been commissioned for a volume on Lask (as had the original version of chap. 2 above), which, after several years of delays, was finally abandoned. I retain the citation here because the present chapter was written with the earlier, unpublished version of Kisiel's essay before me.

3. The phrase is Quine's, but is perfectly applicable to Heidegger's early "logicist" treatment of meaning. See W. V. O. Quine, "Two Dogmas of Empiricism," 22.

4. It is not my intention in this chapter to trace exhaustively the development of Heidegger's reflections on logic and meaning. To do so would require extended treatment of the shift in his position which begins in his early Freiburg period (1919–23) and is documented in the lecture courses from that time (e.g., GA 56/57, GA 61, GA 63). Important studies of this material include Theodore Kisiel, "Das Entstehen des Begriffsfeldes 'Faktizität' im Frühwerk Heideggers"; Carl Friedrich Gethmann, "Philosophie als Vollzug und als Begriff"; and Friedrich Hogemann, "Heideggers Konzeption der Phänomenologie in den Vorlesungen aus dem Wintersemester 1919/1920 und dem Sommersemester 1920." See also Gethmann's recent collection, *Dasein: Erkennen und Handeln: Heidegger im phänomenologischen Kontext.* In addition, full-scale interpretations have been offered by van Buren, *The Young Heidegger,* and Kisiel, *The Genesis of Heidegger's "Being and Time"* (henceforth abbreviated *GH*). The present chapter is limited to identifying certain features of Heidegger's early reception of Lask that remain important throughout his development, though they are not the ones emphasized by Kisiel and van Buren. I will turn very briefly at the end to some consideration of the presence of these themes in *Sein und Zeit* and will have more to say about Heidegger's work during the intervening years in chaps. 7 and 8 below.

5. Karl Lehmann, "Metaphysik, Transzendentalphilosophie, und Phänomenologie in den ersten Schriften Martin Heideggers," 355.

6. This, at any rate, is how Lask interprets the ambiguities inherent in Aristotle's category of ousia (see *LP* 227–29).

7. Lotze originally used the term in his influential interpretation of Plato's Forms in his *Logik—Drei Bücher: Vom Denken, Vom Untersuchungen, und Vom Erkennen;* see esp. vol. 2 of the English translation, Hermann Lotze, *Logic in Three Books: Of Thought, Of Investigation, and Of Knowledge,* 200–23. It would be a mistake to think that in developing his own *Geltungslogik* Heidegger is indebted more to Lotze than to Lask. Anyone who reads Heidegger's dissertation and *Habilitationsschrift* with knowledge of Lask's two major works recognizes immediately how much Heidegger follows Lask—not only in his way of posing problems, but down to the very vocabulary he uses. Nor did Lotze ever interpret the validity character of the object of logic as a theory of meaning; nevertheless, it is precisely Lask's theory of meaning that Heidegger takes up. In his later critical discussion of *Geltungslogik,* Heidegger always targets Lotze because he was the well-known initiator of this way of thinking. But frequently in those very contexts he goes out of his way to praise Lask. See, e.g., the lecture course from WS 1925–26 (GA 21:62–86). And in *Sein und Zeit,* where Heidegger dismisses talk of *Geltung* as an "Urphänomen"

that has been popular "since the time of Lotze," he still praises Lask as the only one from outside the phenomenological movement to have positively appropriated Husserl's sixth logical investigation (GA 2:207, 289/198, 493).

8. See Kisiel's discussion of the various senses bound up in this term in his "Why Students of Heidegger Will Have to Read Emil Lask," 216–17. By the time of *Sein und Zeit,* Heidegger's phenomenology will have developed the resources to elucidate the basis of this substitution of *Bewandtnis* for logical form—namely, in his account of how the "relevances" of things are tied to Dasein's circumspective concern, Dasein's projective abilities to be, or skillful being-in-the-world. Neither Lask nor the young Heidegger, however, had a clear insight into the origin of the *Bewandtnisse,* nor, therefore, into the nature of the "material determination of form."

9. Thus for Lask, as for Rickert, the sciences are rooted in pretheoretical experience, and their "governing categories" (*Gebietskategorien*) will differ according to the way their objects present themselves in such experience. For example, the basic categories of physics, the categories that define the object domain, include "being" (for Lask, "sensible existent") and "causality," whereas the object domain of the science of history is governed by the categories of "value individuality" (*Wertindividualität*) and "motivation." There are complex categorial relations between the sciences, to be sure—relations of what Husserl would call *Fundierung*—but there can be no question of *reducing* the categories of one science to those of another. This antireductionist conception of the geography of the sciences is equally important for Heidegger.

10. Lask is aware of the threat of an infinite regress here: If being is the category that clarifies the domain of "sensible-existent" material, and if validity is the category that, at a second level, clarifies the domain of the logical (to which being, as a logical category, belongs), must there not be a further "meta" category to clarify validity as a categorial form? But here Lask argues that there is no regress: Since validity is itself the *Gebietskategorie* of the logical domain ("the category of categories"), it applies to itself. It alone, of all theoretical categories, has reflexive self-applicability, and this brings a certain closure to the system of sciences. Heidegger praises this aspect of Lask's theory in his 1912 review essay on logical theory (GA 1:25).

11. Some commentators on Lask have recognized this problem of the accessibility of the object. Konrad Hobe, for instance, admits that the Kantian "thing-in-itself" problem will return unless "der Gegenstand selber bereits vor dem urteilsmässigen Erkennen in einer 'Offenheit,' d.h., in einer Beziehung der Erkennbarkeit zum Subjekt steht." But Hobe thinks that Lask's logos-immanent object already secures such a relation since, for Lask, "Gegenstand schon immer Gegenstand für uns ist." See Hobe, "Zwischen Rickert und Heidegger," 364. Appealing as such a view is, however, it is difficult to square with what Lask says about the paradigmatic object "untouched by all subjectivity." This is an unresolved tension in Lask's work, deriving, as we saw in chap. 3, from the fact that he is not clear about how investigation of such "openness," or phenomenological subjectivity, should proceed.

12. See esp. GA 2:111–19/114–22, where the structure of "letting something be involved" (*bewendenlassen*) is analyzed. It would not be too much to say that only at this point is Heidegger's theory of meaning truly transcendental. The involvement (*Bewandtnis*) of the material, which is for both Lask and Heidegger the truth or intelligibility of the thing, remains ungrounded in Lask because he cannot account for the conditions under which such involvements show themselves. In Heidegger, however, the "totality of involvements" is illuminated by (*not* reduced to) the character of Dasein's understanding as projection of possibilities. The genuine transcendental move is thus the analysis of Dasein's disclosedness (*Erschlossenheit*) as the condition for the possibility of the logos-immanent object as meaning.

13. Letter from Lask to Husserl, December 24, 1911, *Briefwechsel,* ed. Schuhmann, 5:34.

14. This task is carried out as a "genealogy of logic" in Edmund Husserl's *Experience and Judgment.* This text, a compilation of sketches and research manuscripts Husserl worked on between 1919 and 1930, was edited by Ludwig Landgrebe and first published (in a German edition) only in 1938. Thus Lask, who died in 1915, could have known nothing of these investigations. The point, however, is not that Lask explicitly rejected some portion of Husserl's work, but rather that his own position contained no resources that could have enabled him to develop in that direction, though his theory of judgment requires it.

15. The phrase is Husserl's, used in *Formal and Transcendental Logic* to chide those (like Lask) who, out of excessive fear of psychologism, refused altogether to explore the genuine transcendental problems of logic that are found at the level of intentional constitution (Hua XVII:159/151).

16. This seems to be Hobe's position in "Zwischen Rickert und Heidegger," 68, but it also seems to be a presumption of most interpretations that emphasize the concept of "facticity" in Heidegger. I, on the contrary, see Heidegger as a phenomenological transcendental idealist, and I shall try to motivate that interpretation in pt. 2 of this book.

17. As we shall see in chap. 7, this step is already taken in the lecture course of WS 1921–22 (GA 61:56–58). Further, in the lecture from the Kriegsnotsemester of 1919, "Die Idee der Philosophie und das Weltanschauungsproblem," Heidegger claims that Lask saw the problem of the origin of the logical in prelogical, pretheoretical "life" without, however, possessing the means to develop this insight (GA 56/57:88).

18. Compare Heidegger in 1915: "To speak of the logical place of a phenomenon is more than a mere logician's idiom" since it reflects the deep fact that "every phenomenon within the realm of the thinkable in general requires, with respect to what it is [*seinem Gehalt nach*], a particular place. Every place rests upon spatial determination, which determination, as order, is itself possible only on the basis of a system of relations [*Bezugssystem*]. Similarly, 'place' in the logical sense implies an *order.* What has its logical place locates itself in a specific way in a particular *totality of relations* [*Beziehungsganzes*]" (GA 1:212).

19. See, e.g., Mark Okrent, *Heidegger's Pragmatism: Understanding, Being, and the Critique of Metaphysics.*

20. This was in fact the view of Oskar Becker ("Para-Existenz: Menschliches Dasein und Dawesen," 261 ff.), who sought to make good on this lack while remaining within the general framework of Heideggerian phenomenological ontology. Interestingly, Otto Pöggeler, who has chronicled this chapter in the early history of the reception of Heidegger's work, notes (in "Hermeneutische und mantische Phänomenologie," 322 ff.) that in a previous essay published in 1927, *Mathematische Existenz: Untersuchungen zur Logik und Ontologie mathematischer Phänomene,* Becker held a different view. There "he still saw Husserlian and Heideggerian phenomenology as a unity," the latter being "a consistent further development, a 'concretization' of Husserl's transcendental point of departure." Though Pöggeler finds this view in error (and if one insists on complete fidelity to Husserl, or on including everything Heidegger ever wrote, it surely is), I believe that the early Freiburg phenomenologist perceived something important that now, after Husserlian and Heideggerian phenomenologies have been pursued in isolation for decades, might once more be accessible to us.

21. Quine, "Two Dogmas of Empiricism," 43.

Chapter 5

1. This was one *systematic* site of the modernism/antimodernism controversy and was crucial to the neo-Scholastic strategy, launched by the encyclical *Aeterni Patris* (1879), of showing that "modern" thinkers and issues—including modern science—could be absorbed into a Scholastic framework. Thus, Gudopp, *Der junge Heidegger,* 21, sees in Heidegger's early work a neo-Scholastic antimodernism. But in his more nuanced look at Heidegger's early milieu, Hugo Ott, *Martin Heidegger: Unterwegs zu seiner Biographie,* 74 f., provides strong evidence that Heidegger was deeply attracted to modernist positions.

2. The "preparatory work" Heidegger mentions in the cited passage has affinities with the task of translating natural language into logical form (symbolic notation). This raises the question of Heidegger's relation to the emergence of symbolic logic, though I shall not discuss that here. In the 1912 logic review, Heidegger takes note of Russell and Whitehead, only to argue that "logistics" is unable to reach the "genuine logical problems" concerning "the conditions of possibility" for the "mathematical handling of logical problems" (GA 1:42–43).

3. Heidegger's reconstruction is based in part on *De modis significandi,* subsequently shown to have been authored not by Scotus but by the Scotist Thomas of Erfurt. Since this has little bearing on Heidegger's text, given its *problemgeschichtlich* approach (GA 1:196, 399), I will continue to refer to "Scotus" in this chapter.

4. Thus, Brelage, *Studien zur Transzendentalphilosophie,* 72–230, has shown that Heidegger's project can be seen as one of several efforts—characteristic of late neo-Kantianism—to complete or go beyond a formal "objective logic" of principles of valid knowledge. Among these efforts to contextualize critical epistemology, in addition to Heidegger's, Brelage discusses Husserl's transcendental phenomenology, the later Natorp's *Denkpsychologie,* Hönigswald's "monadology," and Hartmann's "gnoseology/ontology."

5. Kant, *Critique of Pure Reason,* 98 (A59/B84), 100 (A62–63/B87).

6. Ibid., 97 (A58/B82).

7. The term *Wirklichkeitsbereich* (realm of reality) is Heidegger's usual term for the categorial "sort" to which different objects and object domains (*Gegenstandsgebiete*) belong, though he sometimes uses related terms like *Daseinsform, Wirklichkeitsform,* or *Wirklichkeitsweise.* Given the connection between these concepts and the subsequent ontic/ontological difference, it is noteworthy that here "being" is restricted to the status of a category governing a single realm of reality, that of sensibly existent entities. Heidegger expressly repudiates this usage, "deriving from Lotze," in WS 1925 (GA 21:64).

8. "Categories of nature" include "being," "causality," or "occurrence." The empirical scientist is not concerned with such categories, but with relations in and among the objects of the science. But (and this is how Heidegger understands the "rational" dimension of science) it is evident that in abstraction from the categorial dimension the scientist's "theoretical" approach to objects loses its meaning, as will be discussed below.

9. Compare Brelage, *Studien zur Transzendentalphilosophie,* 103.

10. In the logic review, and then again verbatim in his dissertation, Heidegger credits Husserl with having "broken the psychologistic curse," while at the same time approving Natorp's claim that the neo-Kantians had "little to learn" from Husserl's antipsychologistic arguments (GA 1:19, 64).

11. On my use of the term "ontological difference" above, note the formulations in which Lask directly anticipates those Heidegger will propose (e.g., *LP* 21, 46, 117, 121).

12. Neo-Kantians did not, of course, view categories as *psychic* forms of thought. But they did understand categories to be formal principles of valid *knowledge.* This reference to knowledge is rejected by Lask, however, for whom knowledge implies a knowing subject. The relation between the mode of reality called "validity" and the subject of knowledge is one Lask tries to *determine* rather than assume definitionally—though (as we saw in chap. 4) it is just here that Heidegger holds him to have failed.

13. Though as early as 1912 Heidegger argues that the question of whether Kant's philosophy was in essence psychologistic or transcendental had already been decided "in favor of the transcendental-logical interpretation" (GA 1:19), the very existence of a psychologistic interpretation bespoke an unclarity in Kant's ideas (e.g., in the doctrine of synthesis). Lask did not absolve Kant fully of psychologism (*LP* 243–62). Heidegger is known to have taken renewed interest in Kant around the time of *Sein und Zeit* primarily because he saw a way to interpret Kant *phenomenologically* (GA 25:6). See Daniel Dahlstrom, "Heidegger's Kantian Turn: Notes to His Commentary on the *Kritik der reinen Vernunft.*" Dahlstrom does not deal with the interpretation of Kant in Heidegger's earliest work, where Heidegger seems to have found it convenient to share some of Husserl's contemporaneous reservations about Kant.

14. The *Beziehungsganzes* of logical space is precursor of the *Bewandtnisganzheit* in *Sein und Zeit,* and a crucial moment in the transformation of the

one to the other is Heidegger's appropriation of Lask's term "*Bewandtnis*" in his explication of logical form. We have already noted the difficulty in translating this central term in Heidegger's early work. As Ernst Tugendhat, *Der Wahrheitsbegriff bei Husserl und Heidegger,* 290, points out, "[T]here is probably no other language that contains a single word for the two significations" involved in Heidegger's use of "*Bewandtnis*" in *Sein und Zeit.* I mark this fact by leaving it for the most part untranslated here.

15. Heidegger praised Lask's *LvU* as being "even more significant for the theory of categories than his *Logik der Philosophie*" (GA 1:407), and in his dissertation he expressly invokes Lask's "metagrammatical subject-predicate theory" (GA 1:177–81; GA 1:32 f.).

16. This phrase anticipates the idea, introduced by Heidegger in WS 1921/22, of categories as "formal indicating" concepts that "interpret a phenomenon in a particular way" (GA 61:86). As we shall see in chap. 7, the later texts construe categories as eminent ways "in which life comes to itself" (GA 61:88). Here the *Bewandtnis* of knowing, understanding entities within the world, is traced ever more closely to modes of *self*-understanding.

17. For some discussion see Roderick M. Stewart, "Signification and Radical Subjectivity in Heidegger's *Habilitationsschrift*"; John Caputo, "Phenomenology, Mysticism, and the *Grammatica Speculativa:* A Study of Heidegger's *Habilitationsschrift.*" Theodore Kisiel provides an important critical corrective to Stewart's and Caputo's treatment of the *modi* in "Das Kriegsnotsemester 1919: Heideggers Durchbruch in die hermeneutische Phänomenologie," and see also Kisiel, *GH* 31, 515 f.

18. This is related to Heidegger's observation that medieval thought "exhibits a lack of methodological self-consciousness" in the "modern" sense of "reflecting" on its "problems as *problems,*" on the "possibility and manner of solving them." In a word, "medieval man is not *bei sich selbst* in the modern sense" (GA 1:199). This is not without its advantages, according to Heidegger, for it precludes the errors of psychologism, but it also leads to the above-mentioned lack of a "precise [logically adequate] concept of the subject."

19. Heidegger goes into these matters in his 1912 essay, "Das Realitätsproblem in der modernen Philosophie," which is background for his brief note in the *Schluss* (GA 1:13–15).

20. In the end Heidegger rejects critical—or "scientific"—realism because it collapses the distinction between philosophy and empirical science. On Oswald Külpe's "naturalistic" view (summarized in his 1902 *Die Philosophie der Gegenwart in Deutschland*), problems of knowledge are to be resolved ultimately by an "inductive metaphysics" that projects the results of the sciences of subject (psychology) and object (physics) to their ideal point of intersection. Already in 1912 Heidegger finds the "hypothetical" character of such metaphysics objectionable (GA 1:15). In chap. 12 we shall find Heidegger returning to criticize Külpe's view in 1929, when he is once more tempted by the idea of a "metaphysical conclusion" to the problem of knowledge—this time under the heading of "metontology."

21. In SS 1925, for example, Heidegger identifies categorial intuition as

one of the "fundamental discoveries" of phenomenology (GA 20:63f/47 f.), and the report from the 1973 seminar in Zähringen suggests that Heidegger held the concept of categorial intuition to be the "flashpoint of Husserlian thought." See Martin Heidegger, *Vier Seminare,* 111.

22. In WS 1921–22 Heidegger investigates the "value and limits" of the form/material dichotomy, cautioning that it "is best to keep the concept of form separate from the concept of category" (GA 61:86)—a departure from transcendental "logic" already adumbrated in the idea of categorial form as the *Bewandtnis* of the material.

23. This is the very question Heidegger had raised at the conclusion of his 1914 dissertation: "What is the meaning of meaning? Does it even make sense to ask this? . . . Perhaps we stand here before something ultimate, irreducible, that precludes any further illumination" (GA 1:171).

24. This problem is addressed ultimately in Heidegger's "hermeneutic of facticity." See Kisiel, "Das Entstehen des Begriffsfeldes 'Faktizität' im Frühwerk Heideggers." I would add only that this hermeneutics is still explicitly conceived as *transcendental* philosophy. To allow the transcendental ambition to drop out amounts to the claim that "translogical" principles are no more than *empirical,* and that "facticity" is just a fancy name for "fact."

25. See John Caputo, *The Mystical Element in Heidegger's Thought,* esp. 145–52. Caputo correctly sees Heidegger's turn to Eckehart's mysticism as motivated by the desire for a "solution to the problem of truth, where truth is taken to be the correlativity or belonging together of thought and being" (151), and he speculates—again with good reason—that this solution aimed at a "realism in the form of . . . Husserl's *Logical Investigations*" (152), though such realism is far from Scholastic realism and is quite close to *transcendental* idealism. But mysticism as such becomes an option because of the issue Heidegger specifically mentions: the "principle of the material determination of form" (GA 1:402). Van Buren, *The Young Heidegger,* 87–112, makes this the centerpiece of his interpretation of the *Schluss.*

26. This problem preoccupies Heidegger from the beginning. In 1912 he mentions the suspicion that "the sharp separation of logic from psychology may not be achievable"; furthermore, "the fact that the logical is embedded in the psychological" is a "peculiar and perhaps never fully clarifiable problem" (GA 1:29–30). Again in 1914 he notes the question of "how the relation between the psychical reality and valid subsistence of the judgment is to be characterized" and wonders "whether a deeper solution of this matter can even become a goal" (GA 1:176). In the present context (1916), he suggests that the problem can be solved by a metaphysics of living spirit. In *Sein und Zeit,* however, he implies that "the separation of the real accomplishment and ideal content of the judgment" is altogether unjustified, that "psychologism" may indeed be "right to hold out against this separation" even if it does not clarify the (ontological) relation (GA 2:287/259–60). This of course does not mean that Heidegger now *accepts* psychologism, though Tugendhat argues that he falls victim to a version of it nonetheless. See Tugendhat, *Wahrheitsbegriff,* 331 f., 340 f.

Chapter 6

1. Kisiel, *GH* 59.

2. Kisiel's story thus becomes an extended gloss on Heidegger's self-description, found in a letter to Karl Löwith (August 19, 1921) that Kisiel cites several times: "I am a 'Christian theo*logian*.' " The letter can be found in Dietrich Papenfuss and Otto Pöggeler, eds., *Zur philosophischen Aktualität Heideggers,* 2:29.

3. We shall take up this question in chap. 12.

4. Kisiel does of course draw judiciously from the more biographically oriented works of Hugo Ott and Thomas Sheehan, as well as from Heidegger's correspondence and other important sources. My point concerns a matter of emphasis.

5. The phrase is found in Heidegger's letter to Löwith, August 19, 1921, *Zur philosophischen Aktualität Heideggers,* Papenfuss and Pöggeler, eds., 2:29.

6. Related to this, Kisiel's book clearly shows how right from the start Heidegger saw in philosophy an "admixture of historical with systematic foundations" (*GH* 111). This deeply complicates the question of how an autonomous (and not merely "immanent") critique of "Heidegger's" thought is to proceed. If the systematic and historical are "equiprimordial," they are nevertheless not identical, and in the difference there is room for tension.

7. Kisiel's attention to Heidegger's ongoing fascination with grammatically impersonal sentences, as well as to the importance of prefixes, suffixes, and prepositions in Heidegger's thought, is a noteworthy feature of the book. "The KNS experience" itself might even be said to follow a logic of punctuation: The "primal experience of our beginnings in experience" is "at first bland [.], then exclamatory [!], and finally interrogative [?]" (*GH* 363).

8. The description is Heidegger's, found on a "loose note" that Kisiel dates to "the months following September 1916" (*GH* 73, 520 n. 11).

9. Martin Heidegger, "Mein Weg in die Phänomenologie," 86; translated by Joan Stambaugh under the title of "My Way to Phenomenology," 78.

10. The extent to which formal indication is compatible with Husserl's conception of phenomenological science, from which it can be shown to derive, will be assessed in chap. 7.

11. Rickert, *Die Philosophie des Lebens,* 194. It is time, writes Rickert, to stop "measuring the value of a philosophizing by its liveliness [*Lebendigkeit*]." Heidegger discusses the objection elsewhere (GA 61:80). Kisiel also mentions the exchange (*GH* 509). My argument is that without highlighting the positive role Husserlian notions play in Heidegger's thinking here one cannot sufficiently clarify the *possibility* of distinguishing between living life and philosophical thinking about it.

12. A précis of the issues involved here can be found under the heading "*Verstehen, Seinsverständnis*" in app. D of the *Genesis* (*GH* 507). There Kisiel notes that Heidegger fails to give us "any real hint on how the *Besinnung*" that is supposed to contrast with Husserl's reflection "does not entail reflective intrusion." As I shall argue in the next chapter, the problem is solvable only by

recognizing that not all reflection *is* "intrusion."

13. Is it surprising then that an appropriately Husserlian functional notion of *Sicht* returns in *Being and Time* itself, as a formal indication for "access in general" (GA 2:195/187)?

14. A further question concerns whether any such cognitive-illuminative self-recollection could escape being merely individual, a matter at best of clarifying *this* individual life, and so hardly a theme for science. Doubts on this score were already leveled at Husserl's position by Rickert, for Husserl's "reflection" also thematizes what is originally concrete *individual* experience. To make this a topic for science Husserl employs the eidetic reduction—roughly, the move from fact to essence by way of imaginative variation. So the question is whether Heidegger's method of formal indication excludes such essentializing. My own view of the matter is presented in chap. 10 below. Though the evidence is ambiguous, Heidegger does not intend his analyses to be valid merely for the one who is in his "situation," but to be repeatable by others in principle, even if not in a mechanical way.

15. Thus Kisiel seems to suggest that only with Aristotle does Heidegger find a mode of thinking that is at once sensuous and intellectual (*GH* 237–38, 242, 265–68, 302–6)—when Husserl's concept of intuition obviously does not exclude categorial ("intellectual") moments. Did not the notion of "categorial intuition" contribute to Heidegger's ability to recognize the significance of phronesis and to formulate the role of *aletheia?*

16. One may consult Theodore Kisiel's "On the Way to *Being and Time:* Introduction to the Translation of Heidegger's *Prolegomena zur Geschichte des Zeitbegriffs*" to learn his views of the latter, but here I shall confine myself to the argument in *GH.*

Chapter 7

1. Kant, *Critique of Pure Reason,* 25 (Bxxii). As an inquiry into the possibility of synthetic a priori judgments, Kant's *Critique* is not concerned with the analysis and presentation of everything that can be known by pure reason, but with the conditions of reason's access to it. Kant's failure to account fully for the possibility of transcendental inquiry itself provides the problem to which, for Heidegger, phenomenological method is the answer. For readings of *Being and Time* in the tradition of transcendental philosophy, see Brelage, *Studien zur Transzendentalphilosophie;* Daniel O. Dahlstrom, *Das logische Vorurteil;* and Carl Friedrich Gethmann, *Verstehen und Auslegung: Das Methodenproblem in der Philosophie Martin Heideggers.*

2. Heidegger expresses this clearly in an August 20, 1927, letter to Löwith: "Der 'Ansatz' der Fundamentalontologie sind ja nicht die ersten 10 Seiten, sondern die *ganze* Abhandlung. Gleichwohl sage ich: die Analytik des Daseins ist existenziale, also von der Existenz her geleitet, und zwar deshalb, weil die 'vorbereitende' Analytik des Daseins (*nicht* ontologische Anthropologie!) einzig

zielt auf die Aufklärung des zum Dasein gehörigen Seinsverständnisses. Dieses *Verstehen* gilt es aus dem Dasein zu explizieren. Die Frage ist: wo und wie gewinne ich den Horizont für *dieses Verstehens?* Verstehen aber charakterisiert die Existenz; daher ist das Existenziale inhaltlich und methodisch zentral, aber so, daß zugleich die 'Ganzheit' der Grundstruktur des Daseins heraustritt." And further: "Das Existenziale [hat] für die Möglichkeit der Ontologie überhaupt einen Vorrang." In Papenfuss and Pöggeler, eds., *Zur philosophischen Aktualität Heideggers,* 2:35–36.

3. In *Ideen I,* e.g., we read: "In a certain way, and with some caution in the use of words, we can also say that *all real unities are 'unities of meaning' [Sinn].* Unities of meaning presuppose . . . a meaning-bestowing consciousness which, for its part, exists absolutely and not by virtue of another meaning-bestowal" (Hua III:134/128).

4. See, e.g., the essays by Gethmann, "Philosophie als Vollzug und als Begriff"; Hogemann, "Heideggers Konzeption der Phänomenologie"; Christoph Jamme, "Heideggers frühe Begrundung der Hermeneutik"; and Otto Pöggeler, "Heideggers logische Untersuchungen."

5. See Kisiel, *GH.*

6. In the most closely reasoned and comprehensive work to date on the relation between Husserlian and Heideggerian conceptions of phenomenological method, Burt Hopkins, *Intentionality in Husserl and Heidegger,* clearly shows how each "prerogative" opens up aspects of the things themselves that the other has difficulty with. In particular, in a spirit very much in line with the argument of the present chapter, Hopkins suggests that Heidegger seems to rely on something like phenomenological reflection in order to gain *methodological* purchase on the difference between entities and their meaning (being). The " 'advance regard toward being' " that makes this possible "cannot be suitably accounted for on the basis of either ontico-ontological or explicitly ontological appeals to the 'hermeneutic situation' " (214). On the contrary, from a Husserlian point of view "it cannot help but seem . . . that the disclosure of an unreflective, pre-theoretical understanding of being 'always already there' involves the *reflectively* theoretical comportment of a methodological regard" (183). A central chapter of Hopkins's book is thus devoted to the question, "Phenomenological Method: Reflective or Hermeneutical?" and without trying to resolve the question completely, Hopkins draws the firm conclusion that it cannot be *both* (203–4). Though I cannot respond to Hopkins's trenchant argument here, part of his conclusion seems to be based on the view that hermeneutic phenomenology is committed to "*ground[ing]* the methodological legitimacy of Dasein's theoretical comportment in its pre-conceptual, and hence unreflective comportment" (182), and this seems questionable. One of the most interesting aspects of the early lecture courses—and the one I will try to elucidate in what follows—is that Heidegger's appeal to facticity (the precise *way* it is supposed to function as a ground) already tries to take into account the methodological priority (as regards questions of legitimacy, validity, and evidence) of what is reflectively uncovered, such that phenomenology will be both hermeneutic *and* reflective.

7. Of course, Heidegger here tacitly criticizes an aspect, analyzed in chaps. 4 and 5, of his own earlier adherence to *Geltungslogik.*

8. Compare Edmund Husserl, "Philosophie als strenge Wissenschaft" (Hua XXV:52/136).

9. In a series of articles Theodore Kisiel has thoroughly explored this turning point in the lecture course of *KNS* 1919. See "The Genesis of *Being and Time,*" and "Das Kriegsnotsemester 1919: Heideggers Durchbruch in die hermeneutische Phänomenologie." For a summary, see *GH* 15–25, 38–44.

10. In the next semester's course, *Phänomenologie der Anschauung und des Ausdrucks: Theorie der philosophischen Begriffsbildung* (GA 59), Heidegger returns to these psychological (Natorp) and historical (Dilthey) approaches in more detail, though without, I would argue, changing his position in fundamental ways. For an opposed reading, see Robert C. Scharff, "Heidegger's 'Appropriation' of Dilthey before *Being and Time,*" 106, where it is argued that a proper understanding of the "Dilthey-Heidegger connection" raises "serious questions about the perspicacity of those many current readings of *SZ*'s line of inquiry ('Weg') that privilege its phenomenological and transcendental ideas."

11. Compare Husserl, *Ideen I* (Hua III:52/44).

12. As we saw in the previous chapter, Kisiel argues that Heidegger makes Natorp's objection his own (*GH* 47) while still trying to "salvage, amplify, and deepen" Husserl's idea of the reflexivity built into all experience (*GH* 56). Where I would want to press the point is that this attempt to "salvage" reflection is necessarily at work in Heidegger's reconstruction of phenomenological *method* as well. Because Kisiel does not discuss the 1921–22 lecture in any detail—dismissing it as "verbose, baroque, and turgid" (*GH* 235)—and since this is where Heidegger is most expansive on what he takes phenomenological method to involve, it is hard to know whether he sees the "salvage operation" at work in the method problem.

13. Here I translate *Besinnung* as "reflection." Any translation of a philosophical term must be justified by a philosophical argument, and the present essay constitutes the beginning of one. Heidegger avoids the term *Reflexion* in describing his method because, as we saw, it suggests either introspection or objectification of the *Erlebnisse,* neither of which belongs to Heidegger's procedure. But if the difference between meaning and entities—the topic of philosophy according to the lecture course, as I shall show—is explicitly thematizable only through a *Besinnung* that invokes the experiencing of the experienced, the understanding of the understood (in short, something like a first-person stance), this arguably implicates a crucial aspect of what belongs to the English term "reflection" and so justifies its use in translation. If the phenomenon of reflection need not include the idea of objectification of *Erlebnisse,* it need not exclude the interpretive elements that Heidegger's account of philosophy's method involves. The crucial thing (as I argue in sec. 3) is that to philosophize, to grasp meaning as meaning, one must "accompany" oneself explicitly: In my thinking about *X,* "*my* thinking" about *X* must always also be at issue.

14. Husserl, "Philosophie als strenge Wissenschaft" (Hua XXV:53/137).

15. This "primordial decision" is evidently the precursor of "authenticity"

in *Being and Time*—an isomorphism that attests to the methodological function that the later notion has as a condition of possibility for philosophy. Though I shall have more to say about this in sec. 3 (and in chaps. 8 and 9 below), a full interpretation of the methodological role of authenticity lies beyond the scope of this book.

16. See, further, the accounts in Theodore Kisiel, "Heidegger (1907–1927): The Transformation of the Categorial," and "On the Way to *Being and Time.*"

17. The term "*Vollzug*" and the various forms of "*vollziehen*" play an enormously important role in Heidegger's lecture course. Just how important is demonstrated by Gethmann in "Philosophie als Vollzug und als Begriff." Translating the term is difficult, however, since it has several senses, all of which are in play at various times in Heidegger's usage, sometimes all at once. Daniel O. Dahlstrom, "Heidegger's Method: Philosophical Concepts as Formal Indications," 782, notes that in " 'Vollziehen' there is a sense of executing, carrying out, and performing, but also a sense of accomplishing, perfecting, and fulfilling." I have generally translated the term as "accomplishment," which seems to me best to suggest both the idea of carrying out and the idea of perfecting, but I have sometimes resorted to other terms as the context seemed to demand.

18. In *Being and Time* the concepts used to determine the being of Dasein are designated "formal-indicating." Though never explained there, the term contains an essential clue about how philosophical discourse (the text of *Being and Time*) is to be understood. The term frequently appears when Heidegger breaks the course of his exposition to discuss questions of method explicitly—e.g., GA 2:307/274, where Heidegger is making the crucial transition from division 1 to division 2, and again GA 2:415, 417/361, 362, where Heidegger is discussing the existentiell/existential circle in fundamental ontological interpretation and the idea of presupposition. The English translation does not preserve the fact that this is a quasi-technical term in Heidegger's thought, but the lecture course—where formal indication is discussed in detail—shows just how important it is to Heidegger's conception of hermeneutic *philosophy.* Kisiel makes the concept of formal indication the centerpiece of his interpretation of the early Heidegger in *GH.* See also Otto Pöggeler, "Heideggers Begegnung mit Dilthey"; Dahlstrom, "Heidegger's Method."

19. Compare Dahlstrom, "Heidegger's Method," 780. According to Dahlstrom, formal indication is "a revisable way of pointing to some phenomenon, fixing its preliminary sense and the corresponding manner of unpacking it, while at the same time deflecting any 'uncritical lapse' into some specific conception that would foreclose pursuit of a 'genuine sense' of the phenomenon." This function is clearly at work in terms like "death," "truth," and "guilt" in *Being and Time* and explains why commentators have often had trouble determining the extent to which such terms are meant to invoke the phenomena they "ordinarily" name.

20. I am unable to come up with noncumbersome translations of these technical terms, which are oft-used tools in the conceptual workshop of Heidegger's early Freiburg lectures. Kisiel (*GH* 493, 510) translates them as follows: *Bezugssinn*

(relating sense), *Gehaltssinn* (containing sense), *Vollzugssinn* (actualizing sense), and *Zeitigungssinn* (sense of temporalization). In what follows I shall leave them untranslated and allow their meaning to emerge with the context. For Husserl's distinction between authentic and inauthentic thinking, see *Logische Untersuchungen* (Hua XIX/2:717, 722 ff./821, 825 ff.).

21. For instance, both biology and history are concerned (in part) with the same object, namely, human being, but the noematic aspect or *Gehaltssinn* relevant in these sciences is different. In biology human being would be approached (roughly speaking) under the aspect of organic life, whereas history would concern itself with human being in the sense of "living spirit" (to use the term from Heidegger's *Habilitation* thesis). This example is meant only to illustrate how Heidegger in 1921–22 could not determine how he actually would specify the categories that define these two scientific domains.

22. Kisiel (*GH* 534 n. 4) claims that the term is not used until October 1922 and that the "passage in GA 61:60 postdates the lecture course itself."

23. It is instructive to note that as late as 1927—in *Die Grundprobleme der Phänomenologie* (GA 24:155–56/110–11)—Heidegger can still speak of "reflection" (*Reflexion*) as distinctive of ontological inquiry, using the term precisely to distinguish the "naïveté" of ancient ontology from the modern attempt—including his own—to overcome such naïveté: "Ancient ontology performs in a virtually naive way its interpretation of beings and its elaboration of the concepts mentioned." Though "naive ontology, too, if it is ontology at all, must already always, because necessarily, be reflective—reflective in the genuine sense that it seeks to conceive beings with respect to their being by having regard to the Dasein (puche, nous, logos)," in naive ontology "reflection [*Reflexion*] remains in the rut of pre-philosophical knowledge"—it has not become an explicit issue of method. Heidegger's attempt to revamp the phenomenological concept of reflection, the beginnings of which I am outlining in this chapter, is an attempt to overcome this naïveté and so to reunite Aristotelian with Kantian transcendental philosophy.

24. Heidegger analyzes such breakdown categorially later in the lecture; I shall return to it.

25. The published text reads "von Ausdrücklichkeit zu Unausdrücklichkeit," which is surely a misprint.

26. Before accepting Heidegger's characterization of Husserl, however, one needs to keep in mind Hopkins's indisputable point (*Intentionality in Husserl and Heidegger,* 197, 184, 181) that the "intentional essence of the non-actional fringe and horizonal field that Husserl exhibits in terms of the *Hintergrundsfeld* (background field) of intentional acts is . . . *clearly not* addressed in the Heideggerian account and critique of the phenomenon of intentionality," thus leading to a "foreshortened" understanding of Husserl's concept of reflection "in terms of the cogito" and its "subjectivity . . . determined on the basis of an epistemological understanding of an inward reflective grasping of an immanent, and hence absolute, entity in its Being." For Husserl, such an "ontological" reading of reflection is a prejudice distorting its true essence, neutrally determined "in terms of the phenomenally peculiar uncovering of its reflected theme as 'something

that manifests itself as having already been prior to its coming before the reflective regard' "—a description that would hold of the sorts of things that Heidegger's "hermeneutics" uncovers as well.

27. The theological horizon of the categories found in this text is discussed in Kisiel, *GH,* and especially in van Buren, *The Young Heidegger.* Given the formal indicating character of the categories of factic life—the fact that they are crafted from an evidence situation to which they are to lead us back explicitly—it is certainly a legitimate question as to whether the "fundamental experiences" of Christian life (as explicated by certain forms of Christian theology) are not thereby taken at least as starting points for reflection. At the same time, Heidegger insists that philosophy "must remain *a-theistic* in its radical, self-imposed, questionability" (GA 61:197). This means that the validity of the categorial account is to stand or fall on the basis of its adequacy to the phenomenological evidence. Thus, it does not seem quite right to argue, with Dahlstrom, "Heidegger's Method," 794–95, that Heidegger's method *itself* is "incomprehensible apart from Christian theology." For a fuller account of the categories of factic life in this lecture as they relate to their counterparts in *Being and Time,* see Gethmann, "Philosophie als Vollzug und als Begriff."

28. Here Heidegger already anticipates the crucial innovation of *Being and Time* in relation to the ontological tradition, namely, that the categorial features of Dasein's being (the *existentialia*) "are not present-at-hand 'properties' of some entity which 'looks' so and so and is itself present-at-hand; they are in each case possible ways for it to be" (GA 2:56/67). This means that categories, as existential "possibilities," include reference in their structure to alternatives of (so to speak) success or failure—just as *Existenz,* as *je mein,* is modalized into "authentic" or "inauthentic" possibilities.

29. The modalization, or essential ambiguity, in life's sort of categorial being is indicated in the term Heidegger uses to describe its peculiar self-referentiality, *vorkommen.* For it at once means "to occur" and to "come forth" in the sense of "appear." In the present passage it is used to suggest that in everyday practical affairs, life is there for itself in a way—it "occurs"—though it does not really *come forth* in its ownmost, but only "shines through" (*hindurchscheint*) in the non-ownmost, "worldly" way of the everyday. Thus, in a later passage, analyzed below, Heidegger can call the sort of *Vorkommen* he describes here a *Nichtvorkommen.*

30. A possible philosophical translation of *Nichtvorkommen* might be "the not being there as worldly entities are." In the lecture course it occupies roughly the position filled by uncanniness (*Unheimlichkeit*) in *Being and Time* (GA 2:250/233).

Chapter 8

1. See, in particular, Ott, *Martin Heidegger;* Hans Sluga, *Heidegger's Crisis: Philosophy and Politics in Nazi Germany;* Thomas Sheehan, "Heidegger's Early Years: Fragments for a Philosophical Biography"; Thomas Sheehan, "Reading a Life: Heidegger and Hard Times"; and Kisiel, *GH.*

2. This notion, adumbrated in sec. 4 at the outset of *Sein und Zeit,* becomes methodologically explicit in sec. 63, where Heidegger argues that "the ontological 'truth' of the existential analysis is developed on the ground of primordial existentiell truth" (GA 2:419/364). In the lecture course from the summer semester 1927, *Die Grundprobleme der Phänomenologie,* Heidegger argues that "ontology does not permit of a purely ontological grounding. . . . Ontology has an ontical foundation" (GA 24:26/19). The deep ambiguities in this notion will concern us in chap. 12.

3. See, e.g., Sluga's decisive rejoinder to Bourdieu, whose attempt to refine Ringer's thesis as applied to Heidegger remains "enticingly simple": "The philosophical field in which Heidegger operated was not, in fact, ruled by neo-Kantianism; neo-Kantianism cannot be identified at large with the tradition of enlightened humanism; and Heidegger's 'rebellion' cannot be said to have forced him to embrace a conservative ideology" (*Heidegger's Crisis,* 10).

4. In addition to the works previously cited, see Victor Farías, *Heidegger and Nazism;* Luc Ferry and Alain Renaut, *Heidegger et les modernes;* Dominique Janicaud, *L'ombre de cette pensées: Heidegger et la question du politique;* Philippe Lacoue-Labarthe, *La fiction du politique;* Günther Neske and Emil Kettering, eds., *Antwort: Martin Heidegger im Gespräch;* Tom Rockmore, *On Heidegger's Nazism and Philosophy;* Tom Rockmore and Joseph Margolis, eds., *The Heidegger Case: On Philosophy and Politics;* Richard Wolin, *The Politics of Being;* Michael Zimmerman, *Heidegger's Confrontation with Modernity.*

5. Martin Heidegger, "Only a God Can Save Us," 103.

6. Fritz Ringer, *The Decline of the German Mandarins: The German Academic Community, 1890–1933,* 187–99.

7. Among the accommodationists the names Friedrich Meinecke, Ernst Troeltsch, Paul Natorp, and Max Weber might be taken as representative. Ringer, *Decline of the German Mandarins,* 133, associates this group with the politics of Friedrich Naumann's proposals for "social reform without Marxism," and it is interesting to note that in the *Der Spiegel* interview Heidegger identifies his own activism with the need to find a social "point of view, perhaps of the sort Naumann attempted" ("Only a God Can Save Us," 95). On this, see Otto Pöggeler, "Heidegger's Political Self-Understanding," 210 ff.

8. Among the orthodox one can list the neo-Kantian philosophers Wilhelm Windelband and Heinrich Rickert, the latter of whom directed Heidegger's *Habilitationsschrift.* In addition, one should note the presence of the movement Ringer identifies as "vulgar *Lebensphilosophie,*" a popular movement vaguely associated with the ideas of Bergson, Dilthey, and Nietzsche (*Decline of the German Mandarins,* 334–40). Orthodox mandarins like Rickert saw this as a culturally subversive irrationalism that denied the absoluteness of values. See Rickert's *Die Philosophie des Lebens,* in which both William James and Husserl's phenomenology are identified with *Lebensphilosophie.* In the 1930s this movement began to enter the mainstream of university life in the form of a Nietzsche revival carried out by those whom Sluga, *Heidegger's Crisis,* 125–53, calls "the philosophical radicals," among whom he counts Heidegger. One needs to note, however, that Heidegger's lecture courses from the 1920s show that he was no less critical of *Lebensphilosophie* than

were (in different ways) Husserl, Rickert, and Weber. I return to the significance of this point below.

9. Zimmerman, *Heidegger's Confrontation with Modernity,* 19 f., notes that Heidegger does not neatly fit the mold of either the accommodationist or the orthodox, but he fails to appreciate the extent to which Heidegger's earlier views are not directly assimilable to the form of antimodernism he came to espouse in the 1930s.

10. This is Ringer's designation (*Decline of the German Mandarins,* 357).

11. Max Weber, "Science as a Vocation," 131, 134, 141–42, 152.

12. Compare Charles E. McClelland, *State, Society, and University in Germany, 1700–1914.*

13. Wilhelm von Humboldt, "Über die Innere und Äussere Organisation der höheren wissenschaftlichen Anstalten in Berlin," 377, 381.

14. Compare Herbert Schnädelbach, *Philosophy in Germany, 1831–1933,* 66–109.

15. McClelland, *State, Society, and University,* 273.

16. Ringer, *Decline of the German Mandarins,* 122–27.

17. Ibid., 335.

18. On the prejudice against Catholics from the days of the *Kulturkampf,* and the various "thaws" and changing circumstances, see McClelland, *State, Society, and University,* 248, 295, 319: "Even as late as the first decade of the twentieth century, scholars could still enter into heated debates (mostly one-sided) about whether believing Catholics actually possessed the qualification of *wissenschaftliche Voraussetzungslosigkeit,* that is, whether they were capable of teaching and doing research 'objectively.' " Pierre Bourdieu, *The Political Ontology of Martin Heidegger,* 47 ff., makes much of Heidegger's "ambivalence toward the intellectual world" in which he found himself; indeed, he sees the driving habitus of Heidegger's thought in a kind of *ressentiment* at the cultural deficit represented by his background vis-à-vis the urbane humanism of Protestant (and Jewish) neo-Kantianism. Heidegger's writing thus betrays "a man excluded from the aristocratic elite but unable to suppress his own aristocratic elitism" (53).

19. Compare Joseph Geyser, *Neue und alte Wege der Philosophie: Eine Erörtergun der Grundlagen der Erkenntnis im Hinblick auf Edmund Husserls Versuch ihrer Neubegründung* (1916); and *Grundlegung der Logik und Erkenntnistheorie in positiver und kritischer Darstellung* (1919).

20. Compare Ott, *Martin Heidegger,* 63–65.

21. Ibid., 73.

22. Ibid., 83; cf. Thomas Sheehan, "Reading a Life: Heidegger and Hard Times."

23. Ott, *Martin Heidegger,* 85–87. See van Buren, *The Young Heidegger,* 122–29, for a different account of these issues.

24. Letter from Edmund Husserl to Paul Natorp, October 7, 1917, *Briefwechsel,* ed. Schuhmann, 5:130. On the difficulties for docents in general, see Ringer, *Decline of the German Mandarins,* 54–56; McClelland, *State, Society, and University,* 258–80.

25. Cited in Ott, *Martin Heidegger,* 107.

26. Ibid., 107.

27. Weber, "Science as a Vocation," 155, 151.

28. Martin Heidegger, "The Self-Assertion of the German University," 29; see also p. 30: "The will to the essence of the German University is the will to science as the will to the historical spiritual mission of the German Volk as a Volk that knows itself in its state."

29. Compare Ringer, *Decline of the German Mandarins,* 104–5, 282 ff.

30. Heidegger's way of formulating these issues, as will become evident below, owes a great deal to Husserl's 1911 "Philosophie als strenge Wissenschaft," in which he argues for science's "responsibility to humanity," for its pursuit of timeless validities, and the corresponding renunciation of the goal of "personal wisdom" in the finite (Hua XXV:51–62/131–47).

31. This radical "individualism" should not be seen eo ipso as implying that scientific knowledge is not public or "universal." Heidegger is after a phenomenological description of the scientific *attitude*—an attitude that, if he is right, entails, as an ideal, the willingness to call into question what is merely handed down by others, though it is in fact impossible to question everything all at once. On the basis of its "individualism," science aims at insights that are *justified,* whether shared or not, and thus aims at insights that are sharable by those whose sole duty is to truthfulness.

32. Weber, "Science as a Vocation," 151–52.

33. Herbert Spiegelberg, *The Phenomenological Movement,* 74–75, notes that in this article Husserl "himself took a stand very similar to Weber's, though for very different reasons," on the issue of whether science had anything to say about "questions of meaning for personal existence." However, "this whole situation changed for Husserl after the First World War." The later Husserl sought to mitigate the rigorous distinction between science and value by a new phenomenology of reason. In his essays between 1919 and 1923, this is just the sort of move Heidegger projects in critical confrontation with Husserl's earlier article.

34. Philip Buckley, *Husserl, Heidegger, and the Crisis of Philosophical Responsibility,* usefully details the importance of the "crisis of the sciences" theme for assessing the relation between Husserl and Heidegger and notes in passing (110 n. 40) the similarity between Husserl and Weber in their diagnosis of the crisis, together with the divergence in their recommendations. But because he does not look in detail at the way Husserl's "Philosophy as Rigorous Science" informs Heidegger's earliest approach to the question of university reform, he misses an important reason that there seems to be what he calls an "ambiguity" in Heidegger's response to the crisis prior to 1928 that has all but disappeared by 1933 (216–21).

35. Heidegger's challenge to Husserl here (one that we shall not be able to explore in detail) targets a certain conception of science that makes it depend on a kind of epistemological foundationalism—the notion of an apodictic evidence that is also wholly adequate. Husserl himself came to find this view of science problematic and hinted at the very sort of "existential" solution to the transcendental problem of ultimate grounding (*Letztbegrundung*) toward which Heidegger

is working in this lecture and in *Being and Time.* For my assessment of the limits of this approach see Steven Galt Crowell, "The Project of Ultimate Grounding and the Appeal to Intersubjectivity in Recent Transcendental Philosophy."

36. As Husserl wrote in 1911, "Genuine science, so far as its real doctrine extends, knows no profundity. . . . Profundity is an affair of wisdom; conceptual distinctness and clarity is an affair of rigorous theory" (Hua XXV:59/144).

37. Sluga, *Heidegger's Crisis,* 77, 102, 120, exhibits the Fichtean roots of the appeal, common among philosophers of this period, to *Ursprünglichkeit.* At the same time, it is clear that Husserl's employment of the term—which reflects his quasi-positivist invocation of direct evidence in sources of "intuitive fulfillment" rather than the mystical profundity of Fichtean and life-philosophical usage—is at work in Heidegger's understanding. Husserl's "Philosophy as Rigorous Science" concludes with the claim that "to the extent that philosophy goes back to ultimate origins [*letzten Ursprünge*], it belongs precisely to its very essence that its scientific work move in spheres of direct intuition" (Hua XXV:61/147). For the argument that this places Husserlian phenomenology in the camp of *Lebensphilosophie,* see Heinrich Rickert, *Die Philosophie des Lebens,* 28 ff.

38. Consulting the archives, Kisiel (*GH* pt. 1, chaps. 3 and 4) has shown that appearances of the term *Existenz* in these early lectures are later insertions by Heidegger. It is nevertheless still instructive to note the contexts where Heidegger finds such insertions appropriate—as here, where philosophy, as a radical form of self-questioning that goes against the grain of the natural attitude (*Selbstgenügsamkeit*), is identified with *Existenz* in an eminent sense.

39. Compare the expression of the methodological starting point of fundamental ontology in *Sein und Zeit:* "Philosophy is universal phenomenological ontology, taking its departure from the hermeneutic of Dasein which, as an analytic of *existence,* fixes the end of the guiding thread of all philosophical questioning at the point where it *arises* and to which it *returns*" (GA 2:51/62). What this means shall concern us further in chap. 12.

40. Weber, "Science as a Vocation," 152.

41. Heidegger's turn from "the tradition" as something to build upon echoes Husserl's challenge aimed at the neo-Kantians' call to go "back to Kant": "I do not say that philosophy is an imperfect science; I say simply that it is not yet a science at all, that as a science it has not yet begun" (Hua XXV:4/73).

42. The importance of this early rejection of the *Führerprinzip,* as it were, has been noted by Buckley, *Husserl, Heidegger,* 221, and Rudolf Makkreel, "The Genesis of Heidegger's Phenomenological Hermeneutics and the Rediscovered 'Aristotle Introduction' of 1922," 311.

43. On June 27, 1922, Heidegger wrote to Jaspers that

> either we get serious about philosophy and its possibilities as principled scientific research, or we must, in our self-understanding as scientific men, see it as the most serious shortcoming that we splash around with used up concepts and half-clear tendencies, working randomly. . . . Without any sentimentality it is clear that, for me, the decision for the former alone, for the philosopher as a scientific [man], comes into question. These are

> things about which one does not speak, and in speaking, as here, only indicates. Should one fail to awaken such a consciousness positively and concretely in the youth, then all talk about the crisis of science and the like is just that, talk. If we ourselves are not clear that we must exemplify such things before the youth—precisely as we are in the process of working them out—then we have no right to live in scientific research.

In Walter Biemel and Hans Saner, eds., *Briefwechsel, 1920–1963/Martin Heidegger, Karl Jaspers,* 28.

44. Heidegger's *Kant und das Problem der Metaphysik* (1929), one of the first places where Heidegger publicly linked his own project to "metaphysics" in Kant's sense, was dedicated to Max Scheler, and at the time of Scheler's death (1928), Heidegger was interested enough in him to entertain hopes of collaborating with him on an edition of his collected works. Compare Otto Pöggeler, *Martin Heidegger's Path of Thinking,* 59. We shall encounter this theme again in chap. 12. As for Nietzsche, though Heidegger's interest in Nietzsche goes back to his student years it is barely audible in his work, whereas by the 1930s his "Nietzscheanism" was a well-established idiom. Compare Sluga, *Heidegger's Crisis.*

45. Pöggeler, "Heidegger's Political Self-Understanding," 211.

46. Sluga, *Heidegger's Crisis,* 135–36, rightly notes that "after the collapse" of 1929 Heidegger's previously apolitical concern with his "own I-am" changes into a more activist stance. Otto Pöggeler, "Den Führer führen? Heidegger und keine Ende," 228, 234, sees a kind of path "from Nietzsche to Hitler" when, in 1929, Heidegger "seeks, with Nietzsche, a way back to a tragic experience of the world and so to an historical greatness, by way of the creative act of the great creators"—a path that explicitly turns away from Husserl's scientific philosophizing and is perhaps more consistent with Heidegger's recasting of the "transcendental ego" as "finite." Similarly, Jürgen Habermas, "Martin Heidegger—Werk und Weltanschauung," 57–61, argues that the interest in Nietzsche accompanied a certain transformation of the *theory of Sein und Zeit* into a "*worldview*" that could pretend to effect a passage from "historicality" (as a quasi-transcendental structure of Dasein) to "real history." It was only beginning in 1929, then, that the "reconstruction" of the analytic of Dasein in terms of the demands of the present was suffused with "the worldview motives of a scientifically unfiltered crisis-diagnosis." On the saying attributed to Heidegger, see Otto Pöggeler, "Besinnung oder Ausflucht? Heideggers ursprünglicheres Denken," 241.

Chapter 9

1. Compare Richard E. Palmer, trans., "'Phenomenology': Edmund Husserl's Article for the *Encyclopædia Britannica* (1927)," 21–35. Full documentation of this episode can now be found in Thomas Sheehan and Richard Palmer, eds. and trans., *Edmund Husserl: Psychological and Transcendental Phenomenology and the Confrontation with Heidegger 1927–1931.*

2. Emmanuel Lévinas, "Dialogue with Emmanuel Lévinas," 15.

3. Mohanty, *Possibility of Transcendental Philosophy.* See esp. "The Destiny of Transcendental Philosophy," 215.

4. See, e.g., Walter Biemel, "Husserl's *Encyclopædia Britannica* Article and Heidegger's Remarks Thereon"; James C. Morrison, "Husserl and Heidegger: The Parting of the Ways."

5. For details of the collaboration, see Sheehan and Palmer, *Edmund Husserl: Psychological and Transcendental Phenomenology.* Also see Biemel, "Husserl's *Encyclopædia Britannica* Article," 303; Herbert Spiegelberg, "On the Misfortunes of Edmund Husserl's *Encyclopædia Britannica* Article 'Phenomenology,' " 18–20, and *Phenomenological Movement,* 342–44. The present chapter concentrates on the first two drafts alone, both of which are found in Edmund Husserl, *Phänomenologische Psychologie* (Hua IX).

6. On this point, see Tugendhat, *Wahrheitsbegriff,* 263; and Gethmann, *Verstehen und Auslegung,* 93–107.

7. To grant this, however, does not imply that such a "being-character" will be understood in the same way by Husserl and Heidegger. It is well known, for example, that in *Being and Time* Heidegger revises Husserl's conception of the natural attitude in such a way that "what things are" for practical activity (their *Zuhandensein*) is not derivative—as it is for Husserl—from what they are for simple perceptual consciousness (*Vorhandensein*). Such revisions, however, concern how things are given in a primary sense, and so remain within the phenomenological horizon of investigation into modes of givenness. They do not affect the legitimacy of the reduction as specified here; rather, they take aim at the presuppositions about "being" that Husserl imports into his conception of the natural attitude. We return to this issue in n. 8, in sec. 2, and more extensively in chap. 10.

8. A full account of positing (*Setzung*) and posited being would take us too far afield here. In the context of the theory of the reduction, it is equivalent to the "taken-for-granted" existing of things encountered in the natural attitude—a presupposed givenness that it is the task of the reduction to make explicit for reflection. Thus, in bracketing posited being, such being is not *denied* but made explicit as phenomenon.

9. See Mohanty, *Possibility of Transcendental Philosophy,* xiii–xxxii, 191–212; and chap. 1 above.

10. Compare Tugendhat, *Wahrheitsbegriff,* 101–6, 173–77, 180–81, 189–93, and finally, 199: "Wenn man das nicht festhält, daß für Husserl das transzendentale Ich lediglich den Sinn hat, letzte jeweilige Stätte aller Geltung und Ausweisung zu sein, nicht aber ein letztes Prinzip einer Begründung, kann man dann auch nicht die Lehre von der transzendentale Konstitution verstehen."

11. As we saw in chap. 7, Heidegger from the start was oriented toward the phenomenological concept of *Evidenz* and toward philosophizing from an "original evidence situation."

12. When Biemel, "Husserl's *Encyclopædia Britannica* Article," 303, argues to the contrary that "Heidegger . . . uses the expression 'transcendental constitution' . . . as a favor to Husserl" and that "Heidegger looks on the constitution problematic as an idealistic residue that must be overcome," one might rightly

object that the situation is more complicated. It is true that Heidegger avoids the language of "constitution" in his writings, but the "thing itself" seems to be at work in the transcendental philosophy of *Being and Time*, at least if constitution (for Husserl) is not taken to mean creation, and if the *evidenztheoretisch* character of the constitution problem is kept in mind. As for "idealism," a better term for the residues that Heidegger seeks to overcome in Husserl would seem to be "theoretism." In any case, if *Being and Time* abandons idealism in any sense, it is not in favor of realism. A full interpretation of these issues would have to take into account Heidegger's extensive criticisms of Husserl in *Prolegomena zur Geschichte des Zeitbegriffs* (GA 20), some of which will concern us in chap. 10.

13. Morrison, "Husserl and Heidegger," 50–51, purports to locate a fundamental source of the disagreement between Husserl and Heidegger in the latter's "ultimate rejection of the possibility of a scientific philosophy" and claims that in the second draft of the *Encyclopædia Britannica* article Husserl's "emphasis on subjectivity and science" is "subordinated to an ontological problematic" by Heidegger. However, the previous chapters have tried to suggest that what Heidegger rejects is not scientific philosophy but rather Husserl's conception of what "scientific" means as applied to philosophy. If Heidegger rejected scientific philosophy at all, it was only after *Being and Time*. The issue shall concern us again in chap. 12.

14. See, e.g., Husserl, *Ideen I* (Hua III:11/6).

15. See, e.g., *Cartesian Meditations* (Hua I:126/95).

16. This is not the place for a full examination of the consequences of that thought experiment that Husserl, in *Ideen I* (Hua III:114/109), proposes as "the annihilation of the world of physical things." The intricacies of Husserl's argument, and its motivation, cannot be represented briefly. But even if it is conceivable that a reduction to pure chaos would leave behind a "residuum" of "mental processes" (though these would be processes that would not have unified "concatenations of experience" as their correlates), it is far from clear that they would be mental processes "of an Ego" as Husserl claims. If "Ego" means more than "mental processes"—as it does, for Husserl, both in *Ideen* and in the *Encyclopædia Britannica* article—then it is likely that some phenomenological analogue of Kant's "refutation of idealism" argument, to the effect that ego identity requires object identity (though perhaps not *physical* object identity in Husserl's sense), would come into play here. For an interesting discussion of Husserl's thought experiment, see Karl Ameriks, "Husserl's Realism," 498–519.

17. Indeed, it is Husserl's awareness of this problem that leads to his attempt to motivate the transcendental reduction through the detour of phenomenological psychology: "On essential grounds that are easy to understand, humanity as such, and each individual human being, lives initially exclusively in the positive [*Positivität*], and so the transcendental reduction is an alteration of one's entire form of life, surpassing [*hinübersteigt*] all previous life experience, and on account of its absolute foreignness, it is difficult to understand with respect to its possibility and actuality" (Hua IX:276). Phenomenological psychology is supposed to serve as a propaedeutic to the reduction. But since what motivates *it* (a pure science of

the psyche as worldly entity alongside a pure science of the physical) is altogether different from that which motivates the transcendental-*philosophical* question of the ground of all worldly knowledge, it is hard to see how such a propaedeutic could be of much help unless the mundane being itself ("man") did not already "understand" its "difference" from entities within the world—did not already in some sense understand transcendental reflection as one of *its* possibilities. This issue continued to bother Husserl to the end of his life, and the wisdom of the Heideggerian approach becomes apparent when Husserl's assistant, Eugen Fink, spells out the consequences of Husserl's initial position in his "me-ontology." See chap. 13 below.

18. See *Formal and Transcendental Logic* (Hua XVII:157 ff./149 ff.).

19. Four of these problems will occupy us in chap. 13.

20. For an alternative to Heidegger's epistemological reading of Husserl's absolute being, see Rudolf Boehm, "Das Absolut und die Realität."

Chapter 10

1. See Timothy Stapleton, *Husserl and Heidegger: The Question of a Phenomenological Beginning;* henceforth abbreviated *HH.*

2. Compare Edmund Husserl, *Ideen I* (Hua III:23–40/18–33). Here the logical issues of formal and regional ontologies are handled prior to the main part of the text in which the phenomenological, transcendental standpoint is introduced. The same structure is found in Husserl, *Formal and Transcendental Logic.*

3. On the "transcendental naïveté" of ontology, see Husserl, *Formal and Transcendental Logic* (Hua XVII:159 ff./151 ff.). On the distinction between ontology and phenomenology, see Husserl, *Ideen III* (Hua V:76–89/65–77).

4. As we saw in chap. 3, Lask criticized the early Husserl for failing to include the transcendent object in his phenomenology—thus in effect for failing to provide a genuine account of *Seinsgeltung.* Husserl responded with the transcendental reduction, a move that discloses the space of meaning as such and overcomes the residual naturalism of Lask's position. But because this move is framed in terms of *Evidenz* and givenness, the ontological issue of idealism (which Lask had sought to circumvent with his theory of the "paradigmatic object") takes on new urgency. The ontological status of meaning is not something that Husserl's own transcendental-phenomenological idealism succeeded finally in clarifying—not because it is an idealism, but because the phenomenology is, as Heidegger will suggest, captured by a false picture of our existential situation.

5. "No conceivable theory can make us err with respect to the *principle of all principles:* that every originary presentative intuition is a legitimizing source of cognition, that everything originally (so to speak, in its 'personal' actuality) offered to us in 'intuition' is to be accepted simply as what it is presented as being, but also only within the limits in which it is presented there" (Hua III:52/44).

6. It is not only Husserl who cannot get completely clear about what is

entailed by this sort of phenomenological "dependence." Heidegger also confronts difficulties here, as we shall see in chap. 12.

7. Kant, *Critique of Pure Reason,* 59 (A11–12/B25).

8. This impression is further strengthened by the marginal note Heidegger attached to this part of the text in his own copy of *Being and Time:* "d.h. nicht transzendental-philosophische Richtung des kritischen Kantischen Idealismus" (GA 2:51). However, such notes must be read very carefully. For example, when was it written? And we have already seen that Heidegger goes to some lengths to distinguish Husserlian phenomenology from "critical Kantian idealism" on crucial points that affect the meaning of "transcendental"—even if it is *also* clear that Heidegger resists what might be called Husserl's own drift toward neo-Kantianism. All this just means that when it comes to determining the relation of Heidegger's thought to transcendental philosophy, there is no substitute for careful examination of the actual positions he takes, rather than the general methodological stage setting.

9. Karl Lehmann, "Metaphysik, Transzendentalphilosophie, und Phänomenologie in den ersten Schriften Martin Heideggers," 355.

10. This can be further substantiated by locating Heidegger's work within the context of the then-current debates going on among the various schools of late-stage neo-Kantianism. See, e.g., the detailed studies by Brelage in *Studien zur Transzendentalphilosophie.*

11. Frederick Olafson, "Consciousness and Intentionality in Heidegger's Thought." The "Fregean" interpretation of the noema as an abstract entity goes back to the classical article by Dagfinn Føllesdal, "Husserl's Notion of Noema," and has generated a large literature into which I shall not enter here. For a good canvasing of the issues and a phenomenologically more plausible account of the noema, see John Drummond, *Husserlian Intentionality and Non-Foundational Realism: Noema and Object,* 63–141.

12. A similar concession is found in *Being and Time:* "Perhaps what is given in the mere formal reflective awareness of the 'I' is indeed evident. And this insight even provides access to an autonomous phenomenological problematic which, as 'formal phenomenology of consciousness,' has its fundamental, liminal significance" (GA 2:154/151).

13. This connection was closely explored by Gethmann, *Verstehen und Auslegung.* In my view, it simply extends the transcendental-phenomenological problematic (analyzed in chap. 7) Heidegger had already glimpsed in 1919–22.

14. In this respect Olafson, "Consciousness and Intentionality," 93–94, is quite right to argue that "while [the conception of noesis] is modified in important ways, it clearly survives and forms a part of Heidegger's interpretation of Dasein" in *Being and Time.*

15. Tugendhat, *Wahrheitsbegriff,* 263.

16. Jacques Taminiaux, "From One Idea of Phenomenology to the Other," 42–43, discusses this passage in his perceptive treatment of the Husserl-Heidegger relation.

17. See, e.g., the discussion of this issue in all versions of the *Encyclopædia*

Britannica article (e.g., Hua IX:275 f.). The implications of this "identity" shall concern us again in chap. 13.

18. Of course, many commentators have criticized this as an inconsistency in Heidegger's philosophy, but my concern is not with that but with the character of that philosophy as Heidegger understood it. See, e.g., Charles Guignon, *Heidegger and the Problem of Knowledge;* Pöggeler, *Martin Heidegger's Path of Thinking;* Okrent, *Heidegger's Pragmatism;* among many others.

Chapter 11

1. On metontology, see chap. 12.

2. On this editorial controversy, see Habermas, "Martin Heidegger—Werk und Weltanschauung," 74–77; Pöggeler, *Martin Heidegger's Path of Thinking,* 276–78. For Heidegger's own explanation, and his editor's defense, see GA 40:232–34.

3. The phrase is from Martin Heidegger, "Brief über den 'Humanismus' " (GA 9:357/258).

4. Martin Heidegger, "Zeit und Sein," 25; translated by Joan Stambaugh under the title "Time and Being," 24.

5. Martin Heidegger, "Das Ende der Philosophie und das Aufgabe des Denkens," 70, 73, 77, 80; translated by Joan Stambaugh under the title "The End of Philosophy and the Task of Thinking," 63, 66, 70, 73.

Chapter 12

1. The German reads: "Die Herausstellung der Seinsverfassung des Daseins bleibt aber gleichwohl nur *ein Weg.* Das *Ziel* ist die Ausarbeitung des Seinsfrage überhaupt" (GA 2:575/487). The apposition of emphasized terms—*ein Weg* and *Ziel*—suggests that Heidegger is emphasizing not, as the Macquarrie and Robinson translation has it, that this is one way among others, but that it is in general only on the way, not yet at the goal. Some justification for the translation is found, however, in the sentence I cite next in the text, which is separated from this one by a paragraph. As shall be seen in what follows, Heidegger stands here at a moment of methodological crisis.

2. Kant, *Critique of Pure Reason,* 25 (Bxxii).

3. The execution and implications of these distinct explanatory proposals differ markedly, of course. Heidegger's ontological knowledge is knowledge of meaning. Appealing to a causal theory, the naturalist might offer an account of such "ontological knowledge" that eliminates it altogether. See, e.g., McDowell's account of Quine's notion of "empirical significance" in *Mind and World,* 131–33. The historicist, in contrast, typically argues that the intentional "content" of a claim to ontological knowledge depends upon linguistic conditions obtaining at a particular time and further (if she is a pragmatist) that these conditions are themselves a function of historically contingent social practices, and so on. Here meaning is not eliminated, but justification is tied to what the norms inherent

in current conditions and practices allow. Heidegger is often taken to espouse something like the historicist view, but if he does espouse it, it is on the basis of phenomenological considerations. This means that the differences between naturalism and historicism as *ontic* explanatory proposals are not decisive in context of the present chapter. For the pertinent question after 1927 is whether the situatedness of ontological knowledge, already attested phenomenologically, can become the theme of an ontic *inquiry.* Empirical inquiries into natural and historical conditions are of course possible, but they cannot (on Heidegger's view) yield grounds *for* ontological knowledge since they presuppose such knowledge. Heidegger's failed search for another sort of inquiry into this situatedness—designated "metaphysical" or "metontological"—is the topic of the present chapter.

4. Letter from Martin Heidegger to Karl Löwith, August 20, 1927, *Zur philosophischen Aktualität Heideggers,* Papenfuss and Pöggeler, eds., 2:36.

5. The German reads: "Der fragliche Abschnitt wurde zurückghalten, weil das Denken im zureichenden Sagen dieser Kehre versagte und mit Hilfe der Sprache der Metaphysik nicht durchkam."

6. Kisiel, *GH* 59. Ryioichi Hosokawa, "The Conception of *Being and Time* and the Problem of Metaphysics," 20–21, has seen this quite clearly: During the late 1920s "the conception of fundamental ontology in *Being and Time* is transformed into that of metaphysics," and this "period of Heidegger's own metaphysics can be followed up to the first and second lectures on Nietzsche (WS 1936/37, SS 1937)"; hence, "it is a great mistake if one maintains that Heidegger tries to overcome metaphysics beginning in 1930." See also Hosokawa's extremely valuable essay, "Heidegger und die Ethik," 256.

7. Jean Grondin, "Prolegomena to an Understanding of Heidegger's Turn," 64.

8. David Farrell Krell, *Intimations of Mortality,* 39.

9. Joanna Hodge, *Heidegger and Ethics,* 177.

10. In his 1914 review of Charles Sentroul's *Kant und Aristoteles,* for example, Heidegger rejects the theory of "ontological truth," concluding that "even today the perspective of the theory of science is lacking in Aristotelian scholastic philosophy." In contrast to the Kantian theory of knowledge, Aristotle's is "from the beginning heavily burdened with metaphysics" (GA 1:52, 50).

11. As we saw in chap. 5, an inconsistency already infected Heidegger's earlier hopes for a renewed metaphysics, and a similar one will lead metontology to a dead end.

12. As has been shown in convincing detail by Ryioichi Hosokawa, "*Sein und Zeit* als 'Wiederholung' der Aristotelischen Seinsfrage."

13. The first remark is found in "Letter on Humanism" (GA 9:343/246); the second is from the 1953 "Author's Preface to the Seventh Edition" of *Sein und Zeit,* in which Heidegger announces that the promised second half of the text "could no longer be added" (GA 2:vii/17).

14. In lieu of the lengthy interpretation of Heidegger's later works a defense of this claim would require, I refer to the similar point made by Friedrich-Wilhelm von Herrmann, *Der Begriff der Phänomenologie bei Heidegger und Husserl,*

51, who argues that the later Heidegger no longer reflects on phenomenological method or describes his thinking in those terms, not "because he abandoned phenomenology but because he continued to practice phenomenological seeing and demonstration exclusively." Heidegger still defends phenomenological seeing in his last seminar in Zähringen in 1973. See *Vier Seminare* (1973), 110 ff.

15. Kant, *Critique of Pure Reason,* 297–300 (A293/B349–A298/B355). I leave out of account here Kant's arguments for a kind of *metaphysica specialis* based on practical reason, though it is perhaps not without relevance for the problem at hand. For valuable suggestions (though with little analysis of metontology), see Frank Schalow, *The Retrieval of the Kant-Heidegger Dialogue.* Most recently, there is Sarah Lilly Heidt, "From Transcendence to the Open: Freedom and Finitude in the Thought of Martin Heidegger."

16. Kant, *Critique of Pure Reason,* 318 (A326/B383).

17. David Wood, "Reiterating the Temporal: Toward a Rethinking of Heidegger on Time," 139.

18. Krell, *Intimations of Mortality,* 28.

19. Compare Otto Pöggeler, "Ausgleich und andere Anfang: Scheler und Heidegger," 178.

20. John Sallis, *Echoes: After Heidegger,* 154, e.g., notes that the 1935 lecture, which became *Einführung in die Metaphysik* and which starts from this Leibnizian question, tries to "retrace the way from the question of metontology back to the question of fundamental ontology." The tension between the two questions is also explored in William McNeill's essay, "Metaphysics, Fundamental Ontology, Metontology: 1925–1935." In what follows I show that this tension results from an equivocation on the meaning of "ground."

21. See GA 2:310/ 276, but the first three chapters of division 2 are devoted to this question.

22. In the 1929 essay "Was ist Metaphysik?" (GA 9:110/99), Heidegger insists on "an essential distinction" between "comprehending the whole of beings as such [*des Ganzen des Seienden an sich*] and finding oneself in the midst of beings as a whole [*des Seienden im Ganzen*]. The former," he continues, "is impossible in principle." This leaves the question of what *inquiry* into the latter might be. What Heidegger in this essay calls "metaphysical inquiry" is really still only ontological in the sense of *Being and Time* and provides no evidence for what metontology might be.

23. Pöggeler, "Heideggers logische Untersuchungen," 92–93. Pöggeler further takes the term "metontology" to echo Scheler's proposal for a "metanthropology"—an inquiry "concerned with metaphysical perspectives in the various sciences" (Otto Pöggeler, "Heidegger on Art," 116). Others, however—such as Krell, *Intimations of Mortality,* 38–39, and Hosokawa, "Heidegger und die Ethik," 251—link the term with the idea of a "sudden transition" (μεταβολή, *Umschlag*) of ontology.

24. Compare Krell, *Intimations of Mortality,* 41.

25. Martin Heidegger, "Das Realitätsproblem in der modernen Philosophie" (GA 1:15). This criticism should not blind one to the fact that Heidegger's own position in 1912 is very much like that of Külpe's so-called critical realism,

with all its attendant ambiguities. It is not until his metaphysical decade that Heidegger finally comes to terms with this aspect of his thinking.

26. This in found in the lecture course of SS 1927, *Die Grundprobleme der Phänomenologie* (GA 24:1/1).

27. These four problems are again discussed later in the text, in somewhat different terms (GA 26:191–95/151–53).

28. Heidegger makes a similar phenomenological point later in the text: "If I say of Dasein that its basic constitution is being-in-the-world, I am then first of all asserting something that belongs to its essence, and I thereby disregard whether the being of such a nature factually exists or not" (GA 26:217/169).

29. Similar remarks are frequent in Heidegger's texts of the period; compare, e.g., *Metaphysical Foundations of Logic* (GA 26:194–95/153), and *Basic Problems of Phenomenology* (GA 24:421–22/297).

30. In *Metaphysical Foundations of Logic,* Heidegger writes: "Being is prior neither ontically nor logically, but prior in a primordial sense that precedes both. It is prior to each in a different way; neither ontically nor logically prior but ontologically" (GA 26:186/147). I interpret this to refer to the transcendental-phenomenological priority of meaning (the topic of *Being and Time*) over all empirical, formal, and *metaphysical* modes of knowledge or "encounter" of beings. And, as Heidegger suggests in *Basic Problems of Phenomenology,* this ontological ground "implies nothing about . . . the ontical relations between beings, between nature and Dasein" (GA 24:419/295).

31. See, e.g., *Being and Time* (GA 2:281, 304/255, 272); *Basic Problems of Phenomenology* (GA 24:240, 249, 313/169, 175, 219); *Metaphysical Foundations of Logic* (GA 26:251–52/194–95).

32. Compare Theodore de Boer, *Development of Husserl's Thought;* and chap. 3 above.

33. Henry Allison, *Kant's Transcendental Idealism,* 25, 10.

34. This difference is nicely elaborated by Hubert Dreyfus, *Being-in-the-World: A Commentary on Heidegger's* Being and Time, *Division I.*

35. In Husserl's case this is especially apparent in his collaboration with Eugen Fink on the so-called *Sixth Cartesian Meditation* in which traditional metaphysical issues come to the fore—as I shall argue in chap. 13, largely thanks to Fink's Hegelian way of formulating phenomenological problems.

36. One will object that this reading cannot be right since it imputes to Heidegger an acceptance of the phenomenological reduction (in at least some of its aspects), when he must surely reject it. What is Heidegger's hermeneutic phenomenology, after all, if not a rejection of Husserl's reduction of the world to transcendental subjectivity? And doesn't he specifically repudiate the reduction in the lecture course from WS 1925, *History of the Concept of Time* (GA 20:150/109)? Yet the argument of chaps. 9 and 10 suggests that the problem is quite complicated and cannot be a matter of any simple acceptance or rejection. In fact, *Being and Time* is finally inconsistent on the issue.

37. David Wood, "Reiterating the Temporal," 141, correctly notes that what Heidegger proposes here is something like "the unity of a differentiated set that he has already analyzed transcendentally," a take on Dasein that "cannot, however,

be ontic [i.e., empirical], nor can it be transcendental." He then expresses well-founded worries that in so doing Heidegger threatens to "dispense with certain constitutive rules of intelligibility."

38. A sensitive treatment is found in Robert Bernasconi, "'The Double Concept of Philosophy' and the Place of Ethics in *Being and Time.*"

39. For full elaboration of this suggestion, see Hosokawa, "The Conception of *Being and Time* and the Problem of Metaphysics," and "Heidegger und die Ethik."

40. This does not, of course, rule out an ontological theology; it only rules out taking such theology as ground *of* ontology.

41. This view of Aristotle's "theology" predates Heidegger's metaphysical decade. It is present as early as the lecture course of WS 1924–25, *Platon: Sophistes* (GA 19:222).

42. Pöggeler, "Heideggers logische Untersuchungen," 93.

43. It is tempting to link this suggestion with a retrieval of rational *psychology* from Kant's dialectic.

44. Versions of this view can be found in Hosokawa, "Heidegger und die Ethik"; Krell, *Intimations of Mortality;* Sallis, *Echoes;* McNeill, "Metaphysics, Fundamental Ontology, Metontology"; and Grondin, "Prolegomena to an Understanding of Heidegger's Turn"; among others.

45. For this reason, as we saw above, Heidegger distinguishes here between "comprehending the whole of beings" (which he sees as impossible for a finite being) and "finding oneself in the midst of beings as a whole" (which is accomplished all the time through mood). The question of whether the phenomenon of mood can serve as the basis for metaphysical *inquiry* is explored in the lecture course from WS 1929/30, *Die Grundbegriffe der Metaphysik: Welt, Endlichkeit, Einsamkeit* (GA 29/30). In my view it does not get beyond the impasse of 1928, but the issue is too complex to treat here.

46. Grondin, "Prolegomena to an Understanding of Heidegger's Turn," 69; Sallis, *Echoes,* 145, 148.

47. Bernasconi, "'The Double Concept of Philosophy,'" 33.

48. Wood, "Reiterating the Temporal," 156–57.

49. I mean by this perhaps contentious-sounding statement only that the architectonic drive is more clearly present in *Being and Time* than in anything Husserl ever published.

50. J. L. Austin, "Other Minds," 66.

51. Bernasconi, "'The Double Concept of Philosophy,'" 37.

52. Habermas, "Martin Heidegger—Werk und Weltanschauung," 58.

53. It should be obvious that this chapter has not tried to provide sufficient argument for this claim about an ethical ground. For some discussion of what I mean by it, see Crowell, "The Project of Ultimate Grounding and the Appeal to Intersubjectivity in Recent Transcendental Philosophy."

54. See, e.g., the 1949 "Einleitung Zu: 'Was ist Metaphysik?' Der Rückgang in den Grund der Metaphysik" (GA 9:365–83).

55. Thus, I agree with McNeill, "Metaphysics, Fundamental Ontology, Metontology," 78, that the later Heidegger has "no need" of metontology and

does not thematize "'beings' as such, but, for example, people, things, and nature"—but I would say that this sort of inquiry ("*thoroughly* existentiell" but not an "objectification") is nothing but the practice of phenomenological seeing freed from an "inappropriate concern with 'science' and 'research.' "

Chapter 13

1. Eugen Fink, *Sixth Cartesian Meditation: The Idea of a Transcendental Theory of Method;* henceforth abbreviated *SCM.*

2. Ronald Bruzina, the translator of *SCM,* has in fact demonstrated some significant overlap in the approaches to the question of "origins" found in Fink and Derrida. See Ronald Bruzina, "The Transcendental Theory of Method in Phenomenology: The Meontic and Deconstruction."

3. The English translation of this text is found as an epilogue in Edmund Husserl, *Ideas Pertaining to a Pure Phenomenology and to a Phenomenological Philosophy,* vol. 2. The passages cited above are on 107–8.

4. Alfred Schutz, "Husserl's *Crisis of Western Science,*" 279.

5. This no doubt partly reflects the division of labor that characterized the Husserl-Fink collaboration during the late 1920s and early 1930s. As Bruzina, "The Transcendental Theory of Method in Phenomenology," 7, describes it, the "detail work" of specific phenomenological analyses "was Husserl's special province of mastery," while "disclosing what all that detail meant" by means of a "second-level, systematically synthetic and self-critical (re-)interpretation of first-level findings" was assigned to Fink. For a full account, see Bruzina's "Translator's Introduction" (*SCM*).

6. Cited by Bruzina (*SCM* xxv).

7. Fred Kersten, "Notes from the Underground: Merleau-Ponty and Husserl's *Sixth Cartesian Meditation,*" 58. Kersten sees the *SCM* as uncovering an existential dimension within transcendental phenomenology itself, a reading I find congenial in many ways though I shall not discuss it in the present context.

8. Cited by Bruzina (*SCM* xx) from Husserl's foreword to Eugen Fink's "Die phänomenologische Philosophie Edmund Husserls in der gegenwärtigen Kritik I."

9. Nor is it limited to Bruzina's take on the Fink-Husserl collaboration. A similar idea is proposed by Anthony Steinbock, *Home and Beyond: Generative Phenomenology after Husserl,* 269–70, who claims that "generative phenomenology" cannot be practiced by individual thinkers, but only "as a participation over the generations."

10. See chap. 9 above, as well as the documentation in Sheehan and Palmer, *Edmund Husserl: Psychological and Transcendental Phenomenology.*

11. On appearance truth, see sec. 4 of the present chapter.

12. This is not to say that the position is without its own puzzles. For instance, the thesis that transcendental and mundane subjectivity are the "same" runs into the difficulty of explaining how some things can be predicated of one but not the other. Thus, for Husserl the person is in causal interaction with things and other

persons in the world, whereas the transcendental subject is not. This need not entail an "individuating" distinction if the denial that the transcendental subject is causally involved merely expresses the reduction itself (its "bracketing" of all questions that depend, as this one does, on the positing of existence), and not, as it might appear, a positive assertion about the existing-independently-of-causation of some entity. Something similar would also hold of Heidegger: Dasein is not "human being" but the *being of* human being; hence one might say that "this man" is six feet tall, but it would not imply that Dasein is six feet tall. William D. Blattner, *Heidegger's Temporal Idealism,* 52 ff., seems to argue a similar point (though he would not affirm the connection I see between Husserl and Heidegger here). But the whole issue is important and complicated enough to deserve separate treatment. I mention it simply to suggest that this sort of puzzle seems to me preferable to the paradoxes one gets into by embracing Fink's "individuating distinction."

13. Heidegger asks: "Is not this act [the transcendental reduction] a possibility of man, but precisely because man is never simply on hand; a comportment, i.e., a mode of being, which it secures for itself and so never simply belongs to the positivity of what is on hand" (Hua IX:275)?

14. Burt C. Hopkins, "Review of Eugen Fink, *Sixth Cartesian Meditation,*" 72, 74 n. 11.

15. Bruzina, "Transcendental Theory of Method in Phenomenology," 13 f., notes the connection between the "new and peculiar intelligibility" sought by Fink "precisely in the simultaneous affirmation and rejection of the very same semantic or ideational positivity" and Derrida's notion of a double reading or double gesture, his "self-erasing proto-writing."

16. Hopkins, "Review of Eugen Fink," 71.

17. This is the cosmological Idea of the "Absolute completeness of the *Composition* of the given whole of all appearances," and it yields the thesis that the "world has a beginning in time, and is also limited as regards space," together with the antithesis that the "world has no beginning, and no limits in space; it is infinite as regards both time and space." See Kant, *Critique of Pure Reason,* 390, 396 (A415/B443, A427/B455).

18. Or as Bruzina, "Transcendental Theory of Method in Phenomenology," 4, glosses a similar matter: The potential emptiness of talk about phenomenological origins is avoided because "instead of simply adopting talk of 'the Nothing,' Fink treats the 'nothing' of origins *in intrinsic methodological connection with that which originates from it,*" that is, in connection with what is or is intuitable.

19. Kant, *Critique of Pure Reason,* 99 (A62/B86).

20. In the text (*SCM* 64), Fink suggests a connection between constructive phenomenology and Kant's theory of the "regulative employment" of the Ideas of reason. Yet more than this regulative employment must be at stake in constructive phenomenology if a genuine move beyond the principle of intuitive givenness is to be entailed by it. Neither Kant nor Husserl would see the notion of a regulative Idea as challenging that principle.

21. Kant, *Critique of Pure Reason,* 69–70 (A25/B40). "Space should properly be called not *compositum* but *totum,* since its parts are possible only in the

whole, not the whole through the parts"—which holds mutatis mutandis for time (A438/B466).

22. Ibid., 396–98 (A427/B455–A429/B457).

23. Ibid., 448 (A505/B533).

24. Actually, it is difficult to speak of "the" question Fink raises, since he runs together the problem of the antinomy (the cosmological problem of a beginning and end to the temporal flow) with the paralogism (the problem of "immortality"), which for Kant concerns the putative *simplicity* of the soul. I shall ignore this complication, however.

25. We would need to ask how "human immanence" is being conceived here when Fink says that "the time man in the world has begins at birth and ends in death." Perhaps the time "man" in the world "has" begins *after* birth; perhaps it ends *before* death. What *is* man in the world, and how do birth and death show themselves there?

26. In fact, Fink does not discuss our example, but he does discuss the related question of the "coincidence" between the "transcendental ego" and "man" (*SCM* 116–17). I think the structure of his solution here, something of which I reproduce in the text above, is indicative of how he would approach constructive issues generally.

27. Kant, *Critique of Pure Reason,* 463–64 (A531/B559–A532/B560).

28. Fink is perhaps thinking here of the sort of move Kant makes when discussing how beauty can be a "symbol of the morally good." A "symbolic exhibition" uses an analogy not based on similarity between two things but on "the rules by which we reflect on the two and on how they operate." This too is a kind of second-order analogy, but I shall not pursue the suggestion here. See Kant, *Critique of Judgment,* 227–30.

29. The locus classicus is, of course, the discussion of categorial intuition in logical investigation 6, sec. 45, where we read, e.g., that "the essential homogeneity of the *function* of fulfillment . . . obliges us to give the name 'perception' to each fulfilling act of confirmatory self-presentation, to each fulfilling act whatever the name 'intuition,' and to its intentional correlate the name of 'object' " (Hua XIX/2:671/785).

30. This notion of "anonymity" was central to Maurice Natanson's version of existential phenomenology, found already in his early book, *The Journeying Self: A Study in Philosophy and Social Role,* but developed with progressively more subtlety in his subsequent *Anonymity: A Study in the Philosophy of Alfred Schutz,* and the posthumously published *The Erotic Bird: Phenomenology in Literature.*

31. On Merleau-Ponty's rejection of Fink's absolute, see Kersten, "Notes from the Underground," 48, 55–58.

Bibliography

Allison, Henry. *Kant's Transcendental Idealism.* New Haven, Conn.: Yale University Press, 1983.

Altwicker, Norbert. *Geltung und Genesis bei Lask und Hegel.* Frankfurt: Horst Heiderhoff Verlag, 1971.

Ameriks, Karl. "Husserl's Realism." *Philosophical Review* 86 (1977): 498–519.

Arendt, Hannah. "Martin Heidegger at Eighty." In *Heidegger and Modern Philosophy,* edited by Michael Murray, 293–303. New Haven, Conn.: Yale University Press, 1978.

Austin, J. L. "Other Minds." In *Philosophical Papers,* 44–84. Oxford: Oxford University Press, 1961.

Becker, Oskar. "Mathematische Existenz: Untersuchungen zur Logik und Ontologie mathematischer Phänomene." *Jahrbuch für Philosophie und phänomenologische Forschung* 8 (1927): 439–809.

———. "Para-Existenz: Menschliches Dasein und Dawesen." In *Heidegger: Perspektiven zur Deutung seines Werkes,* edited by Otto Pöggeler, 261–85. Königstein: Athenäum, 1984.

Bernasconi, Robert. " 'The Double Concept of Philosophy' and the Place of Ethics in *Being and Time.*" In *Heidegger in Question: The Art of Existing,* 25–39. Atlantic Highlands, N.J.: Humanities Press, 1993.

Biemel, Walter. "Husserl's *Encyclopædia Britannica* Article and Heidegger's Remarks Thereon." In *Husserl: Expositions and Appraisals,* edited by Frederick Elliston and Peter McCormick, 286–303. Notre Dame, Ind.: University of Notre Dame Press, 1977.

Biemel, Walter, and Hans Saner, eds. *Martin Heidegger, Karl Jaspers: Briefwechsel, 1920–1963.* Frankfurt: Vittorio Klostermann, 1990.

Blattner, William D. *Heidegger's Temporal Idealism.* Cambridge: Cambridge University Press, 1999.

Boehm, Rudolf. "Das Absolut und die Realität." In *Vom Gesichtspunkt der Phänomenologie,* 72–105. The Hague: Martinus Nijhoff, 1968.

Bourdieu, Pierre. *The Political Ontology of Martin Heidegger,* translated by Peter Collier. Cambridge: Polity Press, 1991.

Brandom, Robert. *Making It Explicit.* Cambridge, Mass.: Harvard University Press, 1994.

Brelage, Manfred. "Transzendentalphilosophie und konkrete Subjektivität: Eine Studie zur Geschichte der Erkenntnistheorie in 20. Jahrhunderts." In *Studien zur Transzendentalphilosophie,* 72–229. Berlin: Walter de Gruyter, 1965.

Brentano, Franz. *On the Several Senses of Being in Aristotle.* Edited and translated by Rolf George. Berkeley: University of California Press, 1975.

Bruzina, Ronald."The Transcendental Theory of Method in Phenomenology: The Meontic and Deconstruction." *Husserl Studies* 14, no. 2 (1997): 75–94.

Buckley, Philip. *Husserl, Heidegger, and the Crisis of Philosophical Responsibility.* Dordrecht: Kluwer, 1992.

Caputo, John. *The Mystical Element in Heidegger's Thought.* Athens: Ohio University Press, 1978.

———. "Phenomenology, Mysticism, and the *Grammatica Speculativa:* A Study of Heidegger's *Habilitationsschrift.*" *Journal of the British Society for Phenomenology* 5 (1974): 101–17.

Cassirer, Ernst. *Philosophie der symbolischen Formen.* 3 vols. Vol. 1: *Die Sprache.* Vol. 2: *Das mythische Denken.* Vol. 3: *Phänomenologie der Erkenntnis.* Berlin: B. Cassirer, 1923–29.

Cohen, Hermann. *Kants Theorie der Erfahrung.* Berlin: Dümmler, 1871.

———. *Das Princip der Infinitesmal-Methode und seine Geschichte: Ein Kapitel zur Grundlegung der Erkenntniskritik.* Berlin: Dümmler, 1883.

Crowell, Steven Galt, ed. *The Prism of the Self: Philosophical Essays in Honor of Maurice Natanson.* Dordrecht: Kluwer, 1995.

———. "The Project of Ultimate Grounding and the Appeal to Intersubjectivity in Recent Transcendental Philosophy." *International Journal of Philosophical Studies* 7, no. 1 (1999): 283–95.

Dahlstrom, Daniel. "Heidegger's Kantian Turn: Notes to His Commentary on the *Kritik der reinen Vernunft.*" *Review of Metaphysics* 45, no. 2 (1991): 329–61.

———. "Heidegger's Method: Philosophical Concepts as Formal Indications." *Review of Metaphysics* 47 (June 1994): 775–95.

———. *Das logische Vorurteil.* Vienna: Passagen Verlag, 1994.

D'Amico, Robert. *Contemporary Continental Philosophy.* Boulder, Colo.: Westview Press, 1999.

Davidson, Donald. *Inquiries into Truth and Interpretation.* Oxford: Clarendon Press, 1984.

de Boer, Theodore. *The Development of Husserl's Thought.* Translated by Theodore Plantinga. The Hague: Martinus Nijhoff, 1978.

Dreyfus, Hubert. *Being-in-the-World: A Commentary on Heidegger's* Being and Time, *Division I.* Cambridge, Mass.: MIT Press, 1991.

Drummond, John. *Husserlian Intentionality and Non-Foundational Realism: Noema and Object.* Dordrecht: Kluwer, 1990.

Fariás, Victor. *Heidegger and Nazism.* Edited by Joseph Margolis and Tom Rockmore. Translated by Paul Burrell and Gabriel R. Ricci. Philadelphia: Temple University Press, 1989.

Ferry, Luc, and Alain Renaut. *Heidegger et les modernes.* Paris: Editions Grasset et Fasquelle, 1988.

Fink, Eugen. "Die phänomenologische Philosophie Edmund Husserls in der gegenwärtigen Kritik I." *Kant-Studien* 38 (1933): 319–83.

———. *Sixth Cartesian Meditation: The Idea of a Transcendental Theory of Method.* With textual notations by Edmund Husserl. Translated with an introduction by

Ronald Bruzina. Bloomington: Indiana University Press, 1995.

Føllesdal, Dagfinn. "Husserl's Notion of Noema." *Journal of Philosophy* 66 (1969): 680–87.

Gadamer, Hans-Georg. *Philosophical Apprenticeships.* Translated by Robert R. Sullivan. Cambridge, Mass.: MIT Press, 1985.

———. *Philosophical Hermeneutics.* Edited and translated by David E. Linge. Berkeley and Los Angeles: University of California Press, 1977.

Gethmann, Carl Friedrich. *Dasein: Erkennen und Handeln. Heidegger im phänomenologischen Kontext.* Berlin: Walter de Gruyter, 1993.

———. "Philosophie als Vollzug und als Begriff." *Dilthey-Jahrbuch* 4 (1986–87): 27–53.

———. *Verstehen und Auslegung: Das Methodenproblem in der Philosophie Martin Heideggers.* Bonn: Bouvier Verlag, 1974.

Geyser, Joseph. *Grundlegung der Logik und Erkenntnistheorie in positiver und kritischer Darstellung.* Münster: H. Schöningh, 1919.

———. *Neue und alte Wege der Philosophie: Eine Erörterung der Grundlagen der Erkenntnis im Hinblick auf Edmund Husserls Versuch ihrer Neubegründung.* Münster: H. Schöningh, 1916.

Gram, Moltke S. "Transcendental Arguments." *Nous* 5 (1972): 15–26.

Grondin, Jean. "Prolegomena to an Understanding of Heidegger's Turn." In *Sources of Hermeneutics,* 61–98. Albany: State University of New York Press, 1995.

Gudopp, Wolf-Dieter. *Der junge Heidegger: Realität und Wahrheit in der Vorgeschichte von "Sein und Zeit."* Frankfurt: Verlag Marxistische Blätter, 1983.

Guignon, Charles, ed. *The Cambridge Companion to Heidegger.* Cambridge: Cambridge University Press, 1993.

———. *Heidegger and the Problem of Knowledge.* Indianapolis: Hackett, 1983.

Gurvitch, Georges. *Les tendances actuelles de la philosophie allemande.* Paris: Vrin, 1949.

Habermas, Jürgen. "Martin Heidegger—Werk und Weltanschauung." In *Texte und Kontexte,* 49–83. Frankfurt: Suhrkamp, 1991.

Hartmann, Klaus. "On Taking the Transcendental Turn." *Review of Metaphysics* 20, no. 2 (1966): 223–49.

Hartmann, Nicolai. *Grundzüge einer Metaphysik der Erkenntnis.* Berlin: Walter de Gruyter, 1921.

Haugeland, John. *Having Thought: Essays in the Metaphysics of Mind.* Cambridge, Mass.: Harvard University Press, 1998.

Heidegger, Martin. "Das Ende der Philosophie und die Aufgabe des Denkens." In *Zur Sache des Denkens,* 61–80. Tübingen: Max Niemeyer, 1976. Translated by Joan Stambaugh under the title "The End of Philosophy and the Task of Thinking." In *On Time and Being,* 55–73. New York: Harper and Row, 1972.

———. "Mein Weg in die Phänomenologie." In *Zur Sache des Denkens,* 81–90. Tübingen: Max Niemeyer, 1969. Translated by Joan Stambaugh under the title "My Way to Phenomenology." In *On Time and Being,* 81–90. New York: Harper and Row, 1972.

———. "Only a God Can Save Us." Translated by Maria P. Alter and John D.

Caputo. In *The Heidegger Controversy,* edited by Richard Wolin, 91–116. New York: Columbia University Press, 1991.

———. "The Self-Assertion of the German University." Translated by William S. Lewis. In *The Heidegger Controversy,* edited by Richard Wolin, 29–39. New York: Columbia University Press, 1991.

———. *Vier Seminare.* Translated from the French seminar protocols by Curd Ochwald. Frankfurt: Vittorio Klostermann, 1977.

———. "Zeit und Sein." In *Zur Sache des Denkens,* 1–25. Tübingen: Max Niemeyer, 1976. Translated by Joan Stambaugh under the title "Time and Being." In *On Time and Being,* 1–24. New York: Harper and Row, 1972.

Heidt, Sarah Lilly. "From Transcendence to the Open: Freedom and Finitude in the Thought of Martin Heidegger." Ph.D. diss., Yale University, 1997.

Heimsoeth, Heinz. "Die metaphysischen Motive in der Ausbildung des kritischen Idealismus." *Kant-Studien* 29 (1924): 121–59.

Herrmann, Friedrich-Wilhelm von. *Der Begriff der Phänomenologie bei Heidegger und Husserl.* Frankfurt: Vittorio Klostermann, 1988.

Hobe, Konrad. "Emil Lask: Eine Untersuchung seines Denkens." Ph.D. diss., Heidelberg, 1968.

———. "Zwischen Rickert und Heidegger: Versuch über eine Perspektive des Denkens von Emil Lask." *Philosophisches Jahrbuch der Görres-Gesellschaft* 78 (1971): 360–78.

Hodge, Joanna. *Heidegger and Ethics.* London: Routledge, 1995.

Hogemann, Friedrich. "Heideggers Konzeption der Phänomenologie in den Vorlesungen aus dem Wintersemester 1919/1920 und dem Sommersemester 1920." *Dilthey-Jahrbuch* 4 (1986–87): 54–71.

Hopkins, Burt C. *Intentionality in Husserl and Heidegger.* Dordrecht: Kluwer, 1993.

———. "Review of Eugen Fink, *Sixth Cartesian Meditation.*" *Husserl Studies* 14 (1997): 61–74.

Hosokawa, Ryioichi. "The Conception of *Being and Time* and the Problem of Metaphysics." *Bulletin of the Faculty of Letters Kyushu University.* Forthcoming.

———. "Heidegger und die Ethik." In *Phänomenologie der Praxis um Dialog Zioischen Japan und dem Westen,* edited by Hiroshi Kojimo, 249–62. Würzburg: Königshausen und Neumann, 1989..

———. "*Sein und Zeit* als 'Wiederholung' der Aristotelischen Seinsfrage." *Philosophisches Jahrbuch der Görres-Gesellschaft* 94, no. 2 (1987): 362–71.

Humboldt, Wilhelm von. "Über die Innere und Äussere Organisation der höheren wissenschaftlichen Anstalten in Berlin." In *Die Idee der deutschen Universität,* edited by Ernst Anrich. Darmstadt: Hermann Gentner Verlag, 1956.

Husserl, Edmund. "Epilogue." In *Ideas Pertaining to a Pure Phenomenology and to a Phenomenological Philosophy, Second Book,* translated by R. Rojewicz and A. Schuwer, 405–30. Dordrecht: Kluwer, 1989.

———. *Experience and Judgment.* Translated by James S. Churchill and Karl Ameriks. Evanston, Ill.: Northwestern University Press, 1973.

———. *Philosophie der Arithmetik: Psychologische und logische Untersuchungen.* Halle: C. E. M. Pfeffer, 1891.

Jamme, Christoph. "Heideggers frühe Begrundung der Hermeneutik." *Dilthey-Jahrbuch* 4 (1986–87): 72–90.

Janicaud, Dominique. *L'ombre de cette pensées: Heidegger et la question du politique.* Grenoble: Jérôme Millon, 1990.

Kant, Immanuel. *Critique of Judgment.* Translated by Werner S. Pluhar. Indianapolis: Hackett, 1987.

———. *Critique of Pure Reason.* Translated by Norman Kemp Smith. London: Macmillan, 1968.

Kern, Iso. *Husserl und Kant: Eine Untersuchung über Husserls Verhältnis zu Kant und zum Neukantianismus.* The Hague: Martinus Nijhoff, 1964.

Kersten, Fred, "Notes from the Underground: Merleau-Ponty and Husserl's *Sixth Cartesian Meditation.*" In *The Prism of the Self: Philosophical Essays in Honor of Maurice Natanson,* edited by Steven Galt Crowell, 43–58. Dordrecht: Kluwer, 1995.

Kisiel, Theodore, "Das Entstehen des Begriffsfeldes 'Faktizität' im Frühwerk Heideggers." *Dilthey-Jahrbuch* 4 (1986–87): 91–120.

———. "The Genesis of *Being and Time.*" *Man and World* 25 (1992): 21–37.

———. *The Genesis of Heidegger's "Being and Time."* Berkeley and Los Angeles: University of California Press, 1993.

———. "Heidegger (1907–1927): The Transformation of the Categorial." In *Continental Philosophy in America,* edited by Hugh J. Silverman, John Sallis, and Thomas M. Seebohm, 165–85. Pittsburgh: Duquesne University Press, 1983.

———. "Das Kriegsnotsemester 1919: Heideggers Durchbruch in die hermeneutische Phänomenologie." *Philosophisches Jahrbuch* 99, no. 1 (1992): 105–22.

———. "On the Way to *Being and Time:* Introduction to the Translation of Heidegger's *Prolegomena zur Geschichte des Zeitbegriffs.*" *Research in Phenomenology* 15 (1985): 193–226.

———. "Why Students of Heidegger Will Have to Read Emil Lask." *Man and World* 28, no. 3 (1995): 197–240.

Kisiel, Theodore, and John van Buren, eds. *Reading Heidegger from the Start: Essays in His Earliest Thought.* Albany: State University of New York Press, 1994.

Köhnke, Klaus Christian. *The Rise of Neo-Kantianism: German Academic Philosophy between Idealism and Positivism.* Translated by R. J. Hollingdale. Cambridge: Cambridge University Press, 1991.

Krell, David Farrell. *Intimations of Mortality.* University Park: Penn State Press, 1986.

Krings, Hermann. *Transzendentale Logik.* Munich: Kösel Verlag, 1964.

Külpe, Oswald. *Die Philosophie der Gegenwart in Deutschland.* 6th ed. Leipzig: Teubner, 1914.

Lacoue-Labarthe, Philippe. *La fiction du politique.* Strasbourg: Associations des Publications des Universités de Strasbourg, 1987.

Lang, Friedrich Albert. *Geschichte des Materialismus und Kritik seiner Bedeutung in der Gegenwart.* Iserlohn: J. Baedeker, 1866–73.

Lask, Emil. *Fichtes Idealismus und die Geschichte.* In *Gesammelte Schriften,* edited by Eugen Herrigel, 1:193–273. Tübingen: J. C. B. Mohr, 1923.

———. "Gibt es ein 'Primat der praktischen Vernunft' in der Logik?" In *Gesammelte Schriften,* edited by Eugen Herrigel, 1:347–56. Tübingen: J. C. B. Mohr, 1923.

———. *Die Lehre vom Urteil.* In *Gesammelte Schriften,* edited by Eugen Herrigel, 2:283–463. Tübingen: J. C. B. Mohr, 1923.

———. *Die Logik der Philosophie und die Kategorienlehre.* In *Gesammelte Schriften,* edited by Eugen Herrigel, 1–282. Tübingen: J. C. B. Mohr, 1923.

Lehmann, Gerhard. "Kant im Spätidealismus und die Anfänge der neukantischen Bewegung." In *Materialien zur Neukantianismus-Diskussion,* edited by Hans-Ludwig Ollig. Darmstadt: Wissenschaftliche Buchgesellschaft, 1987.

Lehmann, Karl. "Metaphysik, Transzendentalphilosophie, und Phänomenologie in den ersten Schriften Martin Heideggers." *Philosophisches Jahrbuch der Görres-Gesellschaft* 71 (1964): 333–67.

Lévinas, Emmanuel. "Dialogue with Emmanuel Lévinas." In *Face to Face with Lévinas,* edited by Richard A. Cohen, 13–33. Albany: State University of New York Press, 1986.

Liebmann, Otto. *Kand und die Epigonen.* Stuttgart: Schober, 1865.

Lotze, Hermann. *Logik—Drei Bücher: Vom Denken, Vom Untersuchungen, und Vom Erkennen.* Leipzig: S. Hirzel, 1874 . Translated by Bernard Bosanquet under the title *Logic in Three Books: Of Thought, Of Investigation, and Of Knowledge.* 2 vols. Oxford: Clarendon Press, 1888.

Makkreel, Rudolf. "The Genesis of Heidegger's Phenomenological Hermeneutics and the Rediscovered 'Aristotle Introduction' of 1922." *Man and World* 23 (1990): 305–20.

Malpas, J. E. *Donald Davidson and the Mirror of Meaning.* Cambridge: Cambridge University Press, 1992.

McClelland, Charles E. *State, Society, and University in Germany, 1700–1914.* Cambridge: Cambridge University Press, 1980.

McCormick, Peter, and Frederick Elliston, eds. *Husserl: Shorter Works.* Notre Dame, Ind.: University of Notre Dame Press, 1981.

McDowell, John. "Having the World in View: Sellars, Kant, and Intentionality." *Journal of Philosophy* 95, no. 9 (1998): 431–91.

———. *Mind and World.* Cambridge, Mass.: Harvard University Press, 1994.

———. "Précis of *Mind and World.*" *Philosophy and Phenomenological Research* 58, no. 2 (1998): 365–68.

McNeill, William. "Metaphysics, Fundamental Ontology, Metontology: 1925–1935." *Heidegger Studies* 8 (1992): 63–80.

Mohanty, J. N. *The Possibility of Transcendental Philosophy.* Dordrecht: Martinus Nijhoff, 1985.

Morrison, James C. "Husserl and Heidegger: The Parting of the Ways." In *Heidegger's Existential Analytic,* edited by Frederick Elliston, 47–59. The Hague: Mouton, n.d.

Nachtsheim, Stephan. *Emil Lasks Grundlehre.* Tübingen: J. C. B. Mohr, 1992.

Natanson, Maurice. *Anonymity: A Study in the Philosophy of Alfred Schutz.* Bloomington: Indiana University Press, 1986.

———. *The Erotic Bird: Phenomenology in Literature.* Princeton, N.J.: Princeton University Press, 1998.

———. *The Journeying Self: A Study in Philosophy and Social Role.* Reading, Mass.: Addison-Wesley, 1970.

Natorp, Paul. *Allgemeine Psychologie nach kritischer Methode, Erstes Buch: Objekt und Methode der Psychologie.* Tübingen: J. C. B. Mohr, 1912.

———. *Logik in Leitsätzen zu akademischen Vorlesungen.* Marburg: N. G. Elwertsche Verlagsbuchhandlung, 1910.

———. *Philosophie, Ihr Problem und ihre Probleme: Einführung in den kritischen Idealismus.* Göttingen: Vanderhoek und Ruprecht, 1911.

———. *Platos Ideenlehre: Eine Einführung in den Idealismus.* Leipzig: Meiner, 1903.

Neske, Günther, and Emil Kettering, eds. *Antwort: Martin Heidegger im Gespräch.* Pfullingen: Neske, 1988.

Okrent, Mark. *Heidegger's Pragmatism: Understanding, Being, and the Critique of Metaphysics.* Ithaca, N.Y.: Cornell University Press, 1988.

Olafson, Frederick. "Consciousness and Intentionality in Heidegger's Thought." *American Philosophical Quarterly* 12, no. 2 (1975): 91–103.

Ollig, Hans-Ludwig. *Der Neukantianismus.* Stuttgart: J. B. Metzlersche Verlagsbuchhandlung, 1979.

Ott, Hugo. *Martin Heidegger: Unterwegs zu seiner Biographie.* Frankfurt: Campus Verlag, 1988.

Palmer, Richard E., trans. "'Phenomenology': Edmund Husserl's Article for the *Encyclopædia Britannica* (1927)." In *Husserl: Shorter Works,* edited by Peter McCormick and Frederick Elliston, 21–35. Notre Dame, Ind.: University of Notre Dame Press, 1981.

Papenfuss, Dietrich, and Otto Pöggeler, eds. *Zur philosophischen Aktualität Heideggers.* Vol. 2, *Im Gespräch der Zeit.* Frankfurt: Vittorio Klostermann, 1990.

Pöggeler, Otto. "Ausgleich und andere Anfang: Scheler und Heidegger." In *Studien zur Philosophie von Max Scheler,* edited by Ernst Wolfgang Orth, Heine von Alemann, and Gerhard Pfafferott, 166–203. Munich: Karl Alber, 1993.

———. "Besinnung oder Ausflucht? Heideggers ursprünglicheres Denken." In *Zerstörung des moralischen Selbstbewusstsein: Chance oder Gefährdung?* edited by the Forum für Philosophie Bad-Homburg, 238–72. Frankfurt: Suhrkamp, 1988.

———. "Den Führer führen? Heidegger und keine Ende." In *Neue Wege mit Heidegger,* 203–54. Munich: Karl Alber Verlag, 1992.

———. "Heidegger on Art." In *Martin Heidegger: Politics, Art, and Technology,* edited by Karsten Harries and Christoph Jamme, 106–23. New York: Holmes and Meier, 1994.

———. "Heideggers Begegnung mit Dilthey." *Dilthey-Jahrbuch* 4 (1986–87): 121–60.

———. "Heideggers logische Untersuchungen." In *Martin Heidegger: Innen- und*

Aussensichten, edited by the Forum für Philosophie Bad-Homburg, 75–100. Frankfurt: Suhrkamp, 1989.

———. "Heidegger's Political Self-Understanding." Translated by Steven Galt Crowell. In *The Heidegger Controversy,* edited by Richard Wolin, 198–244. New York: Columbia University Press, 1991.

———. "Hermeneutische und mantische Phänomenologie." In *Heidegger: Perspektiven zur Deutung seines Werkes,* edited by Otto Pöggeler, 321–57. Königstein: Athenäum, 1984.

———. *Martin Heidegger's Path of Thinking.* Translated by Daniel Magurshak and Sigmund Barber. Atlantic Highlands, N.J.: Humanities Press, 1987.

Quine, W. V. O. "On What There Is." In *From a Logical Point of View,* 1–19. New York: Harper and Row, 1961.

———. "Two Dogmas of Empiricism." In *From a Logical Point of View,* 20–46. New York: Harper and Row, 1961.

Rickert, Heinrich. *Der Gegenstand der Erkenntnis: Einführung in die Transzendentalphilosophie.* 3d ed. Tübingen: J. C. B. Mohr, 1915.

———. *Die Grenzen der naturwissenschaftlichen Begriffsbildung.* Tübingen: J. C. B. Mohr, 1902.

———. *Die Heidelberger Tradition und Kants Kritizismus.* Berlin: Junker und Dünnhaupt, 1934.

———. "Persönliches Gleichwort." In *Gesammelte Schriften,* by Emil Lask, edited by Eugen Herrigel, 1:v–xvi. Tübingen: J. C. B. Mohr, 1923.

———. *Die Philosophie des Lebens: Darstellung und Kritik der philosophischen Modeströmungen unserer Zeit.* Tübingen: J. C. B. Mohr, 1922.

Ringer, Fritz. *The Decline of the German Mandarins: The German Academic Community, 1890–1933.* Cambridge, Mass.: Harvard University Press, 1969.

Rockmore, Tom. *On Heidegger's Nazism and Philosophy.* Berkeley and Los Angeles: University of California Press, 1992.

Rockmore, Tom, and Joseph Margolis, eds. *The Heidegger Case: On Philosophy and Politics.* Philadelphia: Temple University Press, 1992.

Rorty, Richard. *Philosophy and the Mirror of Nature.* Princeton, N.J.: Princeton University Press, 1980.

Rosshoff, Hartmut. *Emil Lask als Lehrer von Georg Lukács.* Bonn: Bouvier Verlag, 1975.

Sallis, John. *Echoes: After Heidegger.* Bloomington: Indiana University Press, 1990.

Schalow, Frank. *The Retrieval of the Kant-Heidegger Dialogue.* Albany: State University of New York Press, 1992.

Scharff, Robert C. "Heidegger's 'Appropriation' of Dilthey before *Being and Time.*" *Journal of the History of Philosophy* 35, no. 1 (1997): 105–28.

Schnädelbach, Herbert. *Philosophy in Germany, 1831–1933.* Translated by Eric Matthews. Cambridge: Cambridge University Press, 1984.

Schuhmann, Karl, ed. *Edmund Husserl: Briefwechsel.* Vol. 2, *Die Münchener Phänomenologen.* Dordrecht: Kluwer, 1994.

———. *Edmund Husserl: Briefwechsel.* Vol. 5, *Die Neukantianer.* Dordrecht: Kluwer, 1994.

Schuhmann, Karl, and Barry Smith. "Two Idealisms: Lask and Husserl." *Kant-Studien* 84 (1993): 448–66.

Schutz, Alfred. "Husserl's *Crisis of Western Science,*" letter to Eric Voegelin (1943), edited by Fred Kersten. In *The Prism of the Self: Philosophical Essays in Honor of Maurice Natanson,* edited by Steven Galt Crowell, 277–87. Dordrecht: Kluwer, 1995.

Schweitz, Michael. "Emil Lasks Kategorienlehre vor dem Hintergrund der Kopernikanischen Wende Kants." *Kant-Studien* 75 (1984): 213–37.

Sentroul, Charles. *Kant und Aristoteles.* Translated into German by Ludwig Heinrichs. Kempten: Kösel, 1911.

Sheehan, Thomas. "Heidegger's Early Years: Fragments for a Philosophical Biography." In *Heidegger: The Man and the Thinker,* edited by Thomas Sheehan, 3–19. Chicago: Precedent, 1981.

———. "Nihilism: Heidegger/Jünger/Aristotle." In *Phenomenology: Japanese and American Perspectives,* edited by Burt C. Hopkins, 273–316. Dordrecht: Kluwer, 1998.

———. "Reading a Life: Heidegger and Hard Times." In *The Cambridge Companion to Heidegger,* edited by Charles Guignon, 70–96. Cambridge: Cambridge University Press, 1993.

Sheehan, Thomas, and Richard Palmer, eds. and trans. *Edmund Husserl: Psychological and Transcendental Phenomenology and the Confrontation with Heidegger, 1927–1931.* Dordrecht: Kluwer, 1997.

Sluga, Hans. *Heidegger's Crisis: Philosophy and Politics in Nazi Germany.* Cambridge, Mass.: Harvard University Press, 1993.

Sommerhäuser, Hanspeter. *Emil Lask in Auseinandersetzung mit Heinrich Rickert.* Ph.D. diss. Berlin: Ernst-Reuter-Gesellschaft, 1965.

Spiegelberg, Herbert. "On the Misfortunes of Edmund Husserl's *Encyclopædia Britannica* Article 'Phenomenology.' " In *Husserl: Shorter Works,* edited by Peter McCormick and Frederick Elliston, 18–20. Notre Dame, Ind.: University of Notre Dame Press, 1981.

———. *The Phenomenological Movement.* 3d rev. and enlarged edition. The Hague: Martinus Nijhoff, 1982.

Stapleton, Timothy. *Husserl and Heidegger: The Question of a Phenomenological Beginning.* Albany: State University of New York Press, 1983.

Steinbock, Anthony. *Home and Beyond: Generative Phenomenology after Husserl.* Evanston, Ill.: Northwestern University Press, 1995.

Stewart, Roderick M. "Signification and Radical Subjectivity in Heidegger's *Habilitationsschrift.*" *Man and World* 12 (1979): 360–86.

Stroud, Barry. "Transcendental Arguments." *Journal of Philosophy* (1968): 241–56.

Taminiaux, Jacques. "From One Idea of Phenomenology to the Other." In *Heidegger and the Project of Fundamental Ontology,* 1–54. Albany: State University of New York Press, 1991.

Tugendhat, Ernst. *Der Wahrheitsbegriff bei Husserl und Heidegger.* Berlin: Walter de Gruyter, 1972.

Van Buren, John. *The Young Heidegger.* Bloomington: Indiana University Press, 1994.

Wagner, Hans. *Philosophie und Reflexion.* Munich: Ernst Reinhardt, 1959.

Weber, Max. "Science as a Vocation." In *From Max Weber,* edited and translated by H. H. Gerth and C. Wright Mills, 129–56. New York: Oxford University Press, 1946.

Wiegand, Olav K. *Interpretationen der Modallogik.* Dordrecht: Kluwer, 1998.

Willey, Thomas E. *Back to Kant: The Revival of Kantianism in German Social and Historical Thought, 1860–1914.* Detroit: Wayne State University Press, 1978.

Wolin, Richard. *The Heidegger Controversy.* New York: Columbia University Press, 1991.

———. *The Politics of Being.* New York: Columbia University Press, 1990.

Wood, David. "Reiterating the Temporal: Toward a Rethinking of Heidegger on Time." In *Rereading Heidegger,* edited by John Sallis, 136–59. Bloomington: Indiana University Press, 1993.

Zimmerman, Michael. *Heidegger's Confrontation with Modernity.* Bloomington: Indiana University Press, 1990.

Index